FOR DUMMIES®

The fun and easy way™ to travel!

P9-DMJ-776

U.S.A.

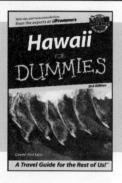

EUROPE

OTHER DESTINATIONS

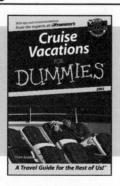

Available wherever books are sold.
Go to www.dummies.com or call 1-877-762-2974 to order direct.

WILEY

Washington, D.C.
FOR
DUMMIES®
2ND EDITION

by Tom Price

WILEY

Wiley Publishing, Inc.

Washington, D.C. For Dummies, 2nd Edition

Published by
Wiley Publishing, Inc.
909 Third Avenue
New York, NY 10022
www.wiley.com

For general information on our other products and services or to obtain technical support, please contact our Customer Care Department within the U.S. at 800-762-2974, outside the U.S. at 317-572-3993, or fax 317-572-4002.

Wiley also publishes its books in a variety of electronic formats. Some content that appears in print may not be available in electronic books.

Library of Congress Control Number: 2002114837

ISBN: 0-7645-5465-4

ISSN: 1531-7587

Manufactured in the United States of America

10 9 8 7 6 5 4 3 2

About the Author

Tom Price has lived in and written about Washington for more than two decades. As a journalist who focuses on government and politics, he knows the ins and outs of official Washington. As the parent of a Washington native who is making the transition from high school to college, he's discovered the best Washington places for kids of all ages. As a long-time D.C. resident, he's found fun and interesting Washington experiences for adults of all ages as well, having repeatedly explored the city with his family and visiting friends. From late 1982 through 1995, Tom was a correspondent in the Cox Newspapers Washington Bureau. Since then, he has been a freelance writer whose work has appeared in books, magazines, and newspapers and on Internet sites. With his wife, Susan Crites Price, Tom is coauthor of *The Working Parents Help Book: Practical Advice for Dealing with the Day-to-Day Challenges of Kids and Careers,* which won a Parents' Choice Award, was a Scholastic Book Club selection, and has been featured by "Today," "Oprah," and other broadcast and print media. Previously, Tom, a Pittsburgh native, reported for newspapers in Pennsylvania and Ohio.

Dedication

For Susan, my partner in writing, family, and life.

Author's Acknowledgments

First, I want to thank Elise Ford, an accomplished travel writer who brought me to this book in the first place and then provided invaluable guidance as I researched and wrote. I also want to thank my editor, Kathleen Warnock; my parents, Anna Mae and Sam Price; my daughter Julie, who helped in the research; Mickey Leibner, who helped as well; and, of course, Susan, who is always my best and most important editor.

Publisher's Acknowledgments

We're proud of this book; please send us your comments through our Dummies online registration form located at www.dummies.com/register/.

Some of the people who helped bring this book to market include the following:

Editorial

Editors: Kelly Ewing, Kathleen Warnock

Cartographer: John Decamillis

Editorial Supervisor: Michelle Hacker

Senior Photo Editor: Richard Fox

Assistant Photo Editor: Michael Ross

Front Cover Photo: John Skowronski/ Folio, Inc.

Back Cover Photo: Ron Jautz/Folio, Inc.

Cartoons: Rich Tennant, www.the5thwave.com

Production

Project Coordinator: Erin Smith

Layout and Graphics: Amanda Carter, Michael Kruzil, Julie Trippetti, Jeremey Unger

Proofreaders: Laura Albert, Susan Moritz, TECHBOOKS Production Services

Indexer: TECHBOOKS Production Services

Publishing and Editorial for Consumer Dummies

Diane Graves Steele, Vice President and Publisher, Consumer Dummies

Joyce Pepple, Acquisitions Director, Consumer Dummies

Kristin A. Cocks, Product Development Director, Consumer Dummies

Michael Spring, Vice President and Publisher, Travel

Brice Gosnell, Publishing Director, Travel

Suzanne Jannetta, Editorial Director, Travel

Publishing for Technology Dummies

Andy Cummings, Vice President and Publisher, Dummies Technology/General User

Composition Services

Gerry Fahey, Vice President of Production Services

Debbie Stailey, Director of Composition Services

Contents at a Glance

Maps at a Glance

Table of Contents

Introduction

● ●

*W*hen you visit Washington, D.C., you're visiting the capital of the world — a city with more power than any other on the planet, and one filled with world-class tourist attractions as well.

It wasn't always this way. Almost nothing stood on the sites of the White House, Capitol, and other current U.S. government buildings when George Washington selected the spot to become the new nation's capital city in 1791, primarily because of its central location between the already quarrelling North and South. As recently as the 1960s, critics described Washington as a cultural backwater, a sleepy Southern town, a place without decent restaurants where the sidewalks were rolled up at dusk.

Washington has long had its shrines to freedom and its halls of government — the Washington Monument, Lincoln Memorial, Library of Congress, and the other government companions to the White House and Capitol. But the city now also has many fine restaurants and hotels, museums, galleries, and performing arts organizations.

Along with New York, Washington was a target of the terrorist attacks of Sept. 11, 2001. American Airlines Flight 77 was flown into the Pentagon, across the Potomac River from D.C. in Northern Virginia. United Airlines Flight 93, which crashed in rural Pennsylvania, was believed to have been destined for the White House or the Capitol. As I write this book, the White House and the Pentagon are closed to public tours, and security has been ratcheted up everywhere. But, like New Yorkers, Washingtonians have been determined to resume normal activities, which include playing host to many visitors. There is little that you could have done here on Sept. 10, 2001, that you can't do today.

I've loved Washington since long before I moved here. For a journalist who focuses on politics and government, there's no better place to be. Having lived in D.C. for 20 years now, I've come to know it as deeply as I love it. I'm thrilled to be able to share that knowledge with you.

About This Book

You probably picked this book because you're too busy to wade through a sea of information or you aren't interested in spending weeks planning a five-day trip. Perhaps you're a first-time visitor to Washington, D.C., and you don't know where to begin. Or maybe you're frustrated by all the detail in conventional guidebooks. (You know what I mean: You want to find out when a museum opens, and the author tells you how to *build* one.) Armed with *Washington, D.C. For Dummies,* 2nd Edition, you'll feel like a capital insider in no time.

Think of this text as a reference book. You can read it from cover to cover if you like (I'll be flattered!), but more than likely, you'll want to dip into the chapters or sections that are the most interesting or important to you at a particular moment. The Table of Contents and Index allow you to find what you need when you need it — hotels, restaurants, sights, stores, nightspots, and more.

This book doesn't overwhelm you with choices, but it does give you enough information so that you can pick what's best for you. When money is involved, you'll find options at various price levels.

I've offered lots of D.C. travel tips to visiting friends and family over the last 20 years, and that's exactly what I'm offering you. When you've finished your visit and are heading back home, I expect you'll have acquired some of the affection that I feel for this town, and that you'll want to come back.

Conventions Used in This Book

To help you get information quickly, I use some abbreviations and symbols throughout this book. Washington, D.C. is referred to as "Washington," "D.C.," or "The District." (Its full name is "Washington, the District of Columbia.")

Hotels and restaurants are listed alphabetically, with prices and evaluations.

Credit cards accepted are listed this way:

- ✔ **AE:** American Express
- ✔ **CB:** Carte Blanche
- ✔ **DC:** Diners Club
- ✔ **DISC:** Discover
- ✔ **JCB:** Japan Credit Bank
- ✔ **MC:** MasterCard
- ✔ **V:** Visa

The dollar signs that accompany the hotel and restaurant reviews give you a sense of their price ranges, as shown in the following table. For a hotel, the dollar signs represent the average of the lowest and highest undiscounted rate for a double-occupancy room for one night during high season. (Chapter 7 explains when high season occurs.) For each restaurant, I've averaged the highest and lowest prices for an appetizer or salad, main course, and dessert at dinner per person, not including taxes and tips.

Cost	Hotel	Restaurant
$	Less than $125	Less than $15
$$	$125–$179	$15–$25
$$$	$180–$275	$25–$35
$$$$	$276–$350	$35–$50
$$$$$	More than $350	More than $50

In the individual reviews, I give more specific information about costs. I can't, of course, tell you about special discounts that hotels and restaurants often offer. And prices, as you know, are subject to change. So it's a good idea to call ahead to confirm hours and prices and to always ask about special offers and discounts when you make your reservations.

Foolish Assumptions

I've written this book for both the frequent flier and the inexperienced traveler. The assumptions I've made about both (and, truthfully, I hope they're not foolish!) are that:

- ✔ You may be an inexperienced traveler who is trying to determine whether or not to visit Washington, or you may be looking for help in deciding when and how to make the trip.

- ✔ You may be an experienced traveler, but you don't want to spend much time planning your trip, or you don't have much time to spend in the city once you arrive. You want expert advice on how to get the most out of your time and how to enjoy a hasslefree visit.

- ✔ You're not looking for a book that provides every piece of information available about Washington sights, or one that lists every hotel and restaurant in the city. Instead, you want a book that focuses on the best places to eat and sleep in all price ranges, and the best ways to enjoy your days here.

If you fit any of these criteria, *Washington, D.C. For Dummies,* 2nd Edition is the book you're looking for.

How This Book Is Organized

Washington, D.C. For Dummies, 2nd Edition is divided into seven parts. Within each part are chapters that delve into specifics. Each chapter is written so that you don't have to read the text before or after it. I refer you to other sections of the book for more information.

Part 1: Getting Started

Here is an overview of Washington and a taste of what you can expect to encounter when you visit. You can find answers to your major questions about the weather, special events, and your vacation budget. I also provide tips for families with children, seniors, travelers with disabilities, and gay and lesbian travelers.

Part II: Ironing Out the Details

Should you use a travel agent? How about buying a package tour? Where can you find the best airfare? How do you go about booking reservations? This part is where I answer these questions and steer you to useful online sources. I introduce you to Washington's best hotels in all price ranges and offer tips about buying travel insurance, renting a car, and packing your bags.

Part III: Settling in to Washington, D.C.

Here's where you find out how to get around and get along. I describe the three airports serving the Washington area, your options for arriving by train or car, and how to find your way once you get here. I also discuss that most important of matters — money.

Part IV: Dining in D.C.

In this part, you find out where the locals eat, what phone numbers you need to make reservations, and how you can save money at mealtime. I list the city's best restaurants in all price ranges. To make your dining choices simpler, I've prepared indexes of restaurants by price, location, and cuisine. And, in case you get an attack of the munchies, I tell you the best places to grab a quick bite, cup of coffee, or scoop of ice cream.

Part V: Exploring Washington, D.C.

This part tells you what you want to know about the top sights (and some particularly interesting lesser known attractions) and gives you the skinny on tours and shopping. I toss in some itineraries at no extra charge (you're welcome), as well as suggestions for excursions nearby.

Part VI: Living It Up After the Sun Goes Down: D.C. Nightlife

Here's where you find out what's going on after the museums close and the government goes to sleep for the night. You explore the theater and performing arts scene. I tell you how to get tickets, where to grab a pre- or post-theater meal, and where to kick back with a cocktail or dance the night away.

Part VII: The Part of Tens

Not as famous as the FBI's Ten Most Wanted list, perhaps, but the *For Dummies* Part of Tens nevertheless is full of cool information. In this part, you find the best places to view the city's breathtaking skyline, as well as places that are worth driving to see — the only time driving is worthwhile in D.C., I may add.

Appendix and Worksheets

You can find two other elements near the back of this book. An appendix — your Quick Concierge — provides handy information you may need while visiting Washington. In it, you can find phone numbers and addresses for area hospitals and pharmacies, tips for finding ATMs, information on where to take a broken camera or which radio station plays your music, and other useful tips. Check out this Appendix when searching for answers to the little questions that may come up as you travel.

You can also find some worksheets that can make your travel planning easier. They help you determine your travel budget, create itineraries, and keep a log of your favorite restaurants so that you can hit them again next time you're in town (or so that you can become a travel advisor and give your friends tips for their trips to DC). You can find these worksheets easily because they're printed on yellow paper near the back of the book. Tear them out and take them along as you trek through Washington.

Icons Used in This Book

You find the following icons (little picture) scattered throughout the margins of this guide. They call your attention to particular kinds of information.

This bull's-eye alerts you to facts, hints, and insider information that can help you make the best use of your time.

This worried fellow warns of tourist traps, rip-offs, hazards, activities that aren't worth your time, and other pitfalls.

These icons call your attention to hotels, restaurants, and attractions that are especially good for children.

Cut your costs with these money-saving suggestions or alerts to great deals.

The Remember icon points to information that bears repeating. Bears repeating.

The Capitol Dome highlights events and attractions that are unique to D.C.

Where to Go from Here

Now that you know what to expect from this book, you can start to plan your visit — or, if you're already in D.C., you can decide what to do right now. See and do all you can. And have fun. Your tax dollars help to pay for much of what you'll encounter here, so you may as well get your money's worth.

Part I
Getting Started

The 5th Wave

By Rich Tennant

In this part . . .

To get the most out of any vacation — with the fewest hassles — knowing what awaits you before you arrive helps. This part highlights the joys of a visit to D.C. and helps you plan your trip. You get a quick tour of the city's top attractions in Chapter 1. Chapter 2 helps you decide when to visit. You can plan your travel budget with help from Chapter 3. And Chapter 4 has tips for travelers with special interests and needs.

Chapter 1

Discovering the Best of Washington, D.C.

When most of the world thinks of Washington, D.C., the city's role as the nation's capital comes to mind: The president, the Congress, the Supreme Court, the Pentagon, and the State Department are all here. But, like all great cities, Washington is much more than just the government.

Inside-the-Beltway Lodging

Hotel choices range from the ultra-ritzy Ritz to the ultra-cheap Hostelling International. Like most visitors, you'll probably choose one of the many options in between. Reasonably priced all-suite hotels can be great for families. You can act like a congressional insider by unpacking your bags on Capitol Hill, or you can settle in near the nightlife of Georgetown, Dupont Circle, or Adams-Morgan.

Capital Dining

As the world's capital, Washington has acquired restaurants that feature many of the world's ethnic cuisines. In Part IV, I introduce you to Brazilian, Chinese, French, Indian, Italian, Malaysian, Mediterranean, Mexican, Moroccan, Spanish, Thai, and Vietnamese restaurants, as well as some others that feature dishes from all around Asia and Latin America. And, of course, you have many varieties of U.S. cooking to choose among, because Washingtonians come from every corner of the nation and bring their dining preferences with them.

D.C. Metropolitan Area

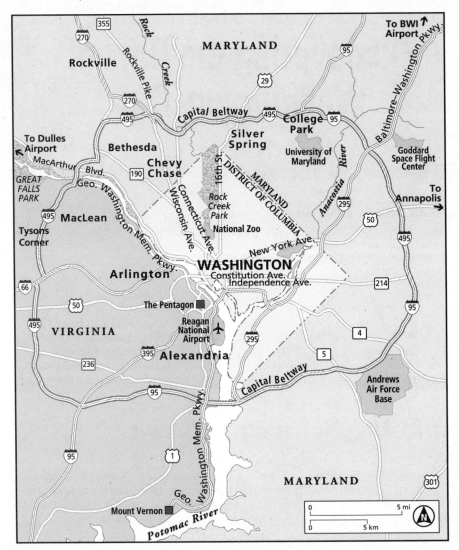

Living History

One of the most striking facts about Washington is that history really has been — and is being — made here. You can walk into and around the places you read about in your history books. And you can watch some of the history that's being created today.

Security won't let you into the Oval Office when the president is making decisions, or into the Defense Secretary's quarters when military actions are being planned, or into the Capitol hideaway rooms when senators and representatives carve out the compromises that become laws. But you *can* sit in on the public hearings where lawmakers grill witnesses about the top issues of the day, attend the congressional committee meetings where legislation is prepared, sit in the House and Senate visitors' galleries when lawmakers vote that legislation up or down, and watch lawyers try to convince the Supreme Court justices that those laws are or are not compatible with the Constitution. And (subject to changing security restrictions) you can tour many government buildings where the people's business is conducted. (I tell you how in Part V.)

The Land of the Free (Attractions)

One of Washington's best selling points is that many of its top attractions are free. Unlike London, Paris, Rome, or other major capitals, you don't have to open your wallet before you can open the doors to most of the popular museums, galleries, and other sights.

Donations are accepted in unobtrusive contribution boxes, but you don't have to pay to visit the Smithsonian's many museums, the National Zoo (another Smithsonian institution), the National Gallery of Art, or some private museums and galleries. Tours of government buildings are free. You don't pay a cent to stroll along the Tidal Basin, ogle the cherry blossoms, fly a kite on the Mall, ride the elevator to the top of the Washington Monument, climb the steps of the Lincoln Memorial, read the words of Thomas Jefferson that are carved into his memorial, or visit the many other monuments to the Americans (and some from other nations) who served the country in the past.

Where Are the Skyscrapers?

In Washington, a high-rise is 180 feet tall. That's because no structure is allowed to exceed the height of the Capitol Dome. This rule has contributed to the suburban sprawl that gives metro Washington some of the worst traffic in the nation. (If you can't build up, you build out.) But it has kept the city on a very human scale. You don't see dark canyons of streets shaded by 100-story skyscrapers. You don't feel overwhelmed walking the streets of the District. And plenty of interesting low-rises are there to capture your attention — the White House, the Capitol, and the Supreme Court, for starters.

D.C.'s landscape is impressive, too. Not only are the buildings kept to a modest size, but an enormous percentage of the city's ground is devoted to parks and gardens.

Washington's many monuments and its monumental government buildings make the city a fascinating place for walking tours.

The car-free National Mall — lawns, gardens, ponds, and walkways — stretches from the Lincoln Memorial to the Capitol and is bordered by many of the Smithsonian's facilities. The cherry trees along the tidal basin are spectacular in the spring. You can glimpse the homes of the rich and powerful by strolling through the quiet brick and cobblestone streets of Georgetown, the city-within-the-city that predates the founding of the republic. You can immerse yourself in the Latin-influenced nightlife of the clubs and restaurants of Adams-Morgan.

For simplicity's sake, this book defines the **Mall** as everything between the Capitol, the Lincoln Memorial, and Independence and Constitution avenues, even though some maps label the Washington Monument Grounds and West Potomac Park (near the Lincoln Memorial) as separate areas.

Leave your car parked, and you'll find that the city is easy to get around. Many sights are within easy walking distance of each other, and Metrorail subway system stations are located near most places you'll want to go. The Cheat Sheet at the front of this book contains a map of the system. For other trips, the 30-series buses carry you along Wisconsin Avenue, M Street, and Pennsylvania Avenue. And D.C.'s cabs are plentiful and cheap when compared with those in other cities, although many are dilapidated and the fare system requires careful study. (See Chapter 3 for a detailed explanation.)

Unofficial D.C.: Arts, Sports, and Nightlife

Washington has rich cultural, historical, scientific, and educational resources. **The Smithsonian Institution's** many museums, the **National Gallery of Art,** the **John F. Kennedy Center for the Performing Arts,** and the **Shakespeare Theatre** are just a few examples. You can experience all the permutations of pop culture around town, from rock concerts at **Robert F. Kennedy Stadium,** to Broadway shows at the **National** and **Warner** theaters, to jazz, folk, bluegrass, country, and hip-hop at the city's clubs. Except for the egregious omission of Major League Baseball, Washington is a world-class sports town, with professional football, hockey, and men's and women's basketball and soccer teams, as well as some perennial college powerhouses. (Someday, maybe Washington will get a baseball team, too!)

Don't Forget About the Shopping

Washington's merchants — in national department store chains or local boutiques — are ready and willing to lighten your wallet. Capitol Hill has an old-fashioned farmers' market, as well as upscale shops in gorgeously renovated Union Station. Georgetown boasts countless boutiques, as well as a traditional flea market. If you're into up-up-up-scale shopping, Upper Wisconsin Avenue has its own smaller version of Beverly Hills' exclusive Rodeo Drive.

Enjoying the Outdoors

The District's climate is friendly to flowering plants in the spring. Azaleas join the cherry trees in bringing color to all parts of town. The Mall and other parkland give Washington a greenway that stretches west from the Capitol to the Potomac River. More greenery runs perpendicular to the mall from the Tidal Basin to Lafayette Square north of the White House. East Potomac Park occupies the land between the Potomac and the Washington Channel in Southwest D.C. Rock Creek Park winds through Northwest Washington from Maryland to the Potomac. Sites of Civil War forts preserve spots of land from development throughout the city. You encounter *vest-pocket parks* (tiny green parks) around any corner. The Capitol grounds are tree-shaded and planted with flowers and flowering shrubs. At the foot of Capitol Hill, the Botanic Garden brings plant life inside what can be called the nation's greenhouse.

The parkland — along with the Tidal Basin, Washington Channel, and Potomac and Anacostia rivers — provides recreational opportunities for hikers, cyclists, and boaters. If you want boating without the work, you can take a cruise on the Potomac. Or you can ride a replica of a 19th-century mule-drawn barge on the C&O Canal. Back on land, a guided tour can be just the ticket for seeing the city while resting your feet. For a couple of side trips outside the Beltway, see Chapters 21 and 25.

Chapter 2

Deciding When to Go

● ●

In This Chapter

▶ Joining (or avoiding) the crowds

▶ Understanding D.C.'s weather

▶ Choosing a season to visit

▶ Exploring Washington's annual events

● ●

Although, by most standards, Washington, D.C. remains a busy town during the year, some seasons are busier than others. Deciding when to visit may affect what you see, how much you pay, and how many people you'll battle at the museums and other attractions. In this chapter, we look at the advantages and disadvantages of visiting during various times of the year so that you can decide which season works best for you.

Discovering the Secret of the Seasons

You can't choose a bad time to visit Washington if your primary goal is to see the sights and you're not concerned about the crowds. You can tour the museums, monuments, and government buildings any season. Cultural, entertainment, and sports activities are always going on. And the stores are glad to sell to you no matter what the season.

The best times to visit D.C. are spring and fall — April through mid-June and September through mid-November. Temperature and humidity tend to be moderate. The flowers are on display in the spring. The weather in the fall can be close to ideal. Congress is likely to be at work, and cultural and entertainment activities are running full force.

Unfortunately, spring also brings crowds. I've always believed that all Americans should visit Washington at least once. But when I was a reporter trying to get from one Capitol Hill building to another on a tight schedule, I used to quietly grumble as I picked my way through gangs of middle-school students blocking sidewalks as they milled about waiting for their tour buses to arrive.

In terms of expense, visiting in the spring means that you find fewer lodging bargains, especially during the work week when business travelers fill the hotels. In addition, events like the Cherry Blossom Festival are so popular that hotels and restaurants can charge top prices and get them.

You can find more bargains in hotter summer months, as hotels try to fill the rooms that empty during Congressional vacations by offering money-saving package deals. You can also enjoy a great deal of free, outdoor entertainment in the summer.

You can choose less-than-ideal times to visit for other reasons, such as the weather. While summer and winter offer much to keep you busy, take the weather into consideration when you're deciding when to visit. If you're anxious to see government in action, also keep in mind that Congress tries to take lengthy recesses in late summer and at year's end, and you can't attend congressional committee hearings or sessions of Congress when the members are out of town.

A strike against August is that, weather-wise, it can feel like an equatorial rainforest — excruciating heat, even more excruciating humidity, and regular, vicious thunderstorms. The first year we lived in Washington, after moving from the Midwest, my wife and I wilted when August hit. We both arranged spur-of-the-moment vacations and just started driving north. The National Weather Service says July is hotter and has more rain, but August always feels worse.

Washington does get a real winter most years, usually with snow and some periods of extreme cold in January and February, even though for many years the city government seemed not to understand the concept of snow and how to plow it. In recent years, the response to inclement weather is much improved. On the other hand, Washington looks gorgeous after a snowfall, especially when the congressional Christmas tree is on display at the foot of Capitol Hill. And D.C.'s latest administration has been doing a much better job of clearing the streets when the snow falls.

That said, why don't you slip Vivaldi into your CD player and consider the pros and cons of Washington's four seasons?

Spring: Blooming beautiful in D.C.

Spring is a popular time for D.C. visits. Some of the best reasons to travel to Washington in spring are as follows:

- The days are clear and comfortable, and Washington is at its most lush and beautiful.
- Gardens in and around the Mall and monuments (around the entire city, for that matter!) bloom with tulips, daffodils, cherry blossoms, dogwoods, and azaleas.

However, keep in mind the following springtime pitfalls:

✔ Washington's weather always is fickle. Scattered among the gorgeous spring days are an occasional preview of summer's heat, humidity, and thunderstorms, along with a sporadic period that feels a bit too cool. Wear layers of clothing and bring rain gear.

✔ Tourists, especially busloads of schoolchildren, pour in like a monsoon. Expect crowds, longer lines, and more traffic.

Summer: Having fun in the D.C. sun

Summer is another popular time to visit because:

✔ The kids are out of school (duh!).

✔ Many hotels offer money-saving packages.

✔ Public buildings are air-conditioned.

✔ Many museums offer extended hours.

✔ Free events, such as outdoor concerts, are plentiful.

But do take into consideration the following:

✔ Summer means *major* heat, folks. And humidity. The 3 Hs — heat, humidity, and haze — make frequent appearances until well after Labor Day. (See Table 2-1 for month-by-month averages of D.C.'s temperature and rainfall.)

✔ The influx of summer vacationers can mean longer-than-usual lines at attractions and cold-drink vendors.

✔ Some theaters are dark (or at least darker) in July and August. Most theater seasons run from fall to late spring, so if you're hoping to see a production by one of Washington's theater companies, check to see whether they have any summer offerings.

Table 2-1	Washington, D.C.'s Average Temperatures (°F)											
	Jan	*Feb*	*Mar*	*Apr*	*May*	*June*	*July*	*Aug*	*Sep*	*Oct*	*Nov*	*Dec*
High	43	47	56	66	75	84	88	86	79	68	57	47
Low	27	30	37	46	56	65	70	69	62	50	40	32
Rain (inches)	3.2	2.6	3.6	2.8	3.8	3.1	3.7	3.4	3.8	3.2	3.0	3.0

(Source: U.S. National Weather Service.)

Fall: Harvest good times in Washington, D.C.

If you don't have to worry about school schedules, fall probably is the best time to travel to D.C.:

- ✔ The weather is as good as it gets. Heat and humidity drop as the calendar wears on.
- ✔ Lines are shorter; crowds are smaller.
- ✔ Entertainment and cultural opportunities abound.

Some things to watch out for include the following:

- ✔ Congress reconvenes and the convention scene heats up, putting more demands on hotels and restaurants, particularly during the work week.
- ✔ Traffic can be worse than in summer. (But you're too smart to drive around D.C. anyway, aren't you?)

Winter: A great place to celebrate the holidays

Winter brings visions of softly falling snowflakes and holiday cheer, although the snow often holds off until the holidays are over. The advantages of a winter visit include the following:

- ✔ You don't need to worry about heat and humidity.
- ✔ Lines at museums and other attractions are short or nonexistent.
- ✔ Colorful, often free, holiday events are plentiful from December into January.

- ✔ Airlines and tour operators offer good deals.
- ✔ When snow surrounds the monuments, you get picture-postcard views of the Capitol, the White House, and other photogenic buildings.
- ✔ Congress and the White House set up their competing Christmas trees. (The congressional tree always is best!)

Winter does have its downsides, however:

- ✔ While its average temperatures look good on paper, Washington always is visited by some extremes. A damp, windy, 40-degree day on the Mall can feel colder than zero in Alaska. And D.C. does get

real cold and windy winter weather — subzero temperatures and
even the occasional blizzard — if only for short spells.

✔ You have fewer opportunities to take advantage of outdoor
activities.

Washington's Calendar of Capital Events

In this section, we list just a few of Washington's many festivals and
special events, month by month. Please double-check before planning
your vacation around any of these events, because they're subject to
change. Also see the "Weekend" section of *The Washington Post* every
Friday for a comprehensive listing of events.

Because the easiest way to get around D.C. is by Metrorail — the local
subway — the event listings include the Metrorail stops closest to
them. The site listings in Part V give detailed directions. Unless otherwise noted, the events are free.

January

Martin Luther King, Jr.'s Birthday, Lincoln Memorial (☎ 202-619-7222;
Internet: www.nps.gov/linc; Metro: Foggy Bottom-George Washington
University), is celebrated in word and music on the third Monday in
January at the Lincoln Memorial, site of the great civil rights leader's
"I have a dream" speech.

Inauguration Day, U.S. Capitol (Metro: McPherson Square, Federal
Triangle, Archives-Navy Memorial, Federal Center Southwest, Capitol
South, Union Station) occurs at noon on Jan. 20 every fourth year, the
day the president is sworn in at the Capitol. A parade along Pennsylvania
Avenue from the Capitol to the White House follows the swearing in. You
need political contacts to get a seat on the Capitol lawn or on the parade
route bleachers. (A friend with an office window or balcony that overlooks the route is good, too.) Otherwise, head for that long stretch
between Congress's and the president's workplaces that morning — the
earlier, the better. The next presidential inauguration is January 20, 2005.
Check *The Washington Post* for parade information. You can also find info
at the campaign Web site of the winning candidate and his/her party
(Internet: www.gop.org or www.democrats.org) or at the White House
site (www.whitehouse.gov) if President Bush wins reelection.

January is Washington's coldest month, so the inauguration can be a
bone-chilling event. Be prepared! I remember wading through the snow
to cover my first inaugural, Jimmy Carter's in 1977. It was so bitterly

cold for Ronald Reagan's inaugural in 1985 that the outdoor events were cancelled.

February

During **Black History Month,** African Americans' struggles and achievements are celebrated in numerous ways throughout the city. Museums, libraries, and other sites feature readings, speeches, musical performances, and other events. Check these Web sites: National Park Service (www.nps.gov/ncro/PublicAffairs/Calendar.htm), Smithsonian Institution (www.si.edu/events), and the Washington Convention and Tourism Corp. (www.washington.org).

On Feb. 12 at noon at the Lincoln Memorial, a wreath-laying, band music, and a dramatic reading of the Gettysburg Address mark **Abraham Lincoln's Birthday,** Lincoln Memorial (☎ 202-619-7222; Internet: www.nps.gov/linc; Metro: Foggy Bottom-George Washington University).

March

As with Black History Month, many Washington institutions commemorate the achievements of women during **Women's History Month,** various locations. You can find information on the Internet from the National Park Service at www.nps.gov/ncro/PublicAffairs/Calendar.htm, the Smithsonian Institution at www.si.edu/events, and the Washington Convention and Tourism Corp. at www.washington.org.

At the **Smithsonian Kite Festival,** Washington Monument grounds (☎ 202-357-3030; Internet: http://kitefestival.org/welcome.htm; Metro: Smithsonian), you can compete, watch the experts, or just find a place to fly your own kite. The Smithsonian Associates and the National Air and Space Museum sponsor this carefree Washington tradition.

Daily events bloom all over town during the **National Cherry Blossom Festival,** various locations (Internet: www.nationalcherryblossomfestival.org.). This two-week festival is scheduled for March 22 through April 7, 2003.

The official highlight is the **parade,** scheduled for April 5, 2003. But the real stars are the cherry blossoms, especially those around the Tidal Basin, and they make their appearances whenever they darn well please. The National Park Service provides updates on the likely timing of the blooms at www.nps.gov/nacc/cherry. The blooms provide a great backdrop and canopy for a picnic around the Tidal Basin or the Washington Monument Grounds.

April

Since 1878, presidents have invited children to roll eggs on the White House lawn on the Monday after Easter. We took our daughter to the **White House Easter Egg Roll** (☎ 202-456-7041; Internet: www.white house.gov; Metro: McPherson Square) during the Clinton and Bush I administrations and have the wooden eggs with the mass-produced presidential signatures to prove it! Modern presidents have added entertainment — inside and outside the White House grounds — to occupy the youngsters during the inevitable waits in line. Free tickets timed for entrance are distributed first-come, first-served at the Ellipse Visitor Pavilion at the southwest corner of 15th and E streets NW. One person can get up to five tickets. Most tickets are distributed beginning at 8 a.m. Saturday, with some additional tickets made available beginning at 7 a.m. Monday. Children of all ages can attend, as long as at least one child is six or younger and no more than two adults are in the group. The egg rolling is restricted to the six-and-younger crowd.

Note: White House egg roll rules are especially subject to change from year to year, so definitely check before you plan your trip.

For four days in late April, more than 100 artisans from around the country, selected from more than 1,000 entrants, display their expertise at such crafts as basketry, ceramics, decorative fiber, furniture, glass, jewelry, leather, metal, mixed media, paper, wearable art, and wood during the **Smithsonian Craft Show,** National Building Museum, 401 F St. NW (☎ 202-357-4000; Internet: www.smithsoniancraftshow.org; Metro: Judiciary Square). The Smithsonian calls this "the nation's premier juried exhibition and sale of contemporary American crafts." Admission runs about $12.

May

What better place to mark **Memorial Day** than Washington, D.C., site of so many memorials? Ceremonies abound at monuments to American heroes of the past. One of the most moving begins with a wreath-laying at 11 a.m. at the Tomb of the Unknowns in Arlington National Cemetery, where members of the Army's 3rd Infantry, the Old Guard, place flags at more than 260,000 graves just prior to the weekend (☎ 703-607-8052; Internet: www.arlingtoncemetery.org).

One of the most pleasant places to be on Memorial Day weekend is on a blanket or a folding chair on the Capitol lawn as the National Symphony Orchestra presents its **Memorial Day Concert** at 8 p.m. on Sunday (☎ 202-467-4600; Internet: www.kennedy-center.org; Metro: Capitol South, Union Station, Federal Center Southwest). The rain date is Memorial Day itself, but the concert is rarely postponed unless the weather is truly terrible. With the performers enclosed in a new band shell and a national audience looking on via PBS, the concert is not postponed lightly. This event is eclectic, with classical, popular, and patriotic music performed by the orchestra and glamorous guest stars.

June

Traditional music, crafts, and ethnic foods from the United States and around the world fill the Mall with enticing sounds, sights, and scents from late June through early July during the **Smithsonian Festival of American Folklife** (☎ **202-275-1150;** Internet: www.si.edu; Metro: Smithsonian). One of Washington's premier outdoor events, the festival, held at the National Mall, typically highlights one or two states and foreign countries.

July

The nation's capital does it up big for the nation's **Independence Day Celebration,** the National Mall (☎ **202-619-7222;** Internet: www.nps. gov/nama/events/july4/july4.htm; Metro: Smithsonian, Federal Center Southwest, Archives-Navy Memorial, Federal Triangle). Highlights include the parade along Constitution Avenue starting a little before noon, the National Symphony Orchestra concert (again with big-name guests) on the Capitol's West Lawn at 8 p.m., and the fireworks launched from around the Lincoln Memorial Reflecting Pool shortly after 9 p.m. Oh, and the Smithsonian folklife festival (see preceding entry) is in full swing! Expect big crowds, especially at the Capitol, for the concert. Other good places for viewing the fireworks, according to the National Park Service, include the Lincoln Memorial, the Mall between 14th Street and the Capitol, the Jefferson Memorial, and the Ellipse behind the White House.

Because of increased security in 2002, the Smithsonian Metrorail station was closed on July 4, and visitors to the Mall had to pass through screening checkpoints. If you want to use that station during your July 4 visit, check in advance to make sure that it's open.

Here's another place the locals go to watch the fireworks: the Key Bridge, which crosses the Potomac River between Georgetown and Arlington. Get there early to grab a railing-side spot. There's no seating, and you can stand on the sidewalks only (not the traffic lanes).

August

On an August evening each year, the U.S. Army Band performs Tchaikovsky's rousing classic, **1812 Overture** (Sylvan Theater at the Washington Monument, ☎ **202-685-2851;** Internet: www.mdw.army. mil; Metro: Smithsonian), accompanied by cannon fire from the

Presidential Salute Gun Battery of The Old Guard (the 3rd Infantry Regiment). Call or check the Web site for the exact date in 2003.

September

Washingtonians mark the end of summer by toting blankets and folding chairs to the Capitol Lawn and listening to the National Symphony Orchestra perform its **Labor Day Concert** (☎ 202-467-4600; Internet: www.kennedy-center.org; Metro: Capitol South, Union Station, Federal Center Southwest) with some guest celebrities. The concert starts at 8 p.m. on the Sunday of Labor Day weekend.

During the **Kennedy Center Open House,** Kennedy Center (☎ 800-444-1324 or 202-467-4600; Internet: www.kennedy-center.org; Metro: Foggy Bottom-George Washington University), the hall and grounds of the performing arts center showcase performances in music, theater, and dance. This event is popular, so be prepared to encounter lines for the inside events.

October

On an evening in October, known as the **Candlelight Open House** (Arlington House, the Robert E. Lee Memorial, Arlington National Cemetery; Metro: Arlington Cemetery), the house where Lee once lived is lighted by candles. Staff and volunteers dress in period clothing and discuss Lee's life while 19th-century music plays. Call ☎ 703-235-1530 or visit www.nps.gov/arho for date, time, and free tickets.

The famous **Marine Corps Marathon** (☎ 800-786-8762; Internet: www.marinemarathon.com) is so popular that you have to enter a lottery to have a chance of being one of the 16,000 runners on the fourth Sunday of October. Nicknamed the Marathon of the Monuments, the race starts at the Iwo Jima statue at the edge of Arlington Cemetery and winds through Georgetown and D.C., passing such landmarks as the Capitol, Union Station, Jefferson Memorial, Lincoln Memorial, Pentagon, and the Smithsonian Museums before returning to the starting point. You don't have to be a world-class runner to participate. Many highly fit amateurs rise to this challenge — my next-door neighbors, for example. If you want to run, register by phone or online. If you're not a runner, stake out a spot along the route and watch.

November

During the **Veterans' Day Ceremony** at Arlington National Cemetery (☎ 703-607-8052; Internet: www.arlingtoncemetery.org; Metro: Arlington Cemetery), the president or another high-ranking government official lays a wreath at the Tomb of the Unknowns at 11 a.m. Nov. 11.

December

In early December, a member of the First Family throws a switch to light the large Christmas tree in the Ellipse. The **White House Christmas Tree Lighting** (☎ **202-208-1631;** Internet: www.nps.gov/whho; Metro: Federal Triangle) ceremony kicks off the Pageant of Peace, which continues most of the month. Features include a Yule Log, a circle of smaller trees — each decorated on the theme of a state, territory, or the District of Columbia — and musical performances from 6 to 8:30 p.m. most nights. You have to apply early to get a free ticket for a seat for the tree lighting. In 2001, the tickets were gone on Oct. 9.

Keep in mind that it gets bitterly cold in Washington in the winter from time to time. If it's cold when you visit, bundle up good, or you may spend all of your time at the pageant huddled beside the burning Yule Log.

During the **Kennedy Center Holiday Celebrations,** Kennedy Center (☎ **800-444-1324** or 202-467-4600; Internet: www.kennedy-center.org; Metro: Foggy Bottom-George Washington University), the performing arts center hosts holiday-themed events throughout the month, including dancing in the Grand Foyer on New Year's Eve.

Chapter 3

Planning Your Budget

● ●

In This Chapter

▶ Managing your dollars and cents

▶ Avoiding surprise expenses

▶ Debating the use of traveler's checks, credit cards, ATMs, and cash

▶ Sharpening your cost-cutting skills

● ●

*W*hen I was a newspaper reporter, a joke around the Washington bureau was that the only guy on staff who thought D.C. living costs were reasonable was the guy who transferred from Tokyo! Washington is not a cheap place to live, especially when it comes to housing. But, believe it or not, the District can be a reasonably priced place to visit. Many attractions and events are free, and you can take cheap public transportation to most places. You can also use *Washington, D.C. For Dummies* to find good deals on food and lodging. The worksheets in the back of this book even help you build a travel budget.

Adding Up the Elements

Several factors come into play when you budget for your trip. To get started, list the following expenses:

> ✔ **The cost of getting from where you are to where you want to be:** Air fare, train fare, or the cost to drive. (See Chapter 5 for tips on finding the lowest fares.)

> ✔ **The cost of getting around once you get here:** Metro, bus, taxi, driving, and parking. Now, cross out driving and parking. (See Chapters 10 and 11 for your local transportation options.)

> ✔ **The cost of sleeping:** Your hotel rate, including tips and (gasp!) room tax, and, if you drive to D.C., the cost of parking your car. (See Chapter 7 for tips on finding the best hotel deal.)

> ✔ **The cost of eating:** Meals and snacks, excluding any that come with your lodging rate.

- ✔ **The cost of looking:** Luckily, D.C.'s top attractions are free. (You pay for them each April 15!)
- ✔ **Theater/entertainment:** See Chapters 22 and 23 for tips on cutting these costs down to size.
- ✔ **Miscellaneous charges:** For example, souvenirs and other shopping you're inclined to do.

To help you estimate your expenses, here's a breakdown of the areas where you can expect to spend most of your vacation dollars.

Lodging

Where to stay is the biggest financial decision you make on your Washington vacation. Rates vary considerably by location, amenities, and a property's reputation. Followers of the "less is more" philosophy can find a dorm bed at a hostel for less than $30 a night. If you make like Sherlock Holmes, you may be able to sleuth your way to a room for less than $100 at a no-frills hotel or a B&B. If your tastes run toward caviar, champagne, and a massage at 3 a.m., prepare to plunk down $300 to $400 and up. Somewhere between the extremes are well-appointed, well-located hotels charging less than $200 a night for couples or families of four. By taking advantage of packages and discounts, you can keep your costs down.

Restaurants

You may dine at the Golden Arches or on prime rib, eat Spanish *tapas* (appetizers) or Thai, order tortillas or tofu, enjoy seafood or chicken, or stick to veggies and fruits. You can find many inexpensive and moderately priced restaurants in Washington, and you can splurge if that's what you want.

You can save big bucks while sampling some of D.C.'s better restaurants by opting for early-bird specials or post-theater menus, choosing fixed-price deals, or eating your main meal at lunch when prices are lower.

Transportation

D.C. offers many forms of local transportation. Some choices definitely are easier on your pocketbook — and stress level — than others.

Driving yourself

No one in his or her right mind should use a car to sightsee in Washington. Here's why:

- ✔ Too many vehicles on too few streets

- ✔ Weird traffic patterns

- ✔ Drivers who think the function of all other vehicles on the road is to get out of the way

- ✔ Inadequate street parking

- ✔ High parking garage fees

- ✔ Relatively cheap cabs

- ✔ One of the best subway systems in the world

Are you a masochist? If not, don't drive in D.C. If necessity dictates that you arrive in the family buggy, I urge you to garage it. Be sure to inquire about your hotel's parking fees; some charge more than $20 a day.

Using the subway, buses, and cabs

The Metrorail (the D.C. subway) is clean, efficient, and reasonably priced. You can find stations near most major attractions. Buses go near the rest. Taxis, which will go anywhere, cost less than in most big cities.

Figure $3 to $5 per day per person to ride the subway and buses. (See Chapter 11 for cost-saving tips.)

Another option is to sit back and relax on **Tourmobile,** an open-sided tram that makes more than 20 stops near top tourist sites. The Tourmobile is a great way to get an overview of the top attractions and is especially attractive to families, the elderly, travelers with disabilities, and the weary of all ages. For one fare, you can get off and reboard as many times as you want during the course of a day. (See Chapter 11 for more details.)

The good news for travelers watching their wallets is that D.C. is pedestrian friendly. Because many of the top sights are close to each other, walking is the best and most efficient way to navigate the District.

Attractions

The top bargain in Washington is everything you want to see. You can walk into almost all of D.C.'s top attractions for free. Try that in New York, London, or Paris!

Shopping

When it comes to shopping, Washington isn't New York. But more than enough D.C. merchants are willing and able to take your cash. Major department stores are scattered around town. Several enclosed shopping areas are filled with boutiques, some affiliated with well-known chains, some unique to D.C. Georgetown's streets offer many interesting shops. And Washington even has a junior version of Beverly Hills' Rodeo Drive on Wisconsin Avenue. If shopping is your thing, you can find details in Chapter 19.

Nightlife

If you want to catch a big show, concert, or major dance performance, you'll pay $20 to $80 for most seats. If your budget won't stretch that far, Washington — the land of the freebee — will come to your rescue. The Kennedy Center's **Millennium Stage** serves up free entertainment nightly throughout the year. The **National Symphony Orchestra** and military bands play free outdoor concerts at several sites throughout the summer. The **Shakespeare Theater** performs outdoors for about a week each summer. And licking an ice cream cone while people-watching in Georgetown or Adams-Morgan provides substantial entertainment. See Table 3-1 for more about approximate and average prices in D.C.

Table 3-1	What Things Cost in Washington, D.C.
Item	*Cost*
Taxi from Reagan National Airport to downtown	$11
Metrorail from National to Metro Center: Rush hour (5:30 9:30 a.m. and 3 7 p.m. weekdays)	$1.35; other times: $1.10
Taxi from Dulles Airport to downtown	$5
SuperShuttle van service from Dulles to downtown	$22 first passenger, $10 each additional
Express Metrobus from Dulles to L'Enfant Plaza	$1.10
SuperShuttle from Baltimore-Washington International Airport to downtown	$30 for first passenger, $10 each additional
Taxi from BWI	$55
Pay telephone call (local)	50¢
Metro	$1.10 1.90 most trips within D.C.
Taxi	$5 (within same zone)
Admission to all Smithsonian museums	Free

Keeping a Lid on Hidden Expenses

Someone once said that travelers should pack half the clothes they think they need and twice as much money. That's a smart someone. As my wife can attest, I haven't mastered this concept and usually arrive home with clean clothing and empty pockets. Vacationers can easily get into trouble if they forget about a trip's hidden costs: surcharges, taxes, tips, and that pricey souvenir you can't live without.

Here are some extras that you should take into account when preparing your budget:

The biggest "ouch" among extra costs in D.C. is the 14.5% tax on hotel rooms. That adds nearly $22 to a $150-per-night room rate.

Other semihidden costs to watch out for as you plan include

- ✔ **Other taxes.** In addition to charging you 14.5% to sleep, D.C. tax collectors tack 10% onto your meals in restaurants and impose a 5.75% sales tax on many other purchases.

- ✔ **Room service rip-offs.** Enjoying that little breakfast or late-night snack delivered to your door can cost a lot more than if you go out to a restaurant to eat or get carryout from a deli.

- ✔ **E.T. (extra tariffs) phone home.** Some hotels charge a dollar or more for a local phone call from your room and impose higher long-distance rates than you're used to. Using a pay phone will cost you 50 cents for that local call. And using your home long-distance carrier's calling card can save you as well.

- ✔ **Minibar moola.** No, Virginia, those minibottles of booze and sacks of snacks in the cute little refrigerator are not gifts. You pay dearly for every nip and munch. Some minibars even have sensors that automatically charge you for an item when you remove it, even if you put it back later. Ask whether this scenario is the case before you start rummaging. (These sensors struck a real blow against one of my own cost-saving habits: emptying the refrigerator, buying beer and soft drinks at a store, chilling them in the fridge, and then putting the original contents back before I checked out!)

Cabbing costs

An unscheduled taxi ride can set you back. Here's a short course in D.C.'s bizarre taxicab zone system, which can be a mystery to long-time residents as well as first-time tourists. (For more details, see Chapter 11.)

- D.C. taxis don't have meters. You're charged according to the zones you travel through.

- A cab ride to a destination within the same zone costs $5. Add $1.90 for crossing into the next zone and so on. You can find a map — with north NOT at the top! — in the back seat of the taxi.

- Add $1.50 for each passenger who accompanies you.

- Add 50 cents for each bag the driver lifts into the trunk.

- Add a $1 for rush hour (7 to 9:30 a.m. and 4 to 6:30 p.m.) rides.

- If you take a D.C. cab into the suburbs (to an airport, for example) you'll be charged by the mile as the cabby reads it on his odometer.

- Humidity, air pressure, and phases of the moon can alter the calculations. (At least, that seems to be the case.)

Given the cost and confusion of taxi travel, you're often better off taking the Metrorail, walking, or boarding a bus.

Tacking on for tickets

Here's another enormous and misleading rip-off: the service charges you pay when you purchase tickets to almost any entertainment event. TicketMaster's charges are bad enough. But if you go to a broker in search of a hot ticket, you'll face an especially painful payment. Be sure to ask about these added costs before you hand over your credit card. Try to book tickets yourself for "must-see" events as far in advance as possible.

Untangling tipping etiquette

A tip says thank you more eloquently than words — at least that's what waiters, bartenders, bellhops, and taxi drivers believe. Although tipping is not obligatory, in polite society (and you're a member, right?) it's expected and appropriate. When dining out, tip 15% for average service. Dig deeper and give 18 to 20% or more for really good service. See Table 3-2 for other tipping tips.

Table 3-2	Tipping in D.C.
Worker	*Amount*
Bartenders	10–15%
Bellhops/porters	$1 per bag
Taxi drivers	15% of fare

Worker	Amount
Hotel maids	$1 a day
Coatroom attendants	$1 per garment
Concierge	$5 (minimum for securing tickets and other services)
Doormen (for hailing a taxi)	$1
Parking attendants	$1

Some restaurants add a gratuity to the bill for large parties. Don't be shy about asking whether this arrangement is the case. When you do figure a tip, calculate the 15 to 20% of the bill *before* the tax has been added.

Choosing Paper or Plastic to Pay the Bills

When it comes time to book the trip, tip the cabbie, buy the perfect souvenir, or check out of the hotel, what form of currency should you use? You'll need a credit card for most reservations, and depending on the lodging, restaurant, or venue, you can pay with plastic, traveler's checks, or plain old cash. In this section, I explore the advantages (and disadvantages) of paying with each method.

Traveling with traveler's checks

Buying traveler's checks used to be a standard part of preparing for a trip. But that was in the days before widespread use of charge cards and widespread availability of ATMs.

Because you can replace traveler's checks if they're lost or stolen, they're a sound alternative to stuffing your wallet with cash. But although they're safe, these checks can be a hassle to exchange. If you still want to carry traveler's checks, rest assured that most banks buy and sell them. American Express has a downtown office near the Farragut North Metro station at 1150 Connecticut Ave. NW (☎ 202-457-1300) and another by the Friendship Heights Metro in the Mazza Gallerie shopping mall at 5300 Wisconsin Ave. NW (☎ 202-362-4000). (See Chapter 9 for more information on acquiring traveler's checks.)

Relying on magic money machines

You can find 24-hour ATMs on nearly every street in D.C., it seems, as well as in hotel lobbies, many public buildings, and some restaurants.

You can use your bank's ATM card to withdraw funds directly from your bank account, or you can get a cash advance with a credit card. To determine which ATM network(s) your bank belongs to, check the back of your bank ATM card. Cirrus (☎ 800-424-7787) and Plus (☎ 800-843-7587) are the most popular networks. Call the 800 number for ATM locations or visit the Web sites for Visa and Plus (www.visa.com) or MasterCard/Cirrus (www.mastercard.com).

If you're not using your own bank's ATMs, many other ATM operators will tack on an extra withdrawal charge. Your bank may assess yet another charge on that transaction. If you use a charge card to get a cash advance, you'll likely start paying interest on it right away.

Regarding the green stuff: Leave it in the coffee can buried in your backyard. It's safer there. Whipping out a wad on a crowded street is a liability. You can encounter pickpockets almost anywhere. For a three- or four-day visit, I suggest bringing no more than $300 cash.

Charge! Carrying the cards

What did Americans do before plastic? Common sense dictates using charge or debit cards, rather than cash or traveler's checks. Plastic doesn't take up much room and is a lot safer than a pocket bulging with cash. The cards are good in hotels, restaurants, and retail stores. Foreign travelers get a better exchange rate when charging or using ATMs than when buying traveler's checks or obtaining currency at a bank. In addition, if you need a cash advance, you can get one at an ATM *if* you have a card.

If you use a credit card for a cash advance, you start to pay interest on the advance *the moment you receive the cash.* If you use an affinity card — one that earns you frequent flyer miles or credits in some other reward program — you won't get the miles or credits with a cash advance.

Here's something else you shouldn't leave home without: your personal identification number(s), or PIN(s), for your bank and charge cards. Commit them to memory and/or hide them somewhere far from where you carry your card, like in your toothbrush case. You can call the number on the back of your credit card for assistance if you forget your PIN and most banks or credit card issuers will mail it to you if you can answer a security question; but that may take up to a week to receive and isn't much help if you suddenly draw a blank at the ATM.

Cutting Costs in D.C.

You can conserve your cash in more than just a couple of ways when you vacation in D.C. Use these tips to keep costs manageable:

✔ **Travel off-season.** In Washington, off-season usually refers to winter or summer. Winter — even during the holidays — is the least popular time to visit. Because hotels hate empty beds, visitors benefit. Good deals also abound in summer, which helps explain why downtown crawls with families from mid-June through August. That's because Congress tries to spend as much of the summer as possible outside of D.C., so fewer business travelers are in town.

✔ **Package it.** You sometimes can save money by booking a package that includes, in many instances, airfare, hotel, sightseeing, and/or restaurant perks, and maybe even ground transportation. For particulars, call your travel agent or visit Travelocity's Web site at www.travelocity.com. (See Chapter 5 for more on package tours.)

✔ **Rent a kitchen.** Dining out three times a day adds up, even if you take all your meals at hamburger joints and pizza parlors. Book a hotel room or suite with a kitchen, and you can make breakfasts and late-night snacks for a lot less than you'd pay at restaurants. A refrigerator and microwave are particularly handy when you're traveling with kids.

✔ **Opt for kids-stay-free hotels.** You can save money by opting for hotels that let kids stay free in their parents' room. Ask whether two double beds or a sofa bed or rollaway is available.

✔ **Feed your faces for less.** Meals can take a bite (ahem!) out of any travel budget. Here are some ideas for trimming the fat off yours. (See Chapter 13 for more ways to save money on dining expenses.)

• **BYOM (bring your own munchies).** Toss prepurchased snacks into your backpack each day. They'll be cheaper than buying them in vending machines or from tourist-area stands. Easy access to appropriate munchies helps keep the younger tourists contented.

• **Bring a water bottle for each member of your party.** Refill the bottles from water fountains as you trek around town. This way, you avoid paying for pricey sodas or bottled H_2O. And it makes it easy for you to stay hydrated — an important health concern in hot weather.

✔ **Take Metrorail or hoof it.** You can get around D.C. on the cheap utilizing the subway and your feet. If you're planning to take at least five Metrorail trips in a day, purchase a $5 all-day fare card, and you can get on and off the subway as many times as you like after 9:30 a.m. on weekdays and all day on weekends and holidays. When you're not taking the subway, walk. Hop the 30-series buses for trips along Pennsylvania and Wisconsin avenues and M Street in eastern Georgetown.

Chapter 4

Tips for Travelers with Special Needs

*W*orried that your kids are too young or that you're too old to enjoy the best that Washington has to offer? Do you need to know the most accessible places in the District? Where to find the gay-friendly activities and venues? Then this chapter is especially for you.

Enjoying Family-Friendly Fun in D.C.

Washington is one of the most family-friendly destinations around. Those yellow school buses migrate here all year round for good reason: Class trips to Washington are rites of passage, like braces and pimples.

Many attractions have special sections and programs for kids. Washington's abundant parkland offers countless places for kids to let off steam. You can even find a dollhouse museum and a children's museum.

Restaurants entice your young and restless with kids' menus or half-portions, booster seats and high chairs, crayons, coloring books, and other pacifiers. The best ones offer menus for children that range far beyond the traditional hotdogs, French fries, and peanut-butter-and-jelly sandwiches.

When you check hotels, ask about special rates for families and perks like free or lower-priced food for kids in hotel restaurants. When you want some time *without* the kids, many hotels can link you up with baby sitters. Ask the concierge.

When you're traveling with kids, a suite with kitchen facilities can be a great place to stay. With a refrigerator and microwave, you can eat breakfast before setting on your adventures, and you can return for a mid-day snack and nap, which is a great way for the little ones to recharge. Separate sleeping areas — perhaps a bedroom and a living room with foldout sofas — let your kids enjoy their own space (and TV), while you relish some peace and privacy. Bring some snacks.

Many Washington attractions offer colorful, age-appropriate workbooks that enhance your youngsters' visit. Some host family film sessions, workshops, and educational programs for children. In museums, ask at the information desk. At National Park Service sites, ask about the Junior Ranger program. Kid-friendly food is available at most museum restaurants as well. (See Chapters 16 and 17 for kid-friendly sights and activities.)

Hands-on exploring in D.C.

Children want to do more than look when they're on vacation. Here is a small sampling of the things kids can *do* in D.C.

- ✔ Use dry ice and their breath to do a laboratory bench investigation of carbon dioxide at the **National Museum of American History.**

- ✔ Pet a tarantula (well, kids think it's cool!) at the **National Museum of Natural History**'s insect zoo.

- ✔ Touch a moon rock and peer into John Glenn's Friendship 7 space capsule at the **National Air and Space Museum.**

- ✔ Attend a **family concert** at the Kennedy Center and touch the musical instruments during the "petting zoo" period.

- ✔ Ride a **carousel** on the National Mall.

And that list is just a teeny-tiny sampling.

Frolicking in wide, open spaces

Washington's parks are an open invitation for your kids to behave like, well, kids. They can run around, ride the carousel, or fly a kite on the mammoth lawn known as the National Mall. If they'd prefer to frolic on water, your family can rent pedal boats under Mr. Jefferson's gaze on the Tidal Basin. Or you can take a hike in the middle of the Potomac River on Theodore Roosevelt Island. For more detailed information on the best activities for families, check out *Frommer's Washington, D.C. with Kids.*

Drafting a plan for your clan

To start your family vacation off right, let your kids get involved in the planning. They can start by writing to the **Washington, D.C., Convention and Tourism Corp.,** 1212 New York Ave. NW, Suite 600, Washington, D.C. 20005 or going to the Web site www.washington.org for general information.

The computer-literate can find useful and interesting information at the Web sites listed throughout this book. A few of the many that have information of special interest to kids are

> ✔ **National Park Service for the Washington, D.C., area:** www.nps.gov/ncro
>
> ✔ **Smithsonian Institution:** www.si.edu
>
> ✔ **White House Web site for kids:** www.whitehouse.gov/kids
>
> ✔ **National Zoo:** http://natzoo.si.edu

After your children toss in their two cents, pencil in your itinerary using the worksheets at the back of this book.

Savings for the Senior Set

If you're a senior citizen, you're (finally!) eligible for some special benefits when you travel. "Senior citizen" can be defined as being a lot younger than many may expect — 50 years old for AARP membership, for example, and 55 for many discount programs.

You may want to check out the benefits of joining **AARP** (known as the American Association of Retired Persons prior to setting its focus on recruiting Baby Boomers *before* they reach retirement age). Various discounts are available to AARP members, and local chapters run programs — including tours — for members. Information is available at ☎ **800-424-3410** or at the AARP Web site at www.aarp.org.

As you plan your trip, and after you arrive, always ask whether any restaurant, lodging, attraction, or form of transport has a senior rate. Carry identification that shows your age, and you may end up with significant savings over your younger counterparts.

Here are some additional ways for you to save money just by revealing your birth date:

> ✔ Many hotel chains offer senior discounts. Always ask when making a reservation. They may require you to register and pay a fee to join a seniors club first.

- ✔ Most U.S. airlines sell discounted tickets to older travelers. A younger traveling companion may qualify for the discount as well.

- ✔ **Amtrak** travelers aged 62 and older receive a 15% discount on most train tickets and 10% off the North America Rail Pass for 30 days worth of travel. The discount doesn't apply to first-class accommodations or the Auto Train between Washington's Northern Virginia suburbs and Florida (☎ **800-872-7245;** Internet: www. amtrak.com).

- ✔ Seniors 65 and older can buy half-price Metrorail fare cards in the Metro Center Station ticket office (12th and F streets NW) and at many stores, including Safeway and Giant grocery stores. You can also ride buses for 50 cents. In both cases, you must provide some proof of your age (driver's license, birth certificate, or passport).

Asking about senior discounts pays off, even if you don't consider yourself to be a senior citizen. You don't necessarily have to be 65. Many establishments — restaurants, theaters, and museums — offer discounts at age 62, while some even begin at age 55.

Traveling without Barriers

Washington is a highly accessible city for disabled visitors, and all major transportation providers offer services to help the disabled traveler get here in the first place.

To scope things out, check out the **Access-Able Travel Source** Web site: www.access-able.com. The site lists travel agents who have experience serving individuals with disabilities and provides some information about accessibility to lodging, transportation, and attractions for major cities around the world, including D.C. It also gives leads for renting wheelchairs and other health-care equipment.

Getting to, and around, town

Definitely let your carrier know ahead of time if you need any assistance — both when you make your reservations and again when you check in at the airport. If you travel with a seeing-eye dog or other service animal, ask about rules for taking it into the airplane cabin with you.

Amtrak asks you to make your reservation by telephone (☎ **800-872-7245**) rather than online if you're going to need assistance. If the regular reservations clerk can't answer all your questions, ask to speak to a customer service agent. The railroad also operates text telephone service (TDD/TTY) from 5 a.m. to 1 a.m. Eastern time at ☎ **800-523-6590.**

If you require the assistance of a personal care attendant, Greyhound (☎ 800-752-4841; Internet: www.greyhound.com) lets the two of you travel for one fare. If you're traveling alone and alert Greyhound 24 hours prior to your travel, the company can arrange "reasonable assistance" along your route.

Visitors with disabilities find **Metrorail** an excellent way to get around D.C. Every station has elevators, as well as fare card vending machines, entrance gates, and telephones, all built to accommodate wheelchairs. For the hearing-impaired, blinking lights along the edge of the track announce the arrival of trains, and (for everyone's convenience) newly installed announcement signs give information about the approaching train. A bumpy surface has been placed along platform edges to help the vision-impaired locate the platform edge. Elevator control-panels and signs in the stations contain Braille. On the train, bells chime and announcements are made when the doors are about to open or close, and the driver announces each station. Lift-equipped and kneeling buses make up more than 70% of the Metrobus fleet. The TDD number for Metro information is ☎ 202-628-8973.

Metro gives passengers with disabilities the same discounts available to seniors, but they must possess valid proof of disability. If the individual doesn't already have a Medicare card, however, the discount probably isn't worth the paperwork for someone who's visiting for a few days or even a few weeks.

Unfortunately, Metrorail's elevators are notorious for breaking down, a minor inconvenience for most passengers but a major problem for anyone with a disability. (Metro management was severely embarrassed not long ago when a frustrated man in a wheelchair — who had encountered several out-of-service elevators — screamed an obscenity and was ticketed. Management quickly apologized, tore up the ticket, and gave the man complimentary passes.) When entering the Metrorail system, ask the attendant whether elevators are working at your destination. You can also call ☎ 202-962-1212 for information on elevator outages. When elevators are out, Metro provides shuttle buses to serve those stations. Ask the attendant where to catch them.

Tourmobile has trams that are accessible to passengers with disabilities. The company also has vans with wheelchair lifts. For information, call ☎ 888-868-7707 or 202-554-5100.

Building accessibility

The **Smithsonian Institution's** museums, as well as most other public museums and attractions, are accessible to individuals with disabilities. Many films aired in museum theaters offer narrated audiotapes for the vision-impaired. Most live theaters have infrared headsets for the vision- and hearing-impaired. Live productions often feature at least one signed performance during the run. Call the theater for specifics. Some older facilities are less accessible than the newer ones, but that's far from universal. The best bet is to call ahead to make sure that the facility can accommodate your needs.

The Smithsonian has published a free guide to accessibility at its facilities. You can obtain it — *Smithsonian Access: A Free Guide for Visitors* — by asking at museum information desks, calling ☎ **202-357-2700** (voice) or 202-357-1729 (TTY), or writing to Smithsonian Information, SI Building 153, Washington, D.C. 20560-0010. The guide is available in large print, audiocassette, Braille, and computer disk versions. You also can read it online at www.si.edu/opa/accessibility/access/index.htm. You can find additional information for Smithsonian visitors with disabilities at the Web site www.si.edu/visit/visitors_with_disabilities.htm.

You may find that some old properties, historic inns, and bed-and-breakfasts are inaccessible, but most major D.C. hotels and restaurants are accessible. Ask specifically when you make a reservation. If you book through a travel agency or tour group, be sure to make your needs known.

Advice for Gay and Lesbian Travelers

Washington has a large and vibrant gay and lesbian community, so the city is a welcoming place for GLBT (gay, lesbian, bisexual, and transgender) visitors. The center of gay life is Dupont Circle, but gay and lesbian Washingtonians are thoroughly integrated into neighborhoods throughout the city. Gay and lesbian tourists are likely to be made welcome wherever they decide to visit.

Gathering gay and lesbian information about Washington

The prime source of news for the GLBT community is the *Washington Blade* (Internet: www.washingtonblade.com), a weekly newspaper that's been hitting the streets of Washington since 1969. It's filled with local, national, and international news, plus information about entertainment and community resources. It's widely available for free throughout the city.

Washington's premier gay and lesbian bookstore is **Lambda Rising** at 1625 Connecticut Ave. NW (☎ 202-462-6969). The **Human Rights Campaign,** the nation's largest GLBT rights political action organization, operates a Corner Store at 1629 Connecticut Ave. NW (☎ 202-232-8621).

Painting the town: D.C.'s gay nightlife

Some of the most popular gay/lesbian nightspots are

- ✔ **Mr. Henry's** (a restaurant with jazz on Friday nights and a mixed gay/straight clientele), 601 Pennsylvania Ave. SE, Capitol Hill (☎ 202-546-8412; Metro: Eastern Market)

- ✔ **Badlands** (mostly men), 1415 22nd St. NW, Dupont Circle (☎ 202-296-0505; Internet: www.badlands.com; Metro: Dupont Circle)

- ✔ **JR's** (mostly men), 1519 17th St. NW, Dupont Circle (☎ 202-328-0090; Internet: www.jrsdc.com; Metro: Dupont Circle)

- ✔ **The Hung Jury** (mostly women), 1819 H St. NW, Downtown (☎ 202-785-8181; Metro: Farragut West)

Getting to and staying in D.C. the gay-friendly way

The **International Gay & Lesbian Travel Association** (IGLTA; ☎ 800-448-8550 or 954-776-2626; www.iglta.org) links travelers up with gay-friendly hoteliers as well as tour operators and airline representatives. **Now, Voyager** (☎ 800-255-6951; www.nowvoyager.com), a San Francisco-based gay-owned travel service, is an excellent source for those who want assistance with trip planning.

The **Gay Hotel Network** (☎ 800-373-8880; Internet: www.gayhotel network.com) classifies the following properties as gay-friendly:

- ✔ **Carlyle Suites,** 1731 New Hampshire Ave. NW (☎ 202-234-3200; Internet: www.carlylesuites.com; Metro: Dupont Circle)

- ✔ **Henley Park,** 926 Massachusetts Ave. NW (☎ 800-222-8474 or 202-638-5200; Internet: www.hotellombardy.com-hph-index.htm; Metro: Gallery Place-Chinatown)

- ✔ **Omni Shoreham,** 2500 Calvert St. NW (☎ 202-234-0700; Internet: www.omnihotels.com; Metro: Woodley Park-Zoo)

- ✔ **Radisson Barcelo,** 2121 P St. NW (☎ 202-293-3100; Internet: www.radisson.com; Metro: Dupont Circle)

Part II
Ironing Out the Details

The 5th Wave   By Rich Tennant

"It's creepin' me out, too, but you're the one who wanted a hotel room close to the Lincoln Memorial."

In this part . . .

In this part, you get down to the nitty-gritty: How do you get from where you are to where I am (in D.C.), which is presumably where you want to be? Where should you stay, and how do you get the best deal on transportation and hotels? And would you like some tips on travel insurance, getting cash in a pinch, and packing like a pro?

Chapter 5

Planes, Trains, and Automobiles: Getting to D.C.

· ·

In This Chapter

▶ Using a travel agent — or not

▶ Checking out the pros and cons of package tours

▶ Comparing the many ways of getting to D.C.

▶ Uncovering the best fares

· ·

*O*ne of Washington's assets is an abundance of ways to get here. There's terrific train service between here and New York. If train travel is your thing, you can find service up and down the East Coast, with less appealing routes to and from the west. Metropolitan Washington also has three major airports, all served by major airlines. And, of course, the city is connected to the Interstate Highway System — though driving into town is no fun, and driving around town is even worse.

This chapter helps you decide which form of transportation to choose, whether to hire a travel agent or plan on your own, and whether you want to join a tour. You also discover how you can keep more of your money in your own pocket, no matter which options you pick.

Figuring Out Travel Agents: Friend or Foe?

A good travel agent is like a good plumber or a good doctor: hard to find but invaluable once you do. The best way to find one is the same way you probably found your plumber and doctor — by word of mouth. Pick the brains of friends and colleagues who use travel agents. Ask them about each agent's strengths and weaknesses and compare each one to your own preferences and needs. And, if you do decide to use an agent, keep evaluating as you work together to make sure that he or she really is right for you.

A good travel agent should know more than you do about your destination and how to get there. He should be able to find options for you that you don't know about, do the research, and make the reservations faster than you can, all the while saving you money.

That's not as true now as it used to be, however. A savvy traveler can get a lot of good information by consulting books like this one and by surfing the Internet. Airlines are trying to cut the costs of intermediaries by cutting the commissions they pay to agents and giving special deals to passengers who buy tickets from the airlines' Web sites. I have found fares on airlines' Web sites that travel agents couldn't match, and the agents have done the honorable thing of advising me to book those flights myself.

As you can see, whether you should use an agent depends primarily on your personal preference. If you have the time, you may actually enjoy making your own arrangements. If you're too busy — or would rather devote your time to other things — an agent's for you.

Even when you use an agent, however, don't just dump the whole job onto the agent's desk. Saying simply, "I want to go to Washington for a week in June" won't produce the itinerary that's perfect for you, and it may cost you more than necessary.

Well-informed travelers benefit the most from a travel agent. You don't need to study world geography, international cuisine, and hotel management, but you should invest some time researching your destination. If you have access to the Internet, check prices on the Web to make some ballpark cost estimates. (See the section "Getting the Best Deals on Airfares: plane and simple," later in this chapter, for ideas.)

Discuss the results of your research with the agent and use your newfound knowledge to evaluate the agent's suggestions. Be sure the agent understands as much as possible about your preferences so that he or she can make recommendations that are best for you.

Ask the agent up front how he or she is compensated. Some agents charge fees because of cuts in the commissions the travel and hospitality companies are paying.

Joining an Escorted Tour or Traveling on Your Own

Some people love escorted tours. The tour company takes care of all the details and tells you what to expect at each attraction. You know your costs up front, and you don't experience many surprises. Escorted tours can take you to the maximum number of sights in the minimum amount of time with the least amount of hassle.

Other people need more freedom and spontaneity. These folks prefer to discover a destination by themselves and don't mind getting lost on the way or finding that a recommended restaurant is no longer in business. They consider these surprises part of the adventure.

If you decide you want an escorted tour, think strongly about purchasing travel insurance, especially if the tour operator asks you to pay up front. *Note:* Don't buy insurance from the tour operator. If the tour company doesn't fulfill its obligation to provide you with the vacation you paid for, it may not fulfill its insurance obligations either. Purchase travel insurance through an independent agency. (See Chapter 9 for more information on the pros and cons of travel insurance.)

When choosing an escorted tour, make sure that you find out whether you need to put down a deposit and when you have to make the final payment. Other questions you should ask include the following:

- ✔ **What is the cancellation policy?** Can the tour operators cancel the trip if they don't get enough customers? How late can you cancel if you're unable to travel? Do you get a refund if you cancel? If *they* cancel? You may rethink your choice of tour operators based on their cancellation policies.

- ✔ **How jam-packed is the schedule?** Do they try to fit 25 hours into a 24-hour day, or do you have time to relax by the pool or shop? If waking up at 7 a.m. every day and not returning to your hotel until 6 or 7 p.m. sounds like a grind, some escorted tours may not be for you.

- ✔ **How big is the group?** The smaller the group, the less time you spend waiting for people to get on and off the bus. Tour operators may evade this issue, because they may not know the exact size of the group until everybody confirms their reservations. But they should give you a rough estimate. Some tour operators require a minimum group size and may cancel a tour if they don't book enough tourists.

- ✔ **How much flexibility do you have?** Can you opt out of certain activities, or does the bus leave once a day with no exceptions? Are all your meals planned in advance? Can you choose your entree at dinner, or does everybody get the same chicken cutlets? If you don't like to be told what to do, then a tour with limited options may not be for you.

- ✔ **What exactly is included?** Don't assume anything. You may need to pay for your transportation to and from the airport. A box lunch may be included in an excursion, but drinks may cost extra. Beer may be included but not wine. Knowing exactly what is included in your tour can help you decide whether the plan is right for you.

Choosing a Package Tour

Package tours aren't the same as escorted tours. You aren't accompanied by a guide on a package tour. Instead, they're simply a way of buying your airfare and accommodations at the same time — at a good price, you hope. Depending on the package, you may even get some "extras" ranging from some meals to discounted or free admission to events or attractions.

For popular destinations like Washington, package tours can be a smart way to go. In some cases, a package that includes airfare, hotel, and transportation to and from the airport costs less than just the hotel charge alone when you book the room yourself. The rates are cheaper because packages are sold in bulk to tour operators who resell them to the public. It's kind of like shopping for your vacation at a buy-in-bulk store — except the tour operator is the one who buys the equivalent of the 1,000-count box of garbage bags and resells them ten at a time at a cost that undercuts what you'd pay at the corner store.

Prices can vary greatly. Some packages offer a better class of hotels than others. Some offer the same hotels for lower prices. Some offer flights on scheduled airlines. Others book charters. In some packages, your choice of accommodations and travel days may be limited. Some let you choose between escorted vacations and independent vacations. Others allow you to add on just a few excursions or escorted day trips (also at discounted prices) without booking an entirely escorted tour.

Each destination usually has one or two packagers that are better than the rest, because they buy in even bigger bulk. The time you spend shopping around may be well rewarded.

The best place to start looking is the travel section of your local Sunday newspaper or in the nearest major newspaper if yours is too small to attract this kind of advertising. **Liberty Travel** (☎ **888-271-1584;** Internet: www.libertytravel.com) is one of the biggest packagers in the Northeast. **American Express Vacations** (☎ **800-346-3607;** Internet: http://travel.americanexpress.com/travel) is another option.

The airlines often package their flights with other accommodations. Among those that offer packages to Washington are

- ✔ **American Airlines Vacations** (☎ **800-321-2121;** Internet: www.aavacations.com)

- ✔ **US Airways Vacations** (☎ **800-422-3861;** Internet: www.usairwaysvacations.com)

The biggest hotel chains also offer packages. If you already know where you want to stay, call the hotel and ask whether it offers land/air packages.

Considering National Tour Companies

More than a million people visit Washington each year as part of a group tour. Some companies provide *fully escorted tours* with a guide or leader who is with you from beginning to end to make sure that everything runs smoothly. This type of tour is for those who like the comfort of being with other people and having someone else at the helm, especially on a first visit.

Other companies make all the arrangements for you; then you're on your own. Many people prefer the convenience of someone else booking airline seats, hotel rooms, rental cars, and sightseeing excursions. If you don't want to travel with a large group and prefer more flexibility, an *unescorted* (also known as an *independent*) *tour* probably is a good fit for you.

Some companies offer you a choice of escorted or independent tours. Here are a few Washington tour providers: (*Note:* These details, including the prices, are subject to change. Sometimes you may be given an option to upgrade, at a higher cost, to fancier hotel rooms or additional activities.)

- ✔ **Contiki** (☎ 800-CONTIKI; Internet: www.contiki.com), which specializes in vacations for 18- to 35-year-olds, offers a seven-day escorted East Coast tour by bus that spends about half the week in Washington. If you're booking the trip by yourself, but want the companionship and economy that comes with sharing a room, Contiki can find you a roommate. The tour, which includes at least one meal a day, costs $769 to $799 per person, double-occupancy. The fee doesn't include transportation between your home and the tour's end points, which are New York and Orlando. Contiki encourages its customers to book through travel agents.

- ✔ **Globus** (☎ 866-755-8581; Internet: www.globusjourneys.com) offers several tours of the Eastern United States that include stops in Washington. Travel is by train as well as bus, and nights are spent in expensive hotels. Starting prices, which include some meals and double-occupancy hotel accommodations, range from $1,099 to $2,299.

- ✔ **Cosmos** (☎ 800-276-1241; Internet: www.cosmosvacations.com), a less-expensive affiliate of Globus, also has several tours that include D.C. Starting prices for these itineraries range from $649 to $1,749.

To induce parents to bring their kids along, Globus and Cosmos grant a 10 percent discount on the land-only price to travelers from 8 through 17 years of age who are accompanied by an adult. You can also get a discount for sleeping three in a room. Children younger than 8 aren't allowed on the escorted tours.

✔ You can spend five days and four nights in Washington and Annapolis with **Tauck World Discovery** (☎ 800-788-7885; Internet: www.tauck.com) for $1,225 double occupancy. An eight-day tour that ends in Washington after traveling through south-eastern Pennsylvania and Virginia costs $1,840. Tauck also offers a three-in-the-room discount.

✔ **Yankee Holidays** (☎ 800-225-2550; Internet: www.yankee-holidays.com) sells three-, four-, and five-day D.C. packages, which include hotel accommodations and several local sightsee-ing tours. You're offered a considerable choice of hotel options, so the prices range from $128 to $547 per person for the three-day package and from $339 to $1,176 for five days.

For Independent Types: Making Your Own Arrangements

Washington is blessed with many transportation options. The city has three major airports, which encourages price competition among the airlines. One airport (Ronald Reagan Washington National Airport) and the train station are legitimate tourist destinations in their own right. For those who prefer making their own travel arrangements, here are the pros and cons of the various means of travel, as well as tips for finding the best fares.

Finding out who flies to D.C.

Washington's airports are **Ronald Reagan Washington National Airport** (the most convenient and known to locals as "National"), **Washington-Dulles International Airport** (25 miles west of downtown in what used to be the Virginia countryside and known, naturally, as "Dulles") and **Baltimore-Washington International Airport** (30 miles northeast of D.C., 8 miles from Baltimore, and known by its acronym "BWI.")

Each airport has its advantages — and disadvantages.

Ronald Reagan Washington National Airport

Republican members of Congress who didn't think enough things had been named for the 40th president bestowed this rather lengthy name on the airport. (It's located in Arlington, Virginia, and is managed by a regional authority.) The locals, for the most part, still call it National.

Nomenclature aside, National is a marvelous airport. The original termi-nal, opened in 1941 on the eve of America's entry into World War II, is a historic structure that is being restored and will stay in use. The new terminal, opened in 1997, is a striking, modern architectural triumph, with picture-window views across the Potomac River to Washington's landmarks. The new terminal was designed by renowned architect Cesar Pelli and has original art incorporated throughout. (The views from planes arriving from the north and west are spectacular, especially after dark, as you can clearly see Washington's most familiar buildings and monuments from the approaching aircraft.)

The food options at National are unusually palatable for an airport, including a number of spots operated by local eateries and a few sit-down restaurants, such as Legal Sea Foods and T.G.I. Friday's. If you find yourself in need of last-minute gifts or souvenirs, your options include shops run by the Smithsonian Institution, the National Geographic Society, and the National Zoo.

The airport is compact and easy to get around. With all the security added in the wake of Sept. 11, 2001, National is probably the safest airport to fly into or out of in the world. And you can't beat the convenience.

You pay $1.10 ($1.25 in rush hour) for a 12-minute ride on Metrorail's Yellow Line from National to the Archives-Navy Memorial Station about halfway between the White House and the Capitol. The trip to Metro Center takes 18 minutes and costs an extra dime because you have to change trains or take a long loop on the Blue Line. A taxi to downtown costs about $11 (before tip) and takes about 20 minutes (depending, of course, on Washington's notorious traffic).

National's downside (I did promise to list the cons) includes the fact that it *is* "national." If you want to fly here nonstop from outside the United States, Canada, or Bermuda, you have to touch down at Dulles or BWI. The airport also has fewer long-distance flights within the United States. Noise restrictions limit traffic late at night and early in the morning. And, because it's so close to the city, the airport has a high demand for its flights, so you find fewer bargains at National than at Dulles or BWI. "Fewer" doesn't mean "none," however. If you book early and follow the tips listed in the section "Getting the best deals on airfares: plane and simple," later in this chapter, you can find good deals at National as well.

The following airlines serve Ronald Reagan Washington National Airport: Air Canada, Alaska Airlines, America West, American Airlines, America Trans Air (ATA), Continental, Delta, Frontier, Midwest Express, North-west, United, and US Airways. (See the Quick Concierge at the back of the book for complete listings of phone numbers and Web sites.)

Washington-Dulles International Airport

Dulles also sports impressive architecture: the soaring main terminal. Designed by well-known architect Eero Saarinen, it opened to many *oohs* and *ahs* in 1962. The airport's main attractions today are its international and long-haul domestic service and its sometimes better fares than you can find at National. At Dulles, you can even catch a flight on Aeroflot . . . should you happen to *want* to catch a flight on Aeroflot.

Dulles' main disadvantage is location — of the airport itself within metropolitan Washington and of the facilities within the airport. The cab ride to D.C. takes about 45 minutes in favorable traffic and costs about $50. Travel within the airport is a bit of a challenge as well.

Dulles has grown and grown. As new terminals were added, airport architects didn't bother to connect them. Not many of Dulles' gates are at the main terminal. As a result, for most travelers, entering the terminal is just the beginning of their airport journey.

If you land at Dulles, you'll probably de-plane at one of the so-called "midfield" terminals. You then make your way to a loading zone where you board a monstrous bus (euphemistically called a "mobile lounge"). You then de-bus at the main terminal. Some of these contraptions take passengers directly to and from the planes.

The last time I flew out of Dulles, I hopped onto the wrong mobile lounge, which took me to the wrong midfield terminal, which left me puzzling for a bit over why I didn't see any signs to my gate. When I figured out what I had done, I had to take another mobile lounge back to the main terminal and then another back to the right midfield terminal. Fortunately, because I had arrived at the airport early, I still caught my flight. This escapade is one of many reasons I always leave myself a lot of extra time when I set out for an airport — and even more when the airport is Dulles.

The cheapest trip from Dulles to D.C. is by the 5A express Metrobus, which drops you at L'Enfant Plaza, a couple blocks south of the National Mall, which has a Metrorail station. You also can get onto the subway earlier, at the Rosslyn station in Virginia. The ride costs $2. It departs Dulles approximately hourly from 6:28 a.m. to 11:40 p.m. weekdays and slightly less often on the weekends.

Airlines serving Dulles Airport are Aeroflot, Air Canada, Air France, AirTran, Alaska Airlines, American, ANA, Atlantic Coast Airlines, Austrian Airlines, British Midland, British Airways, British Airways, BWIA International, Continental, Delta, Ethiopian Airlines, Grupo TACA, Jet Blue, KLM Royal Dutch Airlines, Korean Air, Lufthansa, Midwest Express, Northwest, SAS, Saudi Arabian Airlines, Swiss International, United, US Airways, and Virgin Atlantic. (See the Quick Concierge at the back of the book for complete listings of phone numbers and Web sites.)

Robert

Baltimore-Washington International Airport

BWI's prime attraction is price. It's served by discount carrier Southwest Airlines, which pushes down the prices of other carriers that fly to the same cities. Its distance from Washington means airlines have to try a little harder to attract capital clientele. That means that often — though not always — you can find cheaper airfares at BWI than at National.

BWI's disadvantage is, like Dulles', location. By cab, you're 45 minutes and $55 away from D.C., if the traffic flows smoothly. The SuperShuttle van service sets you back $30 for the first passenger and $10 for each companion. At least when you walk into BWI's terminal, though, you don't have to take a bus to your plane.

Metrobus offers the least expensive trip between BWI and Washington. The B30 express leaves the airport every 40 minutes between 7 a.m. and 10:50 p.m. weekdays (9:40 a.m. to 10:50 p.m. weekends and holidays). It drops you at the Greenbelt Metrorail station in about 30 minutes. Cost is $2.

Consider hiring a limo — a real limo, not a van service that calls itself a limo — if you fly into Dulles or BWI. The price is surprisingly close to a cab, particularly on the trip from D.C. to the airport. (You're charged more money when you're picked up at the airport, because the driver meets you inside the terminal.) My wife and I have used **Airport Car Service** (☎ **301-656-9100**) several times and have been quite happy with the results. It's $47 from downtown D.C. to Dulles, $52 from Dulles to D.C., $57 from D.C. to BWI, and $62 from BWI to D.C. — plus tip. There's nothing like lounging in the back of a Lincoln Town Car during that long ride.

If you take the SuperShuttle van from any airport, ask whether a discount is associated with your hotel.

Airlines serving BWI are Air Canada, Air Jamaica, AirTran, America West Airlines, American, Boston-Maine Airways, British Airways, Continental, Delta, Frontier Airlines, Ghana Airways, Icelandair, Northwest, Pan Am, Southwest, United, and US Airways. (See the Quick Concierge at the back of the book for complete listings of phone numbers and Web sites.)

Getting the best deals on airfares: plane and simple

Deregulation of the U.S. airline industry has brought a flood of discounted fares to the market. The problem is . . . a flood of different fares are on the market. How do you find the best one for you?

If money's no object, you may choose to fly first class or the less pricey but still premium business class. If money is an object, but you must buy a ticket on short notice, you can be stuck with a full-fare coach ticket. The high cost of full-fare coach — theoretically, the low-cost way to travel — can be shocking. My wife and I had to travel between D.C. and Chicago several times on business a couple of years ago. We were able to plan several weeks ahead on all but one occasion, and we were able to buy round-trip tickets for between $200 and $300 each. Once, however, our client summoned us on short notice, and each ticket cost more than $1,200 — on the client's tab, thank goodness.

If you want bargains, then you don't want plain-vanilla coach fares. You want . . . bargain fares. And you, or your travel agent, have to work a bit to find the best ones.

The general rule used to be that the cheapest tickets were for midweek travel purchased at least 21 days in advance and containing a Saturday-night stay. Winter fares were presumed to be the lowest and summer fares the highest. While those assumptions are not completely out of date, life is much more complicated today.

Checking many sources to save

Taking full advantage of the magic of computers, airlines now practice what is called *yield management*. Ticket prices are adjusted day-by-day — hour-by-hour, minute-by-minute — based on what the computer knows about the history of ticket-purchasing on a particular flight and how sales are going right now. The goal is to fill the plane and sell every ticket at the highest possible price. That means you're not going to get a bargain on a flight that's heading toward a sellout. But, because the airline wants to fill every seat — the seat's always there, and if no one's in it, it's not producing any income — you can find cut-rate fares on flights in danger of taking off without a full load.

The way for you to take advantage of this system is to check every possible source of information about ticket prices and to keep your travel plans as flexible as possible. That's because recent studies have shown that the cheapest ticket doesn't always show up in the same information source. To maximize your chances of finding it, you need to telephone the airlines, visit their Internet sites, check for newspaper ads, call a travel agent, and visit online travel agencies as well.

Finding bargains on the Internet

If contacting multiple sources is more hassle than you're willing to endure and you're comfortable on the Internet, checking several Web sites probably is your best bet. Visit a couple online travel agencies, such as Travelocity (Internet: www.travelocity.com) and Expedia (Internet: www.expedia.com). Visit the Web sites of the airlines that the agencies say have the lowest fares to see whether they're even lower there. Check the sites of airlines that you know fly the route you want to travel. And, if you try to collect miles in a particular frequent-flier program, check that airline's Web site, too.

Start your search as early as possible, but check back at the last minute as well; prices can drop on flights that aren't selling well. At the airlines' and travel agencies' Web sites, you can register for e-mail notices that alert you to last-minute deals on routes you specify or on any routes in case you may find one tempting.

If you can be flexible about travel dates or time of day, you increase your chances of finding the best bargain. Be alert for packages that save money by combining airline, hotel, and other reservations in a single purchase.

Be aware that the cheapest tickets are likely to carry the stiffest restrictions — no refunds and high penalties for making changes in your itinerary.

Some airlines offer discounts to older passengers. (Older can be anywhere from ages 55 to 65!) If you think you may qualify, be sure to ask. The discounts may not apply to the lowest fares, however, so it still pays to search. Southwest Airlines, in particular (which uses Baltimore-Washington International Airport as a hub), offers deep discounts on its already low fares.

Many airlines offer free tickets to children younger than two who don't occupy a seat. I urge you to think carefully about the implications of this arrangement before you take advantage of it. There's a reason that airplanes have seat belts and that the pilot urges you to keep your seat belt fastened when you're not standing in line at the potty. Things — including passengers — can get thrown around the cabin if the plane runs into turbulence, and sometimes the turbulence is unexpected. Picture your child flying out of your lap in that situation. The Federal Aviation Administration recommends that children who weigh less than 40 pounds ride in an approved child safety seat (car seat) that is properly belted into the airplane seat. Make sure that your safety seat is labeled "certified for use in motor vehicles and aircraft."

To give your kids — and you! — a little more room on your flight, request seats behind the bulkhead. You'll have to store all your bags in the overhead bins, however, because you won't have a seat in front of you to place them under.

Also known as bucket shops, **consolidators** are a good place to check for the lowest fares. These companies buy large blocks of seats from the airlines at a substantial discount and then resell the seats to travelers. You see their ads in the small boxes at the bottom of the page in your Sunday travel section. Some of the most reliable consolidators include **Cheap Tickets** (☎ 888-922-8849; Internet: www.cheaptickets.com), **1-800-FLY-CHEAP** (Internet: www.flycheap.com), and **Travac Tours & Charters** (☎ 800-872-8800; Internet: www.thetravelsite.com).

Another good choice, **Council Travel** (☎ **800-226-8624;** Internet: www.counciltravel.com), caters especially to young travelers, but offers bargain fares to people of all ages.

The **Transportation Security Administration,** the government agency that now handles air travel security, has devised new restrictions for carry-on baggage, not only to expedite the screening process but to prevent potential weapons from passing through airport security. Passengers now are limited to bringing just one carry-on bag and one "personal item" onto the aircraft. (Previous regulations allowed two carry-on bags and one personal item, like a briefcase or a purse.) The agency also maintains a lengthy list of items that cannot be carried on board. For a copy of the list, visit the TSA's Web site at www.tsa.dot.gov. See Chapter 9 for details on dealing with security.

The comfort zone

It's hard to believe that flying once was considered a luxurious mode of travel and airplanes were appointed like ocean liners. Ah, well . . . flying was more expensive and less reliable then, too. Today, coach-class seats are cramped, the cabin temperature is often too hot or too cold, and the air is as dry as Bob Dole's wit. However, here are a few things you can do — some when you book your flight — to make your trip more tolerable.

- ✔ **Bulkhead seats (the front row of each cabin compartment) allow a little more legroom than the other rows.** However, sitting in the bulkhead also has some drawbacks. For example, bulkhead seats don't provide you with a place to put your carry-on luggage (except in the overhead bin), because you can't place your bag under a seat in front of you. Likewise, you may find that the bulkhead seat isn't the best place to see an in-flight movie.

- ✔ **Emergency exit row seats also offer extra room.** Airlines usually assign these seats at the airport, so ask when you check in. You have to be capable of opening the exit door or window in the unlikely event of an emergency. And that means keeping your cool as well as having enough strength.

- ✔ **Wear comfortable clothes and dress in layers.** You never know what temperature you'll experience during a flight, so you'll be more comfortable with a sweater or jacket that you can put on or take off as needed.

- ✔ **Bring some toiletries on long flights.** Cabins are notoriously dry places. Take a travel-size bottle of lotion to refresh your face and hands near the end of your flight. If you're taking an overnight flight (the red-eye), pack a toothbrush and toothpaste in your carry-on bag to combat morning breath upon arrival.

- ✔ **Chewing gum helps combat ear-pressure discomfort.** Gum particularly helps during takeoffs and landings.

- ✔ **If you're flying with kids, bring toys to keep them entertained.** Throw something new into the carry-on to provide a moment of novelty when the child is feeling particularly unhappy. Don't forget the essentials — bottle, diapers, and so on. And pack some snacks, including beverages that you know your kids like.

Getting to D.C. Without Leaving the Ground

You don't have to fly into D.C. The city has a railway station . . . and highways, too!

Riding the rails

Whenever I travel up the East Coast, as far as New York, I take the train. Rail tickets aren't necessarily cheaper than airfare anymore, but the train is *soooo* much more pleasant. The seats are bigger and much more comfortable. You can walk about with ease. You can sit at a table in the club car and eat, or play cards, or have a cup of coffee or beer while spreading the newspaper out before you. You can work, if you're so inclined. You arrive at and depart D.C. right on Capitol Hill. Union Station — built at the beginning of the 20th century in the heyday of rail travel — is an attraction in its own right, with a Metrorail station inside and a taxi stand outside. The station's food court has a huge selection of places where you can buy great eats for the trip. Whenever the Price family goes to New York for an outing, the vacation starts as the train pulls out, and we picnic on food we bought at the station.

The trip between New York and Washington takes about three hours, give or take 15 minutes depending on which train you choose — the fast and comfortable **Metroliner,** the faster and more comfortable **Acela Express,** or the garden variety trains that make more stops along the way. Regular round-trip fares range from about $140 to about $300. (You pay more for comfort and speed, but the less expensive trains are fine.) Like the airlines, Amtrak offers special deals. Half-price tickets are available to children and seniors on many trains. AAA, AARP, student, and veteran discounts are available. And Amtrak sells packages.

In the Washington-New York corridor, train travel can be faster than flying. You can arrive minutes before the train departs the station. You travel from and to the heart of the city. It's a rare day when rain, fog, or snow disrupts the schedule.

You can catch a train in the Boston-Washington corridor just about any time you want. Service from elsewhere is less frequent and not competitive with air travel in terms of time.

For more information or to make reservations, call ☎ **800-USA-RAIL** or visit Amtrak's Web site, www.amtrak.com.

old Alexandria
waterfront — Bage Blue
Line

Driving to D.C.

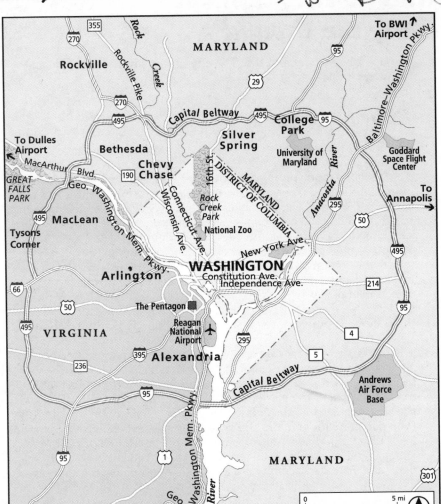

Driving into D.C.
If you drive to Washington, ask your hotel for directions.

In general:
- From the **Northwest**: Take **I-270**, follow **I-495** signs to Virginia,
  go east on **I-66**, which will take you onto Constitution Ave.

- From the **West**: Take **I-66** onto Constitution Ave.

- From the **South**: Take **I-95**, go north on **I-395**, then follow signs into Washington.

- From the **Northeast**: Take **I-95**, then go west on **U.S. 50**, which becomes New York Ave.

- From the **East**: Follow **U.S. 50** into town.

Taking a car

I live in D.C. Therefore, I drive in D.C. But you don't have to, and I advise you not to.

Driving *to* D.C. is another issue. It can be less expensive than air or rail travel, and some people just prefer to drive. The traffic on the region's highways is horrendous, especially at rush hour (which starts earlier and ends later with each passing day). But once you're in town, you can park your car and leave it alone until you're ready to go home. Be aware that parking fees tend to be as horrendous as the traffic. When you make your reservation, ask your hotel whether it offers parking and what it charges. Make sure that you're sitting down when you ask this question.

If you're driving to Washington, you may save money by booking a suburban hotel that offers free parking and is near a Metrorail station. It may take you longer to get to your first sightseeing stop of the day. But Metro remains fast and cheap, even from the farthest suburb. From Shady Grove, at one end of the Red Line in suburban Maryland, for example, it's a 34-minute trip to Metro Center that costs $3.25 in rush hour and $2.10 at other times. When you're researching hotels, ask how long it takes to walk to the Metro station, whether there's free shuttle service, or what it costs to take a cab and how easy it is to get one. You can park at some Metrorail stations, but competition for the spaces is heavy and starts before the rooster crows.

If you do drive to Washington, you encounter the **Capital Beltway** (I-495), which surrounds the city like a medieval moat — filled with raging drivers instead of raging sea monsters. Beware all who enter: There are speeders, chronic lane-changers, and vicious road-ragers . . . or one enormous parking lot. Surviving the Beltway is challenge No. 1. Challenge No. 2 is to actually get into the city.

Assuming that you're traveling to Washington on the Interstate Highway System:

- ✔ If you arrive from the northwest, you'll be on I-270; follow the I-495 signs to Virginia. The simplest route is to stay on I-495 until you come to I-66 East, which takes you into the heart of the city. Locals take the George Washington Parkway to I-66.

- ✔ From the west, I-66 is a straight shot onto Constitution Avenue.

- ✔ From the south, take I-95 to I-395 and then follow signs into Washington.

- ✔ From the northeast on I-95, there is no direct route into town. The easiest (using that term loosely) way probably is to stay on I-95 South after it merges with the Beltway and then take the Baltimore-Washington Parkway south to U.S. 50 West, which runs through the heart of D.C.

✔ From the east, you'll probably be on U.S. 50, which you can take into the middle of town.

Easily accessible on foot and by the Metrorail, Washington is your worst driving nightmare: confusing traffic circles, often poor signage, and streets that dead-end and then resume their course further along. That's not to mention scarce and expensive parking. Traffic is heavy from predawn to post-sunset. One wrong turn, and you may end up in Virginia. I had lived in Washington for years — I do mean years! — before I could consistently negotiate the drive from National Airport to my home in Upper Northwest without missing a turn and finding myself on a freeway to Virginia after I had entered the District.

AAA (☎ 888-859-5161; Internet: www.aaa.com) and some other automobile clubs offer free maps and driving directions to their members. If you're a member, give your club a call.

Riding the bus

Offering express bus service from several northeastern cities, **Peter Pan Bus Lines** (☎ 800-237-8747; Internet: www.peterpanbus.com) has been in business for 65 years. The company features wide-bodied coaches equipped with video cassette players (which show movies during the trip), climate control, and plenty of overhead storage compartments.

For travelers on a tight budget, the bus is probably the cheapest way to reach D.C. from most cities in the Northeast (with discount fares available for seniors, students, and children), usually much cheaper than the train. Travel time from New York City to Washington is listed at just over four hours, but with good road conditions, the drivers can cut some time off the run. Peter Pan's D.C. terminal is at 1005 1st St. NE, a long two blocks from the Union Station Metro stop (or you can take a taxi to your destination).

Once you get to Washington, you can get around via walking, public transportation, and taxis.

If you decide to ride the bus to D.C., make sure you do two things:

✔ Book your trip on an express bus, or you'll spend a few more hours getting there, as well as see the bus stations in places like Newark, New Jersey; Wilmingon, Delaware; and Baltimore, Maryland.

✔ Confirm that the run is on a Peter Pan bus. Greyhound/Trailways runs on the same line and books through the same Web site; their buses aren't as comfortable as Peter Pan buses, and you may end up in the middle of, say, the Maine to Miami run. (The code on the Web site is PPP for Peter Pan, GLI for Greyhound/Trailways.)

Chapter 6

Deciding Where to Stay

· ·

In This Chapter

▶ Finding a hotel, motel, or bed-and-breakfast that meets your needs

▶ Choosing the neighborhood to suit your stay

▶ Selecting a lodging that falls in your price range

· ·

*W*here you set up housekeeping during your vacation helps determine many things about your trip, including how easily you can put together the itinerary that you want, how much money you spend, and whether the hotel experience itself is part of your vacation pleasure.

The factors that determine where you want to rest your head boil down to location, amenities, and price. Although you pay more for the best location — amenities being equal — you may find well-located hotels are worth the extra bucks for their convenience. The closer your hotel is to the things you want to do and see, the less time you spend getting there.

Finding the Right Hotel for You

Accommodations come in many varieties. Options include chain hotels, independent hotels, hotels for business travelers, hotels suited to families, motels, B&Bs, and flophouses. I don't recommend any in the last category!

The chains: Tried and true

Almost all major hotel chains are represented in metropolitan Washington, from the most basic to super luxurious. For those who prefer familiarity when they travel — did someone say "no surprise?" — a chain is the way to go. The Quick Concierge at the back of this book contains a list of toll-free telephone numbers for the major chains located in D.C.

Independent hotels: Basic or luxurious

Independent lodgings tend to exhibit more personality and charm. Their lobbies may be less opulent, but their staff tends to be more personable, less harried, and more attentive to the individual guest. It's the difference between living in a big city, as a face in the crowd, and a small town, where everybody knows your name. Some independents are boutique hotels, which generally target a specific type of traveler (though boutique chains are appearing). People who prefer more intimate surroundings are usually happier in an independent hotel.

Motels and motor inns: No frills

While chain and independent hotels offer service and amenities (at a price, of course), motels are typically no-frills and, therefore, friendlier to your wallet. Motels usually offer free parking (a big plus when you consider downtown parking can cost more than $20 a day), a coffee maker, free ice, soda and snack vending machines, sometimes free coffee and bread or pastries in the morning, also known as the *continental breakfast*, and sometimes a swimming pool. Other than that, you're pretty much on your own. Don't look for a crystal chandelier in the registration area, plush terry robes, or phones in the bathroom. You can't call the manager for theater tickets or a club sandwich at midnight.

Motels are a good choice for budget-conscious travelers willing to trade location for savings. No motels are within walking distance of the major downtown sights in Washington. If you want to stay in a motel during your visit (see the Quick Concierge at the end of the book), head for the hills, in this case the Maryland and Virginia suburbs. From there, you have a 10- to 35-minute Metro ride to the heart of the city.

Bed-and-breakfasts: Close encounters

Bed-and-breakfast, or B&B, accommodations run the gamut from a closet-sized bedroom with a shared bathroom to an antiques-filled site oozing Victorian charm. The prices run the gamut, too. If you come to Washington for an intense, two-day Mall crawl, B&Bs probably aren't your best choice. But if you can spend more time, want to soak up the flavor of the city, and enjoy interacting with your hosts and fellow guests, a B&B may suit you well.

If you want more information on the bed-and-breakfast scene in D.C., you can get in touch with two very helpful B&B groups that have been around a long time — **Bed and Breakfast League/Sweet Dreams & Toast** (☎ 202-363-7767) and **Bed & Breakfast Accommodations, Ltd.** (☎ 202-328-3510; Internet: www.bedandbreakfastdc.com). Both act as reservation services, screening the inns and booking rooms.

Finding the Perfect Location

Tourist Washington is a compact place. You can hike — and it would be a hike — from one end of the prime sightseeing area to the other. From the Capitol to the heart of Georgetown is about 3.3 miles (4km). I walked it once with a visiting editor who really wanted to get a feel for the city. D.C.'s neighborhoods are very different, however, so the following sections offer information to help you decide where you would prefer to become a temporary resident.

Capitol Hill

The Hill, as it is known around Washington, extends from the U.S. Capitol in three directions: north, south, and east. If you bed down in Capitol Hill, you can stroll to the Capitol, the congressional office buildings, the Supreme Court, the Library of Congress, Union Station, the Capital Children's Museum, and the National Postal Museum.

Beyond the impressive stone governmental buildings, this residential neighborhood has brick row houses, local watering holes, mom-and-pop businesses, and a vibrant old marketplace. The neighborhood brims with vitality and a persona uniquely its own.

The perks of staying on Capitol Hill are as follows:

  ✔ In addition to having easy access to the Hill's attractions, you can walk to the Mall or hop Metrorail to anywhere. The Hill is served by Red, Blue, and Orange Line stations.

  ✔ If you arrive and depart by train, your lodging is conveniently close to Union Station, which is a great place to eat and shop as well as to travel from.

  ✔ This area is easier on your pocketbook than many other D.C. neighborhoods.

On the downside:

  ✔ Although the area has its *pocket parks* (small, welcome green spots in the midst of urban surroundings), it has less elbow room than other sections of the city.

  ✔ You won't encounter many problems in the immediate vicinity of the major hotels and attractions, but the farther you go from the Capitol, the less safe you'll be at night.

Washington, D.C. Hotel Neighborhoods

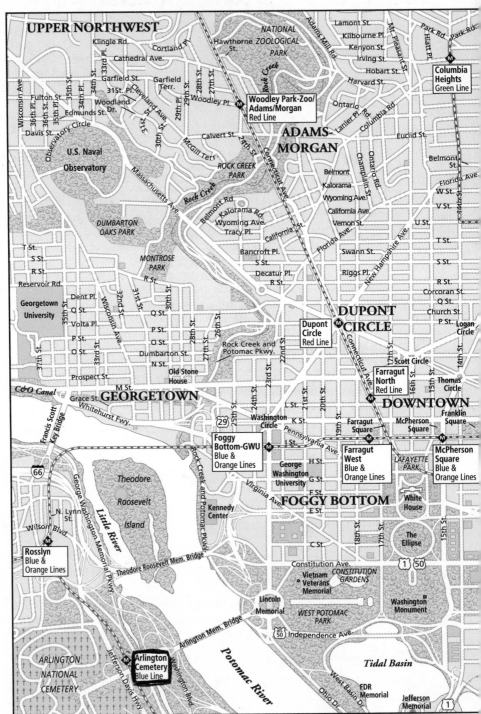

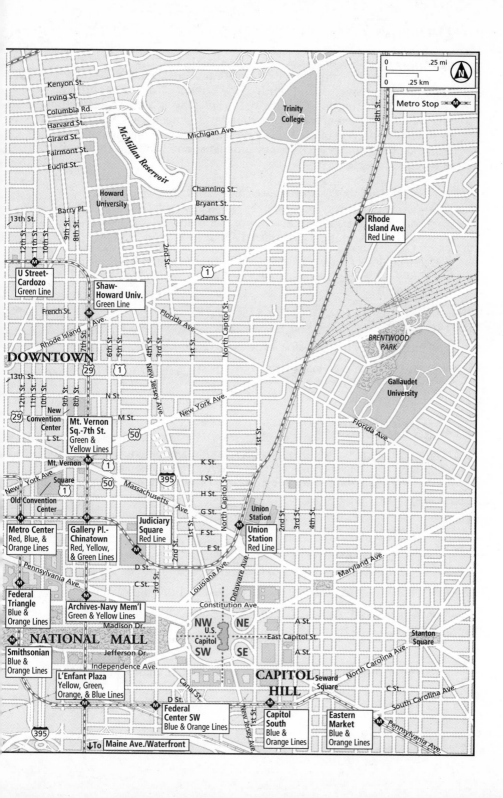

Downtown

Office buildings, shops, hotels, and restaurants vie for space in this central area, which runs roughly from 6th to 22nd streets NW, north of Pennsylvania Avenue and south of the Dupont Circle neighborhood. Once as scintillating as white bread, the area now is a prime destination on evenings and weekends thanks to redevelopment along Pennsylvania Avenue, the addition of the MCI Center sport/entertainment arena, the growth of high-quality restaurants and night spots, and the endurance of long-time theaters.

The perks of staying Downtown are

- ✔ You're within walking distance of major attractions, as well as all those night spots, theaters, and shops.
- ✔ Many of the city's best restaurants are located here, as are a large number of inexpensive eateries frequented by downtown workers at lunch time.

On the other hand:

- ✔ You can pay a high price for the convenient location.
- ✔ Much of the area loses its vitality when the office workers go home for the night.

Dupont Circle

A melting pot known for its bookstores, boutiques, galleries, restaurants, night life, think tanks, activist groups, and nonprofit organizations — as well as the focal point of Washington's gay community — Dupont Circle is an insomniac's dream long after most of D.C. has rolled up the sidewalks.

On the upside:

- ✔ This area is hip, trendy, lively, colorful, more interesting, and less homogenized than most of the other neighborhoods in town.
- ✔ You're close to some of the city's best nightlife and dining.
- ✔ You can find reasonable prices here, too.

The drawbacks include

- ✔ You're further from major tourist attractions than you would be in several other areas.
- ✔ All that after-dark partying means the area can get very noisy at night.
- ✔ In a city full of traffic and parking horrors, this neighborhood can be particularly nightmarish.

Foggy Bottom/West End

This former industrial area west of the White House once was known as Funkstown. Now, more and more of it is becoming known as George Washington University, as that major educational institution gobbles up the neighborhood amid conflict with its neighbors. The area is relatively quiet, with row houses lining brick sidewalks on residential blocks, while hotels, restaurants, and office buildings line Pennsylvania Avenue and are scattered throughout the neighborhood.

The pros:

✔ You're close to the White House, Kennedy Center, State Department, George Washington University, the infamous Watergate, and Georgetown.

✔ You can hop Metrorail or the 30-series Metrobuses for longer trips.

✔ A very pleasing European ambiance pervades the neighborhood.

✔ Foggy Bottom is quieter than other sections of town.

The only con is that the quiet also means that the area usually has less excitement than elsewhere.

Georgetown *Young College*

An instantly recognizable address for eons, Georgetown was a colonial tobacco port situated due west of Foggy Bottom. Georgetown dances to a beat all its own. A rainbow of visitors — from D.C., the suburbs, local universities, and all over the world — frequent the restaurants, pubs, and boutiques along Wisconsin Avenue, M Street, and the K Street waterfront.

Staying in Georgetown is great because:

✔ Like Dupont Circle, Georgetown jumps a lot more than most of the rest of Washington.

✔ An abundance of shopping, dining, and nightlife is within walking distance.

✔ Walk just northwest of the central Wisconsin Avenue and M Street intersection, and you're in another college community — Georgetown University.

✔ Walk just northeast, and you enter Washington's most exclusive residential neighborhood, home to some of the richest, most powerful, and most famous people in the world.

On the other hand:

- ✔ If you seek tranquility, especially at night, stay elsewhere. The noise on weekends (when the student population comes out to party) can grow very loud.

- ✔ Georgetown has no Metrorail station, so you have to hail a cab, hop a bus, or hike to Foggy Bottom or (believe it or not) the Rosslyn Station in Virginia.

- ✔ Georgetown can get very crowded. Traffic is bad at all times and is particularly horrendous during rush hour, on weeknights, and throughout the weekends.

Upper Northwest

The Upper Northwest is where I live, and I love it. It's got lots of residential housing, the city's best public schools, plus hotels, restaurants, movie theaters, stores, and a substantial amount of office space. But the area isn't the first choice for tourists. While several things may draw you here, you're going to want to spend most of your vacation in other parts of town.

The good:

- ✔ Families appreciate the area's proximity to the National Zoo, a major child-pleaser, on Connecticut Avenue.

- ✔ You find Washington's answer to Beverly Hills' Rodeo Drive near the Friendship Heights Metrorail Station.

- ✔ Washington National Cathedral is on upper Wisconsin Avenue.

The only bad thing is that you'll be taking Metrorail, Metrobus, or a taxi to see most of the sights.

Getting Your Money's Worth

When you check out the hotel listings in Chapter 8, you find one to five $ symbols for each hotel. The $ symbols reflect the average of the hotel's high- and low-end rack rates for weekdays during the high season. (*Rack rates* are the hotel's standard rate, before any discounts are applied.)

Price changes are inevitable in this business, so you may be offered a rate that is lower (it could happen!) or higher than the rates listed in this book.

Unless otherwise noted, the hotel accommodations include private bathrooms and air-conditioning, so even if you get hot under the collar about the price, you'll have the opportunity to cool down once you get to your room. You also can expect a radio, TV, and at least one phone. Some phone systems come with Internet access and voice-mail capability. Data ports, once a rarity, are fast approaching standard, as are designated business suites and/or business centers with all the electronic essentials. Not long ago, you had to request irons and ironing boards from housekeeping. Now these aids are as common as pillows in many rooms. When you're done ironing (or maybe while you're ironing), you can tune into your favorite network show and, in most cases, cable channels (HBO, CNN, ESPN, and so on), as well as pay-per-view movies. The list of amenities grows larger as you climb the hotel price ladder.

For an idea of what you get for your money, here's the lowdown on the $ ratings:

- ✔ **$ (Less than $125).** In this category, you may share a dormlike room at a hostel; stay in a smallish room in an older, no-frills hotel; stay at a B&B (perhaps with a shared bathroom); or check into a plain, budget motel. Your room will be clean and probably include a TV and phone. Don't expect room service or chocolates on the pillows.

- ✔ **$$ ($125 – $179).** The rooms in this category may be smallish or in older buildings, but you can count on a TV (most likely with cable) and other amenities (coffee maker, soaps, shampoos). You can find some good bargains in housekeeping suites in this price range.

- ✔ **$$$ ($180 – $275).** These rooms are in full-service hotels minus the most luxurious of amenities, or they're nice all-suite properties. Expect hair dryers, irons, coffee makers, on-site restaurants, health clubs (on- or off-site), and cable TV. You may even have access to room service.

- ✔ **$$$$ ($276 – $350).** Now you're talking luxury. Besides a large, well-decorated room, you can count on a spacious bathroom with ample towels and a terry robe — as a loaner, so don't pack it as a souvenir. Expect a full range of amenities, multiple phones, a data port, minibars, on-site restaurant(s), a health club, and room service. The staff pays great attention to the hotel's appearance and to high-quality service.

- ✔ **$$$$$ (More than $350).** You pay for the prestigious name, location, service, and opulence. Expect round-the-clock concierge and room service, sumptuous lobbies and room furnishings (entertainment centers, heated towel racks, in-room safes), one or more restaurants for fine dining, a bar and/or lobby cocktail lounge, an on-site spa/health club, shuttle service, staff members who trip over themselves to serve you, and an evening turndown of your bedding with chocolates left at the bedside.

Chapter 7

Booking the Best Hotel Room Your Money Can Buy

In This Chapter

▶ Getting a good deal on your hotel room

▶ Shopping for a hotel on the Internet

▶ Arriving in town without a reservation

Some folks call a hotel, ask for a rate, and pay it with no more questions asked. These people are the same folks who go to a car lot and pay sticker price. You, however, aren't going to mimic these people by paying the first price you're quoted, because you're going to use the tips that follow to find the best hotel room for your money.

The Truth about Rack Rates (and Why You Don't Have to Pay Them)

If you walk in off the street and ask for a room for the night, you receive the hotel's maximum charge for that room or its *rack rate*. (During your next overnight stay in a hotel, take a peek at the fire and/or emergency directions posted on the back of your door; the rack rates usually are posted on or near these notices.) If a hotel can get away with collecting its rack rate for a room, the management is very happy. But here's the scoop: Hardly anyone forks over the rack rate. The step you need to take to avoid being charged the rack rate is surprisingly simple: Ask whether the hotel offers a cheaper or discounted rate. You almost always get a better price! Better yet, don't walk in off the street. Make reservations ahead of time.

Getting the Best Room at the Best Rate

Room rates change with the season, as occupancy rates rise and fall. If a hotel is close to full, it's less likely to extend discount rates; if a hotel is close to empty, it may be willing to negotiate. D.C. hotels are more likely to negotiate with you on weekends and during low season.

Room prices are subject to change without notice; therefore, the rates quoted in this book may be different from the actual rate you receive when you make your reservation.

A short course in D.C. hotelnomics

To everything there is a season — and everything includes hotel rates. Here's a short course on how the time of year affects hotel prices in D.C.

Low season — low rates

The three best times of year to find deals on hotel rooms in D.C. are

- **Thanksgiving through New Year's.** Fewer travelers leave home and hearth.

- **July and August.** Congress is in recess, and the city is in siesta mode.

- **Weekends** throughout the year. Politicians (and all the folks who follow them) get outta town on the weekends, leaving space for everyone else.

Between Thanksgiving and early January, the pace slows down. Many members of Congress take very long breaks from Washington. (The House calls them "district work periods." The Senate calls them "recesses.") With fewer people in town, hotels cut their rates. (Someday "Thankmas" may become a national — extended — holiday.) During July and August, when the Senate and House office buildings are morguelike because the elected officials are away, hotels woo visitors with lower charges. (For more on Washington's high and low seasons, see Chapter 2.) And on the weekends, the gang on the Hill takes to the highway, visiting lobbyists go back home, and the rates at the hotels take a dip.

High season — high prices

High season in Washington is

- **Mid-March through June.** Everyone wants to visit D.C. in the spring, and who can blame them? The city blossoms in the warm weather, but, alas, so do hotel prices.

> ✔ **September through mid-November.** Congress is back in session, and Capitol Hill is hopping in fall. The weather outside may be delightful, but it's a safe bet that hotel prices will be frightful.

In spring, the Cherry Blossom Festival, good weather, and spring breaks historically draw visitors to the city in huge numbers. The weather is usually mild into June, and that keeps the crowds coming. High season also occurs when Congress is in session. When the Capitol is a beehive of activity, those who want to influence the Congress converge on the city's hotels. As a result, innkeepers can and do charge higher prices.

Planning strategically for savings

The amount you spend to bed down eats a big chunk of your travel dollars. In all but the smallest accommodations, the rate you pay for a room depends on many factors — chief among them being how you make your reservation. Prices change, sometimes faster than room service can deliver coffee and a bagel.

Calling your friendly travel agent

A travel agent may be able to negotiate a better price with certain hotels than you can get by yourself. Often, the hotel gives the agent a discount in exchange for steering his or her business toward that hotel.

Your travel agent may suggest a package deal (with airfare) and/or traveling with a group. (See Chapter 5 for more on package tours.) Booking with a group can be the best way to get the best deal. Not only do you hand over the responsibility of planning a trip to someone else — the tour operator — you often get a better rate. Hotels, joyful at the prospect of booking 20 rooms instead of one or two, give tour operators a discount that's passed on to you.

Making your own hotel reservations

Hotel chains take telephone reservations through a central toll-free number and at the individual hotels. (See the Quick Concierge at the back of the book for toll-free numbers for the major chains.) Sometimes the toll-free number and the local numbers produce different rates. Your best bet is to call both, to see which reservations agent gives you a better deal.

Be sure to mention membership in AAA, AARP, frequent-flier programs, and any other corporate rewards programs, or if you're a government employee when you make your reservation. You never know when doing so can save you a few dollars off your room rate.

After you make your reservation, ask a few more questions. These inquiries can go a long way toward making sure that you secure the best room in the house.

✔ **Always ask whether a corner room is available at the same price.** Sometimes corner rooms have more space and windows (with views). And the corner location may mean a quieter environment. If you're located at the end of the hall, you don't hear your neighbors passing your room or using the elevator all night.

✔ **Steer clear of construction zones.** Be sure to ask whether the hotel is renovating. If it is, request a room away from the renovation site. The noise and activity may be a bit more than you want to deal with on your vacation.

✔ **Request smoking or nonsmoking rooms.** Be sure to indicate your preference. Otherwise, you may get stuck with a room that doesn't meet your needs.

✔ **Inquire about the location of the restaurants, bars, and night spots.** These areas of the hotel can be sources of irritating noise. On the other hand, if you want to be near the action, or if you have a disability that makes it difficult for you to get around, you may choose to be close to these amenities.

Even if you secure a relatively quiet room, strange noises, loud TVs, and snoring partners can wreak havoc with your sleep. Carry earplugs when you travel.

Surfing the Web for hotel deals

You also can use the Internet to gather information and make hotel reservations. In fact, because so many different deals are available, your best bet is to use both the telephone and the Internet when you search for the best prices.

Online travel agencies, such as Travelocity and Expedia (see Chapter 5 for details), book hotel reservations as well as transportation. Major hotel chains — and many individual hotels — book rooms online the same way that airlines and Amtrak book transportation. (See the Quick Concierge for chains' Web addresses and phone numbers.)

Some Web sites specialize in booking rooms. Two of them are

✔ **Hoteldiscount!com (☎ 800-715-7666)**, which chose a name that's an impossible Web address (no dot!). You find it by surfing to www.hoteldiscount.com. It lists bargain room rates at hotels in hundreds of U.S. and international cities, including — most important — Washington.

✔ **TravelWeb (☎ 866-437-8131;** Internet: www.travelweb.com) is a joint venture of the Hilton, Hyatt, Marriott, Six Continents, and Starwood hotel chains. The reservation service is not limited to those chains' properties. TravelWeb's Click-It Weekends, updated each Monday, offers specially discounted weekend deals.

Taxing matters

Another important factor to remember when booking your hotel room is Washington's hotel tax. The District tacks a hefty 14.5% tax onto your hotel bill. So if your room's rate is $150 a night, you'll pay more than $170. Make sure to ask whether the hotel tax is included in the price when you're quoted a room rate — it probably isn't.

Showing Up without a Reservation

Arriving in D.C. and *then* looking for a place to stay is not the preferred way to find a bargain — or a room, for that matter. If you do find yourself in that bind, start calling the major hotel chains and asking what they have available. (See the Quick Concierge at the back of this book for their phone numbers.) Or try some local reservation services, such as **Capitol Reservations** (☎ **800-847-4832;** Internet: www.hotelsdc. com) and **Washington, D.C. Accommodations** (☎ **800-554-2220** or 202-289-2220; Internet: www.dcaccommodations.com).

Chapter 8

Washington's Best Hotels

· ·

· ·

*B*ecause so many different kinds of people come to Washington with regularity, the city has a wide variety of accommodations. The idealistic young and penniless come here, perhaps to protest, to volunteer for many of the do-gooder groups in town, or just to see the sights. At the other extreme, high-rolling lawyers and lobbyists arrive with no worry about expense accounts because their clients will be picking up whatever tab is presented. The rest of the world, in the gigantic middle between those extremes, are looking for budget, moderate, or moderately luxurious accommodations. And visitors can find them all.

To help you choose, I compiled a concise list of the best Washington hotels in various price ranges and neighborhoods. For quick cost-comparison, you'll find one to five $ symbols beside each hotel's review.

The dollar signs translate into price categories as follows:

> ✔ $ = Less than $125
>
> ✔ $$ = $125–$179
>
> ✔ $$$ = $180–$275
>
> ✔ $$$$ = $276–$350
>
> ✔ $$$$$ = More than $350

First up, you find reviews of the best hotels in alphabetical order. At the end of this chapter, I compiled an index of hotels by price, followed by an index by location. And I also indicate the hotels' locations on the map in this chapter so that you can get an idea of each hotel's neighborhood.

In case these inns are booked, I also include a list of runner-ups.

If you're traveling with kids, note the Kid Friendly icons. These hotels feature amenities that are especially attractive to families.

Hotels in Washington, D.C.

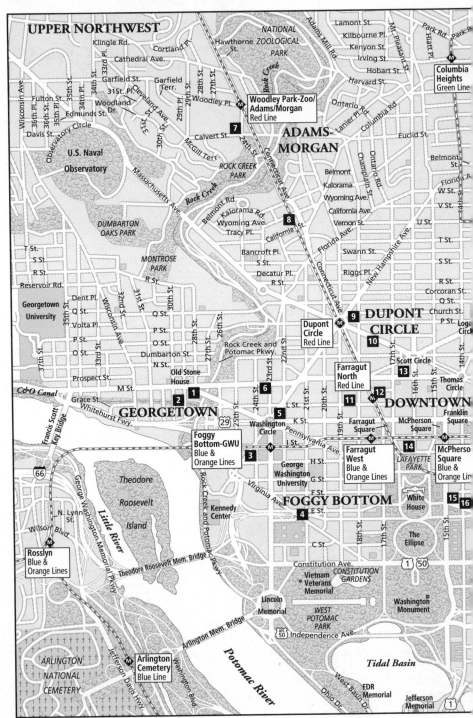

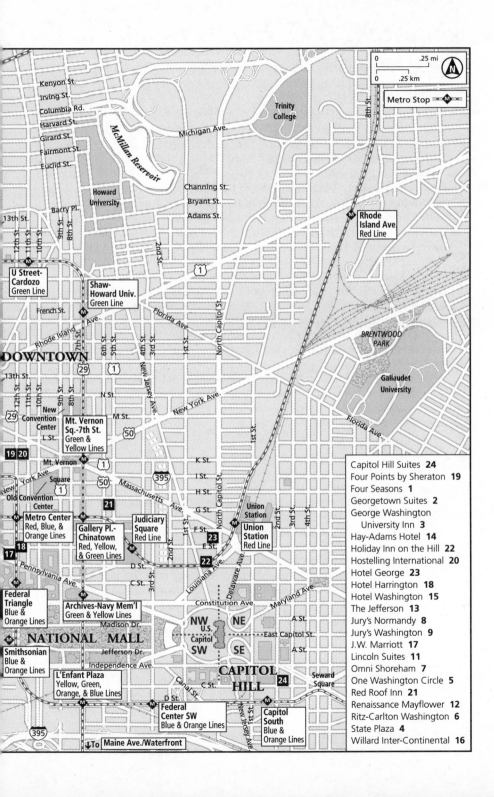

Kenyon St.
Irving St.
Columbia Rd.
Harvard St.
Girard St.
Fairmont St.
Euclid St.

McMillan Reservoir

Michigan Ave.

Trinity College

8th St.

Metro Stop

.25 mi
.25 km

13th St.

Barry Pl.
Howard University

9th St.
8th St.

2nd St.

Channing St.
Bryant St.
Adams St.

Rhode Island Ave. Red Line

U Street-Cardozo Green Line

12th St.
11th St.
10th St.

Shaw-Howard Univ. Green Line

French St.

Florida Ave.

U.S. 1

Rhode Island Ave.

7th St.
6th St.
5th St.
4th St.
3rd St.
1st St.

North Capitol St.

BRENTWOOD PARK

DOWNTOWN

13th St.

29

U.S. 1

New Jersey Ave.

Gallaudet University

12th St.
11th St.
10th St.
9th St.
8th St.

N St.

New York Ave.

Florida Ave.

29

New Convention Center

Mt. Vernon Sq.-7th St. Green & Yellow Lines

50

M St.

1st St.

L St.

19 20

Mt. Vernon Square

U.S. 1

50

Massachusetts Ave.

395

K St.

I St.

H St.

Union Station

Old Convention Center

21

G St.

Union Station Red Line

3rd St.
4th St.

Metro Center Red, Blue, & Orange Lines

Gallery Pl.-Chinatown Red, Yellow, & Green Lines

Judiciary Square Red Line

F St.

23

2nd St.

17   **18**

E St.

22

Pennsylvania Ave.

3rd St.

D St.

Louisiana Ave.

Delaware Ave.

Maryland Ave.

Federal Triangle Blue & Orange Lines

Archives-Navy Mem'l Green & Yellow Lines

C St.

Constitution Ave.

Madison Dr.

NW   **NE**

U.S. Capitol

East Capitol St.

NATIONAL MALL

Jefferson Dr.

SW   **SE**

A St.

A St.

Smithsonian Blue & Orange Lines

Independence Ave.

CAPITOL HILL

Seward Square

L'Enfant Plaza Yellow, Green, Orange, & Blue Lines

Canal St.

C St.

24

395

D St.

Federal Center SW Blue & Orange Lines

New Jersey Ave.

Capitol South Blue & Orange Lines

1st St.

↓To **Maine Ave./Waterfront**

Washington, D.C. Hotels from A to Z

Capitol Hill Suites
$$ Capitol Hill

You become an instant Capitol Hill insider when you bed down at this recently renovated hotel. You'll be two blocks from the Capitol Grounds and across the street from the Library of Congress's Madison Building. You get dining privileges at the nearby Capitol Hill Club, the Republican Party social club that's next door to GOP National Committee headquarters. And you may bump into one of the lawmakers who take advantage of the hotel's long-term rates to make this their Washington home. All suites have kitchenettes. The junior suites are one-room efficiencies, with one queen bed and an armchair with ottoman or sofa bed. Superior suites have two queen beds, an alcove for the kitchenette, and a sitting area with an armchair and ottoman or a sofa bed. The one-bedroom suites have a king or queen bed and a separate living room with a sofa bed. In the 2000 renovation, the hotel's operators tried to capture what they call the "traditional Capitol Hill" look. That look means lots of navy blue and burgundy, leather, marble, and cherry wood. Room rate includes continental breakfast and use of a nearby health club. Valet parking is available. The Capitol South Metrorail Station is about a block away.

200 C St. SE at 2nd Street. ☎ *800-424-9165 or 202-543-6000. Fax: 202-547-2608, Internet:* www.capitolhillsuites.com. *Metro: Capitol South. From escalator exit, walk one block east on C Street to 2nd Street. From elevator exit, walk one block east on D Street and then one block north on C Street. Parking: $20 per night. Rack rates: $119–$239 double. Children under 18 stay free in parents' room. AE, DC, DISC, MC, V.*

Four Points by Sheraton
$$ Downtown

This hotel has a room with a view, but it's not the room you'll be sleeping in. Rather, it's the heated indoor pool on the roof, one of many amenities that makes this recently renovated property a good buy, especially if you can snag one of the lower-priced rooms. From the pool, you get a panoramic look at D.C., including the Capitol dome. Four Points offers concierge services, room service, valet parking, fitness center, business center, and an on-site restaurant. Each room has high-speed Internet access, two-line phones with dataports and voicemail, a coffee maker, and security safe designed to accommodate a laptop computer. You can ask for a microwave and mini-fridge. Rooms come with one queen bed, one king bed, or two double beds. Studio and one-bedroom suites with kitchenettes also are available. This hotel is a place where corner rooms are a bit bigger.

1201 K St. NW at 12th Street. ☎ *888-481-7191 or 202-289-7600. Fax 202-289-3310. Internet:* www.fourpointswashingtondc.com. *Metro: Metro Center. From G* and 12th streets exit, walk three blocks north on 12th to K Street. Parking: $22 per night. Rack rates: $99–$275 double. Children younger than 18 stay free in parents' room. AE, DC, DISC, MC, V.

Four Seasons

$$$$$ **Georgetown**

Where Foggy Bottom meets Georgetown, you'll find one of Washington's most celebrity-friendly (and kid-friendly) hotels. The rich and famous love this place because of its luxury and the staff's discretion and impeccable service. The concierge can rent you a tux, find you a toothbrush, or get you theater tickets. You can take high tea or sip a cocktail in the Garden Terrace. An indoor pool and a health club offer all imaginable amenities. If you want to work — *what?* — the hotel has every imaginable business service as well. George Washington never slept here, but Tom Hanks, Sheryl Crow, and Nicolas Cage have. The hotel also brags about its service to "VICs" (Very Important Children). Kids receive gifts and snacks at check-in. They can use the hotel's board games, videotapes, coloring books, kid-sized terry bathrobes, toddler slippers and Teddy bears. Parents can request baby necessities, such as a crib, high chair, and bottle-warmer. They offer children's menus for meals and at tea. The hotel gets you an experienced, bonded, and insured baby sitter.

2800 Pennsylvania Ave. NW at 28th Street. ☎ *800-332-3442 or 202-342-0444. Fax: 202-944-2076. Internet:* www.fourseasons.com. *Metro: Foggy Bottom-George Washington University. Walk one block north on 23rd Street to traffic circle, left around circle to Pennsylvania Avenue, and then left onto Pennsylvania for four blocks. Parking: $26 per night. Rack rates: $455–$615 double. Children under 16 stay free in parents' room. AE, DC, MC, V.*

Georgetown Suites

$$ **Georgetown**

This Georgetown accommodation can be good for families because the suites with bedrooms allow for some privacy and the kitchens enable you to cook. I know cooking isn't what most vacationers put on their itineraries. But vacationing with kids can be much more pleasant when you can return to your lodgings for meals, snacks, and naps. Here, your options also include a free continental breakfast. You also get dining discounts at some Georgetown restaurants. Your lodging choices include a one-room studio "suite" (queen-size bed and sitting area with loveseat), a "double double suite" (two double beds and a sitting area), or a one-bedroom suite (king bed and separate living room with pull-out queen-size sofa). A two-bedroom suite has two bathrooms, master bedroom with king bed, a second bedroom with full bed, and a living room with queen sofa-bed. All have a kitchen with refrigerator, coffeemaker, microwave, and dishwasher. More luxurious townhouse and penthouse accommodations are available. The hotel has an exercise room, and you can obtain business services at the nearby Georgetown Business Center.

The suites are in two buildings. The main building, at 1111 30th St. NW, is quieter. One final perk: Local phone calls are free.

Main building: 1111 30th St. NW just below M Street; Second building: 1000 29th St. NW at K Street. ☎ *800-348-7203 or 202-298-7800. Internet:* www.georgetown suites.com. *Metro: Foggy Bottom-George Washington University. Walk one block north on 23rd Street to traffic circle, left around circle to Pennsylvania Ave., left onto Pennsylvania for five or six blocks, and then left on 29th or 30th street. Limited parking: $15 per night. Rack rates for studios to one-bedroom suites: $155–$215; others higher. AE, DC, DISC, MC, V. Metro.*

George Washington University Inn
$$ Foggy Bottom

Located in a quiet, tree-lined residential section of Foggy Bottom, the George Washington University Inn is an ideal place to park your suitcase if you're visiting the university or sampling the performing arts at the Kennedy Center. The inn, which is owned by the university, is essentially on the GWU campus; it's about three long blocks from the Kennedy Center. The short walk to the Foggy Bottom-GWU Metrorail Station and to the 30-series bus routes on Pennsylvania Avenue makes visiting the rest of the city easy, too. The 95 rooms (31 of which are one-bedroom suites) are larger than you typically find in moderately priced hotels today, and they come with mini-refrigerators, microwaves, and coffee makers. You get free access to a fitness facility, and valet parking is available if you want it.

824 New Hampshire Ave. NW, between H and I streets. ☎ *800-426-4455 or 202-337-6620. Fax: 202-298-7499. Internet:* www.gwuinn.com. *Metro: Foggy Bottom-GWU. Walk west on I Street, across 24th Street, and then left on New Hampshire. The inn is on the right. Limited parking: $18. Rack rates: $130–$175 double. Children younger than 12 stay free in parents' room. AE, DC, MC, V.*

Hay-Adams
$$$$$ Downtown

The Hay-Adams is such a Washington institution that its 2002 reopening after an $18-million renovation was front-page news in *The Washington Post's* business section. It's hard to imagine a better location for an upscale hotel — directly across picturesque Lafayette Square from the White House. Built in 1928, the Hay-Adams long has been a top choice of the rich, the powerful, and the simply famous. Sure, Warren Beatty, Annette Bening, and Meg Ryan have stayed here. But so have Charles Lindbergh, Amelia Earhart, and Sinclair Lewis. The prime attraction of the Hay-Adams always will be what it always has been — that location. Windows in the higher-level rooms on the south side look across Lafayette Square to the White House, with the Washington Monument in the distance. Now, all the amenities are 21st-century state-of-the art. Impressed by hotel rooms with two telephones? Every Hay-Adams room has *three* two-line phones, including a cordless phone. You also get voice mail, a high-speed Internet connection, a component audio system, 24-hour room service, business services, valet parking, and — of course — the concierge. Will you pay mightily for this luxury? Well . . . if you have to ask. . . .

One Lafayette Square, at 16th and H streets NW. ☎ *800-853-6807 or 202-638-6600. Fax: 202-638-2716. Internet:* www.hayadams.com. *Metro: McPherson Square. From the Vermont Ave.-White House exit, walk south one block on Vermont, turn right on H Street, walk one more block, cross 16th Street, and the hotel is on your right. Valet parking: $28. Rack rates: $345–$545 double. Children younger than 17 stay free in parents' room. AE, DC, DISC, MC, V.*

Holiday Inn on the Hill
$$ Capitol Hill

This Holiday Inn enjoys a choice location, two blocks from the Capitol and Union Station and within walking distance of many other attractions. The rooms were refurbished in 1999 and, if not worthy of *Architectural Digest,* are large and comfortable and have spacious bathrooms. If you desire a separate workspace or your children are traveling with you, you can get a room with an adjoining parlor. The parlor includes a Murphy bed (a bed that can be folded or swung out of the way). A large rooftop pool, which enjoys a great view of the area, is open in summer. The hotel also has a fitness center with steppers, treadmills, stationary cycles, circuit trainers, and free weights. Many of the hotel's employees have been here a long time, and that translates into staff and visitor satisfaction.

415 New Jersey Ave. NW, between D and E streets. ☎ *800-638-1116 or 202-638-1616. Fax: 202-638-0707. Internet:* www.sixcontinentshotels.com/holiday-inn?_franchisee=WASCH. *Metro: Union Station. From the Union Station Shops/Massachusetts Avenue exit, cross Massachusetts, walk around the circle to Louisiana, turn right on Louisiana, right on D, and right on New Jersey. Parking: $18. Rack rates: $99–$270. Children 18 and under stay free with their parents. AE, DISC, JCB, MC, V.*

Hostelling International
$ Downtown

I promised you accommodations in all price ranges, and this one is the lowest price you're gonna get — at least anywhere you'll *want* to stay. If you want candy, you better bring it with you because you don't get Godiva on your pillow here. And you can't watch TV in bed. Whaddaya expect at these prices? Basic basic describes this 270-bed facility. It is, however, clean and comfortable, with dorm-style rooms (all air-conditioned), and it's just three blocks from Metro Center. The rooms, some segregated by sex, sleep 6 to 12 guests. Bathrooms are down the hall. BYO bath soap. Towels, bed linens, blankets, and pillows are provided. You can store your stuff in a locker. The hostel organizes activities for guests, such as walking tours. The savvy staff can help you with your itinerary. The large kitchen and dining room are available for guest use. Families and couples can reserve private rooms for themselves, but you have to do so far in advance.

1009 11th St. NW, at K Street. ☎ *202-737-2333. Fax: 202-737-1508. Internet:* www. hiwashingtondc.org. *E-mail:* reserve@hiwashingtondc.org. *Metro: Metro Center. From 11th Street exit, walk north on 11th Street three blocks. Parking: Use commercial garages in the area. Rack rates: $29 per person. MC, V.*

Hotel Harrington
$ Downtown

When you think bargain and no frills, think Hotel Harrington. Family-owned since it opened in 1914, the Harrington caters to groups, families, and others looking for good value. It's an easy walk to the White House, the National Mall, and many other attractions, such as the FBI headquarters, Ford's Theatre, the National Theater, and MCI Center. In addition, the Metro Center Metrorail Station is conveniently located two blocks away for access to anyplace else you'd like to go. If you're traveling with your kids, a family suite is a good idea. The suite includes two rooms (queen bed in one, twin beds in the other) and two bathrooms. Toss in a load at the self-service laundry on the premises. The hotel has three on-site restaurants, all reasonably priced, and plenty of other nearby food options. Trivia note: In 1938, the Harrington became the first hotel in Washington to air-condition all of its rooms.

436 11th St. NW at E Street. ☎ *800-424-8532 or 202-628-8140. Fax: 202-347-3924. Internet:* www.hotel-harrington.com. *Metro: Metro Center. From 11th Street exit, walk two blocks south to E Street. Parking, four blocks away: $8.50. Rack rates: $89 double to $139 suite. AE, DC, DISC, MC, V.*

Hotel George
$$$$ Capitol Hill

Modernistic posters of the first president adorn the hotel, which attracts lobbyists, celebrities, and others who dig hip surroundings and proximity to power. The George is ideally located — just a block from Union Station and two from the Capitol. The minimalist decor of the guest rooms is refreshing if you're weary of imitation mahogany, swags, and antiques. The amenities — all the latest gadgets you can expect — are tucked away, adding to the spare, uncluttered look. The rooms are equipped for the business traveler, with two-line cordless phones, executive desks, and high-speed Internet access. The clock radio with CD player emits sounds from nature to soothe jangled nerves. Award-winning chef/owner Jeff Buben wields his whisk at **Bistro Bis,** the hotel's French bistro. (See Chapter 14 for the review.) If you're so inclined, you can puff away on your cigar in the hotel's billiards room.

15 E St. NW at North Capitol Street. ☎ *800-576-8331 or 202-347-4200. Fax: 202-347-4213. Internet:* www.hotelgeorge.com. *Metro: Union Station. From Union Station Shops/Massachusetts Avenue exit, turn right on Massachusetts, then left on North Capitol, and then right on E. Parking: $24. Rack rates: $265–$350 double. Children younger than 16 stay free in parents' room. AE, DC, DISC, MC, V.*

Hotel Washington

$$$ Downtown

Overlooking the White House and an easy stroll from the National Mall, the Hotel Washington boasts convenience and one of the city's best views. (I find myself saying that about a lot of D.C. hotels!) From the Sky Terrace open-air restaurant on the hotel's top floor (May to October), you can look down on the president's mansion while eating a light meal or relaxing with a drink. Many of the guest rooms also feature views of the White House and/or the Washington Monument. (Ask about availability and price.) Once every four years, the inaugural parade marches by, as the president makes the quadrennial pilgrimage from the Capitol to 1600 Pennsylvania Ave. Antique reproductions throughout the hotel help to create an atmosphere of historical charm. The full-service **Two Continents** restaurant has two dining rooms in the hotel, on the lobby level and next to the Sky Terrace. If you eat too much there, you can work it off in the fitness center or sweat it out in the sauna.

515 15th St. NW at Pennsylvania Avenue. ☎ *800-424-9540. Fax: 202-638-1595. Internet:* www.hotelwashington.com. *Metro: Metro Center. From the 12th and F streets exit, walk three blocks west on F to 15th. The hotel is on the left. Parking: $20. Rack rates: $185–$275 double. Children younger than 14 stay free in parents' room. AE, DC, MC, V.*

J.W. Marriott

$$$$ Downtown

If you've stayed here before, you probably were attending a convention. This is one of D.C.'s premier convention and meeting hotels. It's *huge* (738 rooms, 34 suites) and centrally located. Next door are the National Press Club, The Shops at National Place, and the National Theatre. Also real close by are the Warner Theatre, Ford's Theatre, the White House, and many other points of interest. The spacious rooms, redecorated in 2000, have cherrywood furnishings and come with all the electronic amenities travelers now expect. This hotel is, of course, full-service, with two restaurants on site and an easy indoor walk to the food court at National Place. The J.W. has a health club, indoor swimming pool, whirlpool, sauna, concierge, business center, and 24-hour room service. For traveling parents, cribs and child care are available. Because this convention hotel is enormous, deep discounts are offered when conventioneers aren't in town. Ask. Then ask again.

1331 Pennsylvania Ave. NW at 14th and E streets. ☎ *800-228-9290 or 202-393-2000. Fax: 202-626-6991. Internet:* www.marriott.com. *Metro: Metro Center. From the F and 12th streets exit, walk two blocks east on F and then turn left on 14th. In bad weather, you can enter the Shops at National Place at 13th and F and follow signs to an indoor hotel entrance. Parking: $25. Rack rates: $289–$359 double. Children under 18 stay free in parents' room. AE, DC, DISC, MC, V.*

The Jefferson

$$$$ Downtown

The Jefferson was my wife's favorite Washington hotel when we lived in Ohio, and she made occasional business trips to D.C. (on a corporate credit card). More than two decades later, it's still considered one of the city's very best hotels because of the same intimate atmosphere and personalized service. It's small, quiet, elegant, and expensive, with a top-notch staff that remembers return guests by name. Antiques, original art, and reproductions grace the 67 rooms and 33 suites, many with balconies. Some rooms include canopied beds, and each room features two-line telephones, speaker-phone, voicemail, fax machine, and Internet access, along with video and CD player. Double-glazed windows mute the traffic noise from 16th and M streets. The hotel has 24-hour room service, 24-hour multilingual concierge service, business services, a good restaurant, and a comfortable lounge. You pay $20 a pop for access to the indoor pool, exercise machines, steam room, and Jacuzzi at the University Club across the street.

1200 16th St. NW, at M Street. ☎ *800-235-6397 or 202-347-2200. Fax: 202-785-1505. Internet:* www.loewshotels.com/hotels/washington_jefferson. *Metro: Farragut North. From L Street exit, walk two blocks east on L, turn left on 16th, and then walk one block to M. The hotel is across M on the left. Parking: $20. Rack rates: $319–$339 double. Children under 12 stay free in parents' room. AE, DC, DISC, MC, V. AE.*

Jurys Normandy

$$ Dupont Circle

This relatively small, homey hotel has 75 guest rooms that were remodeled in 1998. It's a bit out of the way, but not too far. It's about five blocks north of the Dupont Circle Metrorail Station, in the neighborhood known as Kalorama, and about the same distance from the heart of Adams-Morgan, which are two of D.C.'s most popular entertainment districts, with plenty of restaurants and night spots. The hotel is located in a neighborhood of imposing residences and diplomatic facilities. (Check out the French ambassador's digs at 2221 Kalorama Rd., for a truly jaw-dropping example.) If you stay here, you can call this intriguing neighborhood your own for a brief spell. Jurys Normandy also truly is a bargain. For relatively little money (for Washington), you get a comfortable room with high-speed Internet access, two-line phone with dataport, mini-fridge, coffeemaker, and use of the exercise room and outdoor pool at the nearby Courtyard by Marriott. Tea and coffee are served for free in the lounge in the afternoons, and a complimentary wine-and-cheese reception occurs on Tuesday nights. Watch out for diplomats!

2118 Wyoming Ave. NW, at Connecticut Avenue. ☎ *800-424-3729 or 202-483-1350. Fax: 202-387-8241. Internet:* www.jurysdoyle.com/frusa_index.htm. *Metro: Dupont Circle. From the Q Street exit, walk north five blocks on Connecticut Avenue and then turn left on Wyoming. Parking: $10. Rack rates: $79–$175 double. Children under 12 stay free in parents' room. AE, DC, DISC, MC, V.*

Jurys Washington

$$ Dupont Circle

Unlike its sibling, Jurys Normandy, this hotel is not out of the way at all. It's right on the northeastern edge of the Dupont Circle action. With its more convenient location, Jurys Washington naturally is pricier than the Normandy. But it's still a good deal. The Jurys hotels are run by an Irish organization, Jurys Doyle Hotels of Dublin, and that's reflected in the Washington's eatery and drinkery — **Claddagh's Restaurant,** which serves contemporary American cuisine with what the owners describe as "a distinctive Irish flair," and **Biddy Mulligans Bar,** styled as an Irish pub with the bar itself imported from the Old Country. The hostess sported an Irish accent when my wife and I last visited. The rooms at Jurys Washington are large, pretty, and comfortable. They come with the usual amenities, including high-speed Internet access and — this isn't common! — a trouser press. The hotel offers concierge service, 24-hour room service, a business center, and an exercise room.

1500 New Hampshire Ave. NW, northeast of Dupont Circle. ☎ *800-423-6953 or 202-483-6000. Fax: 202-232-1130. Internet:* www.jurysdoyle.com/frusa_index. htm. *Metro: Dupont Circle. From the Dupont Circle exit, walk around the circle counter-clockwise to New Hampshire. Parking: $17. Rack rates: $145–$235 double. Children younger than 18 stay free in parents' room. AE, DC, DISC, MC, V.*

Lincoln Suites

$$ Downtown

The "suites" in this hotel actually are large rooms with kitchen facilities. All have at least a microwave, refrigerator, coffee maker, and wet bar, as well as phones with voicemail and dataports. "Double suites" contain two double beds and an activity table with two chairs. "Executive studio suites" have a full kitchen (full-sized refrigerator, oven, stove, microwave, sink, dishes, pots, and pans) and either two queen-size beds or one king. In 2002, the hotel completed a gradual overhaul that began in 1997 with the upgrading of the rooms and was completed with the entrance, lobby, and front desk. The service didn't need to be upgraded; it's always been great. For a homey touch, you can have free milk and cookies every evening. (Ask nicely.) Guests get free passes to a nearby fitness center. On site is **Mackey's Public House,** which serves tasty fish and chips, other light fare, and your favorite brews.

1823 L St. NW, between 18th and 19th streets. ☎ ***800-424-2970*** *or 202-223-4320. Fax: 202-223-8546. Internet:* www.lincolnhotels.com. *Metro: Farragut North. From the L Street exit, walk one block west on L, crossing 18th. The hotel is on the right. Parking: $16. Rack rates: $129–$199 per suite. Children younger than 16 stay free in their parents' room. AE, DC, DISC, MC, V.*

Renaissance Mayflower
$$$$ Downtown

I'll always have affection for the Mayflower because of some things that happened there long ago. Shortly after I graduated from college, a friend and I came here for a conference and were placed in a suite at no extra cost because of a room shortage. We were so worried about what we might have to pay that we triple-checked before unpacking our bags. The Mayflower also is where I covered my first inaugural ball: It's where Ohio Democrats celebrated Jimmy Carter's move into the White House in 1977. This hotel has been hosting those events since it opened in 1925 and Cal Coolidge's inauguration was celebrated there. The Mayflower is big, luxurious, and the setting for many meetings, conventions, and other public events. You can bump into any big shot here. The guest rooms, as well as the public areas, feature marble and mahogany. They also have your basic modern traveler's necessities — two-line phones, speaker phones, voicemail, and dataports. Parents can obtain cribs and child care. The hotel has a restaurant, coffee shop, lounge, 24-hour room service, concierge services, and exercise room.

1127 Connecticut Ave. NW, between L and M streets. ☎ ***800-228-7697*** *or 202-347-3000. Fax: 202-776-9182. Internet:* www.renaissancehotels.com. *Metro: Farragut North. From the L Street exit, look for the hotel. Parking: $26. Rack rates: $289–$340 double. AE, DC, DISC, MC, V.*

Omni Shoreham
$$$ Upper Northwest

The moment you walk in the door, you know this hotel is spectacular. It's huge! It's opulent! It's historic! You can get some rooms for less than $200. You can get suites for $3,000! Enough exclamation points! Truman played poker here. Inaugural balls, conventions, and major meetings have been routine since 1930. The Omni Shoreham — which completed a three-year, $80-million restoration in 2000 — is essentially an 11-acre self-contained resort. There's a huge heated outdoor pool (April to October), a sauna, and a well-equipped fitness center, as well as easy access to Rock Creek Park out the back door. You can request a "Get Fit Kit" — floor mat, dumbbells, and elastic bands — to work out in your room. For the less active, massages, facials, pedicures, and manicures are available by appointment. The hotel gardens invite a leisurely stroll. The hotel offers a restaurant, lounge, and carryout. The rooms are elegant and large by any standard. You're off the beaten tourist paths here. But you can walk about four blocks to the National Zoo, and the Woodley Park Metrorail Station is just about a block away.

2500 Calvert St. NW, west of Connecticut Avenue. ☎ 800-843-6664 or 202-234-0700. Fax: 202-265-7972. Internet: www.omnihotels.com. *Metro: Woodley Park-Zoo. Walk one block south on 24th Street to Calvert Street. The hotel is to the right across Calvert. Self parking: $19. Valet parking: $22. Rack rates: $179–$309 double. Children younger than 18 stay free in parents' room. AE, DC, DISC, MC, V.*

One Washington Circle
$$$ Foggy Bottom

This all-suite hotel offers a variety of floor plans suitable for business travelers and families. All the suites have kitchens and balconies. The simplest — the "guest suite" — has sleeping and sitting areas in one large room that includes a double bed and fold-out sofa. The grandest — the "suite grande classe" — has a master bedroom with a sitting area, a sleeper sofa in the living room, and a bath-and-a-half. The suites offer a desk, two-line phones, and dataports. *The Washington Post* is delivered each morning. You also can take advantage of a fitness center, an outdoor pool, concierge services, and a good on-site restaurant, the **West End Cafe.** A renovation of the entire property was completed in mid-2002. Georgetown is an easy stroll away, and the Foggy Bottom-George Washington University Metrorail Station is just around the circle. Also across the circle is the GWU Hospital, which is handy should you need medical attention but also attracts ambulance sirens around the clock. Ask about a suite on the quieter side of the hotel.

1 Washington Circle NW, at New Hampshire Avenue. ☎ 800-424-9671 or 202-872-1680. Fax: 202-887-4989. Internet: www.thecirclehotel.com. *Metro: Foggy Bottom-George Washington University. Walk north on 23rd Street one block to Washington Circle and then counterclockwise around the circle to New Hampshire Avenue at the northeast edge of the circle. Valet parking: $18. Rack rates: $219–$319 double. Children younger than 16 stay free in parents' room. AE, CB, DC, DISC, MC, V.*

Red Roof Inn
$$ Downtown

This hotel is not like the Red Roof Inns you breeze by on the Interstate. Hardly. Close to the Convention Center, MCI Center (sports and big-name entertainers), galleries, theaters, restaurants, night spots, and Chinatown, this inn contains 197 rooms on 10 floors. It's a value find for business travelers and families. A king room includes a large desk in work area with dataport and speaker phone. Families can get rooms with two double beds. All rooms feature coffee makers and large bathrooms. The kids can work off excess energy using the in-room Nintendo (hourly charge). The hotel also has an exercise room and an on-site restaurant. Local phone calls are free.

500 H St. NW, at 5th Street. ☎ 800-733-7663 or 202-289-5959. Fax: 202-289-0754. Internet: www.redroof.com. *Metro: Gallery Place-Chinatown. From 7th and H streets exit, walk two blocks east to 5th Street. Hotel is on right. Parking: $11. Rack* *rates: $110–$135 double. Children younger than 18 stay free in parents' room. AE, DC, DISC, MC, V.*

Ritz-Carlton Washington
$$$$$ Foggy Bottom/West End

This hotel may be Washington's most luxurious — in terms of both facilities and services. You can choose, for example, a 2,250-square-foot suite: living room with fireplace, two bedrooms, dining room with seating for ten, Jacuzzi, and private terrace. Or you can stay on the private Club Level, where the lounge offers food and beverage service all day and a concierge is at your beck and call. The standard rooms feature marble in the bathrooms, goose down or non-allergenic pillows to suit your need, dataports, portable phones, and high-speed Internet access. And then you have the "fitness center," the adjacent Sports Club/LA — 100,000 square feet of just about any exercise and sports facility you can dream of. But it's the service that really marks the Ritz. Beyond daily attentiveness, managers here think creatively about what additional services you might want. So, noting increased air-travel hassles, the hotel introduced "luggage-less" travel for frequent guests. Leave your clothes in your room, and the hotel will launder, dry clean, press, store them, and then place them in your room when you return. And, on your way out of D.C., grab some of the hotel's "portable food" to eat on the airplane.

1150 22nd St. NW, at M Street. ☎ *800-241-3333 or 202-835-0500. Fax 202-835-1588. Internet:* www.ritzcarlton.com/hotels/washington_dc. *Metro: Foggy Bottom-George Washington University. Walk one block east on I Street, turn left on 22nd Street, and then walk four blocks to M Street. Self parking: $15. Valet parking: $18. Rack rate: $450 double. No charge for extra person in room. AE, DC, DISC, MC, V.*

State Plaza
$$ Foggy Bottom

The spacious accommodations at the all-suite State Plaza provide a home away from home for diplomats, business travelers, performing artists, and educators headed to the nearby World Bank, State Department, Kennedy Center, and George Washington University. The State Plaza is a find for families, too. Kids younger than 16 stay free in their parents' room, and you can save money by cooking meals in the suites' kitchens. On a quiet Foggy Bottom block, the State Plaza feels like a private residence in a condo or apartment building. Spacious is the operative word. The largest suite (Grand Plaza Suite) has a master bedroom and bathroom, living room (with queen sofa bed), a stylish and well-equipped kitchen, and a separate dining area. Rooms include dataports and dual phone lines. Room service is available. The on-site fitness center has a ballet barre for the dancers who stay here. (Go ahead, ballet up to the barre.) The **Garden Café** serves breakfast, lunch, and dinner, with outdoor dining in season. Two thumbs up for the exceptional Sunday brunch served, weather permitting, on the delightful plant-filled patio.

2117 E St. NW, between 21st and 22nd streets. ☎ **800-424-2859** *or 202-861-8200. Fax: 202-659-8601. Internet:* www.stateplaza.com. *Metro: Foggy Bottom. Walk two blocks east on I Street, turn right on 21st Street, walk four blocks south, and then turn right on E Street. The hotel is on the right. Parking: $12. Rack rates: $145–$245 double. AE, CB, DC, DISC, MC, V.*

Tabard Inn

$$ Dupont Circle

The Tabard is an eclectic and eccentric — and, yes, charming — place. If you've traveled in Europe under Frommer's tutelage, the Tabard will remind you of all those inexpensive but marvelous hostelries that have been cobbled together from adjacent buildings that measure their age in centuries. The Tabard isn't that old, but it was created from three adjacent town houses on a tree-lined street in the Dupont Circle neighborhood. Each of the 40 rooms is different, and they're furnished with a combination of antiques and — uh, well — pre-owned items. They're priced according to their size, view, and location within the hotel. All rooms come with free continental breakfast and free admission to the Tabard's fabulously equipped health club — the Capital YMCA around the corner. The Tabard's restaurant is wonderful, both for the setting and the New American cuisine. You can dine in the garden in warm weather or sip a drink beside a fireplace when it's cold. The lounge is the proverbial comfortable old shoe, a well-worn place for luxuriating by the fire, not for luxury. Be warned that the Tabard has no elevator.

1739 N St. NW, between 17th and 18th streets. ☎ **202-785-1277**. *Fax: 202-785-6173. Internet:* www.tabardinn.com. *Metro: Dupont Circle. From the Dupont Circle exit, walk south on Connecticut Avenue one block, and then turn left on N Street and cross 18th Street. The hotel is on the left. Parking in nearby public garages: $20–23. Rack rates: $92–$190. Additional person: $15. AE, DC, DISC, MC, V.*

Willard Inter-Continental

$$$$$ Downtown

The Willard is another Washington hotel steeped in history. A stone's throw from the White House and the D.C. government's headquarters, it's been a prime spot for the powerful and the power-seekers to hang their hats since even before Henry Willard bought the old hotel that occupied the site in 1850. George Washington didn't sleep here. But Abraham Lincoln stayed for a while in Henry's hostelry. And Calvin Coolidge lived in the current building until Mrs. Harding vacated the White House following her husband's death in 1923. Heads of foreign states stay here now. The current Willard — built in 1901, closed in 1968, opened after thorough restoration in 1986, and given a major face-lift in 2000 — is a large, ornate, and luxurious domicile. Take a walk through Peacock Alley, the first-floor hallway, even if you don't stay here, and take a peek into the opulent **Willard Room** restaurant. If you do stay here, you'll have a room furnished in antique reproductions and equipped with the latest electronics.

You can choose from 299 rooms and 42 suites. The 2,800-square-foot Presidential Suite will set you back just $3,800 or so.

1401 Pennsylvania Ave. NW, at 14th Street. ☎ *800-327-0200 or 202-628-9100. Fax: 202-637-7326. Internet:* www.washington.interconti.com. *Metro: Metro Center. From the F Street exit, walk two blocks west on F to the hotel's rear entrance between 14th and 15th. Parking: $23. Rack rates: $480–$605 double. Children under 18 stay free in parents' room. AE, DC, DISC, MC, V.*

Washington, D.C.'s Runner-Up Hotels

Space limitations prevent me from publishing an encyclopedia of Washington's hotels. If you're stuck and can't find a room, check the Quick Concierge at the back of this book for hotel chains' toll-free reservation numbers, and/or contact the following hotels, all tried and true (until readers of this book tell me otherwise). All offer lower weekend and off-peak rates. How low? Sometimes you can find a room for less than $100 a night, depending on availability.

The Henley Park Hotel
$$$ Downtown

926 Massachusetts Ave. NW (four blocks from Mt. Vernon Square-UDC Metrorail Station). ☎ *800-222-8474 or 202-638-5200. Fax: 202-638-6740. Internet:* www.hotel lombardy.com/hph/index.htm. *Rack rates: $195–$255 double.*

Hotel Lombardy
$$$ Foggy Bottom/West End

2019 Pennsylvania Ave. NW (three blocks to Foggy Bottom Metrorail Station). ☎ *800-424-5486 or 202-828-2600. Fax: 202-872-0503 Internet:* www.hotel lombardy.com/hl/index.htm. *Rack rate: $199 double.*

Phoenix Park Hotel
$$$$ Capitol Hill

520 N. Capitol St. NW (across from Union Station). ☎ *800-824-5419 or 202-638-6900. Fax: 202-393-3236. Internet:* www.pparkhotel.com. *Rack rates: $269–$319 double.*

Washington Plaza Hotel
$$$ Downtown

10 Thomas Circle, (three blocks from McPherson Square Metrorail Station). ☎ *800-424-1140 or 202-842-1300. Fax: 202-371-9602. Internet:* www.washington plazahotel.com/wp. *Rack rates: $199 double.*

Washington Suites Georgetown

$$$ **Foggy Bottom/West End**

2500 Pennsylvania Ave. NW (three blocks from Foggy Bottom Metrorail Station).
☎ *877-736-2500 or 202-333-8060. Internet:* www.washingtonsuiteshotel.com/georgetown.htm. *Rack rates: $269 double.*

Hotel Sofitel Lafayette Square

$$$$ **Downtown**

806 15th St. NW (one block from McPherson Square Metrorail Station) ☎ *800-763-4835 or 202-737-8800. Fax: 202-639-4677. Internet:* www.sofitel.com. *Rack rates: $275–$380.*

Hyatt Regency Washington Capitol Hill

$$$$ **Capitol Hill**

400 New Jersey Ave. NW (three blocks from Union). ☎ *800-233-1234 or 202-737-1234. Fax: 202-737-5773. Internet:* www.hyatt.com. *Rack rates: $260–$325.*

Renaissance Washington, D.C., Hotel

$$$$ **Downtown**

999 9th St. NW (two blocks from Gallery Place Metrorail Station). ☎ *800-468-3571 or 202-898-9000. Fax: 202-289-0947. Internet:* www.renaissancehotels.com. *Rack rates: From $289.*

Hotel Index by Price

$

Hostelling International — Downtown
Hotel Harrington — Downtown
Red Roof Inn — Downtown

$$

Capitol Hill Suites — Capitol Hill
George Washington University Inn — Foggy Bottom
Jury's Normandy — Dupont Circle
Lincoln Suites — Downtown
Tabard Inn — Dupont Circle

$$$

Four Points by Sheraton — Downtown
Georgetown Suites — Georgetown
Holiday Inn on the Hill — Capitol Hill
Hotel Washington — Downtown

Jurys Washington — Dupont Circle
Omni Shoreham — Upper Northwest
One Washington Circle — Foggy Bottom
State Plaza — Foggy Bottom

$$$$

Hotel George — Capitol Hill
J.W. Marriott — Downtown
The Jefferson — Downtown
Renaissance Mayflower — Downtown

$$$$$

Four Seasons — Georgetown
Hay-Adams — Downtown
Willard Inter-Continental — Downtown
Ritz-Carlton Washington — Foggy Bottom/West End

Hotel Index by Location

Capitol Hill

Capitol Hill Suites — $$
Holiday Inn on the Hill — $$
Hotel George — $$$$

Downtown

Four Points by Sheraton — $$
Hay-Adams Hotel — $$$$$
Hostelling International — $
Hotel Harrington — $
Hotel Washington — $$$
J.W. Marriott — $$$$
The Jefferson — $$$$
Lincoln Suites — $$
Renaissance Mayflower — $$$$
Red Roof Inn — $$
Willard Inter-Continental — $$$$$

Dupont Circle

Jurys Normandy — $$
Jurys Washington — $$
Tabard Inn — $$

Foggy Bottom/West End

George Washington University Inn — $$
One Washington Circle — $$$
Ritz-Carlton Washington — $$$$$
State Plaza — $$

Georgetown

Four Seasons — $$$$$
Georgetown Suites — $$

Upper Northwest

Omni Shoreham — $$$

Chapter 9

Tying Up the Loose Ends

● ●

In This Chapter

▶ Buying travel and medical insurance

▶ Renting a car (or not)

▶ Making reservations, ordering tickets, and getting information in advance

▶ Acquiring traveler's checks

▶ Packing smart

● ●

*B*efore you leave for your vacation, you'll probably feel like you need to do a thousand things: make reservations, put the dog in the kennel, pack your bags, and so on. Trust me, if you organize every-thing ahead of time, you can save precious hours otherwise spent wait-ing in line, trying to get show tickets, buying the underwear you forgot to bring, and dealing with all the other annoyances that plague the unprepared traveler.

Buying Travel Insurance: Good Idea or Bad?

Three primary kinds of travel insurance are available: *trip cancellation, lost luggage,* and *medical.* Trip cancellation insurance is a good idea for some people, but lost luggage and additional medical insurance don't make sense for most travelers. Be sure to explore your options and consider the following insurance advice before you leave home:

✔ **Trip cancellation insurance.** If you pay a large portion of expen-sive vacation costs up front, consider purchasing this type of insurance. If you've bought a package trip, insurance comes in handy if the packager or tour company defaults, a member of your party becomes ill, or (heaven forbid!) you experience a death in the family and aren't able to go on vacation.

Trip cancellation insurance costs approximately 6 to 8% of your vacation's total value.

✔ **Lost luggage insurance.** Your homeowner's insurance should cover stolen luggage if your policy encompasses off-premises theft. Check your existing policies or ask your insurance agent before you buy any additional coverage. Airlines are responsible for up to $2,500 on domestic flights.

✔ **Medical insurance.** If you get sick while on vacation, your existing health insurance should cover your expenses. But keep in mind that some HMOs may differ on policy in regard to your benefits when you travel. You may want to review your policy before leaving home.

If you think you need additional insurance, make sure that you don't pay for more coverage than you need. You should also call around to find a good deal on insurance. Here are some reputable issuers of travel insurance:

✔ **Access America,** PO Box 90315, Richmond, VA 23286-4991; ☎ **866-807-3982;** Fax: 800-346-9265; Internet: www.access america.com.

✔ **Travel Guard International,** 1145 Clark St., Stevens Point, WI 54481; ☎ **800-826-4919;** Internet: www.travel-guard.com.

Staying Healthy When You Travel

If you suffer from a chronic illness, consult your doctor before your departure. For conditions like epilepsy, diabetes, or heart problems, wear a **Medic Alert Identification Tag** (☎ **800-825-3785;** www.medic alert.org), which immediately alerts doctors to your condition and gives them access to your records through Medic Alert's 24-hour hotline.

Most health insurance policies cover you if you get sick away from home — but check, particularly if you're insured by an HMO. Always carry your insurance ID card in your purse or wallet.

Pack **prescription medications** in your carry-on luggage and carry prescription medications in their original containers. Also bring along copies of your prescriptions in case you lose your pills or run out. And don't forget sunglasses and an extra pair of contact lenses or prescription glasses.

CVS, Washington's major drugstore chain (with more than 40 locations), has two stores with 24-hour pharmacies: 14th Street and Thomas Circle NW at Vermont Avenue (☎ **202-628-0720**) and at Dupont Circle (☎ **202-785-1466**).

If you need immediate medical attention, head for the **emergency room** at one of the following District hospitals (call for directions):

Children's Hospital National Medical Center, 111 Michigan Ave. NW
(☎ 202-884-5000); **George Washington University Hospital,** 23rd Street
NW at Washington Circle (☎ 202-715-4000); **Georgetown University
Medical Center,** 3800 Reservoir Rd. NW (☎ 202-784-2000); or **Howard
University Hospital,** 2041 Georgia Ave. NW (☎ 202-865-6100).

Deciding Whether to Rent a Car

I live in D.C. Therefore, I drive in D.C. But you don't have to, and I
advise you not to. (See Chapter 5 for reasons why you don't want to
get behind the wheel.) Ask anyone who lives here. They'll tell you that
even with the grid system, getting from place to place can be confusing, and the cost of parking can take a large chunk out of your budget.
Rely on shuttle, taxi, bus, or rail service from the airport or train station. Use Metrorail and your own two feet for sightseeing — or buses
and taxis when necessary.

If you decide you really want or need to drive despite my warnings, see
the next section.

Getting the best rental rate

If you insist on renting a car, keep in mind that car rental rates vary
widely. The price depends on many factors: the size of the car, the
length of time you keep it, where and when you pick it up and drop it
off, where you go in it, and a host of other factors. Asking a few key
questions can save you big bucks. The following are some questions
that may help:

- ✔ **Is the weekend rate lower than the weekday rate?** Ask whether
  the rate is the same for a Friday morning pickup as it is for one on
  Thursday night. If you keep the car five or more days, a weekly
  rate may be cheaper than the daily rate.

- ✔ **Are you charged a drop-off fee if you return the car to a location that's different from where you picked it up?** If, for example,
  you're leaving town from a different airport from the one you
  arrived at or you're driving to another city in a rental car, the
  company may tack on a hefty charge to leave it in a location
  other than the original pickup point.

- ✔ **Is the rate cheaper if you pick up the car at the airport instead
  of a location in town?** One location may be more practical than
  the other, so don't forget to factor convenience into your decision.

- ✔ **Do you get a special rate for being a member of AAA, AARP,
  frequent-flier programs, or other organizations?** Such memberships can entitle you to discounts ranging from 5 to 30%.

✔ **Can you have the discounted rate you saw advertised in the local newspaper?** Be sure to ask for that specific rate; otherwise, you may be charged the standard (higher) rate.

Adding up the costs of renting a car

On top of the standard rental prices, you need to watch out for other charges that may be applied. The *Collision Damage Waiver (CDW)* absolves you of responsibility to pay for damage to the vehicle in exchange for a hefty daily fee. Check with your auto insurance agent and the credit-card company you use to rent the car. You're probably already covered.

Car rental companies also may try to sell you *liability insurance* (to cover you if you harm others in an accident), *additional liability insurance* (to increase the coverage you already have), *personal accident insurance* (to cover injury to yourself or your passengers), and *personal effects insurance* (to cover possessions that you carry in the rental car). If you don't know whether you're already covered, check with your auto and homeowner's insurance agent(s). You may not need to purchase this extra coverage.

Some rental car companies also offer *refueling packages,* which means that you pay for an entire tank of gas up front and don't face extra charges if you fail to return the car with a full tank. This service may be convenient, but the best way to save money is to fill the tank yourself at a gas station just before you return to the rental lot, because the rental car company invariably charges you a lot more per gallon than you'd pay at a local gas station.

Frequent fliers can cheer themselves up with the knowledge that most car rentals are worth at least 500 miles in their frequent-flier accounts.

Booking a rental car on the Internet

As with other aspects of planning your trip, using the Internet can make comparison shopping and renting a car much easier. The major online travel agencies, such as Travelocity (www.travelocity.com) and Expedia (www.expedia.com), have search engines that dig up discounted car rental rates. Enter the size of the car you want, the pickup and return dates, and the city where you want to rent, and you'll be quoted prices. Pick the deal you want and make your reservation at the site. As with buying airline tickets, checking the car rental companies' sites can pay off, too.

Making Reservations and Getting Tickets in Advance

I'm the kind of guy who starts to enjoy a vacation long before I actually leave home. Why? Because I actually like to plan ahead. It gives me the best options for using frequent-flier and frequent-sleeper miles. It can save money. And it assures that my family's not disappointed when we hit a town and discover that the show we wanted to see is sold out.

To find out what's going on in D.C. during your visit (such as museum exhibitions, special events, performing arts, and the like), check out the following Web sites:

- ✔ **Washington Convention and Tourism Corp.** (www.washington.org): Find links to all your basic tourist information — hotels, restaurants, performances, attractions, special events, and shopping.

- ✔ *The Washington Post* (www.washingtonpost.com): Log on to this site to bone up on local and, by extension, world news or to check the congressional and Supreme Court calendars. See the *Post's* online entertainment guide (http://eg.washingtonpost.com) for a slew of current listings.

- ✔ **The Smithsonian Institution** (www.si.edu): Discover most of what you need to know about visiting the Smithsonian's many museums and attending the organization's many programs.

- ✔ **National Park Service** (www.nps.gov/ncro): The Park Service oversees parks, monuments, and many historical buildings in Washington, including the National Mall, Ford's Theatre, and even the White House. This Web site tells you how to tour these places and what special events are going on.

- ✔ **Washington, D.C. Accommodations** (www.dcaccommodations.com): Reserve your room through the site of this reservation service for a large number of Washington hotels.

- ✔ **Capitol Reservations** (www.capitolreservations.com): Peruse the site of this discount hotel reservation service that also has some links to D.C. attractions.

Getting congressional perks

Many members of Congress go out of their way to help visitors from back home. Special "Congressional VIP Tours" are conducted at many government facilities. Your senators and representative can give you passes to watch Congress in action in the House and Senate visitors' galleries. And many members are happy to provide additional tourist information to constituents.

Check out your senators' and representative's Web sites or give them a phone call. To find your representative's Web site, go to `www.house.gov/house/MemberWWW.html` and click his or her name. (Uppercase matters in this Web address.) You can find your senator at `www.senate.gov/senators/index.cfm`. You can phone him or her by calling the House switchboard at ☎ **202-225-3121** and the Senate switchboard at ☎ **202-224-3121.** Write your senators at the U.S. Senate, Washington, D.C. 20510, and your representative at the U.S. House of Representatives, Washington, D.C. 20515. If you don't know your lawmakers' names, but you know your own nine-digit Zip code, you can identify them at the **Project Vote Smart** Web site (`www.vote-smart.org/index.phtml`).

Reserving tickets for performances

If you want to attend a theatrical event during your stay and look forward to seeing a particular show, I strongly suggest ordering tickets ahead. You may be able to amble up to the box office 15 minutes before curtain times and purchase tickets, but the odds aren't in your favor. If you wait until the last minute for seats to pop concerts, major sports events, or ballyhooed Broadway-bound productions, you may be out of luck.

Several ticket companies allow you to order tickets before you leave home. You're in business simply by calling with the name and date of the performance and charging the tickets to your credit card. For this service, expect to pay an unconscionably high surcharge. For tickets to most events, try **TicketMaster** at ☎ **202-432-SEAT** or online at `www.ticketmaster.com`.

You can get information about what's playing from each theater's Web site:

- ✔ **Arena Stage:** `www.arenastage.com`
- ✔ **Ford's Theatre:** `www.fordstheatre.org`
- ✔ **John F. Kennedy Center for the Performing Arts:** `www.kennedy-center.org`
- ✔ **National Theatre:** `www.nationaltheatre.org`
- ✔ **Shakespeare Theatre:** `www.shakespearedc.org`
- ✔ **Warner Theatre:** `www.warnertheatre.com`

Living the sporting life

If you want to catch a game at **MCI Center,** where the Wizards of the NBA and Mystics of the WNBA play basketball, try **TicketMaster** ☎ **202-432-SEAT** or visit the center's Web site at `www.mcicenter.com`.

During hockey season, the NHL's Washington Capitals sell tickets online *without a service charge.* This is an innovation of owner Ted Leonsis, an Internet pioneer who is applying his Web smarts to running his hockey team. One of the best bargains in sports is the Capitals' Eagles Nest, where tickets cost just $10 or a bit more. You have to buy them at the Caps' Web site (www.washingtoncaps.com), and the seats are up where eagles roost, but you can see the action just fine. (Bring your binoculars!)

Getting a table at a trendy restaurant

If you hear about a trendy restaurant and are dying to try it out, make a reservation a week or more ahead, even before you leave home. (Remember to confirm it when you arrive in Washington.) A reservation is an especially good idea for a Friday or Saturday night. If you're staying at a hotel with a concierge, he or she may be able to come up with the hard-to-get reservations.

I indicate which restaurants may require reservations well in advance in Chapter 14.

Packing Like a Pro

As hard as it is to follow this maxim, successful packing unquestionably means traveling light and arriving home with all your clothes dirty. The big mistake any traveler, experienced or otherwise, can make is to overpack. Why schlep all that extra stuff? Do you like lifting weights in airports and along sidewalks? Trust me, no one ever comes back from a trip saying, "Boy, I wish I had brought more stuff with me." The good news is that, unless you reside in a nudist colony, you can dress in Washington pretty much as you do at home. Better to take half the clothing you think you need, an extra credit card, and a packet of detergent. (You always can wash a shirt or shorts in the sink and dry your duds on a towel rack.)

In this day of increased airport security, the light packer has a shorter trip through the terminal. Stuff everything into the carry-on bag and "personal item" (purse, briefcase) you're allowed to take inside the cabin with you, and you can skip the baggage check and baggage claim sections of the airport.

Knowing what to pack

It bears repeating that the less you take, the better. Nevertheless, you need to bring along a few essential items. Here are some necessities:

- ✔ The single most important thing to pack for your visit is a pair of comfortable walking shoes, broken in. You can always pick up toothpaste or deodorant. But you may be sorry if you try to break in a pair of brand new shoes while sightseeing.

- ✔ The next most important thing is raingear. It can rain or storm nearly anytime in this town.

- ✔ D.C. summers can be brutal, especially for those not used to heat and humidity. Because the mercury often climbs from comfortable to unbearable by noon during the months of June through August, I urge you to bring breathable, cool clothing.

- ✔ During the other seasons of the year, Washington's climate can be fickle. You need to wear layered clothing.

- ✔ A light sweater, sweatshirt, or windbreaker is a necessity in all seasons, even in summer when overly air-conditioned buildings may turn your lips blue.

- ✔ To find out D.C.'s weather before you leave home, visit the Weather Channel's Web site, `www.weather.com`.

- ✔ Don't leave home without a camera and film (these items are probably cheaper in your neighborhood), toiletries, and your medications. If you check bags, pack your camera, film, clean underwear, and toilet kit in your carry-on luggage. That way, you have them in case your luggage goes astray. (On a trip from Washington to Atlanta, with a plane change, my bag ended up on an island in the middle of the Pacific, which is how I learned this lesson the hard way!)

- ✔ Unless you're invited to a black-tie affair, you can leave your formal wear in mothballs. In fact, you can dress informally almost anywhere in Washington nowadays. Shorts and T-shirts are perfect for hot-weather traipsing around the monuments and the National Mall. For most restaurants, theaters, and concert halls, a collared shirt and slacks work for the men; a simple dress, a shirt and skirt, or a shirt and slacks are fine for the women.

Knowing how to pack

When choosing your suitcase for Washington, D.C., think wheels. Even with an abundance of bellhops, chances are you'll carry your suitcase at some point, and that sort of thing can wear you down. A fold-over garment bag helps keep dressy clothes wrinkle-free and can be slung over the shoulder if it's not too heavy. Keep in mind that hard-sided luggage may better protect breakable items, but it weighs more than soft-sided bags.

Pack the largest, hardest items, like shoes, on the bottom. Put smaller items in and around them. Put breakables among several layers of clothes or — better — keep them in your carry-on bag. Zip-seal bags are ideal for leaky items like shampoo and suntan lotion. Putting tissue paper or dry cleaning bags between items can reduce wrinkles.

In your carry-on luggage, pack medications, eyeglasses, reading material, CD player, breakable items, and vital documents (like your return tickets, passport, and wallet). I suggest packing a snack, in case you don't like the airline food . . . or don't get any, an increasingly common phenomenon.

Put identification tags on the outside *and* the inside of each bag for easy identification. I also suggest affixing a bright-colored ribbon or tape to the handle for easy spotting in the baggage claim area, especially if your luggage is black like most of the world's.

Nearly all guns are illegal in nearly all circumstances in the District of Columbia. Leave yours at home!

Getting yourself through security

Heightened security also puts new restrictions on air passengers. You have to show a government-issued ID with photo, such as a driver's license. If you use an e-ticket, make sure that you know the documentation that the airline ticket-takers require. Only ticketed passengers are allowed beyond the security checkpoints. (If a child or person with a disability or illness requires assistance, you need to request a special pass at the ticket counter in order to accompany that person to the plane.)

Don't joke about terrorism, or you may find yourself under arrest. The mere mention of words such as "gun" or "bomb" can get you detained and questioned.

Be prepared to remove your laptop computer from its travel case for inspection. Other electronic items also may get extra attention from security personnel.

If a prohibited item is taken from you, security personnel won't ship it back to you. In fact, if you carry banned items through the checkpoints, you may be fined up to $1,100 in a civil action in addition to being subject to criminal penalties. Among the items most often confiscated at checkpoints are scissors, pocketknives, corkscrews, and mace.

After being wanded and frisked at several airport security checkpoints, I adopted the following strategies: When I place my toilet kit and dirty laundry in my carry-on luggage, I put them in clear bags so that the security personnel can see what's in them easily. Before going through the metal detectors, I place all metal objects — keys, cell phone, change, watch, ring, and even chewing gum with foil wrappers — in a clear bag in my carryon. I put them back on my body and in my pockets when I've cleared security.

Knowing what you can — and can't — carry on

Air travelers in the United States now are limited to one carry-on bag, plus one personal bag, such as a purse, briefcase, or camera bag. Airlines also restrict the size of carry-on bags. The dimensions vary, but the strictest airlines say carryons must measure no more than 22 x 14 x 9 inches, including wheels and handles, and weigh no more than 40 pounds.

The **Transportation Security Administration** maintains a list of items passengers aren't allowed to carry into the aircraft cabin. The list is enormous (you can read the latest version at www.tsa.gov/workingwithtsa/aircraft_prohibit.shtm), but it boils down to the following:

✔ **Not permitted:** Items you can use as weapons, such as ammunition, guns, knives (including pocket knives), box cutters, axes, hatchets, hammers, corkscrews, straight razors, razor blades not in a cartridge, metal scissors with sharp points, golf clubs, baseball bats, pool cues, hockey sticks, ski poles, ice picks, disabling chemicals and gases, explosives, and toy weapons.

✔ **Permitted:** Nail clippers, nail files, tweezers, eyelash curlers, safety razors (including disposable razors), syringes (with documented proof of medical need), walking canes, and umbrellas (must be inspected).

You can pack many items that are banned from aircraft cabins in checked luggage. You must unload firearms and declare them to the airline at the ticket counter before you go to the screening checkpoint. Small arms ammunition must be securely packed in fiber, wood, or metal boxes or other packaging specifically designed for it. You can carry one self-defense spray canister of no more than 4 fluid ounces in checked luggage if it has a *positive means* (a safety seal or closure that is part of the product) to prevent accidental discharge. The regulations place strict limitations on the air transport of some items, such as compressed air guns, fire extinguishers, and flare pistols. Some items are banned from all air transportation, including explosives, flares, and disabling gases and chemicals.

The federal government is constantly monitoring these regulations, so they're very much subject to change. The airline you fly may have additional restrictions on items you can carry on board. To obtain the latest rules before you pack, call the airline and check the **Transportation Security Administration's** Web site, www.tsa.gov.

Part III
Settling in to Washington, D.C.

"I want a lens that's heavy enough to counterbalance the weight on my back."

In this part . . .

Navigating your way around Washington, D.C. may be overwhelming at first. The city's maze of sometimes poorly marked roadways, traffic circles, and ever-present traffic jams can be quite intimidating. Don't worry, though. Getting around isn't as complicated as it seems. While the randomly plotted avenues and the traffic circles sow much confusion, they're overlaid by a very logical grid of streets. And the public transit system is world-class. In this part, I walk you through Washington's neighborhoods, show you where to catch the subway and the bus, and ease any apprehensions you may have about finding your way around town.

Chapter 10

Orienting Yourself in Washington, D.C.

. . . .

In This Chapter

▶ Arriving in Washington via the airport, train, or highways

▶ Exploring Washington's neighborhoods

▶ Acquiring visitor information when you arrive

. . . .

*A*rriving in a strange city can be a daunting experience. That's why I'm here — to help relieve your angst. I hope your plane lands on time, your train chugs into Union Station on schedule, or you drive into D.C. without circling the Beltway half a dozen times. Those petty details aside, in this chapter, you discover the best way to get to your hotel, visit Washington's diverse neighborhoods, and locate the best places for gathering maps, brochures, and other useful information. That camera dangling from your neck may mark you as a tourist, but stick with me, and you'll feel like an insider in no time at all.

Arriving in Washington

Three major airports serve Washington, D.C. (see the map in this chapter showing their locations), but none is within the boundaries of the District.

Ronald Reagan Washington National Airport (just say "National") and **Washington Dulles International Airport** ("Dulles") are in Virginia, while **Baltimore-Washington International** (BWI) is in Maryland. All the airports offer several options for getting you into town. (See Chapter 5 for more information on the individual airports.)

Finding the way to your hotel

Signs for taxis, Metrorail (at National only), and other ground transportation are posted in the airports' baggage claim areas, as well as

Washington, D.C. Airports

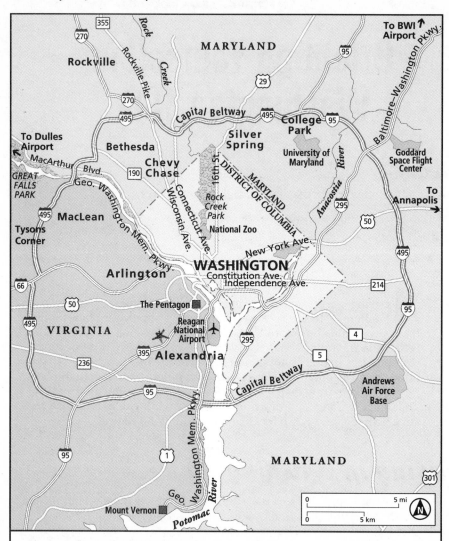

Getting into Town from the Airports

- **From Dulles International Airport:**
  Take the Dulles Airport access road (the only road out) to I-66 east through the Virginia suburbs and over the Theodore Roosevelt Bridge (still I-66), which lands you on Constitution Avenue and the western edge of the national Mall near the Lincoln Memorial.
- **From Baltimore Washington International Airport:**
  Take the airport access road to Highway 295 (Gladys Spellman Parkway; also known as the Baltimore-Washington Parkway) south to Route 50 west (New York Avenue).
- **From Reagan National Airport:**
  Take the George Washington Memorial Parkway north to the 14th Street Bridge, which dumps you onto…14th Street! Just follow the signs to Washington.

outside the terminals. If you experience difficulty finding your way, ask any skycap. The following sections take a look at how you get from flying to sightseeing.

From National Airport

National is Washington's most convenient airport. It's close to town, is easy to get around, and has terrific transportation connections. It's also an attraction in its own right, thanks to the eye-popping terminal that opened in 1997.

Before you leave home, find out whether your hotel offers complimentary shuttle service. If not, the cheapest and quickest way into town is **Metrorail,** which has a station right at the airport. It costs $1.10 ($1.25 in rush hour, which is from 5:30 to 9:30 a.m. and 3 to 7 p.m. on weekdays) to get downtown. The Yellow Line takes you to the Archives-Navy Memorial Station, about halfway between the Capitol and the White House, in about 12 minutes. The ride to Metro Center takes 18 minutes and costs an extra dime, because you have to change trains or take a long loop on the Blue Line.

In general, Metrorail starts running at 5:30 a.m. on weekdays and 8 a.m. on weekends. It shuts down at midnight Sunday through Thursday and stays open until 2 a.m. on Friday and Saturday nights.

If you plan to travel late at night or early in the morning, check the scheduled departure time for the last train between the stations you'll be using. Last train departure times are posted at each station kiosk. You can get Metro information at ☎ **202-637-7000,** Internet: www.wmata.com.

Taxi service from National to downtown runs about $11 before you tip. It takes about 20 minutes, unless you get caught in one of Washington's recurring traffic disasters.

To avoid price gouging, ask for the fare before you get in a cab. D.C. cabs don't have meters. (The suburban cabs do.) Fares are calculated according to an arcane zone system, which is displayed on a nearly indecipherable map in the cab's back seat. To be safe, ask your hotel ahead of time to estimate the fare from the airport. Allow plenty of time to get to the airport for your return flight if you travel weekdays from 6 to 10 a.m. and 3 to 8 p.m.

From Dulles Airport

Dulles is in suburban Virginia, about 26 miles from downtown D.C. To get into town, pick from the following:

 ✔ The **taxi** ride between Dulles and downtown D.C. takes about 45 minutes in nonrush-hour traffic and sets you back about $50 plus tip.

- ✔ **SuperShuttle** van service from Dulles to downtown costs $22 for the first passenger and $10 for each additional passenger. For information, call ☎ **800-258-3826** or visit the company's Web site at www.supershuttle.com.

- ✔ The best bargain is the 5A express **Metrobus** from Dulles to L'Enfant Plaza in D.C. or Rosslyn in Virginia. At both stops, you can enter the Metrorail system or hail a cheaper taxi. The bus departs Dulles approximately hourly from 6:28 a.m. to 11:40 p.m. weekdays, slightly less often on weekends. The fare is just $1.10.

From BWI

BWI often has the least expensive airfares, especially on low-cost Southwest Airlines. But it's also the farthest away from the heart of D.C., so getting from the airport to your hotel takes longer and costs more.

- ✔ By **cab,** you're 45 minutes and $55 away from D.C. if the traffic flows smoothly.

- ✔ The **SuperShuttle** van service charges $30 for the first passenger and $10 for each companion. Call ☎ **800-258-3826** or visit the company's Web site at www.supershuttle.com.

- ✔ A courtesy shuttle operates between BWI Airport and the nearby BWI Rail Station. There, you can board a **MARC commuter train** (☎ **800-325-RAIL;** Internet: www.mtamaryland.com), on *weekdays only*, or an **Amtrak** train (☎ **800-USA-RAIL;** Internet: www.amtrak.com), on any day. The MARC train sets you back $5, while taking Amtrak costs you between $24 and $36. Both trains chug into D.C.'s Union Station on Capitol Hill, where you can enter the Metrorail system or hail a cab.

Arriving by train

Amtrak has great service in the Northeast Corridor. In my experience, it's the most efficient way to arrive from New York and other points between. Trains arrive a few blocks from the U.S. Capitol at historic **Union Station,** a tourist attraction unto itself. You can make taxi and Metrorail connections here. The cab fare to most hotels, which is based on that nutty zone system, is likely to run you from $5 to $10. See Chapter 11 for more on Washington's unique (to put it politely) taxi system.

Arriving by car

They say you shouldn't subject yourself to seeing the making of either law or sausage. To that, I will add driving in Washington. Driving *to*

Washington isn't much fun, either — at least not when you get close to our infamous Beltway. If you do drive on a weekday, try to schedule your arrival at the Beltway between 10 a.m. and 3 p.m. — or after 8 p.m. — to avoid the worst of the rush-hour insanity.

When you make your hotel reservations, ask for directions. To help visualize the territory, see the "Driving to D.C." map in Chapter 5.

Once you get to your D.C. destination, park your buggy and leave it parked until you leave. You'll be much happier if you get around town via Metrorail, Metrobus, taxi, or your own two feet.

If you drive to a hotel in town, be prepared to pay $20 or more to garage your car each day.

Washington, D.C., by Neighborhood

Many first-time visitors are surprised to find that Washington is not all marble and memorials. Even in the most populated areas, you can find grass, trees, flowers, and a place to chill. You can discover much more in Washington than the White House, the Capitol, and the other familiar places featured on the nightly news. In fact, the District has several distinct and distinctive neighborhoods. You can explore their different facets during your visit and leave with a kaleidoscope of impressions. To get you started, here are thumbnail sketches (and a handy map) of D.C.'s major 'hoods.

Adams-Morgan

Vibrant and diverse — that's **Adams-Morgan,** whose crossroads are 18th Street and Columbia Road NW, north of Dupont Circle. This neighborhood's ethnic restaurants, boutiques, and jumping nightlife draw fun-seekers, especially in the evening and on weekends. Then, Adams-Morgan is packed, and parking is nearly impossible. The Dupont Circle and Woodley Park-Zoo Metrorail stations are a hike, but doable for the physically fit. After dark, however, take a taxi or the No. 98 Metrobus, which runs from the Woodley Park-Zoo Metrorail Station from 6 p.m. to 2 a.m. weeknights, from 10 a.m. to 2 a.m. Saturdays, and from 6 p.m. to midnight on Sundays. And exercise your street smarts.

Capitol Hill

Two of the three branches of the federal government live here, as do a lot of people. In addition to housing the Congress and the Supreme Court, **Capitol Hill** is a charming residential neighborhood, with 19th-century

Washington, D.C. Neighborhoods

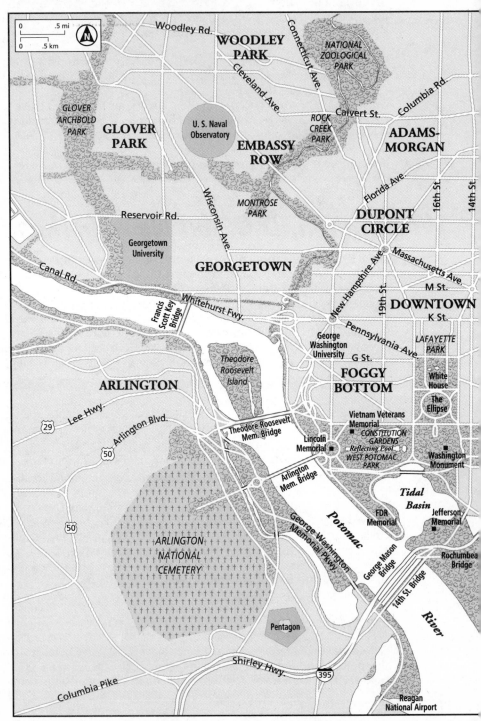

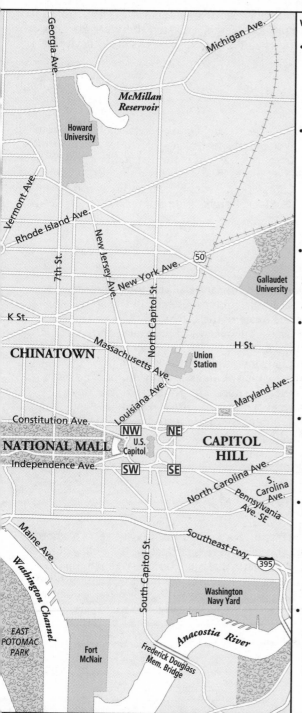

WHAT'S DOING WHERE?

• ADAMS-MORGAN
This neighborhood is vibrant and diverse. Come here to enjoy ethnic restaurants, boutiques, and nightspots. The place really jumps in the evening and on weekends.

• CAPITOL HILL
Congress dominates Capitol Hill, and the Supreme Court has its digs here, too. But the Hill also is a charming residential neighborhood, with a bustling old-fashioned market. And gorgeous old Union Station is filled with shops and eateries as well as gates to trains.

• CHINATOWN
D.C.'s Chinatown is quite small, but it's got some very good restaurants and a large ornamental gateway.

• DUPONT CIRCLE
Day or night, there's always something doing in Dupont Circle. Pop into the galleries, restaurants, and boutiques that abound here. Check out the nightspots or just watch the crazy world saunter by.

• FOGGY BOTTOM/WEST END
As laid back as Dupont is lively, Foggy Bottom boasts quiet residential streets, George Washington University, the State Department, and the Kennedy Center.

• GEORGETOWN
The oldest part of D.C., Georgetown encompasses exclusive residential streets, Georgetown University hangouts, lots of wildly diverse shops, many restaurants, lively nightspots, and an entertaining street scene.

• NATIONAL MALL
The heart of official Washington, the Mall is lined with museums, dotted with memorials, and bordered by government headquarters buildings.

houses, brick sidewalks, and tree-lined streets. You also find Union Station, the National Postal Museum, the Folger Shakespeare Library, the Capital Children's Museum, and the historical — and lively — Eastern Market. This area is another place to watch your step after dark, particularly beyond the Capitol grounds and the first few blocks of Pennsylvania Avenue SE.

Downtown

Washington's **Downtown** is an eclectic amalgam of areas that aren't considered part of Capitol Hill, Foggy Bottom, or Dupont Circle. Downtown encompasses **Chinatown,** as well as D.C.'s theater district, convention area, MCI Center, various federal and city government offices (including the White House), and the Connecticut Avenue/K Street business corridor. You find lots of office buildings, hotels, restaurants, and retail businesses.

Dupont Circle

One of Washington's liveliest neighborhoods all day long, **Dupont Circle** is an ideal spot for people watching. (Check out the street musicians and chess players in the heart of the circle.) Early in the morning, workers arrive at the embassies, businesses, think tanks, and other nonprofit organizations that set up their headquarters here. The area's many restaurants feed people from breakfast through dinner. The neighborhood's filled with art galleries and specialty shops. The night spots keep hopping until well after midnight. Kramerbooks ("open early to late, seven days a week") offered food, drink, and live music long before that became de rigueur for all bookstores. Dupont Circle is the traditional hub of Washington's gay community, which shops — among many other places — at Lambda Rising bookstore and the Human Rights Campaign store.

Foggy Bottom/West End

Insiders call the State Department **"Foggy Bottom"** because that's where its headquarters stand, and the name seems perfect for the obfuscating parlance that marks much diplomatic dialogue. George Washington University also occupies an ever-expanding portion of the neighborhood. That leaves an ever-shrinking piece of the pie to Foggy Bottom's charming residential streets of brick row houses, Lilliputian gardens, and mature trees. Here, you also find the Kennedy Center, the Watergate complex, and quite a few hotels.

Georgetown

One of Washington's best-known neighborhoods was established before the District of Columbia was a gleam in Pierre L'Enfant's eye. Fragments of a former era, when **Georgetown** was a bustling tobacco port, endure in the residential architecture and the cobblestone and brick streets off the main drags.

On Wisconsin Avenue and M Street, however, the mood is far from genteel, especially on weekends. A mix of shops, restaurants, and night spots draws the young — and the young at heart — by the carload. Georgetown University, Dumbarton Oaks, the C&O Canal, the *"Exorcist Steps"* (featured in the movie), and some of the city's most exclusive residences contribute to Georgetown's enduring cache.

Georgetown has no Metrorail station, but 30-series Metrobuses run on Wisconsin and on M to Pennsylvania Avenue. You can hike in from the Foggy Bottom-GWU Metrorail Station. Georgetown Metro Connection shuttle buses run from the Foggy Bottom, Dupont Circle, and Rosslyn stations from 7 a.m. to midnight Monday through Thursday, until 2 a.m. on Friday, from 8 a.m. to 2 a.m. on Saturday, and from 8 a.m. to midnight on Sunday.

The National Mall

Washington's long, long lawn stretches from the Capitol to the Lincoln Memorial and is where you find many museums, monuments, and memorials. The **Mall** is lined by major Smithsonian Institutions and is across the street from major federal government offices. You encounter somber contemplation at places like the Vietnam War Memorial and joyful play on the grass and walkways (kite-flying, cycling, jogging, strolling, and squirrel-watching).

Upper Northwest

The Upper Northwest area is essentially everything north and west of what I describe in the preceding sections. It's mostly nice residential neighborhoods, D.C.'s best public schools, some office buildings, and the restaurants, theaters, and retail establishments that serve them. Some hotels and tourist attractions, notably the Washington National Cathedral and the National Zoo, are here. I live in this neighborhood, but I take visitors elsewhere to sightsee. Where Wisconsin Avenue crosses into Maryland is an area that I refer to as Washington's Rodeo Drive — a number of exclusive stores (plus some discounters) for those who are inclined to expend substantial vacation bucks on shopping.

Gathering Information After You Arrive

Several information sources are available to you after you enter the District. Head for one or more of the following:

- ✔ **Washington, D.C., Visitor Information Center,** on the ground floor of the Ronald Reagan International Trade Center Building, 1300 Pennsylvania Ave. NW, at the Federal Triangle Metrorail Station (☎ 202-328-4748; Internet: www.dcvisit.com). The center is open from 8 a.m. to 6 p.m. on weekdays and from 9 a.m. to 5 p.m. on Saturdays, and it's a full-service spot. Staff members can answer your questions, and you can pick up free brochures. You can buy Metro fare cards, theater tickets, and sightseeing tickets. Information about hotels, restaurants, and events also is available on computers that you can use.

- ✔ **The White House Visitor Center,** on the first floor of the Commerce Department Building, 1450 Pennsylvania Ave. NW, near the Federal Triangle Metrorail Station (☎ 202-208-1631). At press time, the White House has suspended tours for the general public, but the National Park Service continues to operate this visitor center. It's open 7:30 a.m. to 4 p.m. every day except Thanksgiving, Dec. 25, and Jan. 1. You can find information here about other parts of Washington in addition to the White House. You can use restrooms, telephones, and water fountains and obtain first aid if you need it.

- ✔ **The Smithsonian Information Center,** in the "Castle," 1000 Jefferson Dr. SW, on the National Mall, near the Smithsonian Metrorail Station (☎ 202-357-2700; TTY: 202-357-1729; Internet: www.si.edu/visit/infocenter/start.htm; e-mail: info@si.edu). Stop here for information about the Smithsonian and other attractions. Watch a 24-minute video for an overview of the institution. Peruse a model of the Mall to help you locate your first stop. Find attractions and Metro and Tourmobile stops using an electronic map. (See Chapter 11 for information on Tourmobile.) Pick up a free guide in any of seven languages. This center also has information about events elsewhere in the city. Your kids can access information from the video-display monitors while you challenge the staff with your questions. If you're on overload, ask one of the volunteers for help in planning your itinerary. On your way out, you may want to pay your respects to British subject James Smithson, whose bequest gave birth to the institution. His crypt is just inside the Jefferson Drive entrance. The center is open 9 a.m. to 5:30 p.m. daily except Dec. 25.

Chapter 11

Getting Around Washington, D.C.

10-35 min Ride from Arlington to DC Center

In This Chapter

▶ Exploring Washington's transportation options

▶ Driving in Washington . . . or not

▶ Strolling around the city

$$W$$ashington can be a challenge to navigate, particularly for a new-comer. But once you learn the basics, you can negotiate the tourist areas with ease.

D.C. has streets, avenues, roads, drives, places, squares, circles — and probably some other arteries that have slipped my mind. The avenues, roads, drives, and places go every which way. Roadways run into phys-ical barriers and disappear, only to reappear again several blocks away. Circles and squares pop up in your way and leave you searching for your route on the other side. But the street-naming system is based on a grid that extends throughout the city. If you understand how the street-naming system works, you can find almost any address and figure out where you are most of the time.

The Key to the City — Getting from Here to There

When D.C. was created from land ceded by Maryland and Virginia, it was a perfect square, ten miles on a side, with one corner pointing due north. In due course, Virginia was given back most of Southwest D.C. and a portion of Northwest, which is why the district now has an irreg-ular shape defined by the Potomac River along its border with Virginia.

The street-naming system, based on the original square, has endured. The city is divided into quadrants, and all the streets are known by the quadrant they're in: Northwest (NW), Northeast (NE), Southeast (SE), and Southwest (SW).

Understanding the District's Directions

The Capitol dome is the center of D.C. geography. Three streets — North Capitol, East Capitol, and South Capitol — run in those directions from the Capitol grounds. You won't find a West Capitol Street, but you can imagine it running due west from the Capitol down the center of the National Mall. These streets define the boundaries of the four quadrants.

All of Washington's numbered streets run north-south, counting from the Capitol. First Street NE is the first street east of North Capitol Street. First Street NW is the first street west of North Capitol Street. First Street SE is the first street east of South Capitol Street. Just to confuse things, a Half Street SW is closer to South Capitol Street than is a portion of First Street SW.

Washington's east-west-running streets all have names that — in most cases — work through the alphabet as they get further north and south of East Capitol Street and the middle of the National Mall. The streets closest to East Capitol and the middle of the Mall are named for letters — A Street, B Street, and so on. As you continue north and south and the alphabet is exhausted, you run into streets with two-syllable names — Adams, Bryant, Channing, and so on. Then you hit three-syllable names (Allison, Buchanan).

Unfortunately, you will find numerous exceptions to these rules. For some reason — or perhaps for no reason at all — there are no J, X, Y, or Z streets. Some streets break the alphabet and syllable rules. And the roadways that aren't streets — avenues, roads, drives, places — do whatever they feel like doing.

If you understand the basic street grid, you can find almost any address and figure out where you are most of the time. If you're looking for 450 H St. NW, you know it's in the Northwest quadrant of the city, eight streets north of the middle of National Mall, between Fourth and Fifth streets. If you're looking for 850 Fourth St. NE, you know it's in the Northeast quadrant, between H and I streets.

You'll notice I said "almost." The numbered streets don't mess around. But some named streets defy the alphabet and syllable standards. And, because there is no J Street, the block between K and L is the 1000 block. I'm sorry. At least you'll be able to estimate locations within a few blocks. (And then you can ask directions!)

Movin' around on Metro

Washington's extensive public transportation system makes getting around the city a cinch. **Metrorail,** called Metro by locals, is the city's subway system. Rail stations open at 5:30 a.m. on weekdays and at 8 a.m. on weekends. Final trains leave stations around midnight Sunday through Thursday and around 2 a.m. on Friday and Saturday. If you'll be traveling late at night, check the exact time of the last train leaving the station you'll be using. The schedule is posted at the kiosks in each station. You can reach Metro information at ☎ **202-637-7000** (TDD 202-638-3780) or online at www.wmata.com. Request a **Metro Visitor's Kit** by calling ☎ **888-638-7646** or 202-962-2733.

Finding Metrorail stations

Metrorail stations are situated within a few blocks of the vast majority of attractions, hotels, and restaurants recommended in this book. To familiarize yourself with the subway's routes, use the Metrorail map on the Cheat Sheet in the front of this book or the Metrorail map in this chapter.

To find a Metrorail station on Washington's streets, look for the brown pole topped by the letter M and the station name. You should see a *colored stripe* beneath the M to indicate the line or lines that stop there. The different Metrorail lines are named for colors — Red, Blue, Orange, Yellow, and Green. Trains are well marked, but sometimes trains from different lines (such as Blue and Orange) use the same tracks. If you're unsure, ask the station manager or another waiting passenger. If you find yourself on the wrong train, hop off and take a train back to the station where you made the mistake.

Metrorail's cars are air-conditioned, and the seats are upholstered. Stations are clean and well lighted. Trains run every few minutes during rush hour, less often at other times, least often late at night. I always carry reading material for when I'm sitting on the train and waiting at the station. Or you can use your transportation time to people-watch.

Paying your way on Metro

Getting around via Metrorail is relatively inexpensive. Budget $3 to $5 per day per person and use the trains during nonpeak times to save money (9:30 a.m. to 3 p.m. and after 7 p.m. on weekdays and all day on weekends and holidays). Though Metrorail is showing its age (not unlike most people), a major effort is underway to replace tired escalators, refurbish old trains, and bring new trains on line.

Washington, D.C. Metro Stops

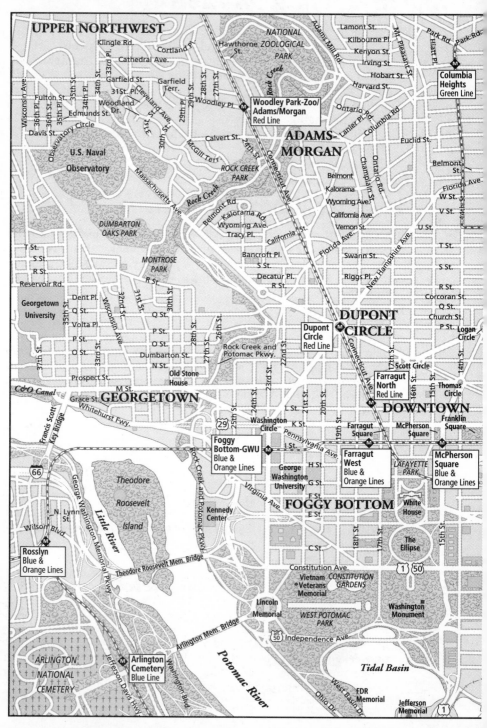

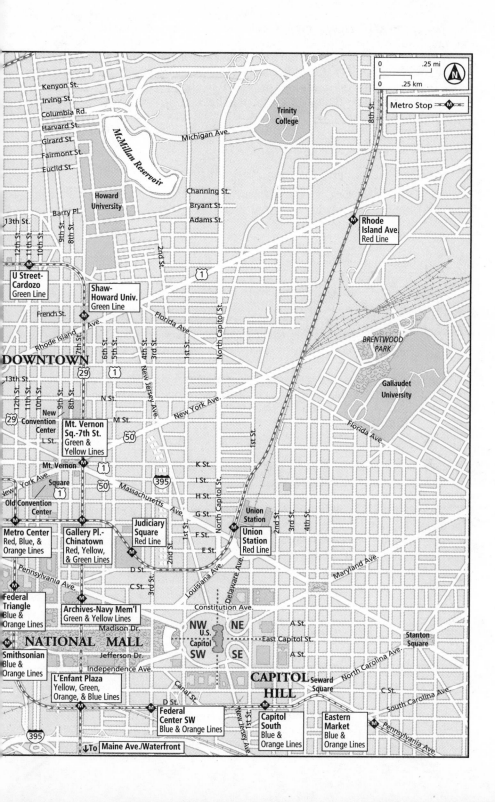

0 .25 mi
0 .25 km

Metro Stop ⊷Ⓜ

Kenyon St.
Irving St.
Columbia Rd.
Harvard St.
Girard St.
Fairmont St.
Euclid St.

McMillan Reservoir

Michigan Ave.

Trinity College

8th St.

Howard University

Channing St.
Bryant St.
Adams St.

Rhode Island Ave.
Red Line

13th St.

12th St.
11th St.
10th St.
9th St.
8th St.

Barry Pl.

2nd St.

US 1

U Street-
Cardozo
Green Line

Shaw-
Howard Univ.
Green Line

French St.

Florida Ave.

Rhode Island Ave.

7th St.

6th St.
5th St.

4th St.
3rd St.

2nd St.

1st St.

North Capitol St.

BRENTWOOD
PARK

DOWNTOWN

29

US 1

Gallaudet
University

13th St.

12th St.
11th St.
10th St.

9th St.
8th St.

N St.

New Jersey Ave.

New York Ave.

Florida Ave.

29

New
Convention
Center

Mt. Vernon
Sq.-7th St.
Green &
Yellow Lines

L St.

50

M St.

50

New York Ave.

Mt. Vernon
Square

US 1

50

Massachusetts Ave.

K St.

I St.

1st St.

395

H St.

Old Convention
Center

G St.

Union
Station

2nd St.

3rd St.

4th St.

Metro Center
Red, Blue, &
Orange Lines

Gallery Pl.-
Chinatown
Red, Yellow,
& Green Lines

Judiciary
Square
Red Line

2nd St.

F St.

E St.

Union
Station
Red Line

Maryland Ave.

Pennsylvania Ave.

D St.

3rd St.

C St.

Louisiana Ave.

Delaware Ave.

Federal
Triangle
Blue &
Orange Lines

Archives-Navy Mem'l
Green & Yellow Lines

Madison Dr.

Constitution Ave.

NW
U.S.

NE

A St.

Stanton
Square

NATIONAL MALL

Jefferson Dr.

Capitol

East Capitol St.

North Carolina Ave.

Smithsonian
Blue &
Orange Lines

Independence Ave.

SW

SE

A St.

L'Enfant Plaza
Yellow, Green,
Orange, & Blue Lines

Canal St.

CAPITOL
HILL

Seward
Square

C St.

South Carolina Ave.

395

D St.

↓To Maine Ave./Waterfront

Federal
Center SW
Blue & Orange Lines

New Jersey Ave.

1st St.

Capitol
South
Blue &
Orange Lines

Eastern
Market
Blue &
Orange Lines

Pennsylvania Ave.

Fares are based on distance traveled and the time of day. Off peak, the minimum fare is $1.10. You'll pay less than $2 for most places you'll go within D.C., even during rush hour. You can buy fare cards from vending machines inside the stations. The machines accept coins (from nickels to quarters) and bills (from $1 to $20). Some machines take credit cards. Bear in mind that the machines return up to only $5 in change — *in coins only*, so make sure that you use small bills when you buy a low-value fare card. Experiencing difficulty? Ask the station manager — or a nearby local — for help.

Estimate the amount of fare you'll need throughout your D.C. stay and buy one fare card per person with that amount on it. That way, you don't have to stop at a fare card vending machine each time you want to take a ride. And, if you buy a fare card worth at least $20, you get a 10% bonus.

Each passenger needs a fare card. One or two children younger than five can ride free with a paying passenger. Disabled persons and seniors 65 and older can ride for half price with a special fare card, but they must possess valid proof of disability or age. For the senior discount, identification can be a driver's license or birth certificate. If the disabled person does not have a Medicare card, however, the discount probably is not worth the paperwork for someone who's visiting for a few days or even a few weeks. A convenient place to purchase the half-price fare cards is the sales office inside the Metro Center Metrorail Station. You can get to it through the station's 12th and F streets entrance or by taking a train to the station. The sales office is open weekdays from 7:30 a.m. to 6:30 p.m. The cards also are sold at many stores, including Safeway and Giant grocery stores.

One-day rail passes cost $5 and allow unlimited rides for a single day after 9:30 a.m. You can buy them at all Metrorail stations.

After you insert your fare card in the entrance gate, it's stamped and returned. Don't walk off without it (as many visitors do). You need to reinsert it in the exit gate at your destination, where the card is returned if value is left on it. If you underestimate the fare, you can add what's necessary at the *Addfare* machines found near the exit and entrance gates.

Hints for smooth riding on Metrorail

First-time passengers sometimes find the system intimidating. Follow these tips, and you should enjoy a smooth ride. (Should you start to hyperventilate, just ask a station attendant for help.)

✔ Wall-mounted **maps** and the lists of station-to-station fares are posted in Metrorail stations. Take your time in locating the station closest to your destination. When in doubt, ask the station manager.

- ✔ Don't forget that you need to hold onto your **fare card** when it's returned to you. Keep it handy for reinsertion at your destination.

- ✔ Don't make the mistake of boarding the wrong train. The minute (or two) that you take to note the station stops, listed on columns inside the stations, is worth it.

- ✔ No eating, drinking, or smoking is allowed on Metro or in the stations. *This rule is serious.* Washington's Metro is one of the cleanest subway systems in the world, and this rule is the reason for it. People are fined — and even arrested — for sipping a soft drink or nibbling on potato chips in a station or on a train. Keep your snacks in your backpacks.

- ✔ If you want a transfer ticket from Metrorail to Metrobus, you need to get it from a machine where you enter the Metrorail system to start your trip. It lets you transfer to a regular bus for 25 cents and to an express bus for $1.15. You can't get any bus-to-subway transfers.

No eating, drinking, or smoking is allowed on Metro or in the stations. Metro has its own police officers, and they fine and arrest people for breaking this rule.

Traveling by Bus

Metrobuses run throughout Washington and its Maryland and Virginia suburbs. Metrorail is faster and more comfortable. But the subway doesn't go to as many places as the buses do. For tourists, the 30-series buses are quite useful.

All 30, 32, 34, 35, and 36 buses travel down Wisconsin Avenue from the D.C.-Maryland border to M Street in the heart of Georgetown. They then go through the heart of downtown and along the National Mall on their way to Capitol Hill.

To find Metrobus stops, look for the red, white, and blue signs with route numbers. You can buy a **map** of all Metrobus Routes in D.C. and Virginia, which probably is all you need to hit the major sights. A map of the D.C. and Maryland routes also is available. Mail $2 for each map to Metro Maps, Office of Marketing, 600 Fifth St. NW, Washington, DC 20001. Or order online for just $1.50 at www.wmata.com/riding/online_sales.cfm.

Bus fare is $1.10, except for some suburban express routes that cost $2. Bus-to-bus transfers are 10 cents. Drivers don't make change, so you need to carry exact fare. Most buses run daily around the clock — frequently during rush hour, infrequently in the wee hours.

Up to two children younger than five ride free with a paying passenger. Seniors 65 and older and persons with disabilities can ride for 50 cents at all times. Valid proof of age or disability must be presented when boarding. For seniors, a driver's license or birth certificate works. A disabled person needs a Medicare card or a special Metro ID that, for a visitor, probably is more trouble to get than it's worth.

Taxi! Cabbing It in D.C.

Hailing a cab in Washington usually is a snap, except for late at night. Stand on a main street, by a busy intersection, or in front of a hotel or large office building to better snag a taxi.

Strangers to D.C. may find the zone fare system baffling — as do the locals. (See the map detailing the zones in this chapter.) But if you ride a Washington cab, you'll have to deal with it. So here's how it works.

The city is divided into zones. When you travel between two points within a zone, your fare is $5. Cross into a second zone, and the fare rises to $6.90. If you continue into a third zone, it's $8.60, and so on until you leave the city. To find out a fare ahead of time, call the **D.C. Taxicab Commission** (☎ **202-645-6018**).

If that system sounds easy to understand, here's why it gets crazy:

✔ The fare increase for crossing from zone to zone is not consistent.

✔ The zone map that's posted in taxicabs is confusing, even to Washingtonians. It's not oriented to the north. It doesn't show many major streets. It doesn't define the zones clearly. In my newspaper days, when I took cabs a lot, I memorized the fares for the trips I took most often — home to office, office to Capitol Hill, and so on.

✔ Zone fares are doubled when the District government declares a snow emergency.

✔ A $1 rush-hour surcharge applies from 7 to 9:30 a.m. and 4 to 6:30 p.m.

✔ For each additional passenger, you pay $1.50.

✔ If you have the driver stop on the way — so that you can mail a letter, for example — you pay an extra dollar.

✔ A surcharge of between 50 cents and $2 is added for luggage, depending on its size.

✔ You pay $1.50 extra if you call to order a taxi.

✔ One child younger than six can ride free with an adult.

Taxicab Zones

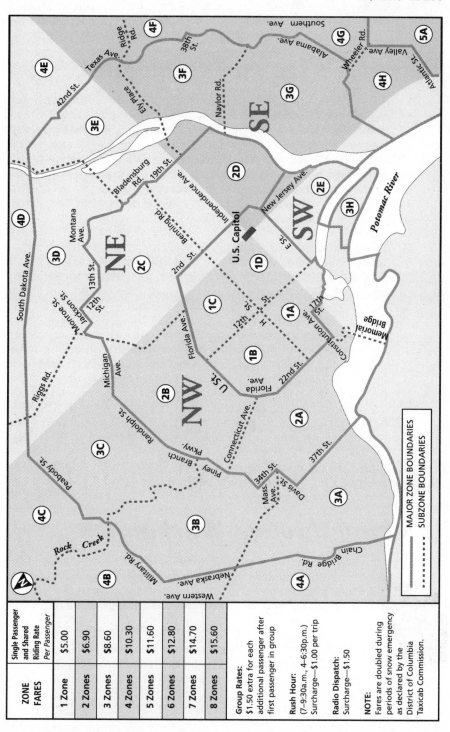

ZONE FARES	Single Passenger and Shared Riding Rate *Per Passenger*
1 Zone	$5.00
2 Zones	$6.90
3 Zones	$8.60
4 Zones	$10.30
5 Zones	$11.60
6 Zones	$12.80
7 Zones	$14.70
8 Zones	$15.60

Group Rates:
$1.50 extra for each additional passenger after first passenger in group

Rush Hour:
(7–9:30a.m., 4–6:30p.m.)
Surcharge—$1.00 per trip

Radio Dispatch:
Surcharge—$1.50

NOTE:
Fares are doubled during periods of snow emergency as declared by the District of Columbia Taxicab Commission.

MAJOR ZONE BOUNDARIES

SUBZONE BOUNDARIES

If you travel to a destination outside D.C., the fare is based on mileage driven. For information on those "interstate" fares, phone ☎ **202-331-1671.**

Taking a Ride on Tourmobile

An excellent alternative mode of transportation for tourists is **Tourmobile** (☎ **202-554-5100;** Internet: www.tourmobile.com), the tram that stops by major tourist attractions and in Arlington Cemetery (see map in Chapter 18). The $18 fare ($8 for children 3 through 11 and free for younger kids) lets you ride all day with unlimited reboarding privileges. That means you can ride the full route, listening to the tour guide's narrative, and get a good overview of most of the big attractions. Then you can use the Tourmobile as a bus to go from place to place for the rest of the day.

Trams stop about every 20 minutes at the red, white, and blue Tourmobile signs from 9:30 a.m. until 4:30 p.m. daily except Dec. 25. Final reboarding is at 3:30 p.m. You can buy tickets from the driver or at Tourmobile ticket booths. (For a list of ticket booths and information about other Tourmobile tours, see Chapter 18.)

All Tourmobile trams are equipped with priority seating for individuals with disabilities and wheelchair storage space. Individuals with disabilities who can transfer from their wheelchairs and climb three steps can board any Tourmobile. Vehicles with lifts are dispatched when a request is made to a Tourmobile driver or at a ticket booth. You can schedule service by a lift-equipped vehicle in advance by calling ☎ **703-979-0690** between 8 a.m. and 5 p.m. daily except Dec. 25. Disabled riders can leave the tram at any stop and arrange a reboarding time with the driver.

After 1 p.m., you can buy a $20 ticket ($9 for kids 3 through 11) that lets you ride the Tourmobile for the rest of that day and all of the next day.

Walking through Washington

Like Nancy Sinatra's boots, Washington is made for walking. In these health- and budget-conscious times, putting mileage on your feet instead of your wallet, fare card, or car makes sense. On foot, you discover things that you may otherwise miss, things that make a trip special. (When you get home, please write and tell me what they are.)

Try a Mall crawl, walking from museum to museum between the Capitol and the Washington Monument. The museums are air-conditioned; you can rest and rejuvenate in a restaurant or snack bar.

Or stroll through the residential side streets of Foggy Bottom and/or Georgetown. (You can find more tips about seeing the sights in Chapters 16 and 17, and information on walking tours in Chapter 18.)

Keep your wits about you when you walk. That's not to say that D.C. isn't safe to walk around in. It is, especially in the major tourist zones. It just pays to be prepared. Stride with a sense of purpose; dawdlers appear vulnerable, which is just what professional pickpockets look for. Be alert in crowds, where a bump from a pickpocket can easily be missed. Be aware of your surroundings. Stow wallets, cash, and credit cards in hard-to-reach pockets or a money pouch worn under your clothing. Wear your purse across one shoulder and over the chest — bandolier style.

The safe zones include the major tourist areas and Metro. At night, use the buddy system and stick to the main commercial blocks when in Adams-Morgan and Capitol Hill. If Metro's service has stopped for the day, and you're still out on the town, take a taxi. Know your destination before you set out. Hold your kids' hands on city streets and sidewalks, on all Metro escalators, and on Metro platforms. Lock your hotel room door, car doors, and trunk. Lock valuables in a safe deposit box (if not in your room, then at the front desk). Keep a close eye on your pocketbook, camera, and wallet. Hold onto your purse in a restaurant. Carry your cash and credit cards in a front pocket or a concealed money pouch. Leave the family jewels at home; what you do bring, don't flash.

On Capitol Hill, you won't encounter many problems in the immediate vicinity of the major hotels and attractions, but the farther you go from the Capitol, the less safe you'll be at night.

Driving Your Car

I have yet to meet a person who enjoys driving in Washington. The traffic is oppressive and constantly getting worse. Washington, D.C. also seems to be cursed by an ever-growing number of drivers who drive as if no one else is on the road.

Street parking is at a premium. Garage parking will consume your family's lunch money.

If you plan on arriving by car, ask about parking rates at your hotel when you make a reservation. It may prevent your requiring treatment for shock when the final hotel tab is totaled up.

Chapter 12

Keeping Your Cash in Check

· ·

In This Chapter

▶ Accessing cash in Washington

▶ Coping with theft

▶ Getting a handle on the local taxes

· ·

*T*he good news for Washington visitors is that most of the city's popular attractions are free. That said, D.C.'s cost of living is high overall, so you may find yourself in danger of emptying your wallet on numerous occasions. The best way to handle this challenge is not to bring suitcases full of cash. In fact, you're better off bringing a relatively small amount. You can reduce your need for cash by using your charge cards wherever you can. And, if necessary, you can replenish your cash supply at an ATM.

Finding Funds in Washington

Washington used to have more monuments than **ATMs.** Now an automated teller machine seems to be on almost every corner. Most, if not all, bank branches house ATMs, many of them outside. In addition, you can find ATMs at attractions, museums, supermarkets, and shopping malls, among other locations.

Before you leave home, ask your bank whether it has branches in Washington where you can use your ATM card with no service fee and find out where they are. It's useful to know locations near your hotel and where you'll be spending your sightseeing time, such as in the Smithsonian Institution museums along the National Mall, for example.

If your bank doesn't have D.C. branches, determine which ATM network(s) your bank belongs to by checking the back of your ATM card. **Cirrus ☎ 800-424-7787** and **Plus ☎ 800-843-7587** are the most popular networks. Call the 800 number for ATM locations or visit the Web sites for Visa and Plus (Internet: www.visa.com) or MasterCard/Cirrus (Internet: www.mastercard.com).

If you're not using your own bank's ATMs, keep in mind that many other ATM operators tack on an extra withdrawal charge. Your bank may assess yet another charge on that transaction. If you use a charge card to get a cash advance, you'll likely start paying interest on it right away.

Every ATM should tell you, on a printed sign, how much the fee is. If no sign is apparent, a message should announce the fee after you punch in your PIN (personal identification number). At that point, you can decide whether to continue with the transaction.

For more information on money matters, see Chapter 3.

Keeping Your Money Safe (and What to Do If It's Stolen)

Washington is about as safe as any other major city in the United States, which means crime does exist, but if you stick to areas frequented by tourists, you should not have any problem. To reduce your chances of losing your cash to a thief, take the following precautions:

- ✔ Always keep a purse or shoulder bag slung diagonally across your chest, under your jacket if you're wearing one. The best kind of purse to take is one that folds over and secures, rather than one that has just a zipper on top. Do not sling your purse or camera over your chair when in a restaurant. If you carry valuables in a fanny pack, turn it into a tummy pack, wearing the pouch in the front.

- ✔ If you don't carry a purse or shoulder bag, put your wallet, cash, credit cards, traveler's checks, and other valuables deep in your front pants pockets. Or use a money belt or money pouch that's worn under your clothing.

- ✔ If your hotel has an in-room safe, use it. Stash excess cash, traveler's checks, and other valuables that you don't need to carry with you. If your hotel room doesn't have a safe, put your valuables and cash inside the hotel's safety deposit box.

In the unlikely event that you become a theft victim, keep the following in mind:

- ✔ Almost every credit-card company has a toll-free emergency number that you can call if your cards are lost or stolen. The credit-card company may be able to wire you a cash advance off your card immediately and send you a replacement card within a day or two.

✔ The issuing bank's toll-free number is usually printed on the back of the credit card. Make note of this phone number and your charge card account number before you leave on your trip and stash them somewhere other than your wallet. If you forget to write down the phone number, call toll-free directory assistance (☎ 800-555-1212) to get your issuing bank's toll-free number.

Because thieves may not swipe this guidebook — though it's surely worth its weight in gold — I'm including these emergency numbers here:

✔ Visa: ☎ 800-847-2911

✔ MasterCard: ☎ 800-622-7747

✔ American Express: ☎ 800-441-0519

✔ American Express traveler's checks: ☎ 800-221-7282

If you opt to carry traveler's checks, make sure that you keep a record of their serial numbers in a safe location, separate from the checks, in case they're lost or stolen. (As examples: Leave the numbers with a relative back home or in the hotel or room safe.) Traveler's checks can be somewhat cumbersome and, considering the number of ATM machines in Washington, they're probably unnecessary. Nevertheless, traveler's checks are the safest way to carry the equivalent of a large amount of cash. Should your checks be stolen, call the issuer, give the serial numbers, and ask for instructions on replacing them.

If your wallet or purse is stolen, head to the nearest phone to cancel your credit cards and inform the authorities. A police report number may come in handy for credit card or insurance purposes later.

Understanding Local Taxes

When you're budgeting for your trip, be sure to make allowances for the local taxes. They can add up, especially on an extended visit. The D.C. sales tax on merchandise is 5.75%, so that $45 painting of the Washington Monument on black velvet actually sets you back $47.59. For each meal in a restaurant, you pay a 10% tax, so it costs you $55 for a $50 dinner check (before the tip). The tax on a hotel room is 14.5% — that's $29 on a $200 room.

Part IV
Dining in D.C.

"Six of Jennifer's goldfish died today, and, well, I just don't think it's worth the three of us keeping our reservations at Takara's Sushi Restaurant tonight."

In this part . . .

*I*n this part, you can find reviews of the city's best restaurants in all price ranges, as well as tips on where to snack. You also discover lots of variety. Washington may not be as renowned for its tables as New York or New Orleans, but it's no longer a bumpkin in this department. After all, this is the city that put the *power* into power lunch. And, as a world capital, it attracts the world's food.

Chapter 13

Getting the Lowdown on D.C.'s Dining Scene

There's a joke around Washington that you can identify the world's trouble spots by checking out the new restaurants in town. People flee trouble overseas, whether it's famine, war, or oppression. Washington — the capital of the free world — is a beacon. Many refugees have started on the road to the American Dream by opening a restaurant. As a result, Vietnamese, Ethiopian, Afghan, and other exotic cuisines took root in the nation's capital. Washington's international influences and community provide a hungry and knowledgeable audience for the Chinese, French, German, Indian, Italian, Japanese, Spanish, Thai, and Middle Eastern restaurants you can find here. And, with Congress representing every corner of America, a variety of regional cuisines from throughout the United States are represented as well.

What's Cooking Now in D.C.

They say that what goes around comes around. Hot in Washington right now are twists on old standards.

✔ **French restaurants,** always at the top of the food chain, are surging in popularity, especially in more reasonable price ranges. In the next chapter, among my reviews of D.C.'s best restaurants, you can find three French establishments where you can order a delicious, moderately priced meal — Bistro Bis, Bistrot Lepic, and La Colline — and one, Café La Ruche, where you can dine downright inexpensively.

✔ **Vegetarianism** is on the march, and not just in purely vegetarian eateries. Most D.C. restaurants offer at least one vegetarian entree. If you prefer not to see meat anywhere on the menu, visit Amma Indian Vegetarian Kitchen in Georgetown. If you don't mind eating in the vicinity of carnivores, try the vegetarian pastas at Al Tiramisu; the fried green tomatoes, house salad, and vegetarian croquette at Georgia Brown's; the vegetarian fixed-price tasting menu at Gerard's Place; the grilled vegetables and vegetarian pasta at Luna Grill & Diner; the Chinese vegetarian dishes at Tony Cheng's *Seafood* Restaurant (he has two eateries on the premises, the other is a grill); or the many organic vegetarian selections at Nora and Asia Nora. (See Chapter 14 for reviews.)

✔ The **martini** has been the ultimate cocktail for ages, but not the way bartenders have been stirring them lately. Want a chocolate martini? Or a sour apple martini? Try the lounge at 701, the restaurant at 701 Pennsylvania Ave. NW. Or head for the Willard Hotel's Round Robin Bar — a highly popular imbibing venue recently — and try an herbal martini. Dill, perhaps, or rosemary?

Let's Do Lunch!

Washingtonians do lunch in just about every way imaginable. The infamous three-martini lunch has pretty much faded into the past. But business lunches remain a big deal — a way for lobbyists, lawmakers, administrators, political operatives, and journalists to share info in a relaxed setting without cutting into their crowded business days. Most Washingtonians on most days, however, gobble quick soups and sandwiches in lunch rooms, grab sandwiches and soft drinks and head for a park bench, or take their eats back to the office and get back to work with their food at their elbows.

What this routine means to you is that you can find lots of spots for grabbing decent quick lunches. And, because many of the top restaurants are open for lunch, you can sample some of the city's best dining in smaller portions for smaller prices at midday.

Eating Like a Local

Both high-class and inexpensive eateries are scattered throughout the city. Here's what makes some neighborhoods a bit distinctive, food-wise.

✔ **Capitol Hill:** Despite their low standing with the general public, members of Congress and their aides are in general a hardworking bunch, so you can find lots of spots for quick lunches on

Capitol Hill. Restaurants, cafeterias, and carryouts are scattered throughout the Capitol and the congressional office buildings. The food court on the bottom floor of Union Station is one of the largest and most diverse you'll find anywhere.

✔ **Downtown:** This area is Washington's business center, so you can find many fine-dining establishments, plus delis and sandwich shops on most corners. Buy a sandwich, chips, and soft drink and find a nearby park for people-watching.

✔ **Georgetown, Dupont Circle, and Adams-Morgan:** These areas are D.C.'s party spots, so lots of vibrant and informal restaurants and saloons line the streets. You can eat, drink, dance, and check out the street scenes.

✔ **The National Mall:** The Mall is lined with museums and galleries, and the bigger ones will feed your stomach as well as your eyes. You can also find a lot of street vendors nearby, hawking hotdogs, sausages, chips, candy, and soft drinks.

Eating Out Without Losing Your Shirt: Tips for Cutting Costs

 Spending oodles on noodles (and steak and swordfish) is easy in D.C., but it's not required. Here are some suggestions for keeping your food bill under control:

✔ **When you want to sample an expensive restaurant, do so at lunchtime.** You can still get the acclaimed food, but you won't pay so much.

✔ **Buy carryout and picnic on a park bench or on the National Mall.** You can find many lovely, shaded spots among the memorials.

✔ **Take advantage of fixed-price, early bird, pretheater, and post-theater menus.** Check your watch as well as the hours restaurants offer specials. If you arrive five minutes late, you'll pay full price. You snooze, you lose.

✔ **Split appetizers and desserts — and even main courses — with your dining companions.** So many restaurants serve sinfully large portions. If you have access to a refrigerator and microwave, ask for doggy bags. You can heat up the leftovers for an in-room meal — like room service without the service (or the service fee).

✔ **Ask the prices of the dishes that are described by the waiter rather than listed on the menu.** They can shock you.

Making Reservations

While you can find lots of spots for lunch without much of a fuss or wait, accomplishing this feat is a bit trickier later in the day. Regarding restaurant dinner reservations: If you can make them, do!

If you know your plans, make your reservations several days in advance — even before you leave home. Reserve for lunch, too, if you can. Otherwise, you can decrease the size of the lines you wait in by arriving before 11:45 a.m. or after 1:30 p.m.

If you're a Web head, you can make reservations at many D.C. restaurants by surfing over to OpenTable at www.opentable.com. OpenTable also provides descriptions of the restaurants, reviews, maps and links to the restaurants' Web sites.

Dressing to Dine

Washington is a working town, so it's filled with suits, wingtips, and "sensible" pumps. You'll encounter them in the restaurants at breakfast, lunch, and dinner, as well as in government, media, and business offices. But Washington has a pretty forgiving dress code. Few restaurants will block your entrance if you're dressed more casually. I doubt you'll get thrown out of many places for wearing jeans, although you may feel out of place at the nicer restaurants. If you love to dress up, go for it. Washingtonians won't look down on you for that, either. Though I wouldn't recommend it, you can wear a tux most places without raising eyebrows. Enough black-tie affairs occur in this town that people are used to seeing the penguin look on Metrorail or hustling down the street.

Chap

Washington's Restaurants

Time to feed your faces, folks! Loosen your belt buckle, I translate the menus. I start with own of my picks for the best restaurants in all price ranges, listed alphabetically for easy referral. The price range, location, and the cuisine follow each restaurant's name. The price included is for your having a salad or appetizer, entree, and dessert.

After the reviews, I list the restaurant by location so that you can find a place near the attractions you visit, by price so that you can budget accordingly, and by **cuisine** so that you can satisfy your individual tastes.

All the listings are for good (or better) restaurants where you can enjoy a satisfying meal and a pleasant dining experience. I based the selections on good quality food for a fair price — in other words, value.

Restaurants designated as kid-friendly in this chapter have a kids' menu and/or cuisine that appeals to a young palate.

What the $ Symbols Mean

The reviews contain two price indicators: a dollar symbol, for a quick look at the price of a dinner without beverages, and the range of prices for main courses. I added up the costs of the least expensive and most expensive appetizer or salad, main course, and dessert at dinner, not including taxes and tips, and then averaged the highest- and lowest-priced meals to come up with the dollar sign ranking.

Prices change over time, and the cost of your meal obviously depends on what you order. One reason I don't include beverage costs in my price categories is that ordering top-shelf cocktails and expensive wines can produce a $$$$$ bill at a $$$ restaurant. Sticking to a lower-priced entree

Dining in Washington

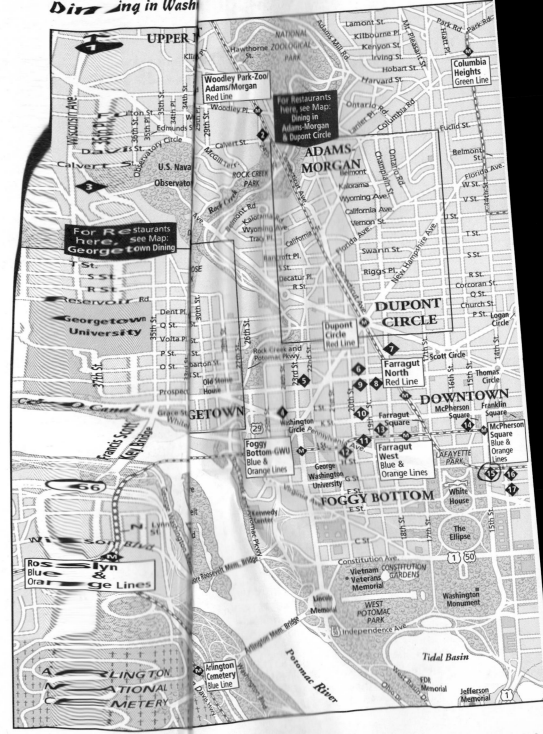

UPPER

Woodley Park-Zoo/
Adams/Morgan
Red Line

For Restaurants
here, see Map:
Dining in
Adams-Morgan
& Dupont Circle

For Restaurants
here, see Map:
Georgetown Dining

ADAMS-
MORGAN

DUPONT
CIRCLE

Dupont
Circle
Red Line

Farragut
North
Red Line

Scott Circle

Thomas
Circle

Logan
Circle

DOWNTOWN
McPherson   Franklin
Square   Square

McPherson
Square
Blue &
Orange
Lines

Farragut
Square

Foggy
Bottom-GWU
Blue &
Orange Lines

George
Washington
University

Farragut
West
Blue &
Orange Lines

LAFAYETTE
PARK

White
House

FOGGY BOTTOM

The
Ellipse

Roslyn
Blue &
Orange Lines

Washington
Monument

Arlington
Cemetery
Blue Line

Vietnam CONSTITUTION
Veterans GARDENS
Memorial

Lincoln
Memorial

WEST
POTOMAC
PARK

Potomac River

Tidal Basin

FDR
Memorial

Jefferson
Memorial

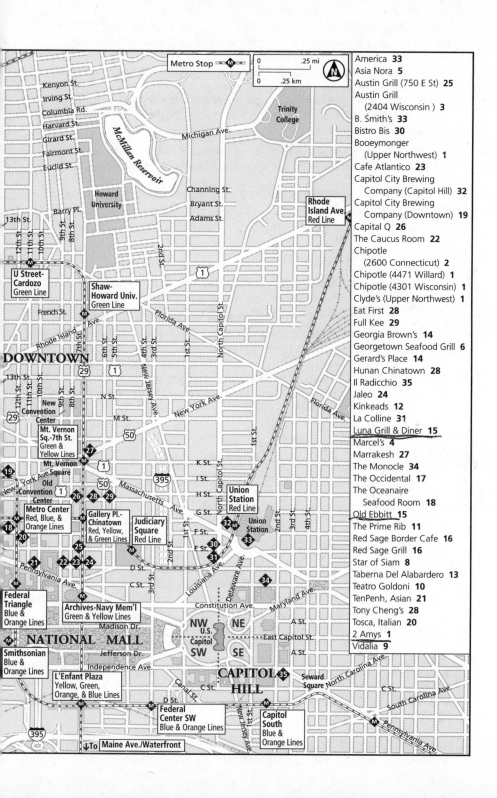

America **33**
Asia Nora **5**
Austin Grill (750 E St) **25**
Austin Grill
(2404 Wisconsin) **3**
B. Smith's **33**
Bistro Bis **30**
Booeymonger
(Upper Northwest) **1**
Cafe Atlantico **23**
Capitol City Brewing
Company (Capitol Hill) **32**
Capitol City Brewing
Company (Downtown) **19**
Capital Q **26**
The Caucus Room **22**
Chipotle
(2600 Connecticut) **2**
Chipotle (4471 Willard) **1**
Chipotle (4301 Wisconsin) **1**
Clyde's (Upper Northwest) **1**
Eat First **28**
Full Kee **29**
Georgia Brown's **14**
Georgetown Seafood Grill **6**
Gerard's Place **14**
Hunan Chinatown **28**
Il Radicchio **35**
Jaleo **24**
Kinkeads **12**
La Colline **31**
Luna Grill & Diner **15**
Marcel's **4**
Marrakesh **27**
The Monocle **34**
The Occidental **17**
The Oceanaire
Seafood Room **18**
Old Ebbitt **15**
The Prime Rib **11**
Red Sage Border Cafe **16**
Red Sage Grill **16**
Star of Siam **8**
Taberna Del Alabardero **13**
Teatro Goldoni **10**
TenPenh, Asian **21**
Tony Cheng's **28**
Tosca, Italian **20**
2 Amys **1**
Vidalia **9**

and drinking coffee (or water) can squeeze a $$$$ restaurant into a $$$ bill (not that I recommend water over wine at gourmet restaurants).

Here's what you can expect, in general, in the different price categories.

- ✔ **$:** Expect simple food in simple surroundings or possibly inexpensive ethnic dishes. Plan on spending less than $15 per person without beverages.

- ✔ **$$:** These restaurants hold down their prices by paying lower rent for being a little out of the way, and they eschew expenses that don't contribute to the quality of the food, such as fresh flowers, linen napkins, and striking art on the walls. A meal goes for $15 to $25 without drinks.

- ✔ **$$$:** You won't blow your budget by eating at one of these fine dining spots. Enjoy nice decor, good service, and better-than-good food for $25 to $35 before drinks.

- ✔ **$$$$:** These restaurants are among the best in D.C. Expect the finest food, chefs, service, decor, and ambiance. Prepare to spend about $35 to $50 per person, not counting your wine and cocktails.

- ✔ **$$$$$:** These restaurants are the very best in town and serve the most expensive foods in the most luxurious surroundings. The restaurants are renowned for their chef, atmosphere, and high-class clientele. It's nearly impossible to imagine that you won't be happy with the food, but you may blanch at the check, which will exceed $50 per diner.

Washington, D.C. Restaurants from A to Z

Al Tiramisu
$$$ Dupont Circle ITALIAN

This good Italian restaurant is known for its fresh fish grilled with olive oil and lemon, as well as dishes with porcini mushrooms, white truffles, risotto, and pasta. The menu also features meat and poultry. Vegetarians can choose among the pastas, and there's a good mixed seafood grill. True to the restaurant's name, the desserts include *tiramisu,* an Italian confection of eggs, cheese, ladyfingers, cream, espresso, chocolate, and spirits. Chef Luigi Diotaiuti, a native of Italy, worked for restaurants in Paris, Venice, and other European cities before moving to Washington in 1990. He opened Al Tiramisu in 1996. He counts among his regulars Placido Domingo, the world-renowned tenor who is artistic director of the Washington Opera.

2014 P St. NW ☎ 202-467-4466. Reservations required. Metro: Dupont Circle. From Q Street exit, walk one block south on 20th Street and turn right on P. Main courses:

Dining in Adams-Morgan and Dupont Circle

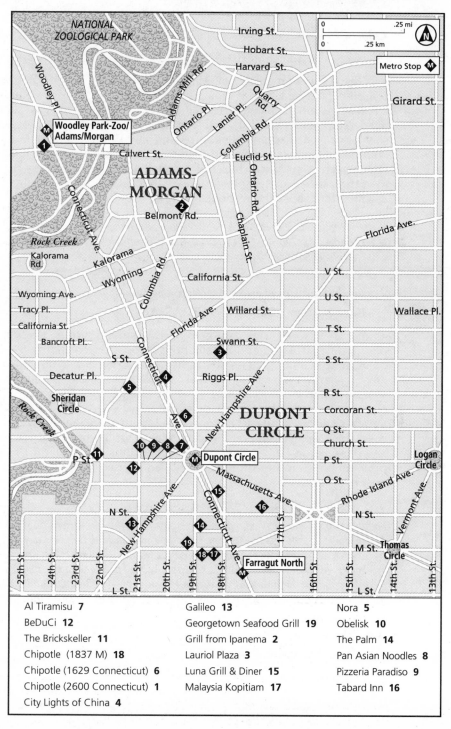

Al Tiramisu **7**	Galileo **13**	Nora **5**
BeDuCi **12**	Georgetown Seafood Grill **19**	Obelisk **10**
The Brickskeller **11**	Grill from Ipanema **2**	The Palm **14**
Chipotle (1837 M) **18**	Lauriol Plaza **3**	Pan Asian Noodles **8**
Chipotle (1629 Connecticut) **6**	Luna Grill & Diner **15**	Pizzeria Paradiso **9**
Chipotle (2600 Connecticut) **1**	Malaysia Kopitiam **17**	Tabard Inn **16**
City Lights of China **4**		

$15–$18. AE, DC, MC, V. Open: Mon–Fri noon to 2:30 p.m. and 5:30–10:30 p.m.; Sat 5:30–10:30 p.m.; and Sun 5–9:30 p.m.

America

$$ Capitol Hill   AMERICAN

This restaurant's gimmick is offering a wide variety of "American" foods in beautiful, historic Union Station. The cover of the oversized menu is the U.S. flag. Inside, the menu is printed on a U.S. map. Selections — all identified, often quite tenuously, with specific parts of the country — include such obvious dishes as peanut butter and jelly, Western omelet, Maryland crab cakes, Cincinnati chili, and Waldorf salad. Best bets are the daily specials, which aren't forced into the theme. If it's on the menu, try the pan-fried trout with tomato, spinach, and crab meat served over saffron rice. Ask for a table upstairs overlooking the activity in the train station.

In Union Station ☎ 202-682-9555. Reservations recommended. Metro: Union Station. Main courses: $8–$20. AE, CB, DC, DISC, MC, V. Open: Mon–Thu 11:30 a.m.–9:30 p.m. and Fri–Sun 11:30 a.m.–10 p.m.

Amma Indian Vegetarian Kitchen

$ Georgetown   INDIAN/VEGETARIAN

Amma is a wonderful example of the serendipitous diversity of Georgetown. This quiet, unassuming second-story restaurant — with quiet, unassuming staff — sits right next to the Jinx Proof Tattoos & Piercing Parlor on bustling M Street. Amma offers you numerous ways to sample Indian vegetarian cooking at bargain prices. The Amma Special comes with rice, salad, bread, pickle, and two vegetables for $6.99. The Kerala Thali House Special features three south Indian curries with mixed vegetables, spicy soup, rice, yogurt, pickle, grilled or deep-fried bread, and dessert for $10.99. The Punjabi Thali House Special, for the same price, is built around three north Indian curries. Or you can mix and match à la carte.

3291 M St. NW near 33rd Street. ☎ 202-625-6652. Reservations accepted. Metro: Foggy Bottom-George Washington University. From the Metrorail station, take the Georgetown shuttle bus to Wisconsin and M and then walk two blocks west on M. Or take a taxi. Or walk west from the 30-series Metrobus stop at Wisconsin and M. Full meals for $11 or less. AE, MC, V. Open: Mon–Thur 11:30 a.m.–2:30 p.m. and 5:30–10 p.m.; Fri 11:30 a.m.–2:30 p.m. and 5:30 p.m.–10:30 p.m.; Sat 11:30 a.m.–3:30 p.m. and 5:30 p.m.–10:30 p.m.; and Sun noon–3:30 p.m. and 5:30–10 p.m.

Asia Nora

$$$$ Foggy Bottom/West End   ASIAN/ORGANIC

Like its older sister Nora (see upcoming listing), Asia Nora cooks with organic ingredients. It's a gorgeous restaurant, decorated and furnished in warm tones, Asian artifacts, and soft chairs. The food, rather than pure

Asian, is modern American with Asian touches. Thus, you may find the menu includes a seared lemongrass flank steak with shallot and black bean sauce, roasted potatoes, garlic shoots, shiitake mushrooms and crispy onions, or pan-seared Alaskan halibut on crispy soba noodle cake. Try the crispy spiced oysters with coriander-jalapeno pesto, Thai basil, plum tomatoes, and pickled scallions as an appetizer. Top it all off with warm Asian pear tartlet and honey-lavender ice cream. I'm drooling as I write!

2213 M St. NW at 22nd Street. ☎ 202-797-4860. Reservations recommended. Metro: Foggy Bottom-George Washington University. Walk north on 23rd Street to M and then right. Main courses: $20–$27. AE, MC, V. Open: Mon–Thur 5:30 p.m.–10 p.m. and Fri–Sat 5:30 p.m.–10:30 p.m.

Austin Grill

$$ Downtown andUpper Northwest   SOUTHWESTERN

Our family hits the Austin Grill often. You get good Tex-Mex food in a festive atmosphere served by friendly staff. The grill gives you lots of choices. My wife tends to pick among the appetizers, while my daughter goes for the Austin Special — one chicken and one cheese enchilada striped with three sauces. If, like me, you're partial to hot stuff, you can take a shot at the Roadhouse Burrito — spicy ground sirloin and red beans, topped with a cheese and jalapeño sauce. It's billed as a "heart attack on a platter." The kids' menu has Tex-Mex dishes, along with burgers and chicken sandwiches. The original Austin Grill is on Wisconsin Avenue above Georgetown. Tourists are more likely to encounter the new and spacious downtown grill in the up-and coming arts-and-entertainment area near MCI Center.

750 E St. NW, between 7th and 8th streets. ☎ 202-393-3776. Reservations not accepted. Metro: Gallery Place. From 7th and F Streets exit, walk one block south on 7th and then turn right on E. Main courses: $8–$19. AE, DISC, DC, MC, V. Open: Mon 11:30 a.m.– 10:30 p.m.; Tue–Thurs 11:30 a.m.–11 p.m.; Fri 11:30 a.m.–midnight; Sat 11 a.m.–midnight; and Sun 11 a.m.–10:30 p.m.

Also 2404 Wisconsin Ave. NW. ☎ 202-337-8080. On the 30-series Metrobus line.

B. Smith's

$$$$ Capitol Hill   SOUTHERN

Under the ornate, soaring Beaux Arts ceiling of what once was the President's Room in Union Station, Washingtonians now dine on Southern, Cajun, and Creole cooking. Share the red beans and rice appetizer before diving into your main courses. B. Smith's house special is called Swamp Thing, and it's mixed seafood over greens in a mustard-based seafood sauce. Other specialties include grilled lamb chops, fried green tomatoes, and spicy Cajun jambalaya. Executive chef Rahman Harper also has come up with a regional dish he calls Chesapeake Bay Surf & Turf — fried chicken and crab cakes. Traditional jazz groups entertain on Friday and Saturday nights and at Sunday brunch.

In Union Station, 50 Massachusetts Ave. NE. ☎ 202-289-6188. Reservations recommended. Metro: Union Station. Main courses: $15–$36. AE, DISC, DC, MC, JCB, V. Open: Mon–Thu 11:30 a.m.–4 p.m. and 5 p.m.–11 p.m.; Fri–Sat 11:30 a.m.–4 p.m. and 5 p.m.–midnight; and Sun 11:30 a.m.–9 p.m.

BeDuCi

$$$$ Dupont Circle   MEDITERRANEAN

BeDuCi (for "Below Dupont Circle") is not just another pretty face. But it *is* a looker, with its sun porch, sidewalk tables, and art-enhanced interior dining rooms. The kitchen turns out Mediterranean-inspired dishes that often taste as good as they look. Your best bet is to pick from the daily specials, especially the pastas. Sinful fudge-frosted brownies are the perfect ending to a meal at BeDuCi. Who cares if the dessert's Mediterranean origins are suspect?

2100 P St. NW, at 21st Street. ☎ 202-223-3824. Reservations recommended. Metro: Dupont Circle. From Q Street exit, walk one block south on 20th Street and then turn right on P. Main courses: $13–$28 AE, DC, DISC, MC, V. Open: Mon–Thur 11:30 a.m.–2:15 p.m. and 5:30 p.m.–10 p.m.; Fri–Sat 11:30 a.m.–2:15 p.m. and 5:30 p.m.–10:30 p.m.; and Sun 5–9:30 p.m. No Saturday lunch in July and August.

Bistro Bis

$$$ Capitol Hill   MODERN BISTRO

The food at Bistro Bis is an excellent modern American interpretation of classic French bistro and brasserie cooking. The setting represents a modern American nod toward classic bistro style. From the zinc bar to the spacious leather booths, Bis is both eye-catching and comfortable. The menu changes frequently, but look for medallions of lamb sautéed with braised onions, tomatoes, beans, and rosemary; trout sautéed with lemon, capers, ham, roasted onions, and wilted spinach; seared sea scallops with garlic, tomato, olives, parsley, and eggplant; or grilled tuna steak with artichoke. The simplest dishes — seared salmon or braised short ribs, for example — often are the best.

15 E St. NW. near North Capitol Street. ☎ 202-661-2700. Reservations recommended. Metro: Union Station. From Union Station Shops/Massachusetts Avenue exit, turn right on Massachusetts, then left on North Capitol, and then right on E. Main courses: $18.50–$29.50 AE, DC, DISC, MC, V. Open: Daily 7–10 a.m., 11:30 a.m. –2:30 p.m., and 5:30–10:30 p.m.

Bistrot Lepic

$$$ Georgetown   CLASSIC FRENCH

This neighborhood hangout is in upper Georgetown and is filled with diplomats, world travelers, and others who revel in real French food. Chef Bruno Fortin began to learn the art of French cooking in his parents' restaurant in Brittany and then hopped around Europe and North

Dining in Georgetown

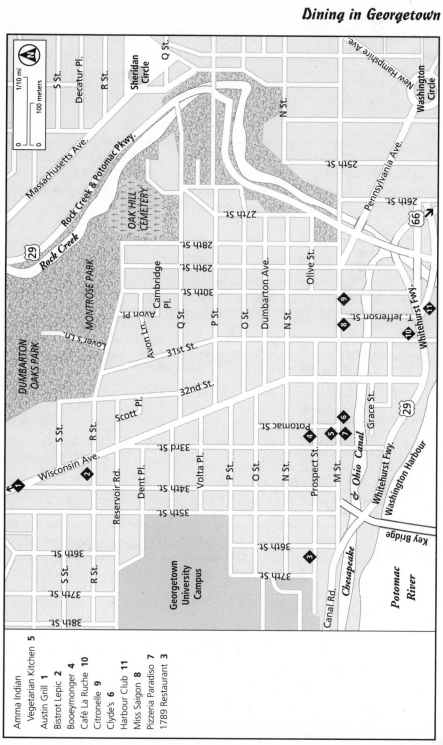

Amma Indian
Vegetarian Kitchen **5**
Austin Grill **1**
Bistrot Lepic **2**
Booeymonger **4**
Café La Ruche **10**
Citronelle **9**
Clyde's **6**
Harbour Club **11**
Miss Saigon **8**
Pizzeria Paradiso **7**
1789 Restaurant **3**

America before settling into Washington and opening Lepic (named for a street he lived on in Paris) in 1995. Like other good French chefs in America, Fortin offers traditional French dishes and his own improvisations on them. Start with the mussel soup with leeks and potatoes, and/or the lemon-lime risotto with shrimp. Then try the grilled trout with carrot sauce, potato-crusted salmon, or sautéed sea scallops with ginger broccoli mousse. The dining room is small, bustling, and pleasant, with sunny yellow walls.

1736 Wisconsin Ave. NW near S Street. ☎ *202-333-0111. Reservations recommended. Metro: Take a taxi or a 30-series Metrobus. Main courses $16–$21. AE, DC, DISC, MC, V. Open: Tue–Thur 11:30 a.m.–2:30 p.m. and 5:30–10 p.m.; Fri–Sat 11:30 a.m.–2:30 p.m. and 5:30–10:30 p.m.; and Sun 11:30 a.m.–2:30 p.m. and 5:30– 9:30 p.m.*

Booeymonger
$ Georgetown and Upper Northwest   AMERICAN

The Wisconsin Avenue Booeymonger is one of our family's hangouts, because it's just a few blocks from home, the eat-in and take-out service is fast, and the food is good. (We've got Booeymonger frequent-eater cards!) My wife and daughter both have a thing for the Manhattan — roast beef, spinach, bacon, cheddar cheese, and dressing on a baguette — and the carrot cake. In delis, I tend to go for hot pastrami on rye with mustard. When in a healthy mood, however, I order the Pita Pan, a veggie and cheese sandwich. The menu has lots of sandwiches, salads, and sides to choose from here (some with silly names), and you can get a full breakfast in the morning.

3265 Prospect St. NW at Potomac Street. ☎ *202-333-4810. Reservations not accepted. Metro: Rosslyn. From the Metrorail station, take the Georgetown shuttle bus to Potomac and M streets and walk up Potomac one block to Prospect. Or take a 30-series Metrobus to Wisconsin Avenue and M, then walk one block west on M, and turn right on Potomac. Or take a taxi. Sandwiches: $4.25–$5.75. Salads: $2.75–$6.25. AE, CB, DC, MC, V. Open: Daily 7:30 a.m.–midnight.*

Also at 5252 Wisconsin Ave. NW at Jenifer Street. ☎ *202-686-5805. Reservations not accepted. Metro: Friendship Heights. From the Jenifer Street exit, walk left on Wisconsin. Open: Sun–Thur 7:30 a.m.–1 a.m. and Fri–Sat 7:30 a.m.–2 a.m.*

The Brickskeller
$ Dupont Circle   AMERICAN

If you've left your college days long behind you, visiting the Brickskeller may make you think you've gone back. Your college town has to have a (smaller) hamburger place like this one. It's got brick walls. It's got checkered tablecloths. It's got bar food. And, my, does it have beer — more than 850 brands are advertised. The emphasis here is on basic dishes that go well with beer: juicy burgers, Buffalo wings, and French fries. If you crave alternatives to standard pub fare, you can get salmon, crab cakes, or a salad, or you can order steak, ribs, or seafood.

1523 22nd St. NW, between P and Q streets. ☎ 202-293-1885. Reservations accepted for six or more people. Metro: Dupont Circle. From Q Street exit, walk west on Q to 22nd and then turn left. Main courses: $5.50 (bacon-cheddar burger)–16.95 (Buffalo steak). AE, CB, DC, DISC, MC, V. Open: Mon–Thurs 11:30 a.m.–2 a.m.; Fri 11:30 a.m.–3 a.m.; Sat 6 p.m.–3 a.m.; and Sun 6 p.m.–2 a.m.

Cafe Atlantico
$$$ Downtown   LATIN AMERICAN

Brightly decorated and filled with greenery and tables scattered over three open floors, Cafe Atlantico is a lively spot within an easy walk of many tourist attractions and cultural and entertainment venues. The Nuevo Latino cooking draws on the cuisines of South America, Central America, Mexico, and the Caribbean. The food is tasty and can be as rainbow-bright as the interior decorations. The *asopao de hongos* (rice and mushroom stew with goat cheese and plantains) is delicious. So is the duck confit with creamed corn, zucchini, squash, and sweet potato chips. The cafe is noted for its exotic mixed drinks and extensive Latin American wine list. Come Saturdays from 11:30 a.m. to 1:30 p.m. for "Latino din-sum" (tapas) and Sunday from 11:30 a.m. to 2:30 p.m. for a New Latin brunch.

405 8th St. NW, between D and E streets. ☎ 202-393-0812. Reservations recommended. Metro: Gallery Place-Chinatown. From From F and 7th streets exit, walk east on F to 8th and then turn left. Main courses: $18–$24. AE, DC, DISC, MC, V. Open: Mon–Thur 11:30 a.m.–2:30 p.m. and 5–10 p.m.; Fri 11:30 a.m.–2:30 p.m. and 5–11 p.m.; Sat 11:30 a.m.–1:30 p.m. and 5–11 p.m.; Sun 11:30 a.m.–3 p.m. and 5–10 p.m.

Café La Ruche
$$ Georgetown   CLASSIC FRENCH

My wife and daughter like to eat in this little restaurant off Georgetown's beaten path because it reminds them of France. From the outside, you can imagine it as a house in the French countryside (if you ignore the surrounding buildings). Inside, it's like a well-worn neighborhood hangout in Paris (though the TV at one end of the dining room intrudes upon the fantasy). Unfortunately, at times, indifferent service can remind you of Paris as well. To start, try the traditional French onion soup. You can make a meal of the salade Niçoise. The quiches are good. And the desserts are wonderful. (Get the fruit tart, and you can pretend it's health food. I do.) Weekend brunch is a treat. When the weather's nice, you can eat outside.

1039 31st St. NW, between M and K streets. ☎ 202-965-2684. Reservations accepted. Metro: Foggy Bottom-George Washington University. Take the Georgetown shuttle bus to K and Thomas Jefferson streets, then walk back on K to 31st, and turn left. Or take a 30-series Metrobus to 31st and M streets and walk south on 31st. Or take a taxi. Main courses: $7–$10. AE, CB, DC, DISC, MC, V. Open: Mon–Fri 11:30 a.m.–3 p.m. and 5–11 p.m. and Sat–Sun 10 a.m.–3 p.m. (brunch) and 5–11 p.m.

Capital Q

$$ Chinatown   TEXAS BARBECUE

How's this for incongruity? In Washington's tiny Chinatown stands a tiny restaurant with autographed pictures of U.S. politicians on the walls and Texas barbecue on the menu. Most of the politicians are Texans, which is appropriate because this restaurant is run by transplanted Texan Nick Fontana. Capital Q is good enough and authentic enough to attract Texas expatriate diners and was picked to cater the party that House Majority Leader Dick Armey (of Texas) threw for 4,000 of his closest friends at the 2000 Republican National Convention in Philadelphia. Order the beef brisket or pulled pork from the sandwich menu. Or try the beef brisket plate, which comes with two side dishes. The "Chinese Cowboy Platter" gives you your choice of barbecued meat over rice. Service is cafeteria style.

707 H. St. NW between 7th and 8 streets. ☎ 202-347-8396. Reservations not accepted. Metro: Gallery Place-Chinatown. From 7th and 8th Streets exit, cross 7th on H and look for the restaurant. Sandwiches: $4.50–$6. Plates: $5.25–$15. No credit cards. Mon–Thurs 11 a.m.–7 p.m., Fri 11 a.m.–8 p.m., and Sat 11:30 a.m.– 8 p.m.

Capitol City Brewing Company

$$ Capitol Hill and Downtown   AMERICAN

The Capitol City's brewpub has been fruitful and multiplied (or fermented), expanding to four locations — two in D.C., one in suburban Arlington, and a fourth in Baltimore. The D.C. digs are big and boisterous. They're located in historic buildings — the old Post Office on Capitol Hill (slip downstairs to see the Postal Museum) and the renovated bus station Downtown — so you get interesting decor with your burger and brew. The beers offered here are made on the premises. The burgers are excellent. So are other items on the long menu, including the chili and the crab and corn chowder. You can order food at the bar, if you're in a hurry.

11th and H streets NW ☎ 202-628-2222. Reservations not accepted. Metro: Metro Center. From 11th Street exit, walk one block north on 11th to H. Main courses: $6.50 (hamburger)–$23 (crab cake platter). AE, DC, DISC, MC, V. Open: Mon–Sat 11 a.m.–11 p.m. and Sun 11 a.m.–midnight.

Also 2 Massachusetts Ave. NE, between North Capitol Street and Union Station, in the old Post Office. ☎ 202-842-2337. Metro: Union Station. From Union Station Shops/Massachusetts Avenue exit, walk across 1st Street.

The Caucus Room
$$$$ Downtown   STEAKHOUSE

This restaurant was created in that grand Washington tradition of Republican and Democratic lawmakers ripping each other's hearts out during the day and then visiting each other's hideaway offices to sip bourbon and swap stories at night. That doesn't happen so much in these highly partisan times, but Democratic lobbyist Tommy Boggs and former Republican National Committee Chairman Haley Barbour joined the ownership group to make it happen at the Caucus Room, just off Pennsylvania Avenue, midway between the Capitol and the White House. The result is a near-caricature of what you'd expect from high-priced lobbyists. Cherry wood, marble, brass, and thick carpet define the decor. On the menu, you find onion soup, Caesar salad, and lots of steak. The food is good, the room is comfortable, and you just may spy some political VIPs moseying about.

401 9th St. NW at D Street. ☎ 202-393-0777. Reservations recommended. Metro: Archives-Navy Memorial. Walk west on Pennsylvania and then right one block on 9th to D. Main Courses: $24–$36. AE, DISC, MC, V. Open: Mon–Fri 11:30 a.m.– 2:30 p.m. and 5:30 p.m. to 10:30 p.m. and Saturday 5:30 p.m.–10:30 p.m.

Chipotle
$ Dupont Circle and Upper Northwest   MEXICAN

To call this "fast food" is to take into account only the speed with which it's delivered. The striking decor and the quality of the food itself say that you're in a modern Mexican restaurant with a limited menu. Burritos and tacos are made fresh as you order them in the cafeteria line and instruct the cooks on which ingredients you want. Pick a beer or margarita to quench your thirst.

All locations: Reservations not accepted. Prices range from $4.75–$5.50. MC, V. Open daily 11 a.m.–10 p.m.

1837 M St. NW between 18th and 19th streets. ☎ 202-466-4104. Metro: Dupont Circle. From Dupont Circle exit, walk two blocks south on 19th Street and then turn left on M.

1629 Connecticut Ave. NW between Q and R streets. ☎ 202-387-8261. Metro: Dupont Circle. From Q Street exit, walk north on Connecticut Avenue.

2600 Connecticut Ave. NW at Calvert Street. ☎ 202-299-9111. Metro: Woodley Park-Zoo. Walk south on Connecticut.

4301 Wisconsin Ave. NW at Warren Street. ☎ 202-237-0602. Metro: Tenleytown. From East Side exit, walk south two blocks on Wisconsin.

4471 Willard Ave. near Friendship Boulevard (in Chevy Chase, Maryland). ☎ 301-654-6661. Metro: Friendship Heights. From Wisconsin and Western Avenues exit, walk north on Wisconsin one block and then left on Willard two blocks.

Citronelle

$$$$$ Georgetown FRENCH/CALIFORNIA CUISINE

Chef Michel Richard has earned a reputation as one of the best French chefs in America. His restaurant actually bills its offerings as "French/California cuisine" — French recipes with American influences. Citronelle offers fixed-price dinners and tasting dinners. The appetizers may include a crab tart or crispy escargot with wild mushrooms, parsley, and basil pesto. For the main course, how about squab cooked four ways or asparagus-encrusted salmon with morel sauce? For dessert, try Richard's famous chocolate bar or a crunchy napoleon in caramel maple sauce. Richard also hosts a chef's table, which starts at $150 per person before beverages.

3000 M St. NW at 30th Street, in the Latham Hotel. ☎ 202-625-2150. Reservations required. Jacket required. Metro: Foggy Bottom-George Washington University. From the Metrorail station, take the Georgetown shuttle bus to Wisconsin Avenue and M and then walk two blocks east on M to 30th Street. Or take a taxi or a 30-series Metrobus. Fixed-price dinner: $70–$82; tasting dinner: $95–$115, without beverages. AE, DC, MC, V. Open: Mon–Thur 6:30 a.m.–10:30 a.m., noon–2 p.m., 6:30 p.m.–9:30 p.m.; Fri 6:30 a.m.–10:30 a.m., noon–2 p.m., 6:30 p.m.–10 p.m.; Sat 6:30 a.m.–10:30 a.m., 6 p.m.–10:30 p.m.; and Sun 6:30 a.m.–10:30 a.m., 6:30 p.m.–9:30 p.m. Closed Sundays in July and August.

City Lights of China

$$ Dupont Circle CHINESE

Good food served by a friendly staff in pleasant surroundings — what more do you want in a Chinese restaurant? City Lights has a large and varied menu, and the owners invite you to ask the chef to accommodate your personal tastes. The restaurant is noted for its Peking duck and crisp-fried Cornish hen. Other favorites include eggplant with garlic, crispy-fried beef, and tangy Szechwan lamb. In addition to serving you inside, City Lights has a substantial takeout menu and delivers to nearby hotels. Keep that thought in mind if you want to picnic on a park bench or collapse in your room after a particularly grueling day of seeing the sights.

1731 Connecticut Ave. NW between R and S streets. ☎ 202-265-6688. Reservations recommended. Metro: Dupont Circle. From the Q Street exit, walk north on Connecticut Avenue past R Street. Main courses: $11–$26. AE, DC, DISC, MC, V. Open: Mon–Fri 11:30 a.m.–11 p.m.; Sat noon–11 p.m.; and Sun noon–10:30 p.m.

Clyde's

$$$ Georgetown and Upper Northwest AMERICAN

Like its sibling Old Ebbitt Grill, Clyde's of Georgetown was one of my favorite places to eat when I managed to find an excuse to visit Washington long before we moved here. Then, it was a comfortable old saloon with some unusually good food, especially (to my taste) the omelets. A 1996 renovation modernized the place, while aiming to maintain a saloon-like atmosphere — oak bar, plank flooring, checkered tablecloths. Clyde's is still a place for hamburgers and other bar fare, but the ever-changing menu is quite ambitious, with special attention to incorporating fresh produce from mid-Atlantic farms. Clyde's is a local chain now, and the Clyde's of Chevy Chase, just across the border in Maryland, is in the midst of the Friendship Heights upscale shopping area, which I describe in Chapter 19.

3236 M St. NW between Wisconsin Avenue and Potomac Street. ☎ *202-333-9180. Reservations recommended. Metro: Foggy Bottom-George Washington University. From the Metrorail station, take the Georgetown Shuttle bus to Wisconsin Avenue and M and then walk a half block west on M. Clyde's is on the left side of the street. Or hop a 30-series bus to Wisconsin and M. Or hail a taxi. Main courses: $11–$24. AE, DC, DISC, MC, V. Open: Mon–Thurs 11:30 a.m.–2 a.m.; Fri 11:30 a.m.–3 a.m.; Sat 10 a.m.–3 a.m.; and Sun 9:30 a.m.–9 p.m.*

Also in Chevy Chase, MD, 70 Wisconsin Circle, in Chevy Chase Shopping Center, at 5400 Wisconsin Ave. ☎ *301-951-9600. Reservations recommended. Metro: Friendship Heights. From Western Avenue and Military Road exit, walk north on Wisconsin, cross Wisconsin Circle, and then turn right into the shopping center parking lot. Main courses: $11–$20. AE, DC, DISC, MC, V. Open: Mon 11 a.m.– 10 p.m.; Tue–Sat 11 a.m.–11 p.m.; and Sunday brunch 10 a.m.–4 p.m.*

Eat First
$ Chinatown   CHINESE

The name and the exterior appearance of Eat First don't scream "gourmet cooking," but the restaurant serves good food popular with the locals. You need to peruse the various sections of the lengthy menu to locate the best dishes. Try the steamed shrimp from among the house specialties, General Tso's chicken in the poultry section, sliced chicken with ginger and scallion from the clay pot preparations, and the barbecued pork and roasted duck entrees from the barbecue and soy sauce dishes. If you know your Chinese cooking, the chefs are happy to prepare items not on the menu. In an early-to-bed town, this place is one where you can satisfy late-late-late hunger.

609 H St. NW between 6th and 7th streets. ☎ *202-289-1703. Reservations accepted. Metro: Gallery Place-Chinatown. From 6th and H Streets exit, walk less than one block east on H. Main courses: $6–$17. AE, MC, V. Sun–Thurs 11 a.m.–2 a.m. and Fri–Sat 11 a.m.–3 a.m.*

Full Kee
$$ Chinatown   CHINESE

Full Kee diners smile a lot. Maybe their fortune cookies prophesy a large inheritance in the near future. Or maybe they smile because this Chinatown bastion rarely disappoints. Consistency is the hallmark of its food and service. If you have a yen for Hong Kong shrimp dumplings in the middle of a Friday or Saturday night, Full Kee is open until 3 a.m. Join the chefs who chow down here after closing their own kitchens.

Cantonese fare is featured, but Full Kee also offers Szechwan and Hunan dishes and is known for its fresh seafood. The decor is basic, and they don't serve alcoholic beverages.

509 H St. NW between 5th and 6th streets. ☎ 202-371-2233. Reservations accepted for six or more people. Metro: Gallery Place-Chinatown. From 7th and H Streets exit, walk east on H. Main courses: $10–$15. No credit cards. Open: Sun–Thurs 11 a.m.–1 a.m. and Fri–Sat 11 a.m.–3 a.m.

Galileo
$$$$$ **Downtown** **NORTHERN ITALIAN**

Galileo has set the bar by which other D.C. Italian restaurants are measured, and you pay for the quality. Award-winning chef Roberto Donna specializes in dishes reflecting the best of the Piedmont region in northern Italy, his birthplace. Risotto, grilled portobello mushrooms, roasted fish, and roasted meat are highlights. In a private dining room known as *Il Laboratorio,* a 10- to 12-course tasting menu is served five nights a week ($98 weekdays, $110 weekends). Epicures are advised to reserve well ahead for one of the 30 coveted seats. The delicious food makes you forget (almost) about the cost.

1110 21st St. NW between L and M streets. ☎ 202-293-7191. Laboratorio ☎ 202-331-0880. Reservations recommended. Metro: Farragut North. Walk west on L Street four blocks and then right on 21st. Main courses $24–$35. AE, DC, DISC, MC, V. Open: Mon–Fri 11:30 a.m.–2 p.m. and 5:30–10 p.m.; Sat 5:30–10:30 p.m.; and Sun 5:30–10 p.m.

Georgia Brown's
$$$ **Downtown** **SOUTHERN**

Ready for "nouveau soul food?" That's how the cuisine is described at Georgia Brown's, a Southern restaurant that bases its cooking on the traditions of South Carolina's Coastal Low Country — with a twist. And just what does that produce? How about fried green tomatoes stuffed with herbed cream cheese, served on green tomato relish with lemon-cayenne mayonnaise and watercress? Or a house salad of baby greens, corn, green onion, croutons, blue cheese, spiced peanuts, and Georgia peach vinaigrette dressing? Or a vegetarian croquette? You can find plenty of traditional home cooking, too, like fried chicken, pork chops, fried catfish, gumbo, shrimp, and grits. Portions are large. The dining room is comfy. A popular jazz brunch is on Sunday. And the place is a hangout for local movers and shakers.

950 15th St. NW between I and K streets. ☎ 202-393-4499. Reservations recommended. Metro: McPherson Square. From the Vermont Ave./White House exit, walk north on Vermont to I, where you bear left on 15th. Main courses: $12–$23. AE, DC, DISC, MC, V. Open: Mon–Thurs 11:30 a.m.–10:30 p.m.; Fri 11:30 a.m.–11:30 p.m.; Sat 5:30–11:30 p.m.; and Sun 11:30 a.m.–4:30 p.m. and 5:30–10:30 p.m. (Sunday brunch 10:30 a.m.– 2:30 p.m.)

Georgetown Seafood Grill
$$$ Downtown   SEAFOOD

The Georgetown Seafood Grill is not in Georgetown, unless you want to extend the boundaries of that neighborhood about seven blocks east. But it does serve seafood. And much of the seafood is good — that's why I recommend it. When you walk in the door, you think you've left Washington for a beach restaurant. Lobster tanks are in the front, aquariums are in the walls, canoes hang from the ceiling, and models of ships are scattered about — and it seems like everything else is sea-blue, including the waiters' outfits. ("Very ocean-y," my daughter describes it.) The service is good. The best bets include the lobster, crab cakes, clams casino, the large variety of oysters, or any of the fresh catch that is offered grilled, sautéed, blackened, or poached.

1200 19th St. NW at M Street. ☎ 202-530-4430. Reservations recommended. Metro: Dupont Circle. From Dupont Circle exit, walk south two full blocks to M Street. Main courses: $15–$25. AE, DC, DISC, MC, V. Open: Mon–Thurs 11:30 a.m.–10 p.m.; Fri 11:30 a.m.–11 p.m.; Sat 5:30–11 p.m.; and Sun 6 p.m.–10 p.m.

Gerard's Place
$$$$$ Downtown   CLASSIC FRENCH

This intimate French restaurant serves top-notch food by Gerard Pangaud, one of the best French chefs in America, at top-notch prices. Pangaud changes the menu every other week. Recommended dishes to look for include roasted chicken with fresh herbs, roasted duck, fricassee of monkfish in red wine sauce, and lobster with ginger, lime, and sauterne. Also recommended are desserts, which you must order with your main course because they're all made to order. Try a fruit soufflé or cake baked just for you. Gerard's proves the value of eating at lunch and ordering fixed-price meals. You can get a three-course, fixed-price lunch for $29.50. A tasting menu at dinner also sets you back $78 or, if you order vegetarian, $58. (All prices are before wine.)

915 15th St. NW, between I and K streets. ☎ 202-737-4445. Reservations recommended. Metro: McPherson Square. From the Vermont Ave./White House exit, walk north on Vermont to I, where you bear left on 15th. Main courses: $28–$43. AE, MC, V. Open: Mon–Thur 11:30 a.m.–2:30 p.m. and 5:30 p.m.–10 p.m.; Friday 11:30 a.m.–2:30 p.m. and 5:30 p.m.–10:30 p.m.; and Sat 5:30 p.m.–10:30 p.m.

The Grill From Ipanema
$$ Adams-Morgan   BRAZILIAN

If you've never enjoyed the complex flavors of Brazilian cuisine, don't miss this favorite, known for its good food and lively neighborhood bar scene. Beneath the palm trees and tropical colors, get into a Latin American mood with Brazil's national dish, *feijoada* — a rich black bean stew with sausages and pork spooned over rice. Wash it down with Brazil's national cocktail, a *caipirinha,* made with lime, sugar, and a sugarcane liquor. Other menu standouts include a light fish stew called *moqueca* and a Brazilian version of paella served with a spicy green sauce in a clay pot. For appetizers, try the conch chowder or the grilled portobello mushroom topped with crab meat. If you want to avoid noise drifting in from the bar, ask for an outdoor table whenever the weather is nice.

1858 Columbia Rd. NW at Mintwood Place. ☎ 202-986-0757. Reservations accepted Sun–Thur, but only until 7:30 p.m. Fri–Sat. Metro: Woodley Park-Zoo-Adams-Morgan. From the Metrorail station, catch the No. 98 Metrobus to Calvert Street and Columbia Road and then walk south on Columbia two blocks. Bus runs 6 p.m.–2 a.m. weeknights; 10 a.m.–2 a.m. Saturdays; and 6 p.m.–midnight Sundays. Or take a taxi. Main courses: $13–$21. AE, MC, V, DC, DISC. Open: Mon–Fri 5–11 p.m. and Sat–Sun noon to 11:30 p.m.

Harbour Club
$$$$ Georgetown   AMERICAN

The new "hip" spot in Georgetown, this restaurant with lounge curves around the fountain at Harbor Place on the waterfront. Opened in 2002, the 280-seat restaurant mixes space-age decor with ocean touches, such as a 3,000-gallon tropical fish tank in the formal dining area. Roomy booths along the exterior windows are equipped with DSL lines. Or choose seats at the counter in front of the open kitchen, in the comfy chairs in the two lounge areas, or on the outdoor patio. The Thai-born chef offers some Asian touches — the Crab Rangoon appetizer is popular — but the menu standouts are the simpler dishes, such as the steaks and chops. You may want to stop here at lunch, when the prices are lower, and you can get really good crab cakes, burgers, or fish and chips.

3000 K St. at Thomas Jefferson Street. ☎ 202-339-9494. Reservations recommended. Metro: Foggy Bottom-George Washington University. From the Metrorail station, take the Georgetown shuttle bus to Washington Harbour. Or take a 30-series bus to M and 30th streets., walk south on 30th to K, and then right on K to Washington Harbour. Or grab a cab. Main courses: $10–$35. AE, V, DC, MC. Open: Mon–Thurs 11:30 a.m.–midnight; Fri–Sat 11:30 a.m.–3 a.m. Sun 11:30 a.m.–11 p.m.

Hunan Chinatown
$$ Chinatown   CHINESE

This has long been one of Washington's most popular Chinese restaurants, not just for the food but also for its refined atmosphere. Quiet music plays in the comfortable dining rooms. The chairs are soft. The tables have tablecloths. Everyone raves about the tea-smoked duck, a dish from southwestern China rarely found in American-Chinese restaurants. Other standouts include General Tso's chicken, Szechwan beef, and two-flavor lobster. When selecting appetizers, don't pass up the dumplings or the hot-and-sour soup.

624 H St. NW, between 6th and 7th streets. ☎ 202-783-5858. Reservations recommended for eight or more people. Metro: Gallery Place-Chinatown. From 6th and H

Streets exit, walk less than one block east on H. Main courses: $10.50–$25. AE, DC, DISC, MC, V. Open: Sun–Thurs 11 a.m.–10 p.m. and Fri–Sat 11 a.m.–11 p.m.

Il Radicchio
$$ Capitol Hill   ITALIAN/PIZZA

Indulge in a pizza with toppings from the long list of possibilities or a bottomless bowl of spaghetti with a variety of sauces. Sandwiches and full meals with salad, meat, and vegetables also are available. The prices are modest, service is efficient, and the wall decorations colorful. (Your kids should enjoy them.) One of chef Roberto Donna's quartet of restaurants (along with Galileo, Barolo, and Vivo), this food is basic Italian that's authentic and good — sometimes *very* good.

223 Pennsylvania Ave. SE between 2nd and 3rd streets. ☎ 202-547-5114. No reservations. Metro: Capitol South. Walk one block north on 1st Street, right on Independence Avenue for just more than a block, and then right on Pennsylvania. Main courses: $6–$16. AE, CB, DC, MC, V. Open: Mon–Thurs 11:30 a.m.–10 p.m.; Fri–Sat 11:30 a.m.–11 p.m.; and Sun 5–10 p.m.

Jaleo
$$ Downtown   SPANISH

Loosely translated, *jaleo* means revelry or racket. Neither is in short supply at this lively, colorful tapas bar and restaurant. Enjoy flamenco music while perusing a menu of 50 tapas and main courses. Because sharing is an unspoken rule, Jaleo is fun with a group. The Sunday brunch (11:30 a.m.–3 p.m.) attracts locals en route to a nearby attraction or an afternoon siesta. Eat your eggs with sausage or atop plantains and rice. You can graze here nightly for a week and not sample everything.

480 7th St. NW at E Street. ☎ 202-628-7949. Reservations accepted until 6:30 p.m. Metro: Gallery Place/Chinatown. From 7th and F Streets exit, walk one block south on 7th to E. Main courses: $13–$20; tapas $4–$8. AE, DC, DISC, MC, V. Open: Sun–Mon 11:30 a.m.–10 p.m.; Tues–Thurs 11:30 a.m.–11:30 p.m.; and Fri–Sat 11:30 a.m.–midnight.

Kinkead's
$$$$ Foggy Bottom   SEAFOOD

This restaurants is one of the very best in Washington. When I had to say a big thank-you to a critic who helped me enormously with this book, I bought her a gift certificate so that she could take her husband here for dinner. Everything is good, but chef Bob Kinkead's signature dishes include Portuguese-style roast monkfish with sausage; crusted salmon with crab, corn, and chilies; and wild mushroom strudel. You can choose from a variety of dining areas at Kinkead's. The main dining rooms upstairs are attractive and formal. There's an informal bar and cafe on the lower level with live jazz from 6:30 to 10 p.m. Tuesday through

Saturday. The "atrium" refers to a few tables outside the restaurant-proper in the adjacent indoor shopping mall.

2000 Pennsylvania Ave. NW (actually on I Street between 20th and 21st streets).
☎ 202-296-7700. Reservations recommended. Metro: Foggy Bottom. Walk two and a half blocks east on I Street. Restaurant entrance is on the right in the middle of the block. Main courses: $21–$29. AE, DC, DISC, MC, V. Open: Daily 11:30 a.m.–10:30 p.m.

La Colline

$$$ Capitol Hill   CLASSIC FRENCH

Back in my newspaper days, La Colline (French for "The Hill") was my favorite place to take Capitol Hill sources for lunch — on the company's tab, of course. Beyond the fine food and the ideal location (the Capitol is practically outside the front door), La Colline has high-backed booths and well-spaced tables that offer some sense of privacy when you're engaged in confidential conversations. The restaurant is known for the classics, such as onion soup or lobster bisque to start a meal and crème brulee for dessert. But you also find more modern creations on the frequently changing menu — free-range chicken and fresh lobster tail with truffle sauce, for example. Being a hangout for lawmakers and lobbyists, La Colline also fires up a grill from which it offers chops and steaks.

400 N. Capitol St. NW, at D Street. ☎ 202-737-0400. Reservations recommended. Metro: Union Station. From Union Station Shops/Massachusetts Avenue exit, walk right on Massachusetts and then left on North Capitol for two blocks. Restaurant is on the right. Main courses: $14–$24. AE, DC, MC, V. Open: Mon–Fri 7 a.m.–10 a.m., 11:30 a.m.–3 p.m., and 6 p.m.–9 p.m. and Sat. 6 p.m.– 9 p.m.

Lauriol Plaza

$$ Adams-Morgan   SOUTHWESTERN

First the warning: This Tex-Mex restaurant is so good and so popular that you're likely to face a wait at mealtime because you can't make reservations. Once you get seated, start sipping your margarita or your Mexican beer and dig into the delicious salsa and tortilla chips, and you'll become a contented diner. The standard Tex-Mex dishes — enchiladas, tacos, burritos, fajitas — are dependable. The daily specials are often quite pleasing, too. Look for offerings from the mesquite-fired grill. During nice weather, you can sit on the sidewalk or the roof, as well as in the dining room. Servings are large, so if you have access to a fridge and a microwave, your visit to Lauriol Plaza can feed you more than once.

1835 18th St. NW between S and Swann streets. ☎ 202-387-0035. Reservations not accepted. Metro: Dupont Circle. From the Q Street exit, walk two blocks east on Q and then left on 18th for four and a half blocks. Main courses $8–$17. AE, DC, DISC, MC, V. Open: Mon–Thurs 11:30 a.m.–11 p.m.; Fri–Sat 11:30 a.m.–midnight; and Sun 11 a.m.–11 p.m.

Luna Grill & Diner

$$ **Dupont Circle** **AMERICAN**

At Luna, you can get bacon and eggs all day — and on weekends nearly around the clock. This diner offers you plenty of comfort food: meatloaf, mashed potatoes, grilled cheese, French fries, cheesesteak with fried onions and mushrooms . . . and burgers. You have alternatives to the traditional meat and potatoes, such as grilled vegetables and vegetarian pasta. Try the fried sweet potatoes or gravied mashed potatoes. Luna is a fun place, with whimsical murals on the walls and booths. The decor, the informality, and the home cooking make this restaurant a good place to take kids.

1301 Connecticut Ave. NW at N Street. ☎ *202-835-2280. Reservations not accepted. Metro: Dupont Circle. From Dupont Circle exit, walk one block south on Connecticut. Main courses: $8–$16. AE, DISC, MC, V. Open: Mon–Thurs 8 a.m.–11 p.m.; Fri–Sat 8 a.m.–6 a.m.; and Sun 8 a.m.–10 p.m.*

Malaysia Kopitiam

$$ **Dupont Circle** **MALAYSIAN**

There's a good chance you've never tasted Malaysian cooking. But, when you do, it will remind you of other Asian cuisines, notably Chinese, Thai, and Indian. Washington is blessed with a good Malaysian eatery ready to help you understand the unfamiliar. First, a photo album shows you what the dishes on the lengthy menu look like. Then owner/host Leslie Phoon is ready to answer questions and offer advice. (His wife Penny is the chef.) Try the *assam sambal* shrimp (stir-fried in a spicy/sour sauce), spicy tamarind beef (with okra, tomatoes, eggplant, and onion) or *nyonya* chicken (with cucumber and another spicy sauce). If you're not into hot stuff, don't worry: An entire menu section lists nonspicy entrees.

1827 M St. NW between 18th and 19th streets. ☎ *202-833-6232. Reservations accepted. Metro: Farragut North. From L Street exit, walk north on Connecticut Avenue and then left on M. Main courses: $7.50–$16. AE, DISC, MC, V. Open: Mon–Thur 11:30 a.m.–10 p.m.; Fri–Sat 11:30 a.m.–11 p.m.; and Sun noon–10 p.m.*

Marcel's

$$$$$ **Foggy Bottom-West End** **FRENCH/FLEMISH**

Chef/owner Robert Wiedmaier describes the fare at Marcel's (named for his son) as "French cuisine with a Flemish flair." That combination produces such recommended dishes as Dover sole with potato puree and baby spinach in a parsley and caper butter; roasted quail stuffed with wild mushrooms in a pinot noir sauce; and pepper-crusted New York steak with a ragout of onions and wild mushrooms in a Zinfandel wine sauce. Diners can hear live jazz drifting from the bar Monday through Saturday. And Marcel's offers a unique pre/post-theater deal. For $42, you can eat dinner, take a complimentary limo to Kennedy Center, and then return in the limo for dessert after the performance.

2401 Pennsylvania Ave. NW at 24th St. ☎ 202-296-1166. Reservations recommended. Metro: Foggy Bottom-George Washington University. Walk west on I Street and then right on 24th one and a half blocks to Pennsylvania. Main courses: $26–$39. AE, MC, V. Open: Mon–Thur 5:30 p.m.–10:30 p.m.; Fri–Sat 5:30 p.m.–11 p.m.; and Sun 5 p.m.–10 p.m.

Marrakesh

$$$ **Downtown MOROCCAN**

This Moroccan restaurant is just plain fun. Suspend your disbelief, and you can imagine you're out for a night with Humphrey Bogart and Sydney Greenstreet in old Casablanca. The adventure starts when you knock on the closed front door, it opens, and you're escorted through a curtain into an enormous dimly lighted dining room decorated from floor to ceiling in intricate colored patterns. After you settle into cushions around a low brass table, you wash your hands, which are your primary eating utensils for the evening. The seven-course meal is served family style, and you scoop up the food with bread or your fingers. Think eggplant, cucumber, phyllo pastry, almonds, cinnamon, olives, dates, raisons, honey, couscous, two meat courses (one perhaps a kebab), fruit, pastries, and mint tea. This restaurant is most fun with a group — I'd say about ten — but the restaurant will serve any number. Oh, and there's a belly dancer.

617 New York Ave. NW between 6th and 7th streets. ☎ 202-393-9393. Reservations required. Metro: Gallery Place/Chinatown. From 7th & H Streets exit, walk two-plus blocks north on 7th and then right on New York. Restaurant is on left, just before 6th Street. Fixed price meal: $25, alcoholic beverages extra. No credit cards accepted. Open: Daily 6 p.m.–11 p.m.

Miss Saigon

$$ **Georgetown VIETNAMESE**

Decorated with potted palms and twinkling lights, Miss Saigon does not look like your typical Vietnamese restaurant. The food is definitely Vietnamese, however, and quite good. Eating in the comfortable dining room, you can choose from such house specialties as *bo luc lac,* which is cubed steak marinated in garlic, butter, and wine and then sautéed with onions; *ga kho xa,* which is chicken marinated with lemon grass, coated in caramel sauce and a touch of chili, and served in a clay pot; or *ca kho tieu,* which is salmon in a caramel sauce with cracked black pepper, also served in a clay pot. For appetizers, try the shrimp-and-pork garden rolls. You also can choose among some very un-Vietnamese desserts.

3057 M St. NW between 30th and 31st streets. ☎ 202-333-5545. Reservations recommended. Metro: Foggy Bottom-George Washington University. From the Metrorail station, take the Georgetown shuttle bus to Wisconsin Avenue and M and then walk two blocks east on M. Or take a taxi or a 30-series Metrobus. Main courses $10–$13. AE, DC, MC, V. Open: Mon–Fri 11:30 a.m.–10:30 p.m.; Sat noon to 11 p.m.; and Sun noon to 10:30 p.m.

The Monocle

$$$$ Capitol Hill AMERICAN

A stone's throw from the Senate office buildings, the Monocle is an old-style Washington institution. Note that the first items on the menu are martinis (with names) priced from $7.50 to $9. (The cheapest, "The 007," is "Beefeaters gin, extra dry, shaken not stirred.") If you're a regular viewer of C-SPAN or CNN, you'll recognize some of the faces you see here (or at least the photos on the walls). The staff is solicitous. You can choose among several steaks, and a two-pound roasted lobster is on the menu. The pork rib chop with pommery mustard sauce is especially good. At lunch, go for the hamburger.

107 D St. NE between 1st and 2nd streets. ☎ *202-546-4488. Reservations recommended. Metro: Union Station. From Union Station Shops/Massachusetts Avenue exit, walk around the circle to 1st Street NE, turn right one block to D, and then turn left. Restaurant is on the right. Main courses $13.75–$36. AE, DC, MC, V. Open: Mon–Fri 11:30 a.m.– midnight. Closed 2 weeks preceding Labor Day.*

Nora

$$$$$ Dupont Circle AMERICAN/ORGANIC

This is PC food for people with lots of organically grown greenbacks. Everything possible on Nora's menu is produced without chemicals, hormones, or other additives. Anything that's not certified organic is marked with an asterisk. Most likely, it's wild fish or foraged mushrooms, for which no certification exists. The water is triple-filtered to remove chlorine, bacteria, and metals. The coffee is purchased from small, farmer-owned cooperatives that grow their crops beneath the forest canopy to protect native trees and wildlife. Even the staff's shirts are made from organic yarn, and Nora strives to patronize winemakers who don't use chemicals in their vineyards. Oh, and did I say the food is sophisticated and delicious and that the dining room — decorated with antique crib quilts — is attractive and comfortable?

2132 Florida Ave. NW at R Street. ☎ *202-462-5143. Reservations recommended. Metro: Dupont Circle. From Q Street exit, walk one block north on Connecticut Avenue and then left on R for two blocks to Florida. Main courses $25–$32. AE, MC, V. Open: Mon–Thur 5:30–10 p.m. and Fri–Sat 5:30–10:30 p.m. Closed two weeks at end of Aug/early Sept.*

Obelisk

$$$$$ Dupont Circle NORTHERN ITALIAN

Before Obelisk opened, you had to hop an Alitalia flight for food this authentic. Pure Italian cooking shines at this tiny Dupont Circle trattoria. The decor is simple, with a basket of fresh vegetables and crusty house-made bread forming the centerpiece. The fixed-price menu features several choices at each course. The pasta is handmade, the wines carefully selected, the ingredients fresh, and the staff knowledgeable and attentive.

The meal includes antipasto, a fish or meat course, cheese, and dessert. Selections on one evening's menu included softshell crab and porcini mushroom crostini among the antipasti; eggplant ravioli and gnocchi with pesto among the pasta choices; and pan-cooked turbot and grilled lamb among the meat dishes.

2029 P St. NW between 20th and 21st streets. ☎ 202-872-1180. Reservations recommended. Metro: Dupont Circle. From Q Street exit, walk south on 20th to P and turn right. Main courses: $55 fixed-price dinner. D, MC, V. Open: Tue–Sat 6 p.m.–10 p.m.

The Occidental

$$$$ **Downtown   AMERICAN**

The Occidental Grill quite likely fits your image of a Washington power hangout. Two blocks from the White House, it projects an old-fashioned atmosphere with its dark wood paneling, classic bar, and spacious booths. The walls are covered with more than 2,000 autographed photos of Occidental diners, from Buffalo Bill Cody through Huey Long and various Kennedys up to Oprah Winfrey and contemporary politicians. The dining rooms (above the grill is a more formal room with the same menu) were opened in 1986, but the restaurant traces its roots on essentially the same site to 1906. The filet mignon is recommended at dinner, with the lobster salad as an appetizer. You can spend a lot less for a hamburger or other sandwich at lunch.

1475 Pennsylvania Ave. NW in the Willard Hotel complex between 14th and 15th streets. ☎ 202-783-1475. Reservations recommended. Metro: Metro Center. From F & 12th Streets exit, walk two blocks east on F to 14th, turn left and walk one block to Pennsylvania, and then turn right. Restaurant is on the right. Main courses: $20–$34. AE, DC, MC, V. Open: Mon–Thurs 11:30 a.m.–10:30 p.m.; Fri–Sat 11:30 a.m.–11:30 p.m.; and Sun 11 a.m.–9:30 p.m.

The Oceanaire Seafood Room

$$$$ **Downtown   SEAFOOD**

My teenage daughter and 11 of her friends had their pre-prom dinner at Oceanaire, because it's a festive place that is an especially good restaurant for larger parties; it also serves good seafood. Many people walk into Oceanaire and feel as if they've stepped onto the set of a 1930s movie; the menu and decor evoke that earlier age. The teens, however, debated whether they were inside a ship — or under water — because of the fish mounted on the walls and the blue cast to the lighting. Whatever the meaning of the décor, oyster lovers can choose among a dozen varieties. The crab cakes are nearly all meat. The fried foods are tops. It's hard to go wrong ordering the fresh fish broiled. Portions are large — for sharing or taking home for another meal.

1201 F St. NW at 12th Street. ☎ 202-347-2277. Reservations recommended. Metro: Metro Center. From the F and 12th Streets exit, look across the street. Main courses: $18–$35. AE, DISC, MC, V. Hours: Mon–Thurs 11:30 a.m.–10 p.m.; Fri 11:30 a.m.–11 p.m.; Sat 5–11 p.m.; and Sun 5–9 p.m.

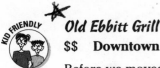

Old Ebbitt Grill
$$ Downtown   AMERICAN

Before we moved to Washington, one of my favorite places to visit was the Old Ebbitt Grill, ensconced in a 19th-century building that made you feel that Teddy Roosevelt might walk through the door. That building was demolished in 1983, and the restaurant moved into new digs just around the corner from the White House. The new Old Ebbitt is a large, handsome establishment that evokes older times with mahogany, velvet, marble, and brass, as well as collections of antique steins, hunting trophies, and decoys. It's known for burgers and other bar fare. But the diverse menu changes daily, featuring what's fresh. The highlight of my latest visit — other than spotting Newt Gingrich with his latest wife — was superb strawberry shortcake with whipped cream. The Virginia farm that produced the berries was credited on the menu. The staff tends to be friendly and nice to kids.

675 15th St. NW between F and G streets. ☎ 202-347-4800. Reservations recommended. Metro: Metro Center. Take 13th Street exit. Walk two blocks west on G., and then left at 15th. Main courses: $11–$19. AE, DC, DISC, MC, V. Open: Mon–Fri 7:30 a.m.–1 a.m.; Sat–Sun 8:30 a.m.–1 a.m.

The Palm
$$$$ Dupont Circle   STEAKHOUSE

This is the ultimate old-school Washington power place, even though it's part of a chain that originated in New York. The walls are covered with autographed caricatures of Palm patrons past and present, many of whom will be familiar to you. And you see many of the regulars seated at their favorite tables, as well as painted upon the walls. (Think Larry King, James Carville, and George Bush the First.) The Palm bills itself as "the place to see and be seen," and that certainly is true. It's also the place to eat large steaks (how about a 36-ounce New York strip for two?) and large lobsters (3 pounds or more). The strip steaks and lobsters are top-notch, by the way, and the fried onions and creamed spinach come highly recommended as well.

1225 19th St. NW, between M and N streets. ☎ 202-293-9091. Reservations recommended. Metro: Dupont Circle. From Dupont Circle exit, walk one and a half blocks south on 19th. The restaurant is on the left. Main courses: $15–$38. AE, DC, MC, V. Hours: Mon–Fri 11:45 a.m. –10:30 p.m.; Sat 5:30–10:30 p.m.; and Sun 5:30–9:30 p.m.

Pan Asian Noodles
$$ Dupont Circle   ASIAN

You could call this Asian comfort food. On a chilly day, this small, cheery restaurant's drunken noodles — with stir-fried minced chicken and spicy basil sauce — warms you faster than an extra sweater. Spring rolls, satay, and tempura whet your appetite for a main course from the two dozen noodle dishes on the menu. Or perhaps you'd like some noodle soup, based on light chicken broth or spicy beef broth. And how about fresh mango with sweet sticky rice for dessert?

2020 P St. NW between 20th and 21st streets. ☎ 202-872-8889. Reservations recommended. Metro: Dupont Circle. From the Q Street exit, walk south two blocks on 20th and then right on P. Main courses: $9–$16. AE, DC, DISC, MC, V. Open: Mon–Thur 11:30 a.m.–2:30 p.m. and 5 p.m.–10 p.m.; Fri 11:30 a.m.–2:30 p.m. and 5 p.m.–11 p.m.; Sat noon–2:30 p.m. and 5 p.m.–11 p.m.; and Sun 5 p.m.–10 p.m.

Pizzeria Paradiso
$$ **Dupont Circle/Georgetown** **PIZZA**

So crowded at meal times that you may not be able to squeeze through the door, the original Pizzeria Paradiso owes its popularity to excellent pizza prepared in the traditional Italian manner. The light, thin crust is baked in a wood-burning oven and topped with whatever you request. To taste real Neapolitan pizza, order the Margherita, which comes with tomato, basil, and mozzerella cheese. The Atomica is spicy, thanks to the hot pepper flakes combined with the tomato, salami, black olives, and mozzerella. Paradiso also serves sandwiches, salads, and desserts. But it's the pizza that sets it apart from Washington's other restaurants, with the exception of the similar 2Amys in Upper Northwest. It's bustling and it serves pizza, so it's obviously a good place to take kids. It's also a good place when you're looking for takeout. Buoyed by the success of her Dupont Circle digs, chef/owner Ruth Gresser was planning to open a new, larger pizzeria in Georgetown, at the end of 2002. Call for details on the move and new location.

2029 P St. NW between 20th and 21st streets. ☎ 202-223-1245. Reservations not accepted. Metro: Dupont Circle. From the Q Street exit, walk two blocks south on 20th and then right on P. Pizzas: $8–$16, higher with added ingredients. DC, MC, V. Open: Mon–Thurs 11:30 a.m.–11pm; Fri–Sat 11:30 a.m.–midnight; and Sun noon–10 p.m.

Also at 3282 M St. NW near Potomac Street. Metro: Foggy Bottom-George Washington University. From the Metrorail station, take the Georgetown Shuttle bus to Wisconsin Avenue and M and then walk a long block west on M. Or hop a 30-series Metrobus to Wisconsin and M. Or take a taxi.

The Prime Rib
$$$$ **Downtown** **STEAKHOUSE**

If you want to visit the first half of the last century during your D.C. vacation, you can eat at Oceanaire one night and Prime Rib the next. Here, the 1940s atmosphere comes from subdued lighting, black lacquered walls, brass trim, leather chairs and booths, tuxedoed waiters, a piano and bass playing supper club music, and the requirement that gentlemen wear jacket and tie. The food is impeccable — prime beef, of course, but also a wide selection of seafood, plus a litte lamb, pork, veal, and chicken.

This place is called the Prime Rib for a reason, so you ought to have a good reason for ordering something else. If you crave seafood, order the crab cake for your appetizer.

2020 K St. NW between 20th and 21st streets. ☎ *202-466-8811. Reservations recommended. Metro: Farragut West. From K Street exit, walk three and a half blocks west on K. Restaurant is on the left. Main courses: $18–$33. AE, DC, MC, V. Open: Mon–Thurs 11:30 a.m.–3 p.m. and 5–11 p.m.; Fri 11:30 a.m.–3 p.m. and 5–11:30 p.m.; and Sat 5–11:30 p.m.*

Red Sage Border Cafe
$$ Downtown   SOUTHWESTERN

This cafe and its sibling Red Sage Grill (see next listing) downstairs defy classification. Certainly, the name and the decor of the cafe proclaim Southwestern. Yet, as I perused the menu, I spotted Peruvian grilled lobster and "classic Caesar" salad. Most of the menu is, indeed, Southwestern or Mexican. Some colleagues and I used to come here after evening meetings in the area for beer and appetizers — a great way to share snacks and chat. (The margaritas get rave reviews, too.) For a real meal, you can select from quesadillas, burritos, chilies, salads, and various entrees. On your way out, take a peek into the strikingly decorated dining rooms of the more expensive Grill.

605 14th St. NW at F Street. ☎ *202-638-4444. Reservations not accepted. Metro: Metro Center. From F and 14th Streets exit, walk two blocks west on F. Main courses: $8.50–$13.50. AE, DISC, MC, V. Open: Mon–Thurs 11:30 a.m.–11:30 p.m.; Fri–Sat 11:30 a.m.–12:30 a.m.; and Sun 4:30 p.m.–11 p.m.*

Red Sage Grill
$$$$ Downtown   AMERICAN

When Red Sage opened, it was the hot spot to dine. The fad has passed, and now it's simply considered a good — and quite interesting — place to eat. The decor remains striking — a sort of Southwestern fantasyland that the designers at Disney World might have dreamed up. The menu, to say the least, is diverse. Forced to classify this place, I call it American — because all nationalities can hop into the American cooking pot, right? On one night alone, the nine entrees included Mediterranean paella, grilled Atlantic salmon, veal scaloppini, roasted red chili pecan-crusted chicken breast, and Maine lobster. If you want to taste what made Red Sage a fad — without emptying your wallet — eat at the Border Cafe upstairs and sneak a peek at the Grill's dining rooms.

605 14th St. NW at F Street. ☎ *202-638-4444. Reservations recommended. Metro: Metro Center. From F and 14th Streets exit, walk two blocks west on F. Main courses: $20–$38. AE, DISC, MC, V. Open: Mon–Thurs 11:30 a.m.–2 p.m. and 5–10 p.m.; Fri 11:30 a.m.–2 p.m. and 5:30–10:30 p.m.; and Sat–Sun 5:30–10:30 p.m.*

1789 Restaurant

$$$$ **Georgetown AMERICAN**

The year 1789 marked the birth of the U.S. Constitution, and of Georgetown University, so it's an appropriate name for this comfortable restaurant, which sits in the nation's capital at the edge of the university's campus. It's an especially attractive place to dine in winter if you can land a table by the fireplace. The restaurant is in a federal-style house built in the mid 1800s and is decorated with antiques and historical prints. It's best known for pretty basic dishes, such as grilled lobster, veal chop, roasted salmon, rack of lamb, beef bourguignon, and seared tuna. A long-time house specialty is pine nut crusted chicken on mashed potatoes with portobello mushrooms, prosciutto, roasted peppers, and lemon-herb sauce.

1226 36th St. NW at Prospect Street. ☎ 202-965-1789. Reservations recommended. Metro: Rosslyn. From the Metrorail station, take the Georgetown Shuttle bus to 34th and M streets, walk up 34th one block to Prospect, and then left to 36th. Or take a taxi. Main courses: $18–$36. AE, CB, DC, DISC, MC, V. Open: Mon–Thur 6 p.m.– 10 p.m.; Fri 6 p.m.–11 p.m.; Sat 5:30 p.m.–11 p.m.; and Sun 5:30 p.m.–10 p.m. June through mid-September: Mon–Friunchanged; Sat 6 p.m.–11 p.m.; and Sun 6 p.m.– 9 p.m.

Star of Siam

$$ **Downtown THAI**

You can eat in the small, softly lighted dining room or — in warm weather — at a sidewalk cafe when you visit the Star of Siam. The regular menu is large, and you also can choose from daily specials. Chef's specialties always on the menu include *pad Thai* (rice noodles with chicken, shrimp, bean sprouts, and egg in peanut sauce), *gai him ma pan* (chicken with cashew nuts, onion, and hot pepper) and *gan keo-wan* (green curry with coconut milk, bamboo shoots, egg plant, green beans, and chicken or beef).

1136 19th St. NW between L and M streets. ☎ 202-785-2839. Reservations recommended. Metro: Dupont Circle. From Dupont Circle exit, walk two and a half blocks south on 19th. Main courses: $8–$13. AE, DC, DISC, MC, V. Open: Mon–Sat 11:30 a.m.–11 p.m. and Sun 5 p.m.–10 p.m.

Tabard Inn

$$$$ **Dupont Circle AMERICAN**

This is one of my wife's favorite Washington restaurants — for the setting as much as for the food. It truly is an Inn, with sleeping, eating, and drinking facilities scattered among three adjoining townhouses near Dupont Circle. The dining rooms are comfortable and lively at meal times. You can have a drink by the fireplace in the winter and dine in the garden when it's warm. Andrew Saba worked for two of Washington's very best chefs — Jean-Louis Palladin and Robert Wiedmaier — before he took over the Tabard's kitchen in late 2001. His New American cooking features organic and regional ingredients. The seafood dishes on the changing menu tend to be the best.

1739 N St. NW between 17th and 18th streets. ☎ *202-833-2668. Reservations recommended. Metro: Dupont Circle. From the Dupont Circle exit, walk south on Connecticut Avenue one block and then turn left on N and cross 18th. The restaurant is on the left. Main courses: $19–$27. AE, DC, MC, V. Hours: Mon–Thurs 7 a.m.–10 a.m., 11:30 a.m.–2:30 p.m., 6 p.m.–10 p.m.; Fri 7 a.m.–10 a.m., 11:30 a.m.– 2:30 p.m., 6 p.m.–10:30 p.m.; Sat 8 a.m.–10 a.m., 11 a.m.–2:30 p.m., 6 p.m.–10:30 p.m.; and Sun 8 a.m.–9:30 a.m., 10:30 a.m. –2:30 p.m., 6 p.m.–9 p.m.*

Taberna Del Alabardero
$$$$ Downtown   SPANISH

This restaurant is more formal than most: Management prefers men to wear jackets and ties. You never know when you may dine across the room from royalty. Spain's King Juan Carlos and his family have eaten here while visiting Washington. Begin your meal with a glass of Spanish sherry. The lobster and seafood paella (for two) or Basque-style crabmeat are signature dishes. The stews, paellas, and tapas also are excellent. Every March, Taberna features a week of flamenco dancing by accomplished artists. Taberna del Alabardero is a Spanish restaurant chain, with only this location outside of Spain. (If you run into King Juan Carlos, do say "*hola!*")

1776 I St. NW, entrance on 18th Street. ☎ *202-429-2200. Reservations recommended. Metro: Farragut West. From 18th Street exit, walk east on I to 18th. Main courses: $19–$32. AE, DC, DISC, MC, V. Open: Mon–Fri 11:30 a.m.–2:30 p.m., 5:30 p.m.–10:30 p.m.; and Sat 5:30–11 p.m.*

Teatro Goldoni
$$$$ Downtown   ITALIAN/VENETIAN

The decor can distract your attention from the usually good food in this theatrically themed Venetian Italian restaurant. "Teatro Goldoni" means "Goldoni Theater;" Goldoni was an 18th-century Venetian playwright and gastronome. In the restaurant, you find a wall of Venetian masks, Harlequin-style panels of colored glass, pillars striped like barber poles, and a glass-enclosed kitchen raised up as if a stage. Chef/owner Fabrizio Aielli calls his food "Venetian world cuisine," which combines traditional Venetian cooking with modern twists and touches of cuisines from other parts of the world. The menu changes daily, but you may find these recommended dishes on the menu: Caesar salad with shaved parmesan cheese; Lobster risotto with roasted tomato, truffle oil, and sweet basil; fried seafood; and tiramisu.

1909 K St. NW between 19th and 20th streets. ☎ *202-955-9494. Reservations recommended. Metro: Farragut West. From 18th Street exit, walk west on I Street, turn right on 19th, and then turn left on K. Main courses: $18–$29.50. AE, DC, DISC, MC, V. Open: Mon–Thur 11:30 a.m.–2 p.m., 5:30–10 p.m.; Fri 11:30 a.m.–2 p.m., 5–11 p.m.; and Sat 5–11 p.m.*

TenPenh

$$$$ **Downtown ASIAN-PACIFIC**

Chef Jeff Tunks describes the food at TenPenh as "Asian-Pacific inspired contemporary cuisine." The restaurant's name can be described in the same fashion. "TenPenh" seems vaguely Asian (like Phnom Penh, the capital of Cambodia?), yet it's a pun on the restaurant's location at the corner of Tenth Street and Pennsylvania Avenue. Tunks and the restaurant's owners visited Bangkok, Singapore, Saigon, and Hong Kong as they planned the restaurant, which opened in mid-2000 — picking up menu ideas, decorating ideas, and artifacts for their striking decor. The best of TenPenh's appetizers include smoked salmon with wonton napoleon, as well as barbecued pork ribs. The best of the entrees include macadamia-crusted halibut, red Thai curry shrimp, and Chinese-style smoked lobster.

1001 Pennsylvania Ave. NW at 10th Street. ☎ *202-393-4500. Reservations recommended. Metro: Archives-Navy Memorial. Walk one and a half blocks west on Pennsylvania, crossing 10th. Main courses: $14–$26. AE, DISC, MC, V. Open: Mon–Thur 11:30 a.m.–2:30 p.m., 5:30 p.m.–10:30 p.m.; Fri 11:30 a.m.–2:30 p.m., 5:30 p.m.–11 p.m.; and Sat 5:30 p.m.–11 p.m.*

Tony Cheng's

$$$ **Chinatown CHINESE**

Tony Cheng couldn't decide between fish and meat, so he put Tony Cheng's Seafood Restaurant on the second floor of this Chinatown building and Tony Cheng's Mongolian Restaurant on the first. The Seafood Restaurant is a bit of a misnomer, because you can order poultry, beef, pork, and vegetarian dishes there as well. But the seafood is the specialty, and it always pays to check what's fresh, including what's swimming in the tank. Downstairs, you pick your own ingredients for two different methods of cooking. Choose meats and vegetables for the chefs to sear quickly on the grill. Or pick vegetables, meats, and seafood that you cook yourself in a pot of boiling stock at your table. You finish the meal by eating the flavorful stock.

619 H St. NW between 6th and 7th streets. ☎ *202-371-8669. Reservations accepted. Metro: Gallery Place-Chinatown. Take 7th & H Streets exit. Walk a half block east on H. Main courses: $10–$28. AE, DC, DISC, MC, V. Open: Sun–Thur 11 a.m.–11 p.m.; and Fri–Sun 11 a.m.– midnight.*

Tosca

$$$$ **Downtown NORTHERN ITALIAN**

Efficient service and good, imaginative food mark Tosca, a contemporary Northern Italian restaurant that opened in 2001. Chef Cesare Lanfranconi worked at Galileo, one of Washington's premier Italian restaurants, and the value of his apprenticeship there shows. The dining room is quiet, low-keyed, and comfortable. The appetizers, pasta, simply cooked fish, and some creative desserts are the best-bet dishes on the changing menu. Lanfranconi has created his own version of tiramisu — with cream, ice cream, and cake soaked in espresso and cappuccino. He also hosts an eight- to ten-course dinner at a chef's table in the kitchen for $85 — beverages not included, reservations required. And he offers multicourse tasting menus in the dining room.

1112 F St. NW between 11th and 12th streets. ☎ *202-367-1990. Reservations recommended. Metro: Metro Center. From F and 12th Streets exit, walk east on F across 12th. Main courses: $15–$28. AE, DC, MC, V. Hours: Mon–Thur 11:30 a.m.–2:30 p.m. and 5:30 p.m.–10:30 p.m.; Fri 11:30 a.m.–2:30 p.m. and 5:30 p.m.–11 p.m.; Sat 5:30 p.m.–11 p.m.; and Sun 5:30 p.m.–10:30 p.m. Closed Sundays in July and August.*

2 Amys
$$ Upper Northwest   ITALIAN/PIZZA

This is real Neapolitan pizza, particularly the "pizze d.o.c." offerings which follow the recipes of the Italian government's "denominazione di origine controllata" regulations. The pizzas here have thin, chewy crust. I like the d.o.c. Margherita, named after Italy's first queen and topped with tomato, cheese, and basil. The d.o.c. versions are meatless, with fewer toppings than many Americans like. You can design your own pie from a list of two dozen toppings if you prefer. Be sure to sample the side dishes, such as the *polpettini al forno* (meatballs) and *suppli a telefono* (breaded rice balls stuffed with cheese and fried). The restaurant is cheery, with shiny black-and-white tile and sunny paint on the walls. The decor makes for noise, which is one reason it's kid-friendly. Others are the food, the highchairs, and the cheerful staff.

3715 Macomb St. NW just west of Wisconsin Avenue near Washington National Cathedral. ☎ *202-885-5700. Reservations not accepted. Metro: Tenleytown and then take a 30-series Metrobus south on Wisconsin. Or take one of those buses from anywhere on Wisconsin, on M Street in eastern Georgetown, or on Pennsylvania Avenue in western Downtown. Pizzas from $8 to $13, or more if you add lots of ingredients. Sides and salads from $4 to $6.75. MC, V. Open: Tues–Sat 11 a.m.–11 p.m. and Sun 11 a.m.–10 p.m. Closed: Mon.*

Vidalia
$$$$ Downtown   SOUTHERN

Maybe it's because I like jazz clubs, but it never bothered me that Vidalia is located below street level. Others, however, seem to hesitate at the top of the stairs. So let me reassure you that at the bottom you find a cheerful restaurant with good food. Vidalia brought modern Southern cooking to Washington as Arkansan Bill Clinton was moving into the White House. And, though the menu now includes variations on Asian and French dishes, what makes Vidalia worth coming to is what proprietor Jeffrey Buben calls "American cuisine with a Southern accent." That means five-onion soup for an appetizer, shrimp and grits for the main course, and Georgia pecan pie with praline ice cream for dessert, for example.

1990 M St. NW between 19th and 20th streets. ☎ 202-659-1990. Reservations recommended. Metro: Dupont Circle. From Dupont Circle exit, walk two blocks south on 19th and then turn right on M. Main courses: $19–$29. AE, DC, DISC, MC, V. Open: Mon–Thur 11:30 a.m.–2:30 p.m. and 5:30 p.m.–10 p.m.; Fri 11:30 a.m.–2:30 p.m. and 5:30 p.m.–10:30 p.m.; Sat 5:30 p.m.–10:30 p.m.; and Sun 5–9 p.m. Closed: Sundays between July 4 and Labor Day.

Index of Restaurants by Neighborhood

Adams-Morgan
The Grill from Ipanema (Brazilian, $$)
Lauriol Plaza (Latin American, $$)

Capitol Hill
America (American, $$)
B. Smith's (Southern, $$$$)
Bistro Bis (Modern Bistro, $$$)
Capitol City Brewing Company (American, $$)
Il Radicchio (Italian/Pizza, $$)
La Colline (Classic French, $$$)
The Monocle (American, $$$$)

Chinatown
Capital Q (Barbecue, $$)
Eat First (Chinese, $)
Full Kee (Chinese, $$)
Hunan Chinatown (Chinese, $$)
Tony Cheng's (Chinese, $$)

Downtown
Austin Grill (Tex-Mex, $$)
Cafe Atlantico (Latin American, $$$)
Capitol City Brewing Company (American, $$)
The Caucus Room (Steakhouse, $$$$)
Georgia Brown's (Southern, $$$)
Georgetown Seafood Grill (Seafood, $$$)
Gerard's Place (Classic French, $$$$$)
Jaleo (Spanish, $$)
Kinkeads (Seafood, $$$$$)
Marrakesh (Moroccan, $$$)
The Occidental (American, $$$$)
The Oceanaire Seafood Room, (Seafood, $$$$)
Old Ebbitt (American/Hamburgers, $$$)

The Prime Rib (Steakhouse, $$$$)
Red Sage Border Cafe (Southwestern, $$)
Red Sage Grill (American, $$$$)
Star of Siam (Thai, $$)
Taberna Del Alabardero (Spanish, $$$$)
Teatro Goldoni (Italian/Venetian, $$$$)
TenPenh (Asian-Pacific, $$$$)
Tosca (Northern Italian, $$$$)
Vidalia (Southern, $$$$)

Dupont Circle
Al Tiramisu (Italian, $$$)
BeDuCi (Mediterranean, $$$$)
The Brickskeller (American, $)
Chipotle (Mexican, $)
City Lights of China (Chinese, $$)
Galileo (Northern Italian, $$$$$)
Luna Grill & Diner (American/ Hamburgers, $$)
Malaysia Kopitiam (Malayasian, $$)
Nora (American/Organic, $$$$$)
Obelisk (Northern Italian, $$$$$)
The Palm (Steakhouse, $$$$)
Pan Asian Noodles (Asian, $$)
Pizzeria Paradiso (Pizza, $$)
Tabard Inn (American, $$$$)

Foggy Bottom/West End
Asia Nora (Asian/Organic, $$$$)
Marcel's (French/Flemish, $$$$$)

Georgetown
Amma Indian Vegetarian Kitchen (Indian/Vegetarian, $)
Bistrot Lepic (Classic French, $$$)
Booeymonger (American, $)
Café La Ruche (Classic French, $$)

Citronelle (French/California Cuisine,
$$$$$)
Clyde's (American, $$$)
Harbour Club (American, $$$$)
Miss Saigon (Vietnamese, $$)
Pizzeria Paradiso (Pizza, $$)
1789 Restaurant (American, $$$$)

Upper Northwest
Booeymonger (American, $)
Chipotle (Mexican, $)
Clyde's (American, $$$)
Austin Grill (Southwestern, $$)
2 Amys (Italian/Pizza, $$)

Index of Restaurants by Cuisine

American
America (Capitol Hill, $$)
Booeymonger (Georgetown/Upper
Northwest, $)
The Brickskeller (Dupont Circle, $)
Capitol City Brewing Company (Capitol
Hill/Downtown, $$)
Clyde's (Georgetown & Upper
Northwest, $$$)
Harbour Club (Georgetown, $$$$)
Luna Grill & Diner (Dupont Circle, $$)
The Monocle (Capitol Hill, $$$$)
Nora (Dupont Circle, $$$$$)
The Occidental (Downtown, $$$$)
Old Ebbitt Grill, (Downtown, $$)
Red Sage Grill (Downtown, $$$$)
1789 Restaurant (Georgetown, $$$$)
Tabard Inn (Dupont Circle, $$$$)

Asian
Asia Nora (Foggy Bottom/West End,
$$$$)
Pan Asian Noodles (Dupont Circle, $$)
TenPenh (Downtown, $$$$)

Brazilian
The Grill From Ipanema
(Adams-Morgan, $$)

Chinese
City Lights of China (Dupont Circle, $$)
Full Kee (Chinatown, $$)
Hunan Chinatown (Chinatown, $$)
Tony Cheng's (Chinatown, $$)
Eat First (Chinatown, $$)

French
Bistro Bis (Capitol Hill, $$$)
Bistrot Lepic (Georgetown, $$$)
Café La Ruche (Georgetown, $$)
Citronelle (Georgetown, $$$$$)
La Colline (Capitol Hill, $$$)
Gerard's Place (Downtown, $$$$$)
Marcel's (Foggy Bottom/West End,
$$$$$)

Hamburgers
The Brickskeller (Dupont Circle, $)
Capitol City Brewing Company (Capitol
Hill/Downtown, $$)
Clyde's (Georgetown & Upper
Northwest, $$$)
Luna Grill & Diner (Downtown, $$)
Old Ebbitt Grill (Downtown, $$)

Indian
Amma Indian Vegetarian Kitchen,
(Georgetown, $)

Italian
Al Tiramisu (Dupont Circle, $$$)
Galileo (Dupont Circle, $$$$$)
Il Radicchio (Capitol Hill, $$)
Obelisk (Dupont Circle, $$$$$)
Teatro Goldoni (Downtown, $$$$)
Tosca (Downtown, $$$$)

Latin American
Café Atlantico (Downtown, $$$)
Lauriol Plaza (Adams-Morgan, $$$)

Malayasian
Malaysia Kopitiam (Dupont Circle, $$)

Mediterranean
BeDuCi (Dupont Circle, $$$$)

Mexican
Chipotle (Dupont Circle/Upper
    Northwest, $)

Moroccan
Marrakesh (Downtown, $$$)

Organic
Asia Nora (Foggy Bottom/West End,
    $$$$)
Nora (Dupont Circle, $$$$$)

Pizza
Pizzeria Paradiso (Dupont
    Circle/Georgetown, $$)
2 Amys (Northwest, $$)

Seafood
Kinkeads (Downtown, $$$$$)
Georgetown Seafood Grill (Downtown,
    $$$)
The Oceanaire Seafood Room
    (Downtown, $$$$)
Tony Cheng's (Chinatown, $$)

Southern
B. Smith's (Capitol Hill, $$$$)

Georgia Brown's (Downtown, $$$)
Vidalia (Downtown, $$$$)

Southwestern
Austin Grill (Downtown & Upper
    Northwest, $$)
Lauriol Plaza (Adams-Morgan, $$)
Red Sage Border Cafe (Downtown, $$)

Spanish
Taberna Del Alabardero (Downtown,
    $$$$)
Jaleo (Downtown, $$)

Steakhouse
The Caucus Room (Downtown, $$$$)
The Palm (Dupont Circle, $$$$)
The Prime Rib (Downtown, $$$$)

Texas Barbecue
Capital Q (Chinatown, $$)

Thai
Star of Siam (Downtown, $$)

Vegetarian
Amma Indian Vegetarian Kitchen
    (Georgetown, $)

Vietnamese
Miss Saigon (Georgetown, $$)

Index of Restaurants by Price

$
Amma Indian Vegetarian Kitchen
    (Georgetown,
Indian/Vegetarian)
Booeymonger (Georgetown/Upper
    Northwest, American)
The Brickskeller (Dupont Circle,
    American)
Chipotle (Dupont Circle/Upper
    Northwest, Mexican)
Eat First (Chinatown, Chinese)

$$
America (Capitol Hill, American)
Austin Grill (Downtown & Glover Park,
    Tex/Mex)
Cafe La Ruche (Georgetown, Classic
    French)
Capitol City Brewing Company (Capitol
    Hill/Downtown, American)
City Lights of China (Dupont Circle,
    Chinese)

Clyde's (Georgetown, Upper
   Northwest, American)
Full Kee (Chinatown, Chinese)
The Grill From Ipanema, (Adams-
   Morgan, Brazilian)
Hunan Chinatown (Downtown,
   Chinese)
Il Radicchio (Capitol Hill, Italian/Pizza)
Jaleo (Downtown, Spanish)
Lauriol Plaza (Adams-Morgan, Latin
   American)
Luna Grill & Diner (Dupont Circle,
   American/Hamburgers)
Malaysia Kopitiam (Dupont Circle,
   Malayasian)
Old Ebbitt Grill (Downtown, American/
   Hamburgers)
Pan Asian Noodles (Dupont Circle,
   Asian)
Pizzeria Paradiso (Dupont
   Circle/Georgetown, Pizza)
Red Sage Border Cafe (Downtown,
   Southwestern)
Star of Siam (Downtown, Thai)
Tony Cheng's (Downtown, Chinese)
2 Amys (Northwest, Italian/Pizza)
Miss Saigon (Georgetown, Vietnamese)
Amma Indian Vegetarian Kitchen
   (Georgetown,
Vegetarian/Indian)
Capital Q (Chinatown, Barbecue)
Eat First (Chinatown, Chinese)

$$$

Al Tiramisu (Dupont Circle, Italian)
Bistro Bis (Capitol Hill, Modern Bistro)
Bistrot Lepic (Georgetown, Classic
   French)
Cafe Atlantico (Downtown, Latin
   American)
Clyde's (Georgetown & Upper
   Northwest, American)
Georgetown Seafood Grill (Downtown,
   Seafood)
Georgia Brown's (Downtown,
   Southern)
La Colline (Capitol Hill, Classic French)

Marrakesh (Downtown, Moroccan)
Old Ebbitt (Downtown, American,
   Hamburgers)

$$$$

Asia Nora (Foggy Bottom/West End,
   Asian/Organic)
B. Smith's (Capitol Hill, Southern)
BeDuCi (Dupont Circle,
   Mediterranean)
The Caucus Room (Downtown,
   Steakhouse)
Harbour Club (Georgetown, American)
The Monocle (Capitol Hill, American)
Nora (Dupont Circle, American)
The Occidental (Downtown, American)
The Oceanaire Seafood Room
   (Downtown, Seafood)
The Palm (Dupont Circle, Steakhouse)
The Prime Rib (Downtown, Steakhouse)
Red Sage Grill (Downtown, American)
1789 Restaurant (Georgetown,
   American)
Tabard Inn (Dupont Circle, American)
Taberna Del Alabardero (Downtown,
   Spanish)
Teatro Goldoni (Downtown, Italian/
   Venetian)
TenPenh (Downtown, Asian-Pacific
Tosca (Downtown, Northern Italian)
Vidalia (Downtown, Southern)

$$$$$

Citronelle (Georgetown, French/
   California Cuisine)
Galileo (Dupont Circle, Northern
   Italian)
Gerard's Place (Downtown, Classic
   French)
Kinkeads (Downtown, Seafood)
Marcel's (Foggy Bottom/West End,
   French/Flemish)
Nora (Dupont Circle, American/
   Organic)
Obelisk (Dupont Circle, Northern
   Italian)

Chapter 15

On the Lighter Side: Top Picks for Snacks and Meals on the Go

● ●

In This Chapter

▶ Chugging coffee and taking tea

▶ Stocking up for a picnic

▶ Searching out sweets

▶ Dining al fresco on the Mall

▶ Drinking with a view

● ●

*W*ashington is full of workaholics who eat at their desks and tourists who eat on the run, so the city is full of places where you can grab snacks and light meals. Because Washington has so many parks — from huge expanses like the National Mall to small green areas suitable for al fresco dining scattered all around town — getting picnic food to go is a great idea.

(Coffee) Break Time

Besides a zillion branches of a certain West Coast coffee empire, Washingtonians have many sources for their caffeine fixes.

A few blocks from the White House, **M E Swing Co., Inc.,** 1702 G St. NW (☎ **202-628-7601**), has been selling coffee and tea in the District since 1916. The coffee is roasted and ground locally. The espresso bar seats 15 for coffee and pastry. M E Swing is open Monday through Friday, 7 a.m. to 6 p.m., and Saturday from 9 a.m. to 5 p.m.

Bookish coffee swillers gather at **Afterwords Café** (inside Kramerbooks), 1517 Connecticut Ave. NW, near the Dupont Circle Metro station (☎ **202-387-1462**). The help leaves you alone to read your political analysis or

Where to Grab a Snack in Washington, D.C.

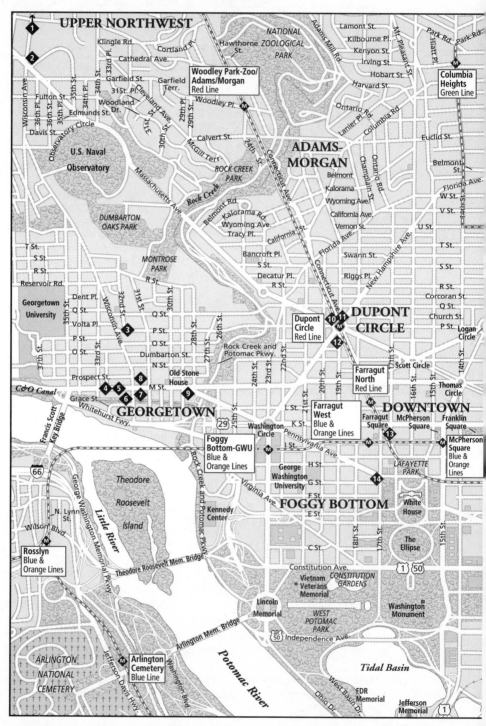

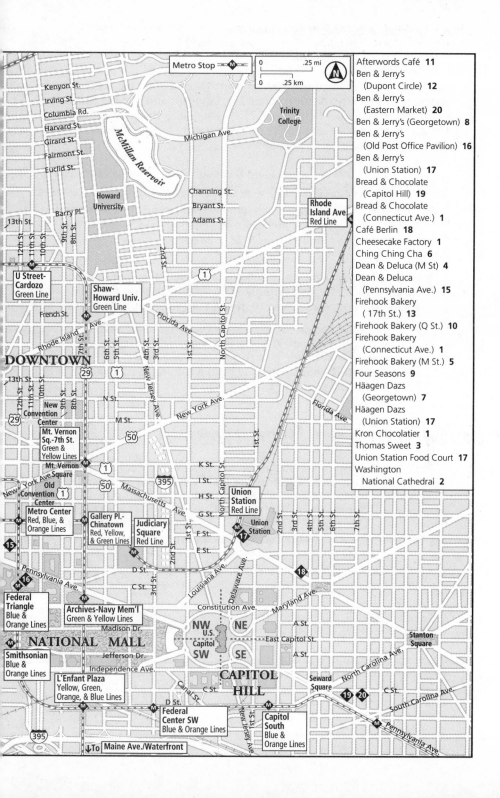

Afterwords Café **11**
Ben & Jerry's
  (Dupont Circle) **12**
Ben & Jerry's
  (Eastern Market) **20**
Ben & Jerry's (Georgetown) **8**
Ben & Jerry's
  (Old Post Office Pavilion) **16**
Ben & Jerry's
  (Union Station) **17**
Bread & Chocolate
  (Capitol Hill) **19**
Bread & Chocolate
  (Connecticut Ave.) **1**
Café Berlin **18**
Cheesecake Factory **1**
Ching Ching Cha **6**
Dean & Deluca (M St) **4**
Dean & Deluca
  (Pennsylvania Ave.) **15**
Firehook Bakery
  (17th St.) **13**
Firehook Bakery (Q St.) **10**
Firehook Bakery
  (Connecticut Ave.) **1**
Firehook Bakery (M St.) **5**
Four Seasons **9**
Häagen Dazs
  (Georgetown) **7**
Häagen Dazs
  (Union Station) **17**
Kron Chocolatier **1**
Thomas Sweet **3**
Union Station Food Court **17**
Washington
  National Cathedral **2**

your trashy novel as you nurse a cup of coffee. Hours are Monday through Thursday from 7:30 a.m. to 1 a.m., and 'round the clock from 7:30 a.m. Friday to 1 a.m. Monday.

The local chain of **Firehook Bakeries** provides a great fix of fresh-made pastries and locally roasted coffee. My daughter and her friends hang out at one that's near her school. Firehook makes the pastries and sells Quartermaine's coffee, which is roasted nearby in suburban Maryland. The restaurant locations are as follows:

- ✔ 912 17th St. NW between I and K streets (open Monday through Friday from 7 a.m. to 7 p.m.); ☎ 202-429-2253.

- ✔ 1909 Q St. NW between Connecticut Avenue and 20th Street (open Monday through Friday from 7 a.m. to 9 p.m. and Saturday and Sunday from 8 a.m. to 9 p.m.); ☎ 202-588-9296.

- ✔ 3411 Connecticut Ave. NW between Newark and Ordway streets (open Monday from 7 a.m. to8 p.m., Tuesday through Thursday from 7 a.m. to 10 p.m., Friday from 7 a.m. to 11 p.m., Saturday from 8 a.m. to 11 p.m., and Sunday from 8 a.m. to 9 p.m.); ☎ 202-625-6247.

- ✔ 3241 M St. NW between Wisconsin Avenue and Potomac Street (open Monday through Thursday from 7 a.m. to 9 p.m., Friday from 7 a.m. to 11 p.m., Saturday from 8 a.m. to 11 p.m., and Sunday from 8 a.m. to 8 p.m.).

Capitalizing on Breakfast

To check out the power breakfast scene, head for a hotel dining room near the White House or Capitol. The **Hay-Adams,** 800 16th St. NW at H Street (☎ **202-638-6600**), and the **Willard Inter-Continental,** 1401 Pennsylvania Ave. NW between 14th and 15th streets (☎ **202-628-9100**), are good places to start. So is the **Old Ebbitt Grill,** 675 15th St. NW between F and G streets (☎ **202-347-4800**).

At **La Colline,** 400 N. Capitol St. NW at D Street. (☎ **202-737-0400**), just down the street from the Capitol, lobbyists meet lawmakers over glasses of OJ. At Kramerbooks & Afterwords Café, 1517 Connecticut Ave. NW, across from the Dupont Circle Metrorail Station Q Street exit (☎ **202-387-1462**), you can crack a book with your soft-boiled egg.

If you want to jump-start *your* engine, not the economy's, try the **Luna Grill and Diner,** 1301 Connecticut Ave. NW at N Street (☎ **202-835-2280**). Another place for a fast, cheap — and good — breakfast is a **Booeymonger.** You can find one in Georgetown, 3265 Prospect St. NW at Potomac Street (☎ **202-333-4810**) and one in Upper Northwest, 5252 Wisconsin Ave. NW at Jennifer Street (☎ **202-686-5805**).

Tea for Two (or One)

The Americans may have beaten the English in the American Revolution, but if the war had been a battle of tea parties, the Brits would have massacred the Yanks. Nevertheless, the United States has come a long way since the Boston Tea Party. Instead of throwing it into the harbor, Americans drink it. In Washington, several hotels are doing their part to perpetuate the upper-crust British tradition of high tea. In this context, *high tea* is a light meal with small, trimmed sandwiches (no crusts!), little cakes, and — of course — pots of fresh-brewed tea.

If you take high tea, you can pass on a big meal at dinnertime and opt for a snack later in the evening.

Get fancy and refined at the **Four Seasons,** 2800 Pennsylvania Ave. NW at 28th Street (☎ **202-342-0444**). Soak up the view of Rock Creek Park from the Garden Terrace and nibble on finger sandwiches, breads, tartlets, scones with double Devonshire cream, fresh-brewed tea, and a nip of sherry (for medicinal purposes only). Teatime is Monday through Friday from 3 to 5 p.m., Saturday from 2 to 5 p.m., and Sunday from 4 to 5 p.m. (Beginning at 4 p.m. Tuesday through Sunday, a pianist performs.) You pay $18.50 per adult and $9 for preteens. Reservations are required.

You can learn Chinese tea ritual at **Ching Ching Cha,** 1063 Wisconsin Ave. NW, near Canal Street in Georgetown (☎ **202-333-8288**). The setting is serene and enhanced by classical Chinese music. The parlor lists more than two dozen teas from China and Taiwan, plus meals, snacks, and desserts. You also can purchase loose tea to take home. The restaurant is open Tuesday through Saturday from 11:30 a.m. to 9 p.m. and Sunday from 11:30 a.m. to 7 p.m.

You can tour and take tea at the **Washington National Cathedral,** Massachusetts and Wisconsin avenues NW (☎ **202-537-8993**), on Tuesdays and Wednesdays. The tour starts at 1:30 p.m. inside the West Entrance on Wisconsin and finishes high up in the Pilgrim Observation Gallery, where you can gaze through arched windows at the city and beyond. Tea is served there at 3 p.m. Cost is $18 per person. Reservations are required — often far in advance — and are accepted up to six months ahead of time.

Picking up Picnic Supplies

Visitors intent on cramming in a lot of sights often prefer quick bites to spending an hour or two in a restaurant. Most delis and coffee shops — as well as many full-service restaurants — gladly pack your order to go.

Don't think of this to-go service as just fast food, however. Think of it as a picnic. You can find park benches all over the place, as well as many small park areas. I particularly like Lafayette Square, across Pennsylvania Avenue from the White House, and you can find lots of room on the Mall and around the Tidal Basin. (I'll pray for the pigeons and squirrels to leave you alone. You can do your part by not feeding them.)

Dean & Deluca is a great place to put together a picnic. There's a downtown cafe, 1299 Pennsylvania Ave. NW at 13th Street (☎ 202-628-8155), open Monday through Friday from 7:30 a.m. to 4:30 p.m. Take your food to Lafayette Square or to Pershing Park (Pennsylvania Avenue and 15th Street) or hike on to the Mall. The Georgetown shop, 3276 M St. NW at 33rd Street (☎ 202-342-2500), is much larger and has a wide selection of sandwiches, salads, and desserts, as well as gourmet groceries. You can picnic in Dean & Deluca's outdoor cafe, take your food south of M to the C&O Canal National Park, or go further south to the Georgetown waterfront.

You can find good, basic sandwich shops throughout the city — several per block in many places. Among those that I can vouch for, should you pass them in your wanderings, are Au Bon Pain, Booeymonger, Bread & Chocolate, Chipotle, Corner Bakery, Firehook Bakery, La Madeleine, Vie de France, and the Wall Street Deli — all with multiple locations.

Satisfying Your Sweet Tooth

Sweet tooth crave a fix? Head for **Bread & Chocolate** on Capitol Hill, 666 Pennsylvania Ave. SE between 6th and 7th streets (☎ 202-547-2875) or in Upper Northwest, 5542 Connecticut Ave. NW at Morrison Street (☎ 202-966-7412).

Also on the Hill, sample the strudels, tortes, and pies at **Cafe Berlin,** 322 Massachusetts Ave. NE (☎ 202-543-7656).

Back in Upper Northwest, buy a Cheesecake at the **Cheesecake Factory,** 5335 Wisconsin Ave. NW between Jenifer Street and Western Avenue (☎ 202-364-4623). Feast on 35 varieties of calorie-laden, artery-clogging desserts. (You may find a slice too rich to consume in one sitting. I can't imagine why.) **Kron Chocolatier** (☎ 202-966-4946) is across the street in the Mazza Gallerie. This shop sells all manner of world-class chocolate. Try the chocolate-dipped strawberries.

I Scream, You Scream

Thank heaven the ice-cream craze drips on. If there's a quicker way to get refreshed and rejoin the human race when the heat beats down and spirits lag, I don't know it. It seems like you can't walk a block in D.C.'s tourist areas without passing a pushcart or store selling ice cream, frozen yogurt, or some other cold concoction. Nearly every restaurant (including those in museums and galleries), deli, and take-out sells the stuff.

You can find branches of the Vermont-based **Ben & Jerry's** in Georgetown, 3135 M St. NW at Wisconsin Avenue, ☎ **202-965-2222;** Dupont Circle, 1333 19th St. NW, south of the circle, ☎ **202-785-4882;** Downtown, in the Old Post Office Pavilion at Pennsylvania Avenue and 12th Street NW, ☎ **202-842-5882;** and on Capitol Hill in Union Station, ☎ **202-842-2887,** and at the Eastern Market, 327 7th St. SE, between Pennsylvania Avenue and C Street, ☎ **202-546-2253.**

Häagen-Dazs competes with B&J in the train station, ☎ **202-789-0953,** and at 3120 M St., ☎ **202-333-3443.**

For local ice cream, visit **Thomas Sweet** (☎ **202-337-0616**), also in Georgetown, 3214 P St. NW at Wisconsin Avenue.

Finding a Food Court Extraordinaire

The lower level of Union Station houses the largest and most diverse **food court** I've ever seen. Sure, you can buy hamburgers and pizzas, and if that's what the kids desire, that's fine. Those with more cosmopolitan tastes will want to take a stroll around the entire court before making their selections.

 You can find the usual national chains, but also branches of local restaurants and a wide range of cuisines — French, Indian, Greek, Cajun, barbecue, seafood, pasta, sushi, deli items, baked goods, and gourmet coffee among the vast selection of edibles. If that doesn't satisfy you, you can take the escalator up to the next level, where other food establishments — from fast-food stands to restaurants reviewed in Chapter 14 — are scattered among the train gates and boutiques.

Enjoying Meals on the Mall

 You'll be spending lots of time in the museums along the National Mall — and trudging from one to the other. You can ease your hunger and quench your thirst in many of them. Some 3 million people eat in the Smithsonian Institution's cafeterias and restaurants each year, and others grab a bite at the National Gallery of Art.

Prices in the Smithsonian cafeterias range from $3 to $8 for sandwiches, burgers, and pizza and from $2.75 to $7.95 for salads and entrees. They all will be happy to add to your AE, DISC, JCB, MC, or V bills.

Here are your options:

- **Arts & Industries Building:** Seattle's Best Coffee kiosk serves coffee, pastries, salads, sandwiches, fruit, juice, and yogurt-granola parfaits.

- **National Museum of American History:** The Cafe and Ice Cream Parlor offers a full lunch menu along with the ice cream. The Palm Court Coffee Bar is self-service, with sandwiches, salads, coffee, and pastries. The Main Street Cafes offer continental breakfast from 10 to 11 a.m. and seafood, burgers, hot dogs, pizza, sand-wiches, and salads the rest of the day.

- **National Museum of Natural History:** At the Fossil Cafe, you can eat sandwiches, salads, desserts, and beverages at tables that themselves are natural history exhibits. The Atrium Café serves continental breakfast burgers, pizza, pasta, rotisserie chicken, soups, salads, and sandwiches.

- **National Air and Space Museum:** The Wright Place, renovated in 2001 and 2002, sells Donato's pizza, Boston Market's rotisserie chicken, and the usual McDonald's stuff. The Mezzanine Café has pastries, salads, and sandwiches. Spring through early fall, food carts on the terrace sell ice cream, soda, snacks, and hot dogs. An outdoor cafe serves panini, coffee, and pastries.

- **The Castle:** The Commons, a 19th-century dining room, serves a lunch buffet Monday through Saturday from 11 a.m. to 2 p.m. The Sunday champagne brunch (10:30 a.m. to 2:30 p.m., with harpist) sets you back $29.95 for adults and $10.95 for preteens. Call 202-357-2957 for reservations.

- **National Gallery of Art:** The Cascade Café, in the concourse between the East and West buildings, with a view of the cascade waterfall, offers a wide range of foods from soups, salads, sand-wiches, and pizzas to full meals and dessert. It's open Monday through Saturday from 10 a.m. to 3 p.m. and Sunday from 11 a.m. to 4 p.m. The Garden Cafe, on the West Building's ground floor, serves traditional lunch fare and is open Monday through Saturday from 11:30 a.m. to 3 p.m. and Sunday from noon to 6 p.m. Terrace Café, on the East Building's upper level, sells light Middle Eastern food at a walk-up station. It's open Monday through Saturday from 11 a.m. to 4 p.m. and Sunday from noon to 5 p.m. The Pavilion Cafe at the Sculpture Garden offers pizzas, sand-wiches, salads, and desserts. It's open Memorial Day through Labor Day Monday through Thursday and Saturday from 10 a.m. to 6 p.m., Friday from 10 a.m. to 8 p.m. (live jazz from 5 p.m.), and Sunday from 11 a.m. to 6 p.m. Its hours the rest of the year are Monday through Saturday from 10 a.m. to 9 p.m. and Sunday from 11 a.m. to 7 p.m.

Drinking in the View

Enjoy a cocktail while drinking in a primo view at the **Sky Terrace** of the Hotel Washington, 151 15th St. NW at Pennsylvania Avenue (☎ **202-638-5900**). Between May and October, this spot is a favorite for catching a sundowner. Keep it simple and stick to a cheese platter or a sandwich if you eat here. While you ogle the landscape, see how many buildings you can identify. You can almost peer into the East Wing of the White House.

For a soothing experience, sip your poison of choice with an appetizer or some light fare by the Potomac River at Georgetown's **Washington Harbour** complex, 3000 K St. at Thomas Jefferson Street. Stop by **Tony and Joe's** (☎ **202-944-4545**) terrace tables and nibble on some appetizers. Or sit at their outdoor bar and watch the people strolling along the riverwalk, the boats sailing on the river, and the planes flying into and out of National Airport.

Part V

Exploring Washington, D.C.

The 5th Wave   By Rich Tennant

Consider yourself lucky. Not everyone gets to meet the national bird when they come to Washington, D.C.

In this part . . .

Now comes the fun part. You didn't decide to visit Washington so that you could sleep and eat, though you need to do both and the eating part can be enjoyable and fulfilling (*heh, heh*). You picked D.C. because you want to see the monuments and the memorials, partake of the culture, and visit major government buildings to observe your tax dollars at work (or not).

This part takes you on a paper tour of Washington's top attractions and shows you which guided tours are worth your while. I also suggest some itineraries that can make your sightseeing easier. If you feel no trip is complete unless you max out your credit card, I clue you in on the most interesting shopping venues. And, in case you'd like a change of scenery, I throw in some day-trip suggestions, too.

Chapter 16

Washington's Top Sights

● ●

In This Chapter

▶ Finding out what you need to know about visiting the top sights

▶ Listing the city's top attractions by location and type

● ●

You came to Washington to see the sights, and this chapter gives you the scoop on Washington's premier attractions (memorials, galleries, topless bars — just wanted to see if you were paying attention — and so on), in alphabetical order. I also list them by location and type to help you figure out the most efficient and logical itinerary.

The reviews give you the lowdown on what you find at each place, as well as the specifics on hours, admission fees (if any), and any specific tips or heads-up you need for an attraction.

The indexes can help you plan your sightseeing trips so that you get the most out of the time you spend in D.C. For example, if you leave the Museum of Natural History, scratch your head, and wonder what other attractions are close by, you can check out the Mall listing and the map to find out what's within a stone's throw — well, almost. When you do, you find that the Museum of American History is the next building to the west and the National Gallery of Art complex is next door in the other direction (toward the Capitol).

The Top Attractions from A to Z

Arlington National Cemetery
Virginia

There's something overwhelming about the tens of thousands of simple grave markers that march in perfect formation across Arlington's hills and valleys. In their presence, it's impossible not to be moved by the enormity of the sacrifice of the military men and women who fought to preserve America's freedom and to enforce its sometimes-controversial foreign policies. More than 260,000 war dead and veterans (and their dependents) are buried here.

The Top Attractions in Washington, D.C.

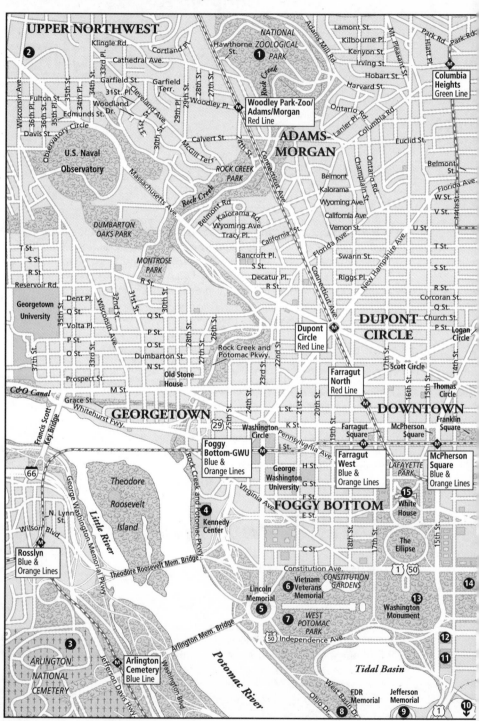

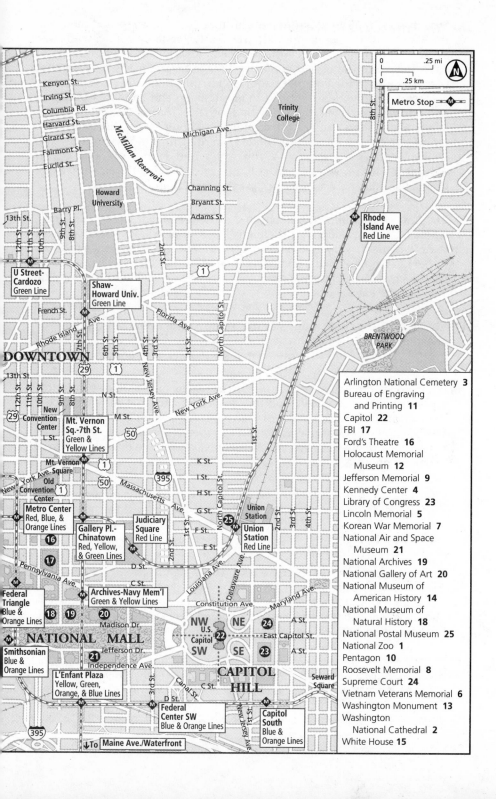

Metro Stop M

Arlington National Cemetery **3**
Bureau of Engraving
and Printing **11**
Capitol **22**
FBI **17**
Ford's Theatre **16**
Holocaust Memorial
Museum **12**
Jefferson Memorial **9**
Kennedy Center **4**
Library of Congress **23**
Lincoln Memorial **5**
Korean War Memorial **7**
National Air and Space
Museum **21**
National Archives **19**
National Gallery of Art **20**
National Museum of
American History **14**
National Museum of
Natural History **18**
National Postal Museum **25**
National Zoo **1**
Pentagon **10**
Roosevelt Memorial **8**
Supreme Court **24**
Vietnam Veterans Memorial **6**
Washington Monument **13**
Washington
National Cathedral **2**
White House **15**

Stop first at the **Visitor Center,** look around, pick up a map, and then take the short walk to the memorial to the nearly 2 million women who have served in the military since the American Revolution; it was opened in 1997. Return to the visitor center and buy a ticket for the **Tourmobile.** (See Chapter 18 for complete Tourmobile information). The sprawling cemetery is hilly. Unless you're in great shape and have lots of time, I don't advise covering it entirely on foot. The Tourmobile stops at the major sights. You can get off, explore it as long as you like, and then reboard to continue your tour. Before boarding for the first time, use the visitor center's restrooms — you won't find more until you get to **Arlington House,** where Robert E. Lee once lived with his wife, Mary Custis Lee, Martha Washington's great-granddaughter.

✓ The first Tourmobile stop is at the grave of President John F. Kennedy, where his widow, Jacqueline Kennedy Onassis, also is buried, along with their two infants who died before the president. The president's brother, Robert F. Kennedy, who was assassinated during his own presidential campaign in 1968, is buried nearby. These gravesites have commanding views of the capital city.

✓ The next Tourmobile stop is at the Tomb of the Unknowns, where the guard is changed every hour on the hour from October to March and every half-hour April to September. It's a somber ceremony.

✹ When you get to Arlington House, also known as the Custis-Lee Mansion, you can take a free self-guided tour from 9:30 a.m. to 4:30 p.m., except Dec. 25 and Jan. 1. The grave of Pierre L'Enfant, who drew up the plans for the capital at George Washington's request, is nearby. He was moved here from a pauper's grave and now enjoys a breathtaking panorama of his masterwork.

After you return to the visitor center, you can take a ten-minute walk to the Marine Corps Memorial, yet another moving scene that portrays the immortal photograph of Marines raising the U.S. flag on Iwo Jima during World War II.

Expect to spend two to three hours at these sights.

✓ Remember that Arlington is a cemetery, so please conduct yourself — and make sure that your children conduct themselves — accordingly. Burials quite likely will be taking place while you visit. An average of 15 burials occur each day.

Arlington, Virginia, across the Memorial Bridge from the Lincoln Memorial. ☎ *703-607-8052. Internet:* www.arlingtoncemetery.org. *Metro: Arlington National Cemetery. Tourmobile stops here. Open: Daily Apr–Sept 8 a.m.–7 p.m.; Oct–Mar 8 a.m.–5 p.m. Admission: Free. Tourmobile tour: Adults $5.25, children 3–11 $2.50.*

Bureau of Engraving and Printing
Tidal Basin

The buck may stop in the White House, but it starts here, where printers and engravers make money, postage stamps, Treasury bonds, and White House invitations. No free samples! But you can purchase a souvenir (such as uncut or shredded currency) in the visitor center, where you can play with interactive displays.

You must get free, timed tickets on the day you tour, and people line up early. One person — with photo ID — can get up to five tickets. The ticket kiosk is on Raoul Wallenberg Place on the 15th Street side of the building. The kiosk opens at 8 a.m. Monday through Friday, except federal holidays, and tickets usually are gone by 9:30 a.m. Evening tours are offered May through August, and the kiosk opens at 3:30 p.m. to distribute those tickets, which also disappear quickly. You can skip the tour and enter the visitor center through the tour entrance on the 14th Street side.

✔ You need a photo ID to get in, and you won't be admitted if you're carrying a backpack, book bag, or anything that may be construed as a weapon. No coat- or package-checking facilities are available.

Figure on spending an hour here (not including the wait to get in).

✔ Security has been tightened substantially at government facilities since the terrorist attacks of Sept. 11, 2001. Please pay attention to requirements for things like photo IDs and restrictions on what you're allowed to carry with you. Also understand that all these procedures are highly subject to change. Call ahead and inquire before you visit or check the Web sites.

Your U.S. representative and senators can help you with tickets to government buildings, such as the Bureau of Engraving and Printing. Phone them way ahead of time, tell them what you want to do, and ask them what they can do for you.

14th and C streets SW. ☎ *866-874-2330 (toll-free) or 202-874-2330. Internet:* www. moneyfactory.gov. *Metro: Smithsonian. From the Independence Avenue exit, walk west on Independence one long block and then left on 14th (to the tour entrance) or two blocks and then left on Raoul Wallenberg Place (for the ticket kiosk). Tours: May–Aug Mon–Fri, except federal holidays, 9 a.m.–1:45 p.m. and 5–6:45 p.m.; Sept–April Mon–Fri, except federal holidays, 9 a.m.–2 p.m. Visitor center: May–Aug 8:30 a.m.–8 p.m., no admission after 6:50 p.m.; Sept–April 9 a.m.–3:30 p.m. Admission: Free.*

U.S. Capitol
Capitol Hill

The Capitol belongs on every visitor's must-see list. It houses the U.S. Congress and symbolizes American democracy. The inspiring architecture, the historic art, and the ornate decoration are other aspects that make the Capitol a necessary stop.

You'll find that the Capitol dominates the Washington landscape. The 180-foot-high dome is topped by a statue titled *Freedom*. Inside, the Rotunda serves as the heart of the Capitol. Above the Rotunda, in the canopy of the dome, you see Constantino Brumidi's fresco, *The Apotheosis of Washington*, which portrays the first president as a godlike character flanked by such allegorical figures as Liberty, War, Victory, and Fame. Statues of prominent Americans — and some not so prominent — fill Statuary Hall and stand throughout the building. Most important, of course, the building contains the House and Senate chambers — which you see on C-SPAN's coverage of congressional floor debates — and the offices of top congressional leaders and some of the most powerful committees.

You can obtain free tickets for guided tours at the Capitol Guide Service Kiosk, just east of the intersection of First Street SW and Maryland Avenue, beginning at 8:15 a.m. Monday through Saturday. Lines can get quite long in spring and summer. Expect to spend one to two hours here, not counting the time you wait to get in.

Your U.S. representative and senators can arrange for you to join a special Capitol Guide Service tour that's conducted before the public tours. Many members of Congress — and their aides — are happy to lead constituents on tours themselves. Call your state's representative or senators far ahead of your visit and ask what they might do for you.

If the House or Senate is in session, you can watch the proceedings from a visitors gallery. Call your representative or a senator for tickets.

If you do take a seat in a visitors gallery, don't be surprised if nothing exciting is going on. While the chambers fill for roll-call votes and during extremely important debates, usually only a handful of members is on the floor. You can witness the surreal scene of a grandiloquent senator propounding profoundly on the greatest issues of the day, with only one or two other members, one or two reporters, a few congressional staffers — and the C-SPAN cameras — looking on.

Capitol Guide Service Kiosk, First Street SW and Maryland Avenue. ☎ *202-225-6827. Internet:* www.aoc.gov. *Metro: Capitol South. Walk north one block on 1st Street SE, turn left on Independence Avenue for three blocks, and then go right on 1st Street SW for one block. Kiosk is on the right. Tours: 9 a.m.–4:30 p.m. Mon –Sat. No tours Sun. Admission: Free.*

FBI

Downtown

The one-hour FBI tour is one of the most popular in Washington among children. The tour covers such topics as the Ten Most Wanted list, famous FBI cases, and how the FBI operates. Participants walk through

The Mall

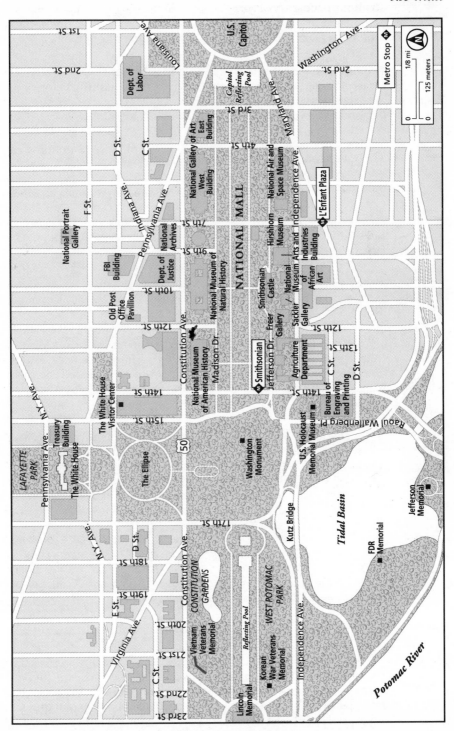

a crime laboratory; don't be surprised to see technicians analyzing hair, fibers, and blood for clues. Usually the tour has a bang-up finish with a demonstration at the firing range — loud and especially popular with little boys (scary for some of the youngest children).

The best way to get into this tour is to ask your representative or senator to make a reservation for you at least three months before your visit. Reservations aren't required, but waits can reach two hours, and high demand can cause the later tours to fill up early.

If you have a reservation, plan on arriving at least 15 minutes early. Be prepared to pass through a security check.

935 Pennsylvania Ave. NW. Tour entrance on E Street at 9th Street. ☎ *202-324-3447. TTY 202-324-1016. Internet:* www.fbi.gov/aboutus/tour/tour.htm. *Metro: Archives-Navy Memorial. Walk west on Pennsylvania and then right on 9th one block to E. Tours: Mon–Fri 8:45 a.m.–4:15 p.m. Closed federal holidays. Admission: Free.*

Ford's Theatre & Lincoln Museum
Downtown

Closed for more than a century after President Lincoln was assassinated here on April 14, 1865, Ford's Theatre became a showcase for plays and concerts again in 1968. You can attend a performance here. And you can tour the scene, viewing the presidential box as it looked the night John Wilkes Booth shot the president during a performance of *Our American Cousin.*

In the small, basement **Lincoln Museum** are Lincoln's death mask and Booth's derringer, along with other presidential memorabilia. Across the street, you can visit the place where Lincoln died, the Petersen House, 516 10th St. NW. The exact hour of his death, 7:22 a.m., is frozen on the bedroom's bedside clock. You can spend about an hour touring the two locations.

511 10th St. NW between E and F streets. ☎ *202-426-6924. Internet:* www.nps.gov/foth. *Performance information: 202-347-4833; Internet:* www.fordstheatre.org. *Metro: Metro Center. From 11th Street exit, walk one block south on 11th, left on F, and then right on 10th. Open: Daily 9 a.m.–5 p.m. except during theater matinees. Closed: Dec 25. Admission: Free.*

Holocaust Memorial Museum
Tidal Basin

I have yet to meet a soul unmoved by a visit to this museum. Prepare to be emotionally drained when you leave. The museum recommends that children younger than 11 not visit the permanent collection, but they can view other exhibits. Prepare your older children for what they'll see and hear.

The museum remembers the 6 million Jews who were murdered and the millions of others who were murdered or oppressed during the Holocaust. Multimedia exhibitions document this obscene chapter of history. Upon entering, each visitor picks up an identity card of a Holocaust victim, which personalizes the museum experience.

The self-guided tour begins with the rise of Nazism. Then, the Nazis' "Final Solution" is depicted. Aboard a freight car that was used to transport Jews to Treblinka, visitors listen to recordings of survivors. Another section is dedicated to the liberation of the concentration camps and to the non-Jews who, at great risk, hid Jews.

Time-specific tickets are required to view the permanent exhibits. They're free at the museum for same-day visits, but usually are depleted quickly. People line up as early as 8 a.m., though distribution doesn't begin until 10 a.m. You can get tickets ahead of time for $1.75 from Tickets.com (☎ **800-400-9373;** Internet: www.tickets.com).

You can visit exhibits on the first floor and concourse without tickets. Among them is "Daniel's Story," which is appropriate for elementary and middle-school children. Most people spend two to three hours in the museum; many visitors spend a lot more time.

100 Raoul Wallenberg Place SW, south of Independence Avenue. ☎ 202-488-0400. TTY 202-488-0406. Internet: www.ushmm.org. *Metro: Smithsonian. From the Independence Avenue exit, walk west on Independence two blocks and then left on Raoul Wallenberg Place. Open: Daily 10 a.m.–5:30 p.m.; extended hours until 8p.m. Tue and Thur from mid-April to mid-June. Closed: Yom Kippur and Christmas. Admission: Free. Fee for advance tickets.*

International Spy Museum
Downtown

The hottest museum in Washington in 2002 was the International Spy Museum — a brand-new private venture that attracted so many visitors that its lines stretched around the block when it opened in July.

Once inside, you encounter the latest in interactive museum technology along with old and new spyware. You can see a Revolutionary War letter written by George Washington to authorize establishment of a spy network in New York in 1777. You can enter a mockup of an intelligence agency's 21st-century operations center, which displays information about the latest developments in espionage. Among the 68,000-square-foot museum's many artifacts are an Enigma cipher machine from World War II Germany, a U.S. Army M-209 cipher machine from the same era, a Soviet overcoat with a buttonhole camera, a CIA disguise kit, and (shades of Maxwell Smart!) a shoe with microphone and radio transmitter concealed in the heel. Instruments of violence, as well as of intelligence-gathering, are on display. A U.S.-made bomb was disguised as a lump of coal to be planted in enemy coal bins during World War II; it exploded when shoveled into a locomotive's engine, a ship's boiler, or a factory's furnace. A double-barreled poison-gas gun enabled KGB agents to kill silently with a spray of cyanide. Another KGB weapon — a single-shot pistol — was disguised as a lipstick tube. On a lighter note, some exhibits explore the public's fascination with espionage — from Junior G-Man toys in the 1930s to James Bond and Austin Powers movies today.

The museum tells the story of spying from Biblical times to the present, with a heavy emphasis on the Cold War. Visitors are invited to adopt a secret identity and try to maintain it under interrogation, to break codes, to identify disguised spies, to eavesdrop, and to be the target of eaves-droppers. There's a museum store, of course, and two eateries operated by the folks who run the popular Red Sage Grill and the Border Cafe (see Chapter 14) — **Spy City Cafe,** for quick meals, and **Zola,** a full-scale Modern American restaurant.

E. Peter Earnest (what a great name for a spy!), the museum's executive director, spent 36 years with the CIA. His advisory board includes two former CIA directors, two former CIA disguise chiefs, and a retired KGB general. The museum is located in five restored buildings, one of which once housed a Communist Party district headquarters. It's within easy eavesdropping distance of the FBI across the intersection.

800 F Street NW between 8th and 9th streets. ☎ ***866-779-6873** or 202-393-7798. Internet:* www.spymuseum.org. *Metro: Gallery Place-Chinatown. From 9th and G Streets exit, walk one block south on 9th, cross F, and then turn left on F. Museum is on the right. Open: April–October daily 10 a.m.–8 p.m. and November–March 10 a.m. –6 p.m. Closed: Thanksgiving, Dec. 25, and Jan. 1. Final tickets sold 1 hour before closing. Admission: Adults $11, seniors 60 and older $9, children 5–18 $8, and under 5 admitted free.*

Jefferson Memorial
Tidal Basin

This memorial is my favorite, partly because Thomas Jefferson is my favorite founding father and partly because the setting is marvelous. A 19-foot statue of Jefferson stands atop a six-foot pedestal inside the memorial's columned rotunda, which is akin to Jefferson's designs for his Monticello home and the University of Virginia. (When we toured U.Va.-rival William and Mary with my college-hunting daughter, the guide said Jefferson founded U.Va. because his children couldn't get into W&M, which Jefferson himself attended!) Jefferson quotations are carved into the memorial's interior.

The memorial, located on the southeast bank of the Tidal Basin, com-mands a spectacular view of the Washington Monument and the White House to the north. The scene is gorgeous in the spring when the cherry blossoms bloom, and awe-inspiring after dark with Jefferson's statue standing behind you and other of Washington's illuminated landmarks

Monuments & Memorials

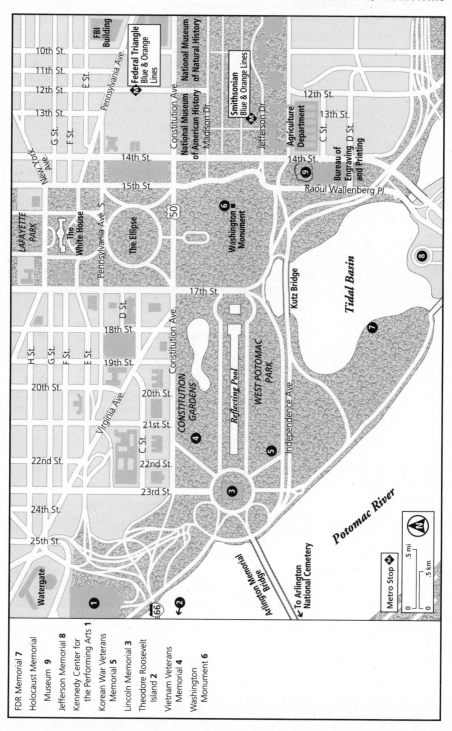

FDR Memorial **7**
Holocaust Memorial
  Museum **9**
Jefferson Memorial **8**
Kennedy Center for
  the Performing Arts **1**
Korean War Veterans
  Memorial **5**
Lincoln Memorial **3**
Theodore Roosevelt
  Island **2**
Vietnam Veterans
  Memorial **4**
Washington
  Monument **6**

glowing in the distance. A bookstore and restrooms are in the basement. Park rangers deliver talks upon request. Count on spending 15 to 45 minutes here depending on whether you listen to a ranger's talk — more if you get mesmerized by the view.

East Basin Drive SW. ☎ **202-426-6841.** *Internet:* www.nps.gov/jefm. *Metro: Smithsonian. From the Independence Avenue exit, walk two blocks west on Independence and then left on Raoul Wallenberg Place to the Tidal Basin path. It's a 15- to 25-minute walk. There's a Tourmobile stop at the memorial, or you can take a taxi. Open: Daily 8 a.m.–midnight. Closed: Dec. 25.*

John F. Kennedy Center for the Performing Arts
Foggy Bottom

This center is Washington's living memorial to a martyred president, and it was a long time a-borning. President Eisenhower signed legislation creating a "national cultural center" in 1958. Kennedy himself was an ardent fundraiser for the project. After his assassination, Congress designated the center as his memorial. President Johnson broke ground in 1965. The center finally opened in 1971, during the Nixon presidency, with a performance of Leonard Bernstein's "Requiem" for Kennedy.

Today, the center is a world-class cultural venue, with concert hall, opera house, movie theater, and other facilities. It's home to the National Symphony, Washington Opera, Washington Ballet, Washington Performing Arts Society, and American Film Institute Theater. The halls outside the performance venues are truly grand. More than 40 nations donated building materials and works of art. Views are grand from the top-floor restaurants and promenade. You can attend performances here, including daily free performances on the Millennium Stage. And you can take a free, hour-long guided tour. You'll spend one to two hours here if you take the tour.

You can obtain tickets for "VIP" tours of the center from members of Congress.

2700 F St. NW between New Hampshire Avenue and Rock Creek Parkway. concerts: ☎ **800-444-1324** *or 202-467-4600; tours* ☎ *202-416-8340, TTY 202-416-8524. Internet:* www.kennedy-center.org. *Metro: Foggy Bottom-George Washington University. Walk west on I St. 1½ blocks and then left on New Hampshire about four blocks. Or take the free Kennedy Center Shuttle from the Metrorail station every 15 minutes from 9:45 a.m.–midnight Mon–Fri; 10 a.m.–midnight Sat; noon—midnight Sun and holidays. Open: Daily 10 a.m.–30 minutes after last performance. Tours: Mon–Fri 10 a.m.–5 p.m., Sat–Sun 10 a.m.–1 p.m. Admission: Free. Fee for most performances.*

Korean War Veterans Memorial
National Mall

Before Vietnam, another undeclared war helped to drive a once-popular president (Truman) from office, cost more than 50,000 American lives, and left the nation in a mood more inclined to forget a conflict than to memorialize it. Finally, on the 42nd anniversary of the armistice that ended the fighting — but which has not yet officially sealed the peace — the Korean War Veterans Memorial was dedicated on July 27, 1995, by the presidents of the United States and South Korea, Bill Clinton and Kim Young Sam. The focal point of the memorial are statues that depict an infantry unit on patrol. Park rangers give talks upon request. A bookstore, restrooms, and concessions are at the site. Allocate at least 15 minutes to this memorial.

French Drive SW and Independence Avenue, southeast of the Lincoln Memorial. ☎ *202-426-6841.* Internet: www.nps.gov/kowa. *Metro: Foggy Bottom-GWU. Walk south eight blocks on 23rd Street to the Lincoln Memorial and then left on French Drive. Or walk from the Tourmobile's Lincoln Memorial stop. Or take a taxi. Open: Daily 8 a.m.–midnight. Closed: Dec. 25. Admission: Free.*

Library of Congress
Capitol Hill

The general public can't borrow books at this library, the world's largest, but you can do research here (and I have). The collection — 120 million items on 530 miles of bookshelves — is built upon Thomas Jefferson's personal library of 6,487 volumes.

The main building, named for Jefferson, is an ornate Italian Renaissance structure that you can tour. If you saw the movie *All the President's Men,* you'll remember a mind-boggling overhead shot of Woodward and Bernstein doing research in the Main Reading Room, which you can view. Another highlight, the Great Hall, soars 75 feet (29 m) from marble floor to stained glass ceiling. The *Gutenberg Bible* and the *Giant Bible of Mainz* are among artifacts on permanent display. The building also houses changing exhibits, as well as film showings and concerts.

Stop first at the Jefferson Building's visitor center, inside the ground level 1st Street SE entrance. Get tour tickets and ask what's going on, not only in the Jefferson Building, but in the library's nearby Madison and Adams buildings as well. Figure on spending one to two hours here if you take the tour. Naturally, at Congress' library, a representative or senator can get you into a special tour.

1st Street SE between East Capital Street and Independence Avenue. ☎ *202-707-8000. Internet:* www.loc.gov. *Metro: Capitol South. Walk north on 1st Street one and a half blocks to Jefferson Building on the right. Open: Jefferson Mon–Sat 10 a.m.–5:30 p.m.; Madison: Mon–Fri 8:30 a.m.–9:30 p.m., Sat 8:30 a.m.–6:30 p.m.; Adams Mon–Thur 8:30 a.m.–9:30 p.m., Fri 8:30 a.m.–5:30 p.m., Sat 8:30 a.m.–5:30 p.m. Tours: Mon–Fri 10:30 a.m., 11:30 p.m., 1:30 p.m., 2:30 p.m., 3:30 p.m.; Sat 10:30 a.m., 11:30 p.m., 1:30 p.m., 2:30 p.m. Congressional tours: Mon–Fri 8:30 a.m. and 2 p.m. Admission: Free.*

Lincoln Memorial
National Mall

Okay, I confess: The Lincoln Memorial is up there with the Jefferson. If you were forced to pick the greatest president, Lincoln would be in the Final Four. And, like Jefferson's, Lincoln's memorial is an awe-inspiring place. Once again, you have an oversized sculpture of the president inside a structure that, in this case, has become as familiar as the Capitol and the White House. The Gettysburg Address and Lincoln's second inaugural address are inscribed on the walls. And the vista is spectacular, looking the length of the Mall, past the Washington Monument to the Capitol. (The World War II Memorial is under construction between Lincoln and Washington, and you'll have to wait to decide whether the advocates or critics are right about its effect on this view.)

The Lincoln Memorial has been the sight of some of America's most important political demonstrations, from Marian Anderson singing here in 1939, to Martin Luther King's "I Have a Dream" speech in 1963, to the Vietnam War protests. The Memorial has a visitor center and restrooms, and rangers give talks on request. You can spend 15 to 45 minutes — or more — here, depending on your interest, and it's awe-inspiring at night. From the back, you look into Arlington National Cemetery and see the perpetual flame on Kennedy's grave.

West end of the Mall at 23rd Street between Constitution and Independence avenues. ☎ *202-426-6841. Internet:* www.nps.gov/linc. *Metro: Foggy Bottom. Walk south eight blocks on 23rd Street. Tourmobile stops here, and you can take a taxi. Open: 8 a.m.–midnight. Closed: Dec. 25. Admission: Free.*

National Air & Space Museum
National Mall

I find the **Milestones of Flight Gallery**, in the center of the first floor, mind-boggling. You stand beside John Glenn's *Friendship 7* capsule (in which he became the first American to orbit Earth), while gazing upon Neil Armstrong's *Columbia* command module and Orville and Wilbur Wright's *Flyer*. There, in a few feet of museum space, the 20th century progresses from "man cannot fly" to "man can walk on the moon" in just 65 years!

This museum is crammed with significant artifacts of flight and exhibits that teach the history and science of flight. You can see Charles Lindbergh's ocean-crossing *Spirit of St. Louis*, Chuck *(The Right Stuff)* Yeager's sound-barrier-breaking *X-1*, a space station, a space rock . . . I have no room to do the collection justice.

 Because the Air and Space Museum is on every visitor's agenda, arriving when the doors open or late in the day is wise. Get a map at the information desk and decide whether you want to take a free guided tour, rent an audio tape tour, or fend for yourself. Next, purchase tickets for the movies on the multistory IMAX screen and consider buying tickets the Albert Einstein Planetarium's tour of the universe.

An hour can slip by in what seems like seconds in this enormous, exhibit-packed place. Allow *at least* two to three hours here. If you're with me or my pilot-in-training nephew, you'll be here all day!

Between Independence Avenue SW, Jefferson Drive and 4th and 7th streets. ☎ *202-357-1400, TTY 202-357-1505. Internet:* www.nasm.edu. *Metro: L'Enfant Plaza. From Smithsonian Museums exit, walk north one block on 7th Street SW, across Independence, and then right. Open: Late May–Aug Daily 9 a.m.–5:30 p.m.; Sept–late May 10 a.m.–5:30 p.m. Closed: Dec. 25. Admission: Free. Fee for Imax Theater, Einstein Planetarium.*

National Archives
Downtown

The Declaration of Independence, the Constitution of the United States, the Bill of Rights, a 1297 version of the Magna Carta, and numerous other historical documents reside in the Archives, which underwent an extensive renovation and were scheduled to reopen in the fall of 2003. (Call ahead or check the Web site for the exact date.) Those familiar with the old Archives, where you squinted to see documentary treasures behind thick glass, are supposed to be bowled over in the new Archives, where the documents are to be explained with multimedia presentations, interactive exhibits, and other state-of-the-art technologies. While I'm focusing on the famous documents, the National Archives and Records Administration preserves *billions* of federal records. As at the Library of Congress, members of the public can conduct research here. Figure on spending at least 20 minutes.

700 Pennsylvania Ave. NW between 9th and 7th streets. ☎ *202-501-5000. Internet:* www.archives.gov. *Metro: Archives-Navy Memorial. Walk across Pennsylvania Avenue. Open: Call or visit the Web site to check. Admission: Free.*

National Gallery of Art
National Mall

The National Gallery is two buildings — East and West — connected by an underground walkway. The Gallery owns more than 100,000 works from the Middle Ages to the present. Important works are on exhibit throughout both buildings, and the gallery always is mounting special exhibitions, some of international importance.

The West Building is a treasure chest of European art from the 13th into the early 20th centuries and American art from the 18th to the early 20th. Notable is the only painting by Leonardo da Vinci in the Western Hemisphere.

ed the starkly modern East Building, which, appropriately,
allery's 20th-century and contemporary art. An immense
e dominates the soaring central court. You also see works by
se, Joan Miró, Pablo Picasso, and Jackson Pollock here.

ro Gallery, near the Mall entrance to the West Building, you can
nputer terminal to identify the works you want to see and then
map that shows you where they're located. In addition to the
exhiu.s, the Gallery presents daily tours of the collection, a concert series,
lectures, and films. The shops sell some of Washington's best souvenirs —
reproductions of the gallery's masterworks in many forms. There's even a
children's shop. You need at least two hours for a cursory taste of the
National Gallery's treasures.

Families take note: Kids — as well as adults — enjoy the outdoor
Sculpture Garden, across 7th Street from the West Building. It even has
an ice-skating rink in the winter.

In addition to housing sculpture, the garden hosts live jazz performances
5 to 8 p.m. on Fridays from Memorial Day through Labor Day.

Constitution Avenue NW between 3rd and 7th streets. ☎ *202-737-4215, TDD
202-842-6176. Internet:* www.nga.gov. *Metro: Archives-Navy Memorial. Walk 1½
blocks east on Pennsylvania Avenue and then right on 6th Street. Open: Mon–Sat
10 a.m.–5 p.m., Sun 11 a.m.–6 p.m. Memorial Day–Labor Day. Sculpture Garden
open until 9 p.m. Fri, 7 p.m. other days. Closed: Dec 25, Jan 1.*

National Museum of American History
National Mall

If the Smithsonian is the nation's attic — as it's often called — then this
is the corner where the heirlooms are kept: three million pieces of vintage
Americana.

A highlight here always has been the original Star-Spangled Banner, the
giant flag that inspired the National Anthem. As I write this book, museum
visitors can take a peek at conservators working to preserve the well-
worn flag, which eventually will go back on normal display. You also can
take a look at first ladies' gowns, a Samuel Morse telegraph, an Alexander
Graham Bell telephone, George Washington's military uniform, Abraham
Lincoln's top hat, Muhammad Ali's boxing gloves, Duke Ellington's sheet
music, Julia Child's kitchen . . . even Howdy Doody. And that's not even
scratching the surface.

Exhibition halls let you concentrate on things (agriculture equipment,
power machinery, musical instruments), while others explore social phe-
nomena (women as political activists, the GI in World War II, the migration
of African-Americans from the South to the North between 1915 and 1940).

The hands-on history and science rooms are designed for youngsters (or oldsters) 5 and older. Kids conduct experiments in the science room. In the history room, they can climb on a high-wheel bicycle or transmit a telegram. When the rooms are busy, you're given timed tickets that let you in later in the day. You can't go wrong taking the kids to the fully functioning ice cream parlor, either.

You need at least two hours here, and this museum is another one in which you could spend an entire day.

Between Constitution Avenue NW, Madison Drive, and 12th and 14th streets. ☎ *202-357-2700. TTY 202-357-1729. Internet:* http://americanhistory.si. edu. *Metro: Smithsonian. From the Mall exit, walk north across the Mall to the museum on your left. Open: Daily 10 a.m.–5:30 p.m. Closed: Dec 25. Admission: Free.*

National Museum of Natural History
National Mall

Kids dig dinosaurs, right? And bugs. And giant 3-D movies. So they gotta love this place! From the moment you walk in and encounter the huge African elephant in the Rotunda, your children will be squealing with delight. And there's plenty to interest the bigger folks, too. While the National Gallery may boast that it has artworks stretching back 800 years, artifacts at the Natural History Museum measure their years in *billions*.

When you're done ogling the elephant, pick up a museum map at the nearby information desk. Then consider buying tickets for the 90-foot-high Imax theater or for the Immersion Interactive Cinema, which is essentially a giant video game. If you'd like to join a tour, they leave from the Rotunda September through June from Monday through Thursday at 10:30 a.m. and 1:30 p.m. and Friday at 10:30 a.m.

Kids go gaga at the insect zoo, where they can touch creepy crawly critters and slither through a model of a termite mound, and they love to explore Dinosaur Hall. Other highlights — for visitors of all ages — include the Hall of Geology, Gems, and Minerals, where you find a moon rock, the 45.5 carat Hope Diamond, and many other baubles; and the marine life exhibit with the 92-foot model whale. Humans are part of natural history, too, so the museum contains exhibits about evolution and various human cultures. Plan on spending two to four hours here.

Between Constitution Avenue N.W., Madison Drive and 9th and 12th streets. ☎ *202-357-2700. TTY 202-357-1729. Internet:* www.mnh.si.edu. *Metro: Smithsonian. From the Mall exit, walk north across the Mall to the museum on your right. Open: Daily 10 a.m.–5:30 p.m.; June–Aug until 8 p.m. Admission: Free.*

National Postal Museum
Capitol Hill

A museum dedicated to the history of stamps and the postal service delivers, by extension, a large slice of American history. Interactive exhibits make it a hit with kids. Tour a Southern Railway mail car, see floating laser images and holograms in the Customers and Consumers Gallery, and find out about the big business of junk — excuse me — *direct* mail that takes up so much room in mailboxes. Plan on spending an hour or more.

2 Massachusetts Ave. NE, next to Union Station. ☎ *202-357-2991. TTY 202-633-9849. Internet:* www.si.edu/postal. *Metro: Union Station. From Union Station Shops/ Massachusetts Avenue exit, walk across 1st Street NE. Open: Daily 10 a.m.– 5:30 p.m. Closed Dec. 25. Admission: Free.*

National Zoo
Upper Northwest.

Hands-down *the* most kid-friendly place in town, the National Zoological Park (that's "zoo" to you) shows off more than 5,800 critters big and small around 163 acres of hills and valleys, most of the animals in compounds designed to resemble their natural habitat. Be sure to wear your walking shoes and comfortable clothing, 'cause you'll be doing lots of hiking here.

Grab a map and schedule of events at the Education Building near the Connecticut Avenue entrance. Zookeepers conduct demonstrations and give talks throughout the park. It's always fun to be around at feeding time. And the elephants and the seals put on performances.

The zoo obtained a new pair of giant pandas from China in 2000, thus assuring that pandas will remain the park's most popular inhabitants. Come meet Mei Xiang and Tian Tian. Here are other highlights.

Think Tank: Look in as scientists study animal thinking, including inquiring into orangutans' language; researchers test apes' ability to use and understand word symbols.

The **Orangutan Transportation System:** The apes use an outdoor overhead cable to commute between buildings.

Amazonia: The Amazon River Basin's tropical habitat is recreated to accommodate macaws, sloths, monkeys, avocadoes, cocoa trees, piranhas, poison frogs, and others; a great place to warm up in the winter.

The **Reptile Discovery Center:** lizards and turtles and snakes, oh my; yucky for grownups, groovy for kids.

The **Pollinarium:** Hummingbirds and butterflies flit about, pollinating plants.

National Zoological Park

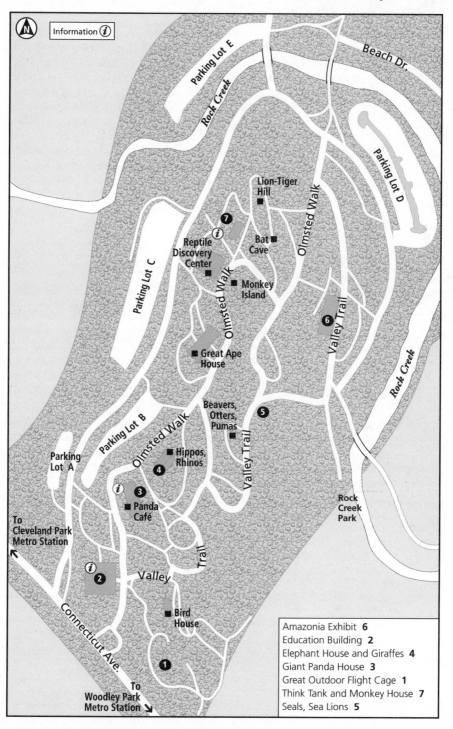

N

Information *i*

Parking Lot E

Beach Dr.

Rock Creek

Parking Lot D

Parking Lot C

Lion-Tiger Hill

i 7

Reptile Discovery Center

Bat Cave

Olmsted Walk

Olmsted Walk

Monkey Island

Valley Trail

6

Great Ape House

Rock Creek

Beavers, Otters, Pumas

5

Olmsted Walk

Parking Lot B

Parking Lot A

Hippos, Rhinos

4

Valley Trail

Rock Creek Park

i 3

Panda Café

To Cleveland Park Metro Station

i 2

Valley Trail

Bird House

Connecticut Ave.

1

To Woodley Park Metro Station

Amazonia Exhibit **6**
Education Building **2**
Elephant House and Giraffes **4**
Giant Panda House **3**
Great Outdoor Flight Cage **1**
Think Tank and Monkey House **7**
Seals, Sea Lions **5**

You can spend two to five hours here. Take it easy. Flop for a while under a tree. Bring some food or grab lunch or a snack at one of the — let's call them "adequate" — refreshment stands.

Despite its name, Woodley Park-Zoo is not the best Metrorail station to use on the way to the zoo. Here's what the locals do: On the way *to* the zoo, use the Cleveland Park station and then walk south on Connecticut Avenue from the East Side exit. When *leaving* the zoo, walk south on Connecticut to the Woodley Park-Zoo station. You walk a tad further, but more downhill and less uphill. The L1 Metrobus runs from Washington Circle to Dupont Circle and then all the way up Connecticut Avenue to Maryland, stopping at the zoo.

3001 Connecticut Ave. NW. ☎ *202-673-4800. Internet:* http://natzoo.si.edu. *Metro: Cleveland Park/Woodley Park-Zoo. Buildings open daily: May 1–Sept. 15 10 a.m.–6 p.m.; rest of year 10 a.m.–4:30 p.m. Grounds open: May 1–Sept. 15 6 a.m.– 8 p.m.; rest of year 6 a.m.–6 p.m. Admission: Free.*

The Pentagon
Virginia

Shortly after the terrorist attacks of Sept. 11, 2001, on weekends, when most of the building's 23,000 employees stay home, members of the public were allowed to drive into a section of the Pentagon parking lots and walk to a grassy rise that overlooks the side of the building that was struck by American Airlines Flight 77. The area became a spontaneous memorial, built by visitors leaving flowers, flags, notes, and other items of tribute. My family went several times and found it quite moving.

Built during the early years of World War II to be U.S. military headquarters, the five-sided building usually is described in terms of its enormous size: 3.7 million square feet of floor space, 100,000 miles of telephone cable, and the like. Unfortunately, the once-popular Pentagon tour was a casualty of the 9/11 attacks. As I write this book, tours are available to some groups, but not to individuals. When you visit Washington, you can call to find out whether the tours have resumed.

Arlington, Virginia. ☎ *703-695-1776. Internet:* http://dod.mil/pubs/ pentagon. *Metro: Pentagon. From the Pentagon exit, take the escalator up. Currently closed to the public. Admission: Free.*

Franklin Delano Roosevelt Memorial
Tidal Basin

This monument to a U.S. president illustrates the latest trend in monument architecture. It is, shall I say, monumental in size — telling the 32nd president's biography as well as honoring him on a 7½-acre site. Walking through four open-air "rooms," one for each of Roosevelt's terms, you revisit the Great Depression, World War II, and other notable aspects of his 12-year presidency, the longest ever. The memorial features statues of his first lady, Eleanor, an important public figure in her own right, and Roosevelt's beloved dog Fala. Note how Fala's statue shines where visitors pet it.

You can see FDR's wheelchair and other memorabilia in the information center. Restrooms are located at each end of the memorial. Allow 30 minutes to an hour to visit.

West Basin Drive at East Ohio Drive. ☎ *202-426-6841. Internet:* www.nps.gov/ fdrm. *Metro: Smithsonian. From the Independence Avenue exit, walk west on Independence until you're sure that you've gone too far and then turn left on West Basin Drive; total walking time about 30 minutes. The Tourmobile stops here, or you can take a taxi. Open: Daily 8 a.m.–midnight. Closed: Dec 25. Admission: Free.*

Supreme Court
Capitol Hill

The majestic Supreme Court building looks as if it has been standing since the birth of the republic — the Roman Republic, that is. In fact, the court was the last of the three government branches to get its own digs. The nine justices didn't move into this classic temple until 1935. Previously, they occupied a nook in the Capitol. This place is another one where a member of Congress — with lots of notice — can get you into a guided tour. Otherwise, you can wander around yourself, check out the exhibits on the ground floor, and attend a lecture in the courtroom.

By far, the best thing to do here is attend a one-hour argument. The topic can be front-page news around the world — defining freedom of speech, setting limits on the death penalty — or it can pick at arcane details of a commercial contract. No matter, it can be grand entertainment — with justices interrupting the lawyers, casting wry asides, or convulsing the courtroom in laughter with an on-the-money wisecrack.

The court hears arguments between 10 a.m. and 3 p.m. (sometimes only in the morning) on many Mondays, Tuesdays, and Wednesdays from October into April. Lines form on the plaza when arguments are being heard — one for listening to an entire argument, the other for taking a three-minute peek. Come early if the argument is big news. You can spend an hour here, more if you attend an argument or take a tour.

1 1st St. NE at Maryland Avenue. ☎ *202-479-3030. Internet:* www.supremecourt us.gov. *Metro: Capitol South. Walk north 2½ blocks on 1st Street. Open: Mon–Fri 9 a.m.–4:30 p.m. Closed: Federal holidays. Admission: Free.*

Vietnam Veterans Memorial

National Mall

Depending on your age and your circumstances, this memorial can be the most emotional spot in Washington. The war divided the country, and the surviving soldiers came home feeling unappreciated. The private Vietnam Veterans Memorial Fund lobbied for a memorial on the Mall and raised money to build it. The organizers wanted to honor the soldiers and steer clear of the war's politics. Maya Lin — a Chinese-American Yale University student who grew up in Ohio — created the winning design.

Like the war, the simple memorial — a black granite V carved into the ground — was controversial. To appease those who wanted a more traditional, patriotic monument, a flagpole and a statute of three soldiers was placed near the wall. Later a statue of three female military nurses, tending to a wounded soldier, was added.

Nevertheless, it's the Wall — with its 58,226 names of the dead and missing — that commands the attention of visitors and eloquently commemorates the soldiers' sacrifice. Park rangers are available to discuss the memorial and help if you're looking for individual names. So, usually, are Vietnam-era vets. You can find a bookstore, restrooms, and concessions in the area. You can spend as little as 15 minutes here, more as you're moved.

Bacon Drive at Constitution Avenue NW, just northeast of the Lincoln Memorial. ☎ *202-426-6841. Internet:* www.nps.gov/vive. *Metro: Foggy Bottom. Walk south 7 blocks on 23rd Street, then left 1½ blocks on Constitution, and then right on Bacon. The Tourmobile stops at the nearby Lincoln Memorial, or you can take a taxi. Open: Daily 8 a.m.–midnight. Closed Dec. 25. Admission: Free.*

Washington Monument
National Mall

This towering marble obelisk is one of the most recognizable sights in America. The view from the top is the most spectacular in Washington. You can get free time-specific tickets at the monument's ticket kiosk for riding the elevator to the top on the day of your visit. They're usually gone before noon, so arrive early. For $2, you can buy tickets from 24 hours to five months in advance at ☎ **800-967-2283** or Internet: http://reservations.nps.gov. The ride to the top takes just 70 seconds. You can stare out the windows as long as you like. You descend at a slower speed so that you can view the monument's interior. The grounds contain exhibits, a bookstore, restrooms, and concessions. On summer evenings, military bands perform here, and the monument provides a gleaming exclamation point for the 4th of July fireworks.

You'll pass through security screening to enter the monument. Prohibited are food, drinks, large bags, strollers, dogs (except guide dogs), and the usual dangerous items. If you wear a pacemaker or other medical device that a magnetometer may affect, tell a ranger so that you can go through alternative screening. Figure on a 30-minute visit, not counting time in line.

Between Constitution Avenue NW, Independence Avenue SW, and 15th and 17th streets. ☎ *202-426-6841. Internet:* www.nps.gov/wash. *Metro: Smithsonian.*

From the Mall exit, walk west on Jefferson Drive two long blocks. Open: Daily 9 a.m.–4:45 p.m.; ticket kiosk 8 a.m.–4:30 p.m. Closed: July 4 and Dec 25. Admission: Free.

Washington National Cathedral
Upper Northwest

The cathedral, founded to serve all faiths (though it's affiliated with the Episcopal denomination), raises its towers higher than anything else in Washington and can be seen throughout D.C. and into the Virginia suburbs. President Theodore Roosevelt and the bishop of London participated in the laying of the foundation stone, which came from a field near Bethlehem, in 1907. Like its European predecessors, this cathedral wasn't built in a day. Constructed in the traditional "stone-on-stone" method (no structural steel), the building was completed in 1990.

You can find much to see and do here, outside as well as inside. You can catch a 30- to 45-minute guided tour at the Cathedral's west end Monday, Tuesday, Thursday, Friday, and Saturday from 10 to 11:30 a.m. and 12:45 to 3:15 p.m.; Wednesday 10 to 11:30 a.m. and 1:15 to 3:15 p.m.; and Sunday 12:45 to 2:30 p.m. ($3 adult, $2 senior, $1 child). Several other specialized tours also are offered; phone or check the Cathedral's Web site for details. You can rent an audio tour or wander about on your own. Whatever you do, be sure and check out the gardens as well as the interior.

The real business of the church — weddings, funerals, worship services, and the like — supercedes touring. Some programs are offered on irregular schedules, so calling before you visit is wise.

Kids 5 and older enjoy the medieval crafts workshop, held in the Crypt Saturday from 10 a.m. to 2 p.m.; they can work on an anvil, carve limestone, create a clay gargoyle, illuminate a manuscript, make a brass rubbing, and build a stone arch. Tours for youngsters to explore the cathedrals gargoyles and grotesques (including Darth Vader!) run from April through Halloween (boo!); bring binoculars. You can find out about other special youth and family tours by calling ☎ 202-537-2934.

The cathedral is a bit off the standard tourist path, but you can grab a good lunch or dinner at several neighborhood restaurants: **2 Amys** (see review in Chapter 14); **Cactus Cantina,** 3300 Wisconsin Ave. NW, ☎ 202-686-7222 (large, boisterous Tex-Mex spot with outdoor dining area); or **Cafe Deluxe,** 3228 Wisconsin Ave., ☎ 202-686-2233 (stylish bistro with indoor and outdoor tables, eclectic menu of New American and traditional comfort foods with a twist: burgers, pasta, chicken pot pie, grilled meatloaf with Creole sauce, lemon pepper-crusted sea bass, and penne pasta with chicken and asparagus).

Massachusetts and Wisconsin avenues NW. (You can't miss it!) General info ☎ 202-537-6200, recorded info ☎ 202-364-6616, tour info ☎ 202-537-5596. Internet: www.cathedral.org/cathed*ral. Metro: Dupont Circle. Take an N-series*

The White House Area

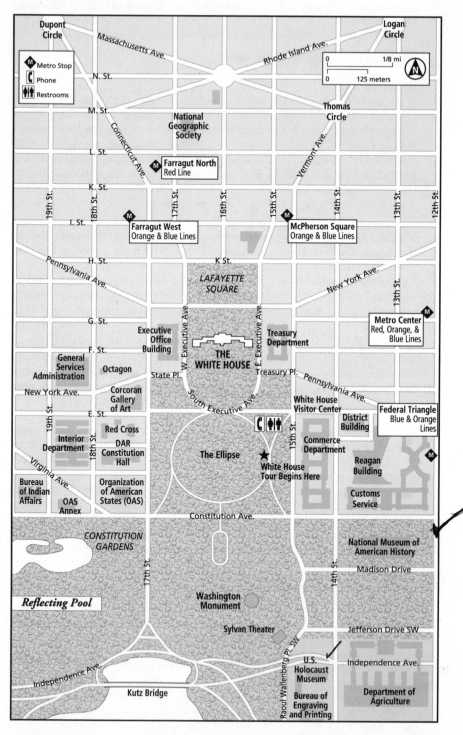

Dupont Circle

Massachusetts Ave.

Rhode Island Ave.

Logan Circle

M Metro Stop
C Phone
Restrooms

N. St.

0 ——— 1/8 mi
0 ——— 125 meters

M. St.

National Geographic Society

Thomas Circle

Vermont Ave.

Connecticut Ave.

L. St.

M Farragut North
Red Line

K. St.

19th St.
18th St.
17th St.
16th St.
15th St.
14th St.
13th St.
12th St.

I. St.

M Farragut West
Orange & Blue Lines

M McPherson Square
Orange & Blue Lines

Pennsylvania Ave.

H. St.

K St.

New York Ave.

13th St.

LAFAYETTE SQUARE

G. St.

Executive Office Building

W. Executive Ave.
E. Executive Ave.

Treasury Department

Metro Center
Red, Orange, & Blue Lines

F. St.

General Services Administration

Octagon

THE WHITE HOUSE

State Pl.

Treasury Pl.

Pennsylvania Ave.

New York Ave.

Corcoran Gallery of Art

South Executive Ave.

White House Visitor Center

District Building

Federal Triangle
Blue & Orange Lines

E. St.

Red Cross

Commerce Department

19th St.
18th St.

Interior Department

DAR Constitution Hall

The Ellipse

15th St.

Reagan Building

M

Virginia Ave.

Bureau of Indian Affairs

Organization of American States (OAS)

White House Tour Begins Here

Customs Service

OAS Annex

Constitution Ave.

CONSTITUTION GARDENS

National Museum of American History

17th St.

Madison Drive

14th St.

Reflecting Pool

Washington Monument

Sylvan Theater

Jefferson Drive SW

Raoul Wallenberg Pl. SW

U.S. Holocaust Museum

Independence Ave.

Independence Ave.

Kutz Bridge

Bureau of Engraving and Printing

Department of Agriculture

Metrobus up Massachusetts Avenue. Or catch a 30-series bus, which runs along Pennsylvania Avenue, M Street, and Wisconsin Avenue. Or take a taxi. Open: Mon–Fri 10 a.m.–5 p.m. (May through Sept until 9 p.m. main floor only); Sat 10 a.m.– 4:30 p.m.; and Sun 8 a.m.–5 p.m. Gardens open until dusk. Admission: Free. Fees vary for tours, programs.

White House
Downtown

Is it just me, or does everybody wonder why, if security can screen people to get on airplanes, why can't they screen them for White House tours? As I write this book, the White House is one of the very few places in Washington to remain closed to the public in the wake of the terrorist attacks of Sept. 11, 2001.

For now, you have to content yourself with visiting the **White House Visitor Center,** which, strangely enough, is located in the Great Hall of the Commerce Department building, about three and a half blocks from the White House visitors entrance. There, you find ranger talks, exhibits, a gift shop, and restrooms. You also can stroll the perimeter of the White House complex, take pictures through the fence, and marvel at the bizarre architecture of the Old Executive Office Building.

I find it hard to imagine that the White House will remain closed for an extended period of time. Congress is open. The Supreme Court is open. How long can the executive branch stay boarded up? When you come to D.C., I suggest calling the visitor center to find out whether tours have started again. If they have, ask a member of Congress for VIP tickets.

1600 Pennsylvania Ave. NW. ☎ 202-208-1631. Internet: www.nps.gov/whho. Metro: McPherson Square. From the Vermont Avenue-White House exit, walk one block south on Vermont and then across Lafayette Square. It's that big white house in front of you.

Visitor Center: 1450 Pennsylvania Ave. NW. Metro: Federal Triangle. Walk half block north on 12th Street and then left on Pennsylvania two and a half blocks. Keep the parks on your right, and the visitor center will show up on your left. Open: Daily 7:30 a.m.–4 p.m. Closed: Thanksgiving, Dec. 25, Jan. 1. Admission: Free.

Index of Attractions by Location

Foggy Bottom

Kennedy Center for the Performing
   Arts
National Mall ·
Lincoln Memorial
Korean War Memorial ·
National Air and Space Museum ✓
National Gallery of Art ✓
National Museum of American History✓
National Museum of Natural History
Vietnam Veterans Memorial✓
Washington Monument

Tidal Basin

Bureau of Engraving and Printing
Holocaust Memorial Museum ✓
Jefferson Memorial
Roosevelt Memorial

Upper Northwest

National Zoo
Washington National Cathedral ·

Virginia

Arlington National Cemetery
Pentagon

Index of Attractions by Type

Memorials/Monuments

Arlington National Cemetery, Virginia
Jefferson Memorial, Tidal Basin
Korean War Memorial, National Mall
Lincoln Memorial, National Mall
Roosevelt Memorial, Tidal Basin
Vietnam Veterans Memorial, National
   Mall
Washington Monument, National Mall

Museums/Galleries

· Holocaust Memorial Museum, Tidal
   Basin
✦International Spy Museum
✦National Air and Space Museum,
   National Mall
National Archives, Downtown
National Gallery of Art, National Mall
✦National Museum of American History,
   National Mall
National Museum of Natural History,
   National Mall
National Postal Museum, Capitol Hill

Government Buildings

Bureau of Engraving and Printing, Tidal
   Basin
Capitol, Capitol Hill
FBI, Downtown
Library of Congress, Capitol Hill
Pentagon, Virginia
Supreme Court, Capitol Hill
White House & White House Visitor
   Center, Downtown

Others

Ford's Theatre, Downtown
Kennedy Center for the Performing
   Arts, Foggy Bottom
National Zoo, Upper Northwest
Washington National Cathedral, Upper
   Northwest

Chapter 17

More Cool Things to See and Do

. . . .

In This Chapter

▶ Entertaining your kids and teens

▶ Exploring the nation's history

▶ Viewing magnificent art

▶ Visiting D.C.'s ethnic museums

▶ Stopping to smell the roses

▶ Checking out Washington Architecture

. . . .

*A*s a world capital — arguably *the world's capital* — Washington really does have something to interest everyone, or at least *nearly* everyone. In this chapter, I identify places of particular appeal to kids, historians, art buffs, and folks of various ethnicities. The last category really should be of interest to everyone. As the old Levy's Bread ads used to say: You don't have to be Jewish to like the B'nai B'rith Klutznick National Jewish Museum.

Especially for Kids

If you have kids with you, you should make a point to check out the following sights, perfectly suited for young visitors. Washington, D.C. is both a fun and important destination for the younger members of the family, with most of the national monuments and museums having a child-focused aspect. Here are a few museums that are specifically for the young (and those who never grew up).

Capital Children's Museum
Capitol Hill

The Capital Children's Museum's hands-on activities and interactive displays are a big hit with kids 2 to 12. Preschoolers can drive a bus and explore what's underneath city streets, while older siblings do the

More Cool Things to See and Do

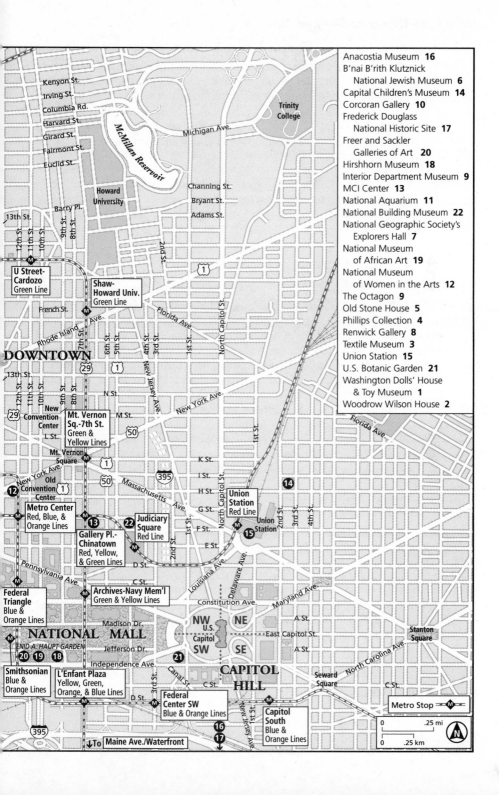

Anacostia Museum **16**
B'nai B'rith Klutznick
National Jewish Museum **6**
Capital Children's Museum **14**
Corcoran Gallery **10**
Frederick Douglass
National Historic Site **17**
Freer and Sackler
Galleries of Art **20**
Hirshhorn Museum **18**
Interior Department Museum **9**
MCI Center **13**
National Aquarium **11**
National Building Museum **22**
National Geographic Society's
Explorers Hall **7**
National Museum
of African Art **19**
National Museum
of Women in the Arts **12**
The Octagon **9**
Old Stone House **5**
Phillips Collection **4**
Renwick Gallery **8**
Textile Museum **3**
Union Station **15**
U.S. Botanic Garden **21**
Washington Dolls' House
& Toy Museum **1**
Woodrow Wilson House **2**

Mexican hat dance and make tortillas in the International Hall. Cartoon lovers create their own animations in the exhibition devoted to Bugs Bunny's creator, Chuck Jones. The museum hosts special weekend activities, workshops, and performances. Call or visit the museum's Web site to find out what's going on. Most kids will want to spend at least an hour here. Sometimes you'll have to get yourself a lasso and drag them away!

800 3rd St. NE, at H Street. ☎ *202-675-4120. Internet:* www.ccm.org. *Metro: Union Station. From inside the station near the train gates, take the escalators up into the parking garage and walk through the garage to H Street. Walk right on H 1½ blocks and then left on 3rd. Museum is on the left. Or take a taxi. Open: Memorial Day–Labor Day. Daily 10 a.m.–5 p.m. Rest of year closed Mondays except Martin Luther King Day, President's Day, Easter Monday, Columbus Day, Veteran's Day, and the Monday between Dec 25–Jan 1. Closed: Jan 1, Thanksgiving, Dec 25. Admission: Ages 2 and younger free, ages 3 and up, $7, seniors (55 and over) $5.*

Washington Dolls' House & Toy Museum
Upper Northwest

Kids may forget all about Santa Claus and his workshop when they get a load of this museum. The Washington Dolls' House and Toy Museum houses collections of dollhouses and antique toys that enthrall kids and those who are kids at heart. Serious collectors can find doll-related periodicals, dollhouses, and miniature accessories (new and consigned) in the second-floor shops. Youngsters can celebrate their birthdays in the tearoom with reservations. Be forewarned: This is a place to look, not touch. Plan on spending 45 minutes or more here.

5236 44th St. NW, between Harrison and Jenifer streets. ☎ *202-244-0024. Metro: Friendship Heights. From the Jenifer Street exit, walk left on Wisconsin Avenue a half block, left on Jenifer one block, and then left on 44th. The museum is on the right. Open: Tues–Sat 10 a.m.–5 p.m., Sun noon–5 p.m. Admission: $4 adults, $3 seniors (65 and over), $2 under 12.*

National Aquarium
Downtown

Locals bring their tadpoles here long before they're ready for the heavy-duty museums. At the National Aquarium, hidden in the Commerce Department building, youngsters can watch sharks, eels, and koi (Japanese carp) get along swimmingly. (It's lucky for the rest of the fish that a separate tank holds the piranhas.) Although this aquarium doesn't boast the latest in technological advances, you can find 1,000 species of aquatic life here, including alligators. Kids can dip their hands into the touch tank and pet a horseshoe crab. Feeding time is 2 p.m. A visit here sets you back a half-hour or more.

14th Street NW between Constitution and Pennsylvania avenues, lower level of Commerce Department building. ☎ *202-482-2825. Metro: Federal Triangle. Walk half block north on 12th Street, left on Pennsylvania two blocks, and then left on*

14th. Aquarium is on the right. Open: Daily 9 a.m.–5 p.m. Closed: Dec 25. Admission: 10 and up $3, ages 2–10 75 cents, under 2 free.

National Geographic Society's Explorers Hall
Downtown

The National Geographic Society explores the universe, so you can encounter exhibits on just about anything in Explorers Hall. Kids can be enthralled by some of the changing topics. As I'm writing this book, for example, visitors can see exhibits of model ships, paintings and sculptures of animals, and what the *National Geographic* magazine's editors picked as the best photos of America that they've published. Call to find out what's on display before you decide to attend. While you're here, you also can check out the National Geographic Store's stock of nature books, photography, globes, maps, and back issues of the magazine. Plan on spending at least an hour.

17th and M streets NW. ☎ *202-857-7588. Internet:* www.nationalgeographic. com/explorer. *Metro: Farragut North. From L Street exit, walk east on L one block, and go left at 17th. Open: Mon–Sat 9 a.m.–5 p.m., Sun 10 a.m.–5 p.m. Closed: Dec 25. Admission: Free.*

Especially for Teens

I have it on good authority, from teenagers who wish to remain anonymous, that the zoo is a cool place for teens to hang out. So is the Air and Space Museum. And the FBI is a cool tour. Here are some other places where local teenagers like to go and that visiting teens likely would enjoy as well.

Georgetown

Teens have been making Georgetown their own since the days of pegged pants and poodle skirts. Shops, restaurants, and the overall scene entertain teenagers in this historic neighborhood, which is centered on the intersection of Wisconsin Avenue and M Street NW. You can eye a wide variety of people for people-watching. And — teens can be cruel — some youngsters get great joy from observing the frustration of drivers inching along in Georgetown's always-gummed-up traffic.

Commander Salamander (1420 Wisconsin), **Urban Outfitters** (3111 M), and **Up Against the Wall** (3219 M) are among the shops that cater to younger shoppers. The Commander offers punk-style clothing, colored wigs, and off-the-wall gifts — think "devil ducks," red rubber duckies with devil's horns. The Outfitters stock slightly offbeat clothing and accoutrements in a wide price range — fuzzy lamps (why not?) for decorating a teen's bedroom and lots of CD accessories. The Wall folks may be distinguished primarily by what's free — lots of loud music.

Check out **Deja Blue** (3005 M) for used blue jeans, **Shake Your Booty** (3225 M) for shoes, and **Beyond Comics** (3060 M) for comic books and related toys, dolls, T-shirts, and other such stuff. If your kids are suffering shopping mall withdrawal, they can find scores of chain stores in **Georgetown Park** (3222 M). I won't tell them about **the Jinx Proof Tattoos and Piercing Parlor** (3281 M) or **Mrs. Natalie the palm reader** (1500 Wisconsin).

A kajillion restaurants are in Georgetown, give or take a few bazillion, and many of them inexpensive and many ideal for carryout food. My teenage daughter and her chums like to sample college life by getting sandwiches at **Wisemiller's Grocery & Deli** (1236½ 36th St.), near the Georgetown University campus and then finding a seat on a convenient wall or set of steps or heading to the little park south of M near 34th. **Dean & Deluca** (3276 M) is a great place for gourmet carryout, and it has outdoor tables. And Georgetown is well-stocked with ice cream parlors — **Ben & Jerry's** (3135 M), **Häagen-Dazs** (3120 M), and the local **Thomas Sweet** (3214 P St. NW at Wisconsin).

The 30-series **Metrobuses** run along Pennsylvania Avenue, M Street, and Wisconsin Avenue. **Georgetown Shuttle** buses connect with the Dupont Circle, Foggy Bottom-George Washington University, and Rosslyn Metrorail Stations. Energetic teens have no trouble walking from the Foggy Bottom station, north on 23rd Street to Washington Circle, left around circle to Pennsylvania Avenue, and then left on Pennsylvania to M.

Dupont Circle

Like Georgetown, Dupont Circle has all the necessities for people-watching, eating, and shopping. The park in the circle is a haven for chess players, recuperating bicycle messengers, and assorted other characters. Teens can buy all the latest music at **Kemp Mill Records. Kramerbooks & Afterwords** is a bookstore where you can eat, drink, listen to music, and . . . well . . . browse for books. **Pizzeria Paradiso** (2029 P St.) is one of the two best pizza parlors in the city and also makes sandwiches to go. Look at three doorways, and one probably leads into a place to eat. Dupont Circle has its own Metrorail Station, so it's really easy to get to.

Union Station

Young people are drawn to Union Station like iron filings to a magnet. Come here any afternoon or weekend if you don't believe me. Who'd have thought that a train station would morph into an upscale mall and entertainment center? Union Station has all the right stuff that young people crave: a nine-screen movie theater complex, more than 50 retailers, and a lower-level food court with dozens of vendors. You can eat in a restaurant or in the brightly decorated food court. Or you can carry your food outside to the fountain.

Sports

If your teens are sports buffs, they'll find Washington to be one of the best professional sports towns in the country. With the exception of baseball (might D.C. get a team before the next edition of this book is published?), Washington has it all — the NFL **Redskins,** the NBA **Wizards,** the NHL **Capitals,** the WNBA **Mystics,** the Major League Soccer **D.C. United,** and the Women's United Soccer Association **Freedom.** Georgetown University also plays big-time basketball, soccer, and lacrosse.

MCI Center is a superb arena and home to the Wizards, Capitals, Mystics, and some Georgetown games. RFK Stadium is a beautiful setting for soccer (and for baseball as well . . . hope springs eternal!). A Metrorail station is practically in MCI Center's basement, and RFK has a station, too. The Redskins' Fed Ex field is not easily accessible, but 'Skins tickets are nearly impossible to get a hold of anyway.

Music

MCI Center and RFK Stadium also are venues for big-time pop-music concerts, as are other stages around town. To keep up with who's performing, check the ads and listings in *The Washington Post* — particularly the Friday "Weekend" section — as well as *The Post's* online entertainment guide (http://eg.washingtonpost.com).

Especially for History Buffs

Deciding which attractions fall into this category is a tough call, because history infuses everything here. When you're done with the monuments, memorials, and federal buildings, I suggest investigating the following sites:

Old Stone House
Georgetown

In the heart of Georgetown — and easy to pass given its diminutive size — is Washington's oldest house. Built in 1765, it predates the United States and the District of Columbia. It's furnished as it was when Georgetown was a thriving tobacco port. Ask the ranger to tell you about the place. Most visitors are struck by the interior space, or lack thereof. Be sure to look out back at the lovely garden, abloom from April to November. You're invited to bring lunch and join picnickers who brown-bag it on the lawn. Plan to spend 15 minutes here, more if you do lunch.

3051 M St., between 30th and 31st streets. ☎ *202-426-6851. Internet:* www.nps. gov/olst. *Metro: Dupont Circle. From the Metrorail Station, take the Georgetown Shuttle bus to 30th and M. Or catch a 30-series bus. Or grab a taxi. Open: Memorial*

Day–December Wed–Sun 10 a.m.–4 p.m.; Jan–Memorial Day Wed–Sun noon–5 p.m. Closed: Jan. 1, July 4, Thanksgiving, and Dec. 25.

Woodrow Wilson House
North of Dupont Circle

After his term ended in 1921, Woodrow Wilson, America's 28th president, lived the last three years of his life in this Georgian Revival home, which was built in 1915. Many of the gifts Wilson received from world leaders — as well as his inaugural Bible, specs, and a shell casing from World War I — are among the artifacts displayed in the house. According to the docents, the residence/museum looks very much as it did when Wilson lived in it. Touring the place properly takes about an hour.

2340 S St. NW., between 23rd and 24th streets. ☎ *202-387-4062. Internet:* www. woodrowwilsonhouse.org. *Metro: Dupont Circle. From the Q Street exit, walk two blocks west on Q, right on Massachusetts Avenue four blocks, right on 24th St. one block, and then right on S. (Note: It's uphill.) Or take an N-series Metrobus up Massachusetts. Or take a taxi. Open: Tue–Sun 10 a.m.–4 p.m. Admission: $5 adults, $4 seniors, $2.50 students, free under 7.*

Especially for Art Lovers

Private art galleries paint many D.C. neighborhoods, but the biggest concentration is in Georgetown, and along 7th Street NW. For the Georgetown galleries, take the Metro to Foggy Bottom, walk north to Pennsylvania Avenue, and then go left. Continue onto M Street. Many galleries are on M and along Wisconsin Avenue between M and R streets. To reach the 7th Street galleries, between D and G streets, take Metro to the Archives-Navy Memorial station and walk north on 7th.

Corcoran Gallery
Downtown

You can find Washington's first art museum — and D.C.'s largest private art museum — just a block from the White House. The Corcoran was founded in 1869 "for the purpose of encouraging the American genius." Its collection traces America's artistic development from colonial times to the present. It also contains a significant number of European works. My teenage daughter, a budding artist, likes to come here to see the works of students in the Corcoran College of Art and Design. The Corcoran has a cafe, a noteworthy museum shop, and an auditorium, which hosts concerts, films, and other activities. Tours of the collection leave from the information desk daily at noon except Tuesday, plus 7:30 p.m. Thursday, and 2:30 p.m. Saturday and Sunday. Figure on spending about an hour here.

500 17th St. NW between New York Avenue and E Street. ☎ *202-639-1700. Internet:* www.corcoran.org. *Metro: Farragut West. From the 17th Street exit, walk five* _blocks south on 17th. Open: Wed–Mon 10 a.m.–5 p.m.; Thur until 9 p.m. except Thanksgiving. Closed: Tue, Dec 25, and Jan 1. Admission: $5 (seniors and students $3, ages 13–18 $1, Younger than 13 free, families $8). Free for all on Mondays and Thursdays after 5 pm._

Freer and Sackler Galleries of Art
National Mall

Although these neighboring galleries store and display their collections in separate buildings, they're connected by underground exhibition space and together comprise the Smithsonian's museum of Asian art. The Freer also contains the world's finest collection of Whistlers (James McNeill Whistler, that is). If you've never seen The Peacock Room, that alone is reason to visit the Freer. Take the guided tour (daily 11:30 a.m. except Wednesday and July 4) to discover the fascinating history behind Whistler's stunning dining room, created for a London town house and moved to the Mall after the owner's death.

The Freer houses a world-renowned collection of art from Asia and the Near East. Highlights include Chinese paintings, Japanese folding screens, Korean ceramics, Buddhist sculpture, and Indian and Persian manuscripts. The Sackler's highlights include early Chinese bronzes and jades, Chinese paintings and lacquerware, ancient Near Eastern ceramics and metalware, South and Southeast Asian sculpture, and Islamic arts. Budget at least a half-hour for each museum.

The Freer's auditorium hosts music, dance, film, lectures, and dramatic presentation relating to the collections.

Between the Smithsonian "castle," Independence Avenue and 12th Street. ☎ _202-357-4880. Internet:_ www.asia.si.edu. _Metro: Smithsonian. From The Mall exit, walk across Jefferson Drive and 12th Street. Open: Daily 10 a.m.–5:30 p.m. Closed: Dec 25. Admission: Free._

Hirshhorn Museum and Sculpture Garden
National Mall

I get a charge out of standing directly beneath Kenneth Snelson's 60-foot-high "Needle Tower," just outside the Hirshhorn, and looking straight up. I must admit that much abstract and contemporary art is not to my taste. But some of it turns me on, and this aluminum-and-steel, TV-tower-like structure is one example.

If modern and contemporary art is _your_ thing, then the Hirshhorn is your museum. All the top guns are here: Benton, Christo, Close, Gorky, Miró, O'Keeffe, Warhol, Bacon, DeKooning, Matisse . . . you get the — uh — picture. And, of course, the museum has many special exhibits. Across Jefferson Drive is the sunken Sculpture Garden, with more than 60 works by Rodin, Moore, Calder, and others.

You can catch a museum tour weekdays at 10:30 a.m. and noon and weekends at noon and 2 p.m., except on federal holidays. Inquire at the information desk about tours of the garden and special exhibitions.

Independence Avenue at 7th Street SW. ☎ *202-357-3091. Internet:* http://hirshhorn.si.edu. *Metro: L'Enfant Plaza. From Smithsonian Museums exit, walk north one block on 7th and cross Independence. The museum is on the left. Open: Daily 10 a.m.–5:30 p.m., until 8 p.m. Thur June–Aug; Plaza: 7:30 a.m.–5:30 p.m.; Sculpture Garden 7:30 a.m.–dusk. Closed: Dec. 25. Admission: Free.*

National Museum of African Art
National Mall

Art from throughout Africa — traditional and contemporary — is the focus of this Smithsonian museum. In addition to mounting exhibits, the museum serves as a research and reference facility, with photo archives and a library. The museum's wide reach is evident in its permanent exhibits, such as "Images of Power and Identity," with symbols of royalty, and "The Art of the Personal Object," which explores the artistic content of everyday objects.

950 Independence Ave. SW, midway between 7th and 12th streets. ☎ *202-357-4600. Internet:* www.nmafa.si.edu. *Metro: Smithsonian. From Independence Avenue exit, cross Independence and walk to the right. Open: Daily 10 a.m.–5:30 p.m. Closed: Dec 25. Admission: Free.*

National Museum of Women in the Arts
Downtown

Housed in a landmark Downtown building that once served as a Masonic Temple, the privately managed National Museum of Women in the Arts has compiled a collection of 2,700 works by more than 800 artists since Wilhelmina Cole Holladay and Wallace F. Holladay began compiling their personal collection in the 1960s. That collection comprised the core of the museum when it was incorporated in 1981 and moved into its current quarters in 1987. The museum seeks to acquire the works of women artists of all periods and all nationalities.

New York Avenue and 13th Street NW. ☎ *202-783-5000. Internet:* www.nmwa.org. *Metro: From 13th Street exit, walk two blocks north on 13th. Open: Mon–Sat 10 a.m.–5 p.m.; Sun noon–5 p.m. Closed Thanksgiving, Dec. 25, Jan. 1. Admission: $5 (60 and older $3, students with ID $3, 18 and younger free.)*

Phillips Collection
Dupont Circle

In the former home of collector and benefactor Duncan Phillips, you find the works of modern artists and of earlier artists who influenced them. The Phillips bills itself as America's first museum of modern art, but it also believes in showing "the continuum of art and artists influencing their successors through the centuries." Duncan Phillips collected El Greco, for example, because he was the "first impassioned expressionist."

The Phillips is noted for impressionist and post-impressionist paintings. You find Renoir's *Luncheon of the Boating Party* here, as well as works by such other notable artists as van Gogh, Monet, Degas, Gauguin, Cézanne, Rothko, Matisse, do Kooning, Hopper, and O'Keeffe. The museum has a shop, cafe, and Sunday concerts at 5 p.m. September through May.

1600 21st St. NW at Q Street. ☎ *202-387-2151. Internet:* www.phillips collection.org. *Metro: Dupont Circle. From Q Street exit, walk one block west on Q. Open: Sun noon–7 p.m., until 5 p.m. in summer; Tue–Sat 10 a.m.–5 p.m., until 8:30 p.m. on Thur. Closed: Mon. Admission: Weekends $7.50 ($4 students and seniors older than 62); weekdays contributions requested; younger than 18 always free. Additional fees for some special exhibitions.*

The Renwick Gallery
Downtown

Across from the White House, this striking Second Empire building shows off American crafts from the 19th century to the present. Rotating exhibits from the gallery's permanent collection are displayed in the second floor galleries.

Among the more notable are Larry Fuente's *Game Fish,* with its glittering scales of game pieces, buttons, and beads, and Albert Paley's *Portal Gates,* made from forged steel, brass, copper, and bronze. Temporary exhibits of American crafts and decorative arts are shown on the first floor. Wood turning, leaded glasswork, and quilts are just a few of the crafts to be featured. Tours start in the lobby Monday through Friday at noon, May through August, except Memorial Day and July 4.

Pennsylvania Avenue NW at 17th Street. ☎ *202-357-2700. Internet:* american art.si.edu. *Metro: Farragut West. From 17th Street exit, walk two blocks south on 17th. Open: Daily 10 a.m.–5:30 p.m. Closed: Dec. 25. Admission: Free.*

The Textile Museum
North of Dupont Circle

More than 17,000 objects, dating from 3,000 B.C. to the present, are held in the Textile Museum's collection. It all started with George Hewitt Myers's Chinese silks, tapestries, and hand-woven Oriental rugs. The gift shop is noteworthy, too, featuring silk scarves and ties, Tibetan rug squares, and other interesting items.

2320 S St. NW between 23rd and 24th streets. ☎ *202-667-0441. Internet:* www. textilemuseum.org. *Metro: Dupont Circle. From Q Street exit, walk two blocks west on Q, right on Massachusetts Avenue four blocks, right on 24th Street one block, and then right on S. (Note: It's uphill.) Or take an N-series Metrobus up*

Massachusetts. Or take a taxi. Open: Mon–Sat 10 a.m.–5 p.m., Sun 1–5 p.m. Closed: Federal Holidays and Dec. 24. Admission: Suggested donation $5.

Exploring Museums of Many Cultures

When you consider how many cultures created the nation's character, you won't be surprised to find that Washington has many ethnic attractions. A visit to one or more of these institutions can round out any capital experience.

Anacostia Museum
Anacostia

With a special focus on the Washington area, the Anacostia Museum studies and explains American history, society, and creativity from an African-American perspective. This Smithsonian museum, named after Washington's lesser-known river, manages a large permanent collection of historic documents, art, and sheet music. The museum presents special exhibitions, talks, workshops, and educational programs. Budget about an hour here.

1901 Fort Place SE between Bruce Place and 18th Street. ☎ **202-287-3306.** *Internet:* www.si.edu/anacostia. *Take a taxi. Open: Daily: 10 a.m.–5 p.m. Closed Dec. 25. Admission: Free.*

B'nai B'rith Klutznick National Jewish Museum
Downtown

Jewish contributions to popular culture, the arts, public service, and social welfare are a prime focus of this museum. The collection includes Jewish ceremonial and archaeological objects, coins, and works by contemporary Jewish artists. You need to call ahead for tickets for admission.

2020 K St. NW between 20th and 21st streets NW. ☎ **202-857-6583.** *Internet:* http://bbi.koz.com. *Metro: Farragut North. From K Street exit, walk three-plus blocks west on K. Open: Call for details. Admission: Free.*

Frederick Douglass National Historic Site
Anacostia

This 21-room house on the Anacostia River was home to Frederick Douglass, the 19th-century abolitionist and civil rights leader, who was born a slave and eventually served as a District of Columbia Council member, D.C.'s U.S. marshal, and U.S. minister to Haiti. The home and visitor center feature original furnishings and tell the story of Douglass' remarkable life. Be sure to see the short film for an overview of his life. A bookstore and restrooms are on site. Space is limited, so call ahead to find the best time to visit and to make a reservation. Plan to spend an hour here.

1411 W St. SE at 1th Street. ☎ *800-426-5961. Internet:* www.nps.gov/frdo *Take a taxi. Or take Tourmobile's Frederick Douglass tour (see Chapter 18). Open: April 15–Oct. 15 9 a.m.–5 p.m.; Oct. 16–April 14 9 a.m.–4 p.m. Closed Jan. 1, Thanksgiving, Dec. 25. Admission: Free. Fee for groups of five or larger.*

Interior Department Museum

Downtown

Despite what one wag suggested, this museum isn't devoted to the decoration of government offices. The Interior Department, of course, is the Cabinet agency responsible for the interior of the country, notably America's natural resources and Indian affairs. One section of the museum contains exhibits about Native American history and life. You can view pottery, baskets, other traditional crafts, and contemporary art. The museum also has a crafts shop. A much more extensive facility — the Smithsonian's National Museum of the American Indian — is scheduled to open on the Mall in 2004. Figure on spending 30 minutes here.

18th and E streets NW. ☎ *202-208-4743. Internet:* www.doi.gov/museum/museum. *Metro: Farragut West. From 18th Street exit, walk south five blocks on 18th and then right on E. Open: Mon–Fri and third Sat of each month 8:30 a.m.–4:30 p.m. Closed: Federal holidays. Admission: Free. Adult visitors must show photo ID, such as a driver's license.*

Smelling the Roses: Gardens and Other Places to Rest

You can find a lot of green spaces in and around Washington, D.C., many dating back to the founding of the city, and some even before that time. The temperate climate (well in the spring, anyway) means that the gardens are blooming pretty much throughout the year.

Dumbarton Oaks

Georgetown

I can give you a lot of reasons to visit Dumbarton Oaks. If you're interested in Byzantine art, pre-Columbian art, landscape architecture, gardens, or history — or any combination of thereof — you'll enjoy a visit to Dumbarton Oaks, on the northern edge of residential Georgetown. I could easily have put this place in just about any other section in this chapter. I chose this one because the gardens are what prompted my wife and me to bring our daughter here when she was little. It's a great place for little ones to run around and let off steam.

Robert and Mildred Bliss — wealthy collectors of Byzantine and pre-Columbian art and of books on gardens — purchased this 19th-century mansion in 1920 and then restored and expanded it over the years. In

1940, they donated the building, some of the grounds, their collections, and an endowment to Harvard University, which uses the property as a study center and museum.

The mansion hosted the Dumbarton Oaks Conversations — international discussions that laid the foundations for the United Nations — in 1944; that's the attraction for history buffs. The art from the Byzantine Empire is considered by many the most important Byzantine collection in America. Mildred Woods employed noted landscape gardener Beatrix Farrand to design the gardens, which were envisioned as a unique American incorporation of elements from traditional French, English, and Italian gardens. They're in bloom from early spring through fall. Blooming starts in mid-March and April with cherry trees, forsythia, wisteria, azaleas, dogwood, lilacs, and magnolias and ends in October with chrysanthemums. The museum shop sells postcards, note cards, slides, and books about the gardens and the collections.

1703 32nd St. NW between R and S streets. (Garden entrance at R and 31st.) ☎ *202-339-6401. Internet:* www.doaks.org. *Metro: Foggy Bottom-George Washington University. From Metrorail station, take Georgetown Metro Connection shuttle bus to Wisconsin and R streets and then walk one block east on R. Or take a 30-series Metrobus to Wisconsin and R. Or catch a cab. Garden open: Daily Mar 15–Oct from 2–6 p.m.; Nov–Mar 14 from 2–5 p.m. Closed in inclement weather and national holidays. Museum open: Tue–Sun 2–5 p.m. Closed national holidays. Garden admission: Adults $5, children and seniors $3. Museum admission: $1 donation suggested.*

Enid A. Haupt Garden
The Mall

This 4.2-acre park, located between the Smithsonian Castle and Independence Avenue, is a pleasant place to rest when you're touring the National Mall. It's named for the woman who endowed it, an heir to the Annenburg publishing fortune and a one-time editor and publisher of *Seventeen* magazine who loved gardens and could afford to finance them.

The Haupt Garden actually is a collection of gardens that grow above the underground sections of the Arthur M. Sackler Gallery of Asian Art, the National Museum of African Art, and the S. Dillon Ripley Center's International Gallery. The Parterre is a large flower bed, lined with benches, in which designs are formed with the dirt, grass, shrubs, and flowers. The Moorish-style Fountain Garden, near the African Art Museum, was inspired by the Alhambra Palace garden in Granada, Spain, which was constructed when the Moors ruled that section of Europe. The inspiration for the Island Garden was the Temple of Heaven in Beijing; it features a circular granite "island" and granite walkways that bridge the water. Catch your breath, rest your feet, and reflect before moving on to the next museum.

Independence Avenue SW at 10th Street ☎ *202-357-2700. Internet:* www.si.edu/ horticulture/gardens/Haupt/hpt_home.htm. *Metro: Smithsonian. From* _the Independence Avenue exit, cross Independence and walk to the right. Open: Memorial Day–Labor Day from 7 a.m.–8 p.m.; rest of the year until 5:45 p.m. Closed Dec. 25. Admission: Free._

Lafayette Square
Downtown

Once part of the White House North Lawn and now separated from the lawn by Pennsylvania Avenue, Lafayette Square is a marvelous place for sitting, snacking, or even stretching out on the grass. Gazing to the south, you see the White House with the Washington Monument peeking over the roof in the near distance. To the west are historic houses that lead you to feel you're visiting a 19th-century town square. You can check out an ethnically diverse collection of statues — Marquis de Lafayette, for whom the square is named, the Comte Jean de Rochambeau, Thaddeus Kosciusko, Baron Frederick von Steuben, and Andrew Jackson on horseback.

The park attracts lunching workers from nearby office buildings, resting tourists, and a diverse collection of demonstrators who like to display their signs at the president's door. Over the centuries, the land has accommodated a farmhouse, an apple orchard, a cemetery, and a racetrack. According to the National Park Service, it's also home to "the highest density of squirrels per square acre ever recorded."

Bordered by Pennsylvania Avenue NW and 15th, 17th, and H streets. ☎ _202-208-1631. Internet:_ www.nps.gov/whho/lafayettepk/index.htm. _Metro: McPherson Square. From the Vermont Avenue-White House exit, walk south one block on Vermont Avenue, cross H Street, and enter the park. Open: 24 hours. Admission: Free._

United States Botanic Garden
Capitol Hill

The nation's greenhouse sits in a sort of no-man's land just west of Capitol Hill, but not really on the National Mall. Because it's run by Congress, I call it a Capitol Hill attraction. And attractive it is, having just been through a major-major-major renovation.

About 4,000 plants are on display inside the Conservatory. More are across Independence Avenue in Bartholdi Park, which also contains the Bartholdi Fountain, created for the 1876 International Centennial Exhibition in Philadelphia by Frederic Auguste Bartholdi — the French designer of the Statue of Liberty. Construction of a three-acre National Garden, just west of the Conservatory, began in 2001 and is scheduled for completion in spring 2004.

Free 45-minute tours of the Conservatory are conducted every day at 11 a.m. and 1:30 p.m., or you can just wander about on your own. The conservatory is particularly appealing in winter, when it serves as a tropical respite from the cold. It's a great place to visit in the Christmas season, when poinsettias brighten holiday spirits.

Maryland Avenue SW at 1st Street. ☎ *202-225-8333. Internet:* www.usbg.gov. *Metro: Federal Center Southwest. Walk three blocks north on 3rd Street and then turn right on Maryland. Conservatory open: Daily 10 a.m.–5 p.m. Bartholdi Park open: Daily dawn to dusk. Admission: Free.*

Especially for Architecture Buffs

Just about every building on the D.C. tourist itinerary has something to offer architecture enthusiasts. You can spend hours — days — studying the details of the great government buildings, such as the Capitol, the White House, the Supreme Court, and the Library of Congress. Many of the monuments are architectural triumphs, like the Jefferson Memorial, the Lincoln Memorial, the Vietnam Veterans Memorial, and the Washington Monument, to name a few. If you take the train to Beaux Arts Union Station or fly into National Airport, you're instantly exposed to fascinating architecture.

National Airport
Virginia

Because travelers often heed advice to get to the airport early, they find themselves with lots of time on their hands. If you find yourself in those shoes, you may want to tour National Airport on your way out of town. Here's how much of an attraction this place is: Just before the new terminal opened in 1997, thousands of Washingtonians (including our family) showed up for an open house.

What you find here is the historically interesting old Terminal A and the modern new terminal. Because of heightened security, only ticketed passengers are allowed access to the gate concourses. But you can see much of the interesting stuff from outside those security checkpoints.

State-of-the-art when it opened in 1941, Terminal A was designed to be both "modern" and reflective of the area's Colonial and Neoclassical architecture. It was built on curve and featured a multilevel waiting room with picture windows that looked over the runways to the Washington skyline across the Potomac River. It will be restored to its 1941 condition and continue to house gates, ticket counters, and concessions.

The new terminal also offers picture-window views of Washington landmarks. The first things you notice, of course, are the glass and metal in the walls, ceilings, and roof, with 54 domes designed to suggest Thomas Jefferson's contributions to architecture. Works by 30 artists are incorporated into the floors, walls, windows, and other elements of the terminal in various materials, including stained glass, marble, and glass mosaics; terrazzo; cast bronze; hammered aluminum and copper; painted steel; porcelain enamel; paint on board; and paint on canvas. As a practical, functioning airport, it's easy to navigate and has an unusually good collection of eating and shopping spots.

Off George Washington Memorial Parkway in Arlington, Va. ☎ *703-417-8000. Internet:* www.metwashairports.com/national. *Metro: National Airport. Open: 24 hours. Admission: Free.*

National Building Museum
Downtown

The best place to begin an architecture tour of Washington is the National Building Museum, dedicated to architecture, design, engineering, construction, and urban planning. The museum itself occupies a fascinating building. Designed in 1881 and opened in 1887, it was constructed to house the Pension Bureau, a predecessor of today's Department of Veterans Affairs.

Among the building's most striking features is a three-foot-high terracotta frieze that wraps for 1,200 feet around the entire exterior. Designed by Caspar Buberl, the frieze depicts a parade of Civil War soldiers. Working before the advent of modern air-conditioning and efficient electric lighting, architect Montgomery C. Meigs employed a system of windows, vents, and open archways to bathe the Great Hall in light and air. The great hall has a central fountain and eight 75-foot-tall Corinthian columns that are among the tallest interior columns in the world. Its monumental dimensions and spectacular appearance make the Great Hall a popular site for major events, including presidential inaugural balls. (If you'd like to host a party here, rental fees start at $11,000.)

The focus of the museum is on the building process, architectural styles, and construction techniques. The collection contains 40,000 photographs, 68,000 prints and drawings, 100 linear feet of documents, and 2,100 objects such as construction materials and architectural fragments. Recent topics included design proposals for a new New York World Trade Center, do-it-yourself home improvement in America, 20th-century architecture drawings, transit in the American city, and an exhibit called "Tools as Art: Instruments of Change." Planned for 2003 and 2004 are exhibits on environmentally friendly architecture, the preservation of Mount Vernon, windows in the American home, and elevators, escalators, and moving sidewalks.

At the information desk, you can get free activity booklets for children ages 6 to 13. Family-oriented programs are scheduled throughout the year; call or check the museum's Web site for details. Exhibits sometimes contain interactive elements aimed at youngsters. Brief hands-on programs are conducted from 2:30 to 3 p.m. each Saturday and Sunday.

401 F Street NW between 4th and 5th streets. ☎ *202-272-2448. Internet:* www.nbm. org. *Metro: Judiciary Square. From the F Street exit escalator, look in front of your nose. Open: Mon–Sat 10 a.m.–5 p.m. and Sunday 11 a.m.–5 p.m. Closed: Thanksgiving, Dec, 25, Jan. 1, and for occasional special events. Admission: Free, but a $5 donation is requested.*

The Octagon Museum
Downtown

The Octagon is a museum of architecture and an architecturally interesting building; it's also a place where international history was made. The Treaty of Ghent, which ended the War of 1812, was signed here. During that war, President and Mrs. Madison fled here after the British set fire to the White House. The OSS, predecessor to the CIA, set up shop in the Octagon during World War II, and the National Trust for Historic Preservation was headquartered here immediately afterward.

Built between 1799 and 1801, the Octagon is one of the oldest structures in the Capital and one of the best examples of Federal architecture in the country. The Octagon was designed by William Thornton, the first architect of the U.S. Capitol. Strangely, it doesn't have eight sides. While it's not known how the Octagon acquired its name, it may have come from the round entrance hall. According to the architectural foundation, round rooms in the 18th century often were formed from eight angled walls that were plastered smooth in a circle and were referred to as "octagon salons." The house was built for John and Ann Ogle Tayloe, who raised 15 children in the Octagon and continued to live here until their deaths — John's in 1828, Ann's in 1855.

Visitors can tour the house and explore exhibits. If you tour the building, you see the Octagon as it looked during the last 11 years of John Tayloe's life. The museum collection includes more than 100,000 architectural drawings, 30,000 historic photographs, 760 pieces of decorative arts, and nearly 14,000 archeological artifacts and architectural fragments from the building and its grounds, as well as scrapbooks, sketchbooks, manuscripts, and models.

1799 New York Avenue NW at 18th Street. ☎ *202-638-3105. Internet:* www.arch foundation.org/octagon. *Metro: Farragut West. From the 18th Street exit, walk five blocks south on 18th. Open: Tue–Sun from 10 a.m.–4 p.m. Closed: Mon, Thanksgiving, Dec. 25, and Jan. 1. Admission: Adults $5, children and seniors $3.*

Union Station
Capitol Hill

This is Washington's back-to-the-future headquarters. After years of blight, Union Station has become the most bustling hub in town. The train is the very best way to travel in the Washington-New York corridor today.

Hordes of subway travelers use the Metrorail station here daily. Maryland and Virginia commuter trains converge here. Cabs line up for business. Tour buses come and go. And — as I detail in other chapters — Union Station is a great place for shopping, eating, movie-going, and teens hanging out. More than 25 million people pass through this place every year.

The building is, indeed, a railroad palace. It was designed in grand Beaux-Arts style by Daniel Burnham, who gathered inspiration from the Diocletian Baths and the Arch of Constantine in Rome. When construction was completed in 1908, Union Station occupied more land area than any other U.S. building and there was no bigger train station in the world. Presidents really used the Presidential Suite (now home to B. Smith's Restaurant), and kings, queens, and other world leaders passed through with regularity.

Airplanes and interstate highways drove the station into a long decline. But a monumental renovation campaign led to a spectacular reopening in 1988, and now you can gaze upon the grandeur that welcomed travelers nearly a century ago — with a lot of new amenities.

A fountain and statue of Columbus stand outside the building, along with a replica of the Liberty Bell. The facade is festooned with eagles. Inside, sculptures of Roman soldiers by Augustus Saint-Gaudens stand guard over the Main Hall, which features a 96-foot high barrel-vaulted ceiling. The East Hall boasts stenciled skylights. At the east end of the East Hall, be sure to peek into B. Smith's to see the soaring ceilings and ornate architecture of the Presidential Suite.

50 Massachusetts Ave. NE. ☎ *202-371-9441. Internet:* www.unionstationdc. com. *Metro: Union Station. Open: All the time. Admission: Free.*

Chapter 18

Seeing Washington by Guided Tour

· ·

In This Chapter

▶ Evaluating guided tours

▶ Taking a special-interest tour

· ·

*T*ravelers with limited time and/or limited mobility can benefit from taking a general orientation tour. So can visitors who like to check out the forest before inspecting the trees. Guided tours also make sense for those with kids in tow, seniors, and travelers with special interests. In Washington, you can tour historic, cultural, and even scandal-ridden sites. And you can do it by bus, bike, boat, and foot — for an hour or for a day or more.

Seeing the City on General Orientation Tours

Tourmobile (☎ **888-868-7707** or 202-554-5100; Internet: www.tourmobile.com) takes the prize as the best general tour operator in the city. The area's largest sightseeing organization is licensed by the National Park Service and operates its tram trains year-round.

The company's **American Heritage Tour** makes about two dozen tram stops on or near the Mall and Pennsylvania Avenue and then heads off to Arlington Cemetery for another four stops. You can get off and on the trams as often as you like. Some visitors remain on board for an entire loop, listening as the Tourmobile guide points out places of interest and discusses their history. Then they take a second go-round, getting off at spots that interest them.

Using Tourmobile is an excellent way to familiarize yourself with the major tourist areas. The tour costs $18 for adults, $8 for kids 3 to 11, and is free for younger tots. You can purchase tickets from the driver or at ticket booths at select boarding points along the tram route.

Tourmobile Route

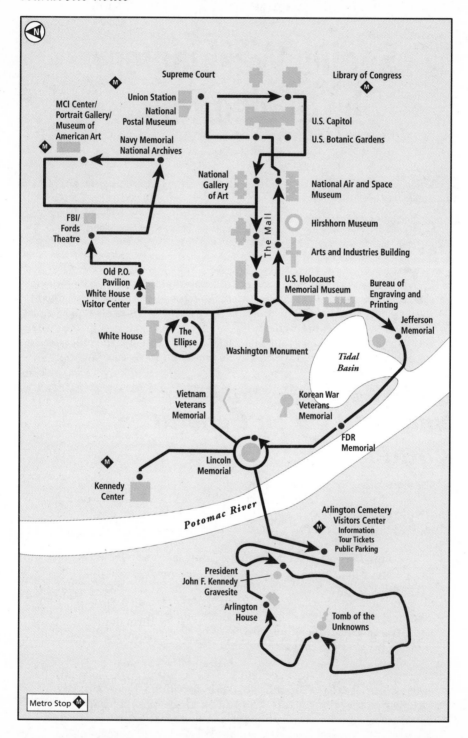

If you find the prospect of tackling both D.C. and Arlington in the space of a day too taxing, Tourmobile offers a separate Arlington Cemetery Tour. The cost is $5.25 for adults, $2.50 children 3 to 11, and is free for those younger. You can purchase tickets at the Arlington Cemetery Visitors Center.

You also can take the Tourmobile to the Frederick Douglass National Historic Site (see Chapter 17), which is off the beaten tourist path. This black heritage tour takes you through Capitol Hill and past Lincoln Park and the Mary McLeod Bethune Memorial on your way to a guided tour at Douglass' house and the visitor center there. The three-hour tour costs $7 for adults, $3.50 for children 3 to 11.

 After 1 p.m., Tourmobile sells "advance tickets" good for the rest of that day and all the next. Because you have unlimited reboarding rights, advance tickets are a great way to get around the major tourist attractions. Cost is $20 for adults and $9 for kids ages 3 to 11.

Old Town Trolley (☎ 202-832-9800; Internet: www.historictours. com/washington) has an advantage over Tourmobile in that it offers pick-up and drop-off service at several hotels — Grand Hyatt, Capital Hilton, Marriott Metro Center, and Hyatt Regency. These buses, outfitted to look like old-time trolley cars, also stop at places farther away, such as Georgetown and the National Cathedral. For a full list of boarding stops, see the company's Web site or call. As with Tourmobile, you can get on and off the trolley whenever the spirit moves you. It takes about 2¼ hours for a trolley to complete one loop. First departure from Union Station is 9 a.m. Trolleys stop running at 5:30 p.m. (Inquire about the final departure from the last stop you plan to use.) Prices are $24 for adults, $12 children 4 to 12, and younger kids free.

 The Trolley also takes you on a 2½-hour **Monuments by Moonlight** tour that lets you see D.C.'s memorials and monuments illuminated in all their nighttime glory — at least during part of the tour. The guides let you in on such secrets as which president's ghost haunts Congress. (Which ones don't?) The tour departs nightly from Union Station and costs $25 for adults and $13 for children 4 to 12. Reservations are suggested. Times vary according to season, so call ahead. The more time you actually spend in the dark, the more impressive the tour will be.

Gray Line Sightseeing Tours (☎ 800-862-1400; Internet: www.grayline. com) offers an extensive array of D.C. tours as well as trips to Maryland and Virginia attractions by motor coach, usually from the Gray Line terminal in Union Station. Always call ahead to confirm departure times and points because they're subject to change. Here's a sampling of the company's touring options:

> ✔ **L'il Red Trolley Tours** are similar to Tourmobile and Old Town Trolley and make a 2½-hour continuous loop around Washington. Some stops include the Capitol, the National Zoo, Arlington

Cemetery, and Georgetown. Riders can hop on and off as they choose. The tour costs $28 for ages 12 and older and $12 for kids ages 3 to 11.

✔ The **Public Buildings Tour** is a nine-hour trek past and through monuments, museums, memorials, government buildings, and historical sites. The tour starts at 8:30 a.m. Monday through Saturday and costs $38 for ages 12 and older and $19 for kids 3 to 11.

✔ Gray Line starts its three-hour **after-dark tour** nightly at 7:45 p.m. except on Jan. 1, July 4, Thanksgiving, Dec. 24, Dec. 25, and Dec. 31. Cost is $28 for ages 12 and older and $14 for 3 to 11.

✔ A nine-hour **Combination Tour** takes in top D.C. sites plus visits to Arlington National Cemetery, George Washington's Mount Vernon home, and Old Town Alexandria, Va. The tour departs at 8:30 a.m. daily except Thanksgiving, Dec. 25, and Jan. 1. It costs $48 for those 12 and older and $24 for kids 3 to 11.

Gray Line also offers multilingual tours and tours to Monticello, Colonial Williamsburg, and Gettysburg.

DC Ducks (☎ **202-966-3825;** Internet: www.historictours.com/washington) supply an entertaining combination of history and silliness. Utilizing amphibious vehicles that transported troops and supplies during World War II, each Duck ferries up to 28 visitors to several major D.C. sights before plunging into the Potomac for a half-hour swim. The 90-minute keels-on-wheels tours depart daily on the hour from Union Station 10 a.m. to 3 p.m. in spring and summer. Tours may be cancelled in bad weather, so it pays to phone ahead. The narrated 90-minute ride is $25 ages 13 and up, $12 for children 4 to 12, and free for younger kids. The drivers will be wise-quacking, and eventually so will you.

Pounding the Pavement with Walking Tours

If your feet aren't too tired, consider a walking tour to discover historic sights and architectural gems up close. **Anthony S. Pitch** — author, historian, journalist, and charming guide with encyclopedic memory — doles out an impressive amount of historical and architectural information during the various tours he leads around town. C-SPAN filmed one of his treks. His various walking tours include Lincoln's assassination, Georgetown homes of the famous and infamous, A, and the and White House area, and the British burning of the Capitol and the White House. Pitch leads public tours, which you can join for $10 to $15, as well as tours for groups for $200 to $300. Get details at www.dcsightseeing.com or ☎ **301-294-9514.**

Riding the Waves on River Tours

Hit the deck and see the capital city's pretty face from the Potomac. For a 50-minute narrated float, take Capitol River Cruises' *Nightingale* riverboat from Georgetown's Washington Harbour dock (end of 31st Street). The cruise runs hourly 11 a.m. to 9 p.m. every day. The cost is $10 for adults and $5 for kids 3 to 12. Call ☎ **800-405-5511** or 301-460-7447 or visit its Web site at www.capitolrivercruises.com.

Cruising on the C&O Canal

Board a mule-drawn canal boat for a trip along the historic C&O Canal. *The Georgetown* is berthed in (where else?) Georgetown, near the Chesapeake and Ohio Canal National Historical Park visitor center, 1057 Thomas Jefferson St. NW, just south of M Street. From spring into early fall, the boat plies the canal for delightful hour rides, manned (and womaned) by volunteers in period clothing, while National Park Service rangers narrate. Schedules vary, so call (☎ **202-653-5190**) or check the Web (www.nps.gov/choh) for details. Tickets are $8 ($6 seniors 62 and older), $5 kids 4 to 14, and free 3 and younger.

Wheeling (and Dealing?) around D.C.

Several guided bicycle tours are available through **Bike the Sites** (☎ **202-966-8662**; Internet: www.bikethesites.com). The three-hour Capital Sites Tour passes 55 landmarks, and the guide stops frequently so that bikers can consume some history and humor with their granola bars. You'll ride about eight miles, almost all on flat trails. The tour costs $40 ($30 for children 6 to 12) and includes a bike, helmet, snack, and water bottle. Tours start at 10 a.m. and 2 p.m. March through December. Call ahead to make sure that the tour has room when you want to go.

Chapter 19

A Shopper's Guide to Washington, D.C.

. . . .

In This Chapter

▶ Getting a feel for the shopping scene

▶ Visiting the outdoor markets

▶ Exploring great shopping neighborhoods

▶ Finding shops for specific needs

. . . .

I know that shopping wasn't your top reason for coming to Washington. And I know that, to the extent you'd like to taste some of the shopping Washington has to offer; you don't want to visit the same national chains that you can find back home. So as I consider the shopping that you may want — or need — to do here, I clue you in to the local shops, as well as the familiar names.

Surveying the Shopping Scene

You won't find much clothing, furniture, or fashion made in D.C. Washington focuses more on making laws, rules, regulations, and headlines. But the Washington area does have artists and craftsmen whose work is displayed in D.C. galleries. Certain shops seek out interesting products that aren't found in run-of-the-mill retail establishments.

You can find the best buys in D.C. at the museum and gallery shops, because they make an effort to sell things related to their collections and that you can't locate in your average suburban shopping mall.

It's impossible to talk about the best times to find sales or general shopping hours anymore. Shoppers demand sales, so the typical retailer puts on some kind of sale most of the time. Retailers also set their shopping hours according to their perceptions of their customers' work schedules and shopping habits and as part of special promotions. During the week that I'm writing this chapter, for example, Hecht's downtown store

Shopping in Washington, D.C.

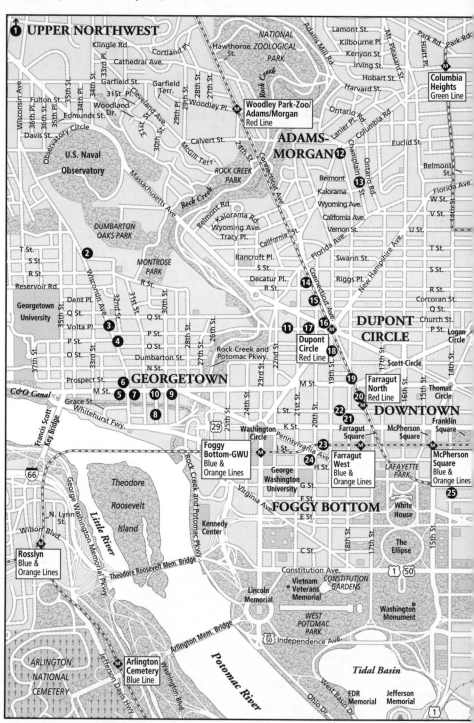

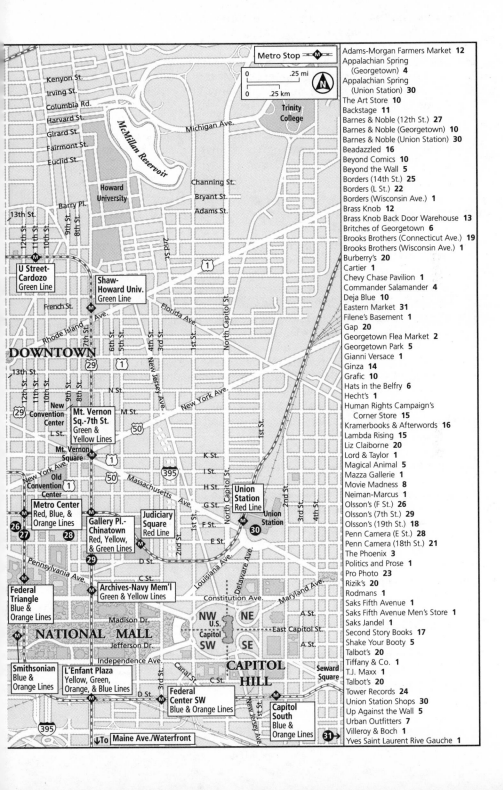

Adams-Morgan Farmers Market **12**
Appalachian Spring
  (Georgetown) **4**
Appalachian Spring
  (Union Station) **30**
The Art Store **10**
Backstage **11**
Barnes & Noble (12th St.) **27**
Barnes & Noble (Georgetown) **10**
Barnes & Noble (Union Station) **30**
Beadazzled **16**
Beyond Comics **10**
Beyond the Wall **5**
Borders (14th St.) **25**
Borders (L St.) **22**
Borders (Wisconsin Ave.) **1**
Brass Knob **12**
Brass Knob Back Door Warehouse **13**
Britches of Georgetown **6**
Brooks Brothers (Connecticut Ave.) **19**
Brooks Brothers (Wisconsin Ave.) **1**
Burberry's **20**
Cartier **1**
Chevy Chase Pavilion **1**
Commander Salamander **4**
Deja Blue **10**
Eastern Market **31**
Filene's Basement **1**
Gap **20**
Georgetown Flea Market **2**
Georgetown Park **5**
Gianni Versace **1**
Ginza **14**
Grafic **10**
Hats in the Belfry **6**
Hecht's **1**
Human Rights Campaign's
  Corner Store **15**
Kramerbooks & Afterwords **16**
Lambda Rising **15**
Liz Claiborne **20**
Lord & Taylor **1**
Magical Animal **5**
Mazza Gallerie **1**
Movie Madness **8**
Neiman-Marcus **1**
Olsson's (F St.) **26**
Olsson's (7th St.) **29**
Olsson's (19th St.) **18**
Penn Camera (E St.) **28**
Penn Camera (18th St.) **21**
The Phoenix **3**
Politics and Prose **1**
Pro Photo **23**
Rizik's **20**
Rodmans **1**
Saks Fifth Avenue **1**
Saks Fifth Avenue Men's Store **1**
Saks Jandel **1**
Second Story Books **17**
Shake Your Booty **5**
Talbot's **20**
Tiffany & Co. **1**
T.J. Maxx **1**
Talbot's **20**
Tower Records **24**
Union Station Shops **30**
Up Against the Wall **5**
Urban Outfitters **7**
Villeroy & Boch **1**
Yves Saint Laurent Rive Gauche **1**

opened at 7 a.m. three days, 10 a.m. three days, and 11 a.m. one day. It closed on different evenings at 7, 8, 9, and 11 p.m.

Call ahead if you want to know a certain store's hours. Otherwise, you can be fairly confident that most D.C. stores will be open at least from late morning to early evening. You're more likely to find late-night shops in late-night entertainment areas.

Don't forget to factor in your contribution to the local government's coffers when you consider the price of an item. The sales tax is 5.75% in Washington, 5% in Maryland, and 4.5% in Virginia.

Checking Out the Big Names

Hecht's (Internet: www.hechts.com) is the only local name left in the Washington department store scene, and it's part of the May Co. chain. The other department stores within the city are Lord & Taylor and Neiman Marcus, in the Upper Northwest/Maryland neighborhood that I describe later in this chapter as Washington's Rodeo Drive. Saks Fifth Avenue has a men's store on Wisconsin Avenue just south of the Washington-Maryland border and a women's store just north.

Hecht's flagship store is at 1201 G St. NW, at the Metro Center Metrorail Station (☎ 202-628-6661). Another store is located just north of the Washington-Maryland line at 5400 Wisconsin Ave. NW, at the Friendship Heights Metrorail Station (☎ 301-654-7600). Hecht's is Washington's most comprehensive department store and also the most moderately priced, so I shop here often.

Neiman-Marcus — the Texas-based emporium that sells six-figure Christmas gifts and is picketed regularly by anti-fur activists — anchors one side of the Mazza Gallerie, an urban shopping mall at 5300 Wisconsin Ave. (☎ 202-966-9700; Internet: www.neimanmarcus.com). It's across Western Avenue from Hecht's and right at the Friendship Heights Metrorail Station.

Lord & Taylor, best known for women's clothing, is at 5255 Western Ave. NW, also near the Friendship Heights Metrorail Station (☎ 202-362-9600; Internet: www.lordandtaylor.com).

Saks Fifth Avenue's Maryland store is a rather regal structure that stands oddly alone in the midst of its own large parking lot at 5555 Wisconsin Ave. (☎ 301-657-9000; Internet: www.saksfifthavenue.com). The Saks Fifth Avenue Men's Store sits across Mazza Gallerie's main lobby from Neiman-Marcus, at 5300 Wisconsin NW (☎ 202-363-2059).

Taking It to the Street

Old-fashioned markets of various kinds are still alive and kicking in Washington. The early dog gets the flea — or something like that — when shoppers battle for bargains at flea markets. And don't be afraid to bargain for your bargain. A lot of folks think that's the main reason to frequent flea markets. Here are a couple of interesting markets:

✔ Capitol Hill's **Eastern Market** (☎ 202-546-2698; Metro: Eastern Market) is a riot of activity on weekends. Scores upon scores of farmers, grocers, artists, craftsmen, and vendors peddle their wares inside the historic market building and in the open spaces and storefronts that surround it. Chefs join the locals and party-givers who shop here on Saturday, when the produce and flowers are especially plentiful. Activity occurs all week long inside the 130-year-old building, where various butchers, bakers, fishmongers, and grocers have their permanent stands in the South Hall. The North Hall has been turned into the Market 5 Gallery, a center for artists and the community. The market is at 7th Street SE between C Street and North Carolina Avenue. The South Hall is open Tuesday through Friday from 10 a.m. to 6 p.m., Saturday from 8 a.m. to 6 p.m., and Sunday from 8 a.m. to 4 p.m. The Gallery is open Tuesday through Friday from 11 a.m. to 5 p.m. and Saturday and Sunday from 10 a.m. to 5 p.m. Both are closed Mondays.

✔ The **Georgetown Flea Market** is flooded every Sunday from March through December with frenzied shoppers hoping for that once-in-a-lifetime bargain. Nearly 100 vendors sell antiques, furniture, clothing, and the odd knickknack. Former Secretary of State Madeleine Albright and Supreme Court Justice Stephen Breyer are among the bargain-hunting and antique-questing Washingtonians who have been spotted here. The flea market takes place in a parking lot west of Wisconsin Avenue NW on Georgetown's north end, S Street. Metro: Foggy Bottom. From the Metrorail station, take the Georgetown Shuttle bus to Wisconsin and R streets and then walk north on Wisconsin. Or catch a 30-series Metrobus. Or hail a cab. The market is open from 9 a.m. to 5 p.m. from March through December.

Hunting Down Bargains in D.C.'s Prime Shopping Zones

During your time in D.C., perhaps as a break from all that sightseeing, you may want to check out the following shopping areas. Each neighborhood has its own unique characteristics.

Adams-Morgan

Adams-Morgan is jammed with restaurants, clubs, and interesting shops — and with people trying to get into them. You can enjoy a number of secondhand and one-of-a-kind stores here selling clothing, antiques, foodstuffs, and other items. On Saturday, you can find a **farmers' market** at 18th Street NW and Columbia Road. Check out a haunt of decorators and do-it-yourselfers at **The Brass Knob,** 2311 18th, and the Brass Knob's **Back Door Warehouse,** 2329 Champlain St. (☎ 202-332-3370), for architectural acquisitions recovered from demolished houses and office buildings.

You can find the heart of this ethnically diverse neighborhood at the intersection of 18th and Columbia. Take Metrorail to the Woodley Park-Zoo-Adams-Morgan Station and walk south one long block on Connecticut Avenue, left five long blocks on Calvert Street., and then bear right a half block to 18th and Columbia. In evenings and on weekends, you can take the No. 98 Metrobus from the station to Calvert and Columbia. The bus runs weeknight from 6 p.m. to 2 a.m., Saturday from 10 a.m. to 2 a.m., and Sunday from 6 p.m. to midnight. Many people prefer to take the bus or a taxi after dark.

When you enter a Metrorail station to begin your trip, get a transfer ticket from the machine on the mezzanine level. Hand the bus driver the transfer and 25 cents.

Carry exact fare; the drivers do not make change. You don't get a discount when you transfer from bus to train.

Connecticut Avenue/Dupont Circle

The shopping on Connecticut Avenue changes flavor as you walk north from the Farragut North Metrorail Station at K Street to Dupont Circle and beyond. Between K and M streets, where many lawyers and lobbyists ply their not-unrelated trades, you can browse such traditional clothiers as **Brooks Brothers** (1201 Connecticut; ☎ 202-659-4650); **Talbot's** (1122 Connecticut; ☎ 202-887-6973); **Burberry's** (1155 Connecticut; ☎ 202-463-3000); and **Liz Claiborne** (1144 Connecticut; ☎ 202-785-8625). For casual wear, stroll into the **Gap** (1120 Connecticut; ☎ 202-429-0691). Women who need a little something to wear to a black-tie affair at the White House shop at **Rizik's** (1100 Connecticut; ☎ 202-223-4050), which has been offering designer garments and excellent service for nearly a century.

As you get closer to Dupont Circle, shoppers and shopkeepers are less likely to be wearing suits and carrying briefcases and more likely to be outfitted in jeans and unnatural hair colors. Check out the galleries, booksellers, secondhand stores, and specialty boutiques in this lively neighborhood, which is one of Washington's major entertainment centers, home to many nonprofit organizations, and the heart of D.C.'s gay community. Try **Kramerbooks & Afterwords** for books, drink, and food into the wee hours (1517 Connecticut; ☎ **202-387-1400**) or **Backstage** (2101 P St.; ☎ **202-775-1558**) for scripts, sheet music, and theatrical makeup. The staff at **Beadazzled** (1507 Connecticut; ☎ **202-265-2323**) can help you make a necklace from a large selection of beads. In search of a kimono and fan? Look no further than **Ginza** (1721 Connecticut; ☎ **202-331-7991**). **Lambda Rising** (1625 Connecticut; **202-462-6969**) is D.C.'s leading gay/lesbian-oriented bookstore. The **Human Rights Campaign,** America's largest gay rights political action organization, runs a store at 1629 Connecticut (☎ **202-232-8621**).

Georgetown

Many art galleries and specialty shops help make Georgetown one of Washington's liveliest neighborhoods from morning until after midnight. This community is truly diverse, sporting some of the city's most expensive residences, Georgetown University and its student rooming houses, and folks from all walks of life strolling the commercial blocks defined by M Street NW, Wisconsin Avenue, and nearby side streets. You see old women with blue hair and young women with blue hair — just different tints.

You'll recognize the major national chain stores when you walk past them, so let me concentrate on some others — local, or at least unusual.

- ✔ **Movie Madness** (1083 Thomas Jefferson St.; ☎ **202-337-7064**) sells movie posters.

- ✔ **Commander Salamander** (1420 Wisconsin; ☎ **202-337-2265**) sells punkish clothing, colored wigs, and off-the-wall gifts. This store is popular with teens.

- ✔ **Hats in the Belfry** (1237 Wisconsin; ☎ **202-342-2006**) sells a large selection of stylish and bizarre chapeaux from its tiny, but successful shop.

- ✔ **The Phoenix** (1514 Wisconsin; ☎ **202-338-4404**) has been selling Mexican folk art and bric-a-bracs, handcrafted silver jewelry, and those peasant blouses once favored by Joan Baez since 1955.

- ✔ **Grafic** (2904 M; ☎ **202-965-4747**) sells vintage posters.

- ✔ At **Deja Blue** (3005 M; ☎ **202-337-7100**), you can buy used blue jeans and other clothing.

- ✔ My daughter, the budding artist, tells me that **The Art Store** (3019 M; ☎ **202-342-7030**) stocks a huge selection of very good art supplies.

✔ It's not unique to Georgetown, but if you're in the market for a book, try the giant **Barnes & Noble** at the corner of M and Thomas Jefferson streets (3040 M; ☎ 202-965-9880).

✔ For another kind of bookstore — and more — check out **Beyond Comics** (3060 M; ☎ 202-333-8650) for comic books and the toys, dolls, T-shirts, and other paraphernalia that the comic characters spawn.

✔ **Urban Outfitters** (3111 M; ☎ 202-342-1012) outfits the young with clothing and accoutrements.

✔ **Up Against the Wall** (3219 M; ☎ 202-337-9316) sells clothes for teens and young adults.

✔ **Shake Your Booty** (3225 M; ☎ 202-333-6524) supplies boots — and shoes — to folks inclined to shake their thing.

✔ You can find posters, prints, and frames at **Beyond the Wall** (3281 M; ☎ 202-333-7790).

✔ **Britches of Georgetown** (1247 Wisconsin; ☎ 202-338-3330), which started as a local store and has widened its reach, still sells clothing here.

If you suffer mall withdrawal, you can find a slew of upscale national chains at **Georgetown Park** (3222 M; ☎ 202-298-5577). To explore something a bit different in the mall, check out the **Magical Animal** (☎ 202-337-3265), which features contemporary American jewelry and crafts, many with an animal theme. Billing itself as "the gift shop for people who love animals," this establishment is quick to assure shoppers that its gifts are "not made from any animal-derived materials."

Union Station

Union Station, a magnificent railway station, serves Washington in multiple ways as it approaches its 100th birthday in 2007 — train station, Metrorail station, intercity bus depot, tour bus departure point, fast-food station, full-service restaurant station, and super shopping destination. National chains are well represented here. But you also encounter some unique shops as well.

The most interesting spot here is the **East Hall Gallery.** The gallery's central open area contains small stands that sell a variety of jewelry, arts, and crafts. Encircling the open area are stores, one of which, **Appalachian Spring** (☎ 202-682-0505), is a favorite of my family. My daughter acquired a wonderful monkey puppet (named "Fred") here when she was much younger, and it still commands a prominent place in her bedroom. (Fred's younger siblings have taken his place in the store.) Appalachian Spring, founded in D.C. in 1964, originally dealt exclusively in arts and crafts from the Appalachian Mountains. Now it carries original works from throughout the United States.

Right outside the East Hall is a **coin shop** operated by the **U.S. Mint** (☎ 202-289-0609). Elsewhere in the station are a cigar shop that goes by the moniker **President Cigars** (☎ 202-289-3778) and a **Discovery Channel Store** (☎ 202-842-3700), run by the TV/Internet empire that's headquartered in Washington's Maryland suburbs.

If you get hungry here, you'll have no trouble finding something to eat. Several full-service restaurants are scattered around the station. (See Chapter 14 for reviews of America and B. Smith's.) The lower-level food court is enormous and offers a wide variety of cuisines.

Upper Wisconsin Avenue

The Upper Wisconsin Avenue area contains what I call Washington's Rodeo Drive. A few blocks of Wisconsin Avenue, on both sides of the Washington-Maryland border, provide retail space for some of the best-known names in up-up-up-scale shopping. (I happen to live near here, so I tell you about the downscale stores that I shop at as well.)

If Tiffany and friends appeal to you, gather up your titanium credit cards and follow me to **Saks Fifth Avenue** (5555 Wisconsin; ☎ 301-657-9000); **Saks Jandel** (5510 Wisconsin; ☎ 301-652-2250); **Saks Fifth Avenue Men's Store** (5300 Wisconsin; ☎ 202-363-2059); **Tiffany & Co.** (5500 Wisconsin; ☎ 301-657-8777); **Gianni Versace** (5454 Wisconsin; ☎ 301-907-9400); **Cartier** (5454 Wisconsin; ☎ 301-654-5858); **Neiman-Marcus** (5300 Wisconsin; ☎ 202-966-9700); **Brooks Brothers** (5504 Wisconsin; ☎ 301-654-8202); **Yves Saint Laurent Rive Gauche** (5510 Wisconsin; ☎ 301-656-8868); and **Villeroy & Boch** (5300 Wisconsin; ☎ 202-364-5180). **Lord & Taylor** (☎ 202-362-9600) is just two blocks southwest of Wisconsin at 5255 Western Ave. NW.

Now, just so you don't get the wrong idea about my neighborhood, let me tell you that you can have an eclectic shopping experience here if you want it. Neiman's and Saks' men's stores are major anchors of the **Mazza Gallerie** shopping mall. So is discounter **Filene's Basement** (☎ 202-966-0208). Across Jenifer Street from Mazza and across 44th Street from Lord & Taylor sits another discounter, **T.J. Maxx** (☎ 202-237-7616). This area also contains Washington's major local department store, **Hecht's** (5400 Wisconsin; ☎ 301-654-7600). Across Wisconsin from Mazza is another indoor mall, **Chevy Chase Pavilion.** You'll notice other familiar names on the storefronts along the avenue.

The easiest way to get to the area is to take Metrorail to the Friendship Heights Station and follow the signs to the Western Avenue Exits. After you go through the Metro gate and up the escalator, you find yourself in a sort of rotunda, with four exits to choose from. The hard left takes you to the Western Avenue and 44th Street exit and Mazza Gallerie. The soft left takes you to the Wisconsin and Western avenues exit, where you can enter Hecht's or continue up to the sidewalk, turn left, and walk up Wisconsin toward the upscale stores in Maryland. Straight ahead is the Western Avenue and Military Road exit, which takes you toward Clyde's restaurant and, during the life of this book, probably a major construction project as the Chevy Chase Center strip mall is rebuilt into a larger retail/office complex. (Clyde's may have to close for a while during 2004 because of the work.) The doors to your right take you right into Chevy Chase Pavilion.

This neighborhood presents you with numerous dining options. See Chapter 14 for reviews of Clyde's, Booeymonger, and Chipotle. You can get good, *huge* meals at the **Cheesecake Factory** (5335 Wisconsin; ☎ 202-364-4623) in the Pavilion, but you may have to wait at meal times because they don't take reservations. At **Maggiano's Little Italy** (5333 Wisconsin; ☎ 202-966-5500), they take reservations but don't seem to know what they're for; you can make a reservation, show up on time, and still have to wait. In the front end of Maggiano's, the **Corner Bakery** (☎ 202-237-2200) serves sandwiches, salads, and pastas. **Chadwick's** (5247 Wisconsin, ☎ 202-362-8040) is a neighborhood hangout; stick to burgers and salads, and you'll do okay. Fancier and more expensive is the French/Mediterranean restaurant Matisse (4934 Wisconsin; ☎ 202-244-5222). The Pavilion has a small food court.

For a look at a real Friendship Heights neighborhood institution, walk south on Wisconsin Avenue to Garrison Street and check out **Rodman's** (5100 Wisconsin; ☎ 202-363-3466). It's sort of a 21st-century general store. Someone from our house comes here nearly every day — to buy milk or wine or toothpaste or bath beads or toilet paper or a kitchen gadget or a birthday card or to get a watch repaired or to pick up a prescription. This place is, after all, a pharmacy . . . and an international food emporium and an electronics shop. Okay, you get the picture. (And you can get film and developing services.) If you need something that fits on a shelf, you just may find it here. If you're here at the right time, you might catch Roy Rodman roaming the aisles, negotiating a deal with a wholesaler on his portable phone. I was here once, after a blizzard, when grocers around town were running out of basics, and I noticed with surprise that Rodman's had lots of milk. I commented on this irony to a clerk, who told me that a milk truck had broken down in front of the store the day before, and Mr. Rodman had negotiated to buy the whole load.

Shopping for Specialties in D.C.

Are you looking to buy a specific product rather than to browse a shopping area? Check this section to find what you're looking for.

Bookstores

Washington is a literary town, so you can buy books in lots of places. Here's a sampling.

✔ It's off the beaten tourist path, but **Politics and Prose** (5015 Connecticut Ave. NW; ☎ **202-364-1919**) is a wonderful bookstore. It's a neighborhood institution in a neighborhood that happens to have lots of writers. So, beyond the books for sale, something is always going on here. C-SPAN is taping a writer who's reading from or talking about his book. An author is signing books or celebrating a new publication. (The coming-out party for the first book my wife and I wrote was here.) You may bump into George Will or Tim Russert while browsing in the current affairs section. A funky coffee house is in the lower level. Take an L4 Metrobus from the Dupont Circle Metrorail Station or catch a cab.

✔ Before it became a universal requirement that bookstores house cafes, **Kramerbooks & Afterwords** (1517 Connecticut Ave. NW; ☎ **202-387-1400**) was serving up food, drink, and live music with its printed products. I'm talking full bar, breakfast, lunch, dinner, and late supper. This place is open from 7:30 a.m. to 1 a.m. daily, and around the clock from Friday morning until Sunday night. Brunch is served Saturday and Sunday, including all night. Did I mention that they sell books?

✔ **Ollson's Books & Records** is Washington's local bookstore chain, with three shops in the city and others in the suburbs, including at National Airport (☎ **703-417-1087**). The stores survive in an era dominated by national chains by focusing on their communities. Each store's manager stocks reading matter and music that he knows his clientele is most interested in. You can find more theater, film, and history at the location that's next door to the Shakespeare Theater (418 7th St. NW; ☎ 202-638-7610 for books, ☎ 202-638-7613 for music), more ecology and politics for the activists who work around Dupont Circle at that branch (1307 19th St. NW; ☎ 202-785-1133 for books, ☎ 202-785-2662 for music), and more business and legal books downtown (1200 F St. NW; ☎ 202-347-3686 for books, ☎ 202-393-1853 for music).

✔ Bargain hunters and collectors browse the shelves of **Second Story Books** by Dupont Circle (2000 P St. NW; ☎ **202-659-8884**). It's Washington's premier used and rare books store and also has locations in the suburbs. Proprietor Allan Stypeck is a host of NPR's "The Book Guys." Together, the three stores have more than a million books, manuscripts, maps, prints, paintings, and vintage posters.

✔ You can get your **Borders Books & Music** fix downtown at 600 14th St. NW (☎ **202-737-1385**) and 1801 L St. NW (☎ 202-466-4999) and in Upper Northwest's Friendship Heights shopping district (5333 Wisconsin Ave. NW; ☎ 202-686-8270).

✔ **Barnes & Noble** stores are downtown (555 12th St NW; ☎ **202-347-0176**), in Union Station (☎ 202-289-1724), and in Georgetown (3040 M Street NW; ☎ 202-965-9880).

Cameras

If you need to get a camera repaired, want to buy some photographic equipment, or need expert advice on the best film for what you plan to shoot, here are two reputable companies that buy, sell, and repair equipment and sell and process film.

✔ **Penn Camera Exchange** has two shops downtown: 915 E St. NW (☎ 202-347-5777) and 1015 18th St. NW (☎ 202-785-7366).

✔ I've bought a camera, other equipment, and film from **Pro Photo** (1902 I St. NW; ☎ 202-223-1292). I was referred there in the first place by a professional photographer.

Music

So, what you really want is music for your ears? Here are some places to find it.

✔ **Tower Records** has an enormous store inside 2000 Pennsylvania Ave. NW (☎ 202-331-2400). You can browse music in all its styles — and videos — over two floors.

✔ Ollson's, Borders, and Barnes & Noble sell music as well as books. See the previous section for details.

Bibliophiles, music lovers, and collectors shouldn't overlook the museum and gallery stores.

Chapter 20

Itineraries for Cutting Washington Down to Size

● ●

In This Chapter

▶ Planning a three-day exploration

▶ Getting a fix on the government

▶ Having fun in Washington with kids

▶ Discovering time-tested tourist tactics

● ●

*S*o many sights, so little time! Is that your problem? Allow me to help with some suggested itineraries for seeing the top Washington sights in just three days, for seeing government in action, and for exploring D.C. with kids.

Refer to Chapter 14 for restaurant reviews and Chapter 16 for details about the top sites.

Exploring Washington in Three Days

Direct from the rectangular office (sorry, mine's not oval), here is a three-day agenda for visiting the cream of Washington's top sights and getting a taste of the city.

As of this writing, the **White House** is not open for tours. But if it reopens to the general public, you'll want to put it on your itinerary, too. Call ☎ 202-208-1631 for information and updates. And ask one of your members of Congress for VIP tour tickets.

Day one

If the **Supreme Court** is hearing arguments today, get in line on the court plaza before 10 a.m. and take a look. One line lets you take a quick peek; the other enables you to see the entire hour-long performance. Whether or not you take in an argument, plan on touring the Court, the **Capitol,** and the **Library of Congress.**

Before you leave home, contact your representative or a senator for tickets to the special congressional tours conducted in each of these buildings.

Act like an insider and grab lunch in a congressional cafeteria. Enter any House or Senate office building and ask a guard for directions. (You can't get into the cafeterias between 11:30 a.m. and 1 p.m.) Or grab a bite in **Union Station's** spacious lower-level food court.

After 1 p.m., buy an advance day-and-a-half **Tourmobile** ticket at Union Station. Ride the Tourmobile around town, taking in the sights from the comfort of your seats. At **Arlington National Cemetery,** transfer to Tourmobile's Arlington tour. Get off at each of the stops to visit the Kennedy gravesites, witness the changing of the guard at the Tomb of the Unknowns, and explore Arlington House.

Go back to your hotel to freshen up.

Have dinner in **Georgetown.** (See Chapter 14 for reviews.) After dinner, stroll M Street and Wisconsin Avenue to absorb the Georgetown nightlife. Treat yourself to an ice cream cone.

Day two

Go first to the **Washington Monument** to get timed tickets to ride the elevator to the top. Before or after you go up the monument, use your Tourmobile tickets to visit the **Jefferson Memorial, Franklin Roosevelt Memorial,** and **Lincoln Memorial.** From the Lincoln Memorial Tourmobile stop, take the short walks to the **Vietnam** and **Korean war veterans memorials.**

Ride the Tourmobile to the **Smithsonian Institution** museum that most interests you and have lunch there or at a nearby museum. (See Chapter 15 for details.) After lunch, tour one or two Smithsonian museums and then head back to your hotel room to take a break.

Have dinner in Union Station — either informally in the food court or in one of the full-service restaurants there, America or B. Smith's. After dinner, take Gray Line's three-hour **Washington-at-Night tour,** which leaves from the bus line's terminal in Union Station.

Day three

Send at least one member of your party, first thing in the morning, to get timed tickets for the **Holocaust Museum.** The timing for today's itinerary depends upon the time you get into the Holocaust Museum. Also today, plan on touring the **National Gallery of Art.** Depending on the time and your energy level, visit one or more **Smithsonian** museums that you haven't gotten to yet. Have lunch at the gallery. (See Chapter 15.)

If fine dining interests you, and you don't mind paying for it, eat at **Kinkead's,** one of Washington's very best restaurants and one of my favorites. Otherwise, check out the reviews for the $ and $$ restaurants listed in the indexes at the beginning of Chapter 14.

In warm weather, cap off your Washington visit by having a drink with a view — on the **Sky Terrace** at the top of the Hotel Washington downtown or at Georgetown's **Washington Harbour** complex on the Potomac waterfront.

Washington for Government Groupies

Many put their faith in oysters and chocolate, but Henry Kissinger declared that — based on personal experience — power is the greatest aphrodisiac. Should you agree with Henry — the former secretary of state, national security adviser, and all-around powerful person — join the government groupie patrol at the following sights. (Even if you're not a government groupie or a political junkie, you may want to tag along just to see where all those tax dollars of yours go.)

Contact your U.S. representative or one of your senators far in advance of your visit to Washington. Ask him or her for **VIP touring tickets.** Also ask about stopping by to see the office — or all three of them — while you're in town.

Government Groupie Morning is much like Day One of the three-day tour. If the Supreme Court is hearing arguments today, get in line on the court plaza before 10 a.m. As a government groupie, you'll want to witness the entire hour-long event. When you're not in the courtroom, tour the Court, the Capitol, and the Library of Congress. You'll definitely want to have lunch in a congressional cafeteria.

Ask a guard in any House or Senate office building for directions. Arrive before 11:30 a.m. or after 1 p.m., because the eating spots are reserved for the true insiders during that period. If you feel more judicial than legislative, eat in the Supreme Court cafeteria. Before you depart Capitol Hill, walk to the West Front of the Capitol for an unobstructed view of the Mall, all the way to the Lincoln Memorial.

If you contact one of your members of Congress at least three months before your D.C. visit, you can secure a reservation for an afternoon **tour of the FBI;** arrive at least 15 minutes before your tour is to start. If the **White House** is offering tours to the general public when you're in Washington, you can also obtain a congressional reservation for that and have factored it into your day. Otherwise, stop by the White House **visitor center** and then take a stroll over to 1600 Pennsylvania Ave. and gaze longingly through the fence.

Now, head back to the Hill and grab a drink at **Bullfeathers** (410 1st St. SE at D Street), a popular hangout for House staffers. After taking a break back in your hotel room, head out for dinner at one of these government groupie gathering places:

- ✔ **The Monocle,** a dining spot for senators, Senate staffers, and others who have business on the Senate side of Capitol Hill

- ✔ **The Palm,** where you may run into Larry King or James Carville or at least see their caricatures on the wall

- ✔ **The Caucus Room,** a fairly new restaurant owned by Democratic and Republican lobbyists who are out to prove that Washington powerbrokers still can eat and drink together in bipartisan conviviality

Touring Washington, D.C. Family Style

Don't despair if the grandparents change their minds about staying with the children so that you can enjoy a nice, relaxing adult vacation. Bring the younger generation along! Washington is a very kid-friendly place. Just take lots of breaks and carry snacks.

With kids younger than 8 . . .

Go directly to the **National Zoo.** Do not pass go. Do not collect $200. Go to the zoo. Pick up a map and schedule of events at the Education Building near the Connecticut Avenue entrance when you arrive. Children particularly enjoy watching the animals being fed and the training sessions. The more active the animals, the more enthralled the kids will be. That makes the seals and the monkeys good bets. Check out the **Orangutan Transportation System,** to see whether any apes are using their overhead cable to swing from building to building right over your head. Small kids sometimes find it easier to identify with the small animals in the **Small Mammal House.** Children like the lizards and snakes at the **Reptile Discovery Center** so much that I wonder if they also identify with slippery slime. Everyone, of course, loves the **pandas.**

After some quiet time back at your hotel, head for the other must-visit place for the little ones — the **Capital Children's Museum.** (See Chapter 17 for details.) Lots of hands-on, made-for-kids activities are here. Then it's on to Capitol Hill, so that you can lunch in the Union Station food court — if you haven't already eaten at the zoo.

If you still have time and energy, head for the **National Mall** and the old-fashioned **carousel** in front of the Smithsonian's Arts and Industries Building. Other kid-friendly happenings on the Mall include

- ✔ The **Insect Zoo** and **Dinosaur Hall** in the Museum of Natural History

- ✔ The hands-on history and science rooms — and the **ice cream parlor** — in the American History Museum

- ✔ Just about any of the airplanes and space vehicles in the **Air and Space Museum**

- ✔ The **sculpture gardens** outside the National Gallery and the Hirshhorn Museum

In addition, not far from the Mall is the **National Aquarium,** where children can pet a horseshoe crab in the touch tank. (See Chapter 17.)

With kids 8 and older . . .

The National Zoo and the Air and Space Museum work for kids of all ages (including me!). So do the **IMAX Theater** presentations in Air and Space and the Natural History Museum. Buy a **kite** in Air and Space and fly it on the Mall — a long-standing tradition. These older kids also like the **FBI** and **Bureau of Engraving and Printing** tours.

The beauty of Washington for families is that it's hard to have an interest that isn't represented in the city somewhere. Ask your youngsters what they're interested in, and you should be able to find a museum — or at least a museum section — that's dedicated to the subject. Washington also has sports, music, movies, and pizza.

With teens . . .

Touring Washington with teens is easy, because they're developing mature interests that will be piqued by many museums and other Washington attractions. Help them understand what's available in D.C. and let them take the lead in planning some of your family's activities. See Chapter 17 for ideas.

Avoiding Common Sightseeing Hassles

To make sure that you get the most out of your sightseeing excursions, try these time-tested tourist tactics:

✔ Most important, **budget your time** wisely. Bear in mind every traveler's first commandment: Thou shalt spend more time and money than anticipated.

✔ Get a feel for the city on a **guided tour.** Then play political consultant and do what's politically expedient: develop a strategy.

✔ Ricocheting like a stray bullet gets old fast. If you zigzag from the White House to the Capitol to Georgetown to the Mall, you waste time and wear yourself out. **Concentrate your sightseeing on one neighborhood at a time** whenever possible.

✔ Visit no more than three or four museums in a day (and that's pushing it!), fewer if your kids are under 10 or if you tire easily.

✔ Earmark an average 1 to 2 hours for each site (that means for *each* Smithsonian museum). Some attractions — the monuments and memorials, for example — can take a half-hour or less. Make sure that you include commuting time and standing-in-line time when you make your sightseeing schedule.

✔ If possible, show up at the busiest museums and attractions (the Air and Space, American History, and Natural History museums) when the doors open or after 3 p.m. Take advantage of extended summer and holiday hours. Pick up tickets for special exhibitions and IMAX movies *before* touring.

✔ **Allow downtime** for meals, shopping, phoning home, and, yes, even quiet reflection. Prevent brain drain by alternating museums with outdoor activities (a stroll along the Tidal Basin, kite flying on the Mall, or a Potomac River cruise, perhaps).

✔ **Wear comfortable shoes** and layered clothing, except in summer when you should wear the minimum allowed by law — and oceans of sunscreen.

Take advantage of all the special tickets you can get from members of Congress. Don't be shy about asking what your representative and senators can do for you. The worst they can say is "nothing." And you can remember that the next time you vote!

Chapter 21

Exploring Beyond Washington: Three Great Day Trips

*I*f time permits, you may want to get out of Dodge for a day or longer. Excursion opportunities abound in the region. You can reach historic sites, shopping outlets, state parks, national parks, and theme parks faster than Congress can answer a roll call. This chapter describes three destinations within an hour or so of the White House (in case that's where you stay). Using your hotel as a base, you can spend a day at one of the following locations and still return in time for a nightcap and the news.

Day Trip #1: Discovering Old Town in Alexandria, Virginia

With its scenic riverfront setting, historic sites, and myriad dining and shopping choices, Alexandria's **Old Town** charms all who visit. George Washington was a teenage surveyor's assistant when Alexandria became a city in 1749. The once-thriving colonial port on the western shore of the Potomac River is about seven miles south of D.C. (See the map in this chapter.) Picturesque and steeped in history, Old Town boasts fine 18th- and 19th-century buildings on cobblestone streets, an active waterfront, an artists cooperative, boutiques, and fine and casual dining. In February, locals and visitors unpack their powdered wigs for the giant Washington's Birthday Parade.

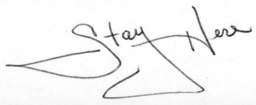

Old Town Alexandria

To Reagan National Airport and Washington, D.C.

Powhatan St.

First St.

Montgomery St.

Madison St.

Wythe St.

■ Alexandria Black History Resource Center

Pendleton St.

❶ Oronoco St.

Princess St.

Quay St.

FOUNDERS PARK

Queen St.

Carlyle House ■

Henry St. (Rte. 1 South)

Patrick St. (Rte. 1 North)

Cameron St. ❷

Market Square ■

King St. ❸

❹

WATERFRONT PARK

❺

Prince St.

Alfred St.

Columbus St.

Washington St.

St. Asaph St.

Pitt St.

Duke St.

Wolfe St.

Wilkes St.

Royal St.

Fairfax St.

Lee St.

Union St.

← To I-95 and U.S. 1

Gibbon St.

← From I-95 and U.S. 1

To Mount Vernon, Woodlawn, and Gunston Hall

Franklin St.

Potomac River

0   1/8 mi
0   125 meters

WASHINGTON, D.C.

VIRGINIA

Old Town Alexandria

Gadsby's Tavern Museum **2**

Lee-Fendall House **1**

Ramsay House Visitor Center **3**

Stabler-Leadbeater Apothecary Museum **4**

Torpedo Factory/ Alexandria Archaeology **5**

Getting there

If you drive to Old Town, go west on Independence Avenue. As you approach the Lincoln Memorial, watch closely for signs to Arlington Memorial Bridge. After you cross the bridge, turn right out of the traffic circle and then exit left, following signs to National Airport. After the parkway becomes Washington Street in Alexandria, turn left on King Street, which goes all the way to the waterfront.

Thumbs down on driving here in rush hour, when the seven miles from D.C. may feel more like 70.

Free short-term parking permits, good for two hours at a meter, are available at the Ramsay House Visitors Center. More convenient are the parking garages and lots. (The city lot charges $8 per day.) Traffic creeps on the narrow streets, and parking can be a hassle, especially on weekends.

To travel by Metrorail, hop on a Yellow line train headed in the direction of Huntington. Get off at the King Street Station and transfer to a DASH (Alexandria's public transportation system) bus to King and Fairfax (at the door of the Ramsay House).

Seeing the sights

Write, call, or stop at the **Ramsay House Visitors Center** (221 King St.; ☎ 703-838-4200; Internet: www.funside.com), the oldest structure in Alexandria. The center provides brochures, maps, and a special events calendar. You also can purchase admission tickets for many historic homes and sights. The Ramsay House is open every day but Thanksgiving, Dec. 25, and Jan. 1 from 9 a.m. to 5 p.m.

A self-guided **walking tour** is outlined in a brochure available at the visitor center. Or you can join a guided walking tour in the garden of the center at 10:30 a.m. Monday through Saturday and 2:30 p.m. Sunday from April through October. The cost is $10.

Because Alexandria enjoys a waterfront setting, beginning your visit with a **Potomac Riverboat Co. cruise** (☎ 703-548-9000) makes sense. Take a 40-minute narrated cruise on the *Admiral Tilp*. Tickets cost $8 for adults, $5 for children. Cruises depart from the Alexandria City Marina, at Union and Cameron streets behind the Torpedo Factory.

Gadsby's Tavern (134 N. Royal St.; ☎ 703-838-4242) reportedly hosted Founding Fathers Washington, Madison, and Jefferson. The tavern now is a museum of colonial furnishings and artifacts. Strolling minstrels play period music during dinner and Sunday brunch in the first-floor restaurant (☎ 703-548-1248).

The **Lee-Fendall House** (614 Oronoco St.; ☎ **703-548-1789**) was built in 1785. Generations of the Lee family lived here until 1903, except when the Union Army captured and used it as a hospital during the Civil War. Labor leader John L. Lewis lived in the house from 1937 to 1969. It's open Tuesday through Saturday from 10 a.m. to 4 p.m. and Sunday from 1 p.m. to 4 p.m. The last tour starts at 3:45 p.m.

You can't fill a prescription at the **Stabler-Leadbeter Apothecary Shop** (105 107 S. Fairfax St. between Prince and King; ☎ **703-836-3713**), but you can read a request for cod liver oil written by Mrs. Bushrod Washington, wife of G.W.'s nephew. Built in the 18th century, this shop now is an apothecary museum, complete with hand-blown medicine bottles and bloodletting paraphernalia. To find out more history, take the self-guided audio tour. The museum is open Monday through Saturday from 10 a.m. to 4 p.m. and Sunday from 1 p.m. to 5 p.m. Admission costs $2.50 for adults, $2 for ages 11–17, and younger children are free.

Late in World War I, the **Torpedo Factory** (105 N. Union St. at Cameron; ☎ **703-838-4565**) did manufacture torpedoes. Now, it's an arts center where more than 160 painters, sculptors, weavers, and other artists work in full view of the public. Visitors are invited inside the artists' studios to observe and make purchases (great shopping opportunity!). While you're here, take a look at the unearthed artifacts on display in the **Alexandria Archaeology Research Lab,** which occupies space in the Center. The factory is open daily from 10 a.m. to 5 p.m., and admission is free.

Where to dine

It may be touristy, but the waterside setting of the **Chart House Restaurant** (1 Cameron St.; ☎ **703-684-5080**) floats many diners' boats. Steer clear of the beef and cruise straight toward the coconut shrimp ($22). A slab (this is no slice) of the famous ice cream mud pie is big enough for two consenting adults. You can easily create a meal from the 50-or-so items on the salad bar. The menu for kids 11 and younger features chicken strips, spaghetti, and other mini-portions. Reservations are recommended. The restaurant is open Monday through Thursday from 5 p.m. to 10 p.m.; Friday and Saturday from 5 p.m. to 11 p.m.; and Sunday from 4 p.m. to 10 p.m., with Sunday brunch from 10:45 a.m. to 2:15 p.m.

Head for the **Warehouse Bar & Grill** (214 King St.; ☎ **703-683-6868**) for a sandwich, full dinner, or Sunday brunch in a casual setting that in former lives served as a trolley warehouse, boat repair business, and pool hall. Best bets are grilled fish or steak. The fried clams enjoy a rep for being crunchy and greaseless. On Sundays, the popular à la carte brunch fills up faster than church. Lunch runs from $7 to $17; dinner entrées $7 to $26; and brunch entrées $8 to $12. Its hours are Monday through

Thursday from 11 a.m. to 4 p.m. and 5 to 10:30 p.m.; Friday and Saturday from 11 a.m. to 4 p.m. and 5 to 11 p.m.; and Sunday from 10 a.m. to 4 p.m. (brunch) and 5 to 9:30 p.m. Reservations are recommended.

The **Hard Times Cafe** (1404 King St.; ☎ **703-837-0050**) earns a spot in our family's heart because of the bizarre focus of its menu — Texas and Cincinnati chili. When we lived in Dayton, Cincinnati chili parlors were all around, and I developed a fondness for the spicy stuff. For the uninitiated, Texas chili is made with coarse-ground or chunked beef. Cincinnati chili, originally concocted by Greek immigrants, uses fine-ground beef in a tomato sauce with sweeter spices, including cinnamon. Adding to Cincinnati chili's uniqueness is the tradition of serving it with spaghetti, beans, onion, and cheese — or any combination thereof. Keeping up with the new times, the Hard Times folks now offer a vegetarian chili. It's open daily from 11 a.m. to 11 p.m. No reservations are necessary.

The **Union Street Public House** (121 S. Union St. between King and Prince; ☎ **703-548-1785**) has long been a favorite for its casual, neighborhood saloon ambiance, bar food, and local beer. Old brick-work, gas lamps, and polished wood enhance the pubby-clubby atmosphere. Dinner entrees range from $9 to $20, sandwiches from $7 to $11.50. A kids' menu is available. It's open Monday through Thursday from 11:30 a.m. to 10:30 p.m.; Friday and Saturday from 11:30 a.m. to 11:30 p.m.; and Sunday from 11 a.m. to 10:30 p.m., with Sunday brunch from 11 a.m. to 3 p.m. and lighter fare available until 1 a.m. Reservations are required for parties of eight or more people.

Day Trip #2: Exploring Mt. Vernon

Mount Vernon lies on the Potomac River, about 15 miles and more than 200 years away from modern-day D.C. A stop at George Washington's riverfront estate, meticulously restored down to the original paint colors on the walls, is the perfect complement to a visit in the federal district bearing his name. The land was granted to Washington's great-grandfather in 1674. G.W. lived here most of his life, with time out for being a soldier and a president. He died and was buried here in 1799. What a setting! He certainly had an eye for prime real estate. The house is restored to look as it did the last year that he lived here.

Getting there

Drive to Alexandria (see the section "Day Trip #1: Discovering Old Town in Alexandria, Virginia," earlier in this chapter) and keep going. The George Washington Parkway ends at Mount Vernon. It's that easy. **Gray Line** (☎ **800-862-1400**) offers a four-hour excursion to Alexandria and Mount Vernon, with about two hours spent at Washington's home. The tour departs Union Station at 8:30 a.m. daily all year and also at 2 p.m. from late June to late October. Cost is $28 for adults, $14 for children 3 to 11. No tours are offered Thanksgiving, Dec. 25, and Jan. 1. From mid-March to late November, the *Potomac Spirit* (☎ 866-211-3811) carries passengers on a Potomac River **cruise** between Washington and Mount Vernon. The cruise departs from Pier 4, at 6th and Water streets SW at 8:30 a.m. Tuesday through Sunday and returns at 3 p.m. Three and a half hours are allocated to touring Mount Vernon. Tickets — which must be reserved — are $29.95 for those 55 and older, $30.95 for ages 12 through 54, and $20.95 for 6 through 11. Kids younger than 6 are free. Admission to Mount Vernon is included.

Seeing the sights

For information before you arrive, contact the **Mount Vernon Ladies' Association,** which runs the place. You can reach them at P.O. Box 110, Mount Vernon, VA 22121 (☎ 703-780-2000; Internet: www.mountvernon.org). Mount Vernon is open daily April through August from 8 a.m. to 5 p.m.; March, September, and October from 9 a.m. to 5 p.m.; and November through February from 9 a.m. to 4 p.m.

Aside from the addition of air-conditioning in 1998, Mount Vernon is a typical 18th-century aristocratic estate. Explore the house and grounds on your own. Guides are stationed throughout the mansion to answer your questions. Take a minute, especially with youngsters, to inspect the family kitchen and outbuildings where baking, weaving, and washing took place. George and other family members are interred in a tomb a short walk from the mansion. Mount Vernon commemorates the **Presidents' Day** holiday, the third Monday in February, by admitting visitors for free and hosting a wreath-laying at Washington's tomb, music, and military exercises by the U.S. Army Old Guard Fife and Drum Corps. On Feb. 22, Washington's actual birthday, anyone who is named George or was born on that date gets free admission. Admission to the mansion is $8.50 for seniors 62 or older, $9 for ages 12 to 61, $4.50 for ages 6 through 11, and free for children younger than 6. You can rent an audio tour recording for $3.

Mount Vernon hosts special events throughout the year, including hands-on activities especially for children. Call to find out what's going on during your visit. The grounds are a great place for youngsters to explore while their parents take turns touring the house.

Where to dine

Outside the main gate are a **food court** (☎ 703-799-8688) and the **Mount Vernon Inn** restaurant (☎ 703-780-0011). The inn is open daily for lunch from 11 a.m. to 3:30 p.m., except Dec. 25. Candlelight dinners are served every day from 5 to 9 p.m. Reservations are suggested.

Picnicking is allowed 1 mile north at Riverside Park. Or stop on the way back to D.C. and dine in Old Town, Alexandria. (See "Day Trip #1: Discovering Old Town, Alexandria, Virginia," earlier in this chapter.)

Day Trip #3: Visiting Annapolis, Maryland

Cruise up to Annapolis, located about 30 miles as the gull flies, from downtown D.C. (Betcha your heart rate slows.) A port since the 18th century, Annapolis still supports hundreds of maritime-related businesses and is a magnet for boaters from all over the world. This home of the **U.S. Naval Academy,** Maryland's state capitol, St. John's College, and exemplary 18th- and 19th-century architecture has a small-town feel. With more than 30,000 registered pleasure craft, Annapolis stakes claim to the title "sailing capital of the United States."

A vocal and active preservation group oversees the historic district, some think with an iron fist. But the efforts have paid off handsomely: No high-rises, billboards, fast food restaurants, or out-of-place modern buildings interfere with the architectural integrity of downtown. A map of Annapolis in this chapter helps you understand the layout of the city.

Getting there

Traveling to Annapolis is one time during your Washington visit when a car comes in handy. The drive from downtown D.C. takes about an hour. Exit Washington to the east via New York Avenue, which is U.S. 50, and follow 50 all the way. As you approach Annapolis, take Exit 24, Rowe (rhymes with cow) Boulevard. Continue about 1 mile, hang a right at the governor's mansion (or you'll crash the iron fence), and go half-way around Church Circle. Take a right at the Maryland Inn (Duke of Gloucester Street) and follow signs to Main Street, City Dock, and the Historic District. On-street parking is 50 cents an hour, with a two-hour max.

The local traffic agents are as vigilant as vultures awaiting fresh road kill. You really don't want to park in an illegal spot. **Parking** also is available in the Hillman Garage (entrances on Duke of Gloucester and Main streets) or Gott's Court Garage (enter on Calvert Street between Rowe and West streets). All-day parking at the Navy-Marine Corps Stadium (Rowe Boulevard and Taylor Avenue) costs $3 weekdays and $4 weekends. For 75 cents, you can ride a **shuttle** from the lot to downtown daily from 6:30 a.m. to 7 p.m. mid-October through May and until 8 p.m. the rest of the year.

Annapolis

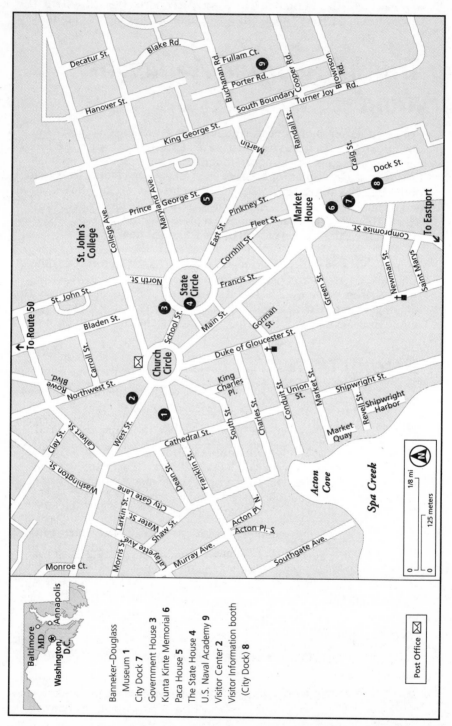

Banneker–Douglass
    Museum **1**
City Dock **7**
Government House **3**
Kunta Kinte Memorial **6**
Paca House **5**
The State House **4**
U.S. Naval Academy **9**
Visitor Center **2**
Visitor Information booth
    (City Dock) **8**

Dillon's Bus Service (☎ **800-827-3490** or 410-647-2321) operates limited service between D.C. and Annapolis for $3.35 one way. **Greyhound's** (☎ **800-229-9424**) limited service is $14.25 one-way, $28.25 round trip.

Seeing the sights

Annapolis is a working state capital whose history stretches back more than 300 years; more than 1,500 historic buildings are scattered among the narrow brick streets and alleys — more colonial buildings than in any other town in the country. The city is almost always crowded with people working, playing, sailing, eating, and studying.

To work out how you want to spend your time in Annapolis, write to the **Annapolis and Anne Arundel County Conference and Visitors Bureau,** 26 West St., Annapolis, MD 21401 (☎ **410-280-0445**), open 9 a.m. to 5 p.m. daily, or surf over to www.visit-annapolis.org. You can get comprehensive information from the walk-in visitor center, off Church Circle. Access the "Whiz Bang Machine," a touch-screen video guide, for more information about sights and special events. If you land downtown, pick up a brochure or calendar of events and ask questions at the visitor information booth (next to the public restrooms at the City Dock) in the heart of town, open daily from 9 a.m. to 5 p.m.

Three Centuries Tours (☎ **410-263-5401**) leads two-hour walking tours of the historic district and the Naval Academy daily April through October. Reservations aren't available, so just show up at 10:30 a.m. at the visitor center, 26 West St., or at 1:30 p.m. at the City Dock information booth. Thursday through Saturday, a sunset tour departs the dock at 6:30 p.m. During November through March, the tours are offered only at 1:30 p.m. on Saturdays from the dock. Tickets are $10 for adults, $5 for children 18 and younger.

Discover Annapolis Tours (☎ **410-626-6000**) shuttles visitors through 350 years of history and architecture aboard minibuses with big windows. The hour-long tours depart several times a day from the visitor center April through November and most weekends December through March. You can make reservations. The cost is $12 for adults, $6 for ages 11 to 15, $3 for kids 6 to 10, and free for preschoolers. This tour is good for persons with disabilities, those who can't walk long distances, and the terminally lazy. All others should get out there and walk!

For $5, you can rent an **audio tour** narrated by Walter Cronkite, or an **African-American heritage tour**, from the Historic Annapolis Foundation Museum Store at 77 Main St. (☎ **410-268-5576**). The recordings are available daily.

Watermark Cruises (☎ **410-268-7600**) sails from the City Dock to view Annapolis Harbor, as well as the U.S. Naval Academy on the banks of the Severn River. Go with the flow. Weekdays, the 40-minute narrated tour leaves every hour on the hour from noon to 3 p.m. April through mid-May; from 11 a.m. to 4 p.m. mid-May through August; and from noon to 4 p.m. in September. On weekends and holidays, the on-the-hour departures run from 11 a.m. to 6 p.m. April through mid-May; from 11 a.m. to 7 p.m. mid-May through August; and from 11 a.m. to 6 p.m. in September. You can catch a cruise the rest of the year as weather permits. Cost is $7 for adults and $4 for ages 3 to 11. Kids younger than 3 cruise free.

Walk the length of City Dock to the water and enjoy the panorama from **Susan Campbell Memorial Park.** Get a double-scooper from **Storm Brothers Ice Cream Factory,** 130 Dock St., and drip across the street to the seawall along **Ego Alley,** appropriately named for the informal parade of boats and flesh that takes place on summer weekends. Where Ego Alley dead-ends, across from Market House, is a life-size bronze of *Roots* author Alex Haley reading to several children. The sculpture commemorates the landing of Haley's ancestor, Kunta Kinte, aboard the slave ship *Lord Ligonier* in 1767.

Check out the architecture as you ascend Main Street from City Dock to Church Circle and the harbor view from the Maryland Inn. Among the independently owned businesses are **A.L. Goodies General Store,** 112 Main St., for souvenirs, T-shirts, and fudge; **Avoca Handweavers,** 141 Main, for woolens and household accessories from the British Isles; **Snyder's Bootery,** 170 Main, with the area's largest selection of boat shoes; and **Chick and Ruth's Delly,** 165 Main, an Annapolis institution since the 1960s. (See the section "Where to dine," later in this chapter).

History buffs may want to detour to the **Banneker-Douglass Museum** (84 Franklin St.; ☎ 410-216-6180), dedicated to preserving Maryland's African-American heritage; it's named for Benjamin Banneker, the mathematician who helped survey and lay out the District of Columbia, and Frederick Douglass, who escaped slavery to become a leader of the abolition movement. From the top of Main Street, go left at Church Circle and then left at Franklin. The museum is housed in the old Mount Moriah A.M.E. Church. The museum's exhibits change periodically; call ahead to find out about current shows. It's open Tuesday through Friday from 10 a.m. to 3 p.m. and Saturday from noon to 4 p.m. Admission is free.

If you go right onto Church Circle from Main Street and right again at School Street to State Circle, you discover Annapolis as state capital. The **State House** (☎ 410-974-3400), the oldest state capitol building in continuous use, still watches over the town below. Construction began in 1772, and the original section was completed in 1789. It served as the U.S. Capitol from November 1783 to August 1784 when the Continental Congress met in the Old Senate Chamber. View the grounds and public areas on your own or take the free tour, daily at 11 a.m. and 3 p.m. When you exit the rear of the building, cross **Lawyers Mall,** with its statue of Thurgood Marshall, to **Government House,** the official residence of

Maryland's governor. Because the governor lives here, you can't just walk in to tour.

On State Circle are some of the town's premier shops and galleries. **The Annapolis Pottery** (No. 40) (☎ 410-268-6153; Web site: www.annapolis pottery.com) is a workshop/gallery with a wide selection of attractive and functional pieces. At **Nancy Hammond Editions** (No. 64) (☎ 410-267-7711; Web site: www.nancyhammondeditions.com), the award-winning local artist sells her limited-edition silk-screen prints, watercolors, note cards, clothing, and gifts. The **Maryland Federation of Art Gallery** (No. 18) (☎ 410-268-4566; Web site: www.mdfedart.org), in a restored 1840 building with exposed brick and modern lighting, mounts solo and small group exhibits of multimedia works and three national shows per year.

From State Circle, turn down Maryland Avenue, with its many home design and antiques shops, boutiques, and galleries. Reminiscent of a gentler era, and a lot less touristy than Main Street, Maryland Avenue merits exploration. Shops line the cobblestone street from State Circle to Prince George Street. Stop in the **Aurora Gallery** (No. 67) (☎ 410-263-9150) a few doors from the State House, with its American-made crafts, pottery, jewelry, paintings, and sculpture (some created by the artist-owners). Across the street is the **Briarwood Book Shop** (No. 88) (☎ 410-268-1440) for used and out-of-print books. **The Dawson Gallery** (No. 44) (☎ 410-269-1299) sells 18th-, 19th-, and early 20th-century American and European paintings. Among the gallery's better-known customers is Harrison Ford, who purchased paintings here while filming *Patriot Games* in Annapolis several years ago.

Anyone who's been in Annapolis five minutes knows it's a sailing mecca. Many people come here from all over the country to learn to sail. If you're one of them, try the **Annapolis Sailing School,** 601 6th St. (☎ 800-638-9192 or 410-267-7205), where I'm told you can learn the basics in a weekend.

If you're not going to take the helm yourself, feel the wind on your face aboard the 74-foot schooner *Woodwind,* which sails from Pusser's Landing (behind Marriott Waterfront Hotel, 80 Compromise St.; ☎ 410-263-7837). Several cruises run daily Tuesday through Sunday, May through October. Call for details. On weekdays, the two-hour cruise costs $25 for adults, $23 for seniors, and $15 for kids 2 to 11. Sunset and weekend cruises are $29, $27, and $15.

Annapolis lays claim to numerous fine examples of 18th- and 19th-century architecture. As you tour, notice the colored plaques on many buildings designating their historic status and the period in which they were built. (An explanation is provided in the *Annapolis Visitors Guide,* available at the visitor center) Check out the **William Paca House and Gardens** (186 Prince George St.; ☎ 800-603-4020 or 410-267-7619). Paca (pronounced *Pay-ca*) was a wealthy planter who signed the

Declaration of Independence. The Georgian mansion, built between 1763 and 1765, nearly succumbed to the wrecker's ball in 1965. The Historic Annapolis Foundation stepped in, restoring the house and gardens to their former grandeur. The mansion is open 10 a.m. to 5 p.m. Monday through Saturday and noon to 5 p.m. Sunday from mid-March through December and from 10 a.m. to 4 p.m. Saturday and noon to 4 p.m. Sunday January through mid-March; It's closed Dec. 25 and Jan. 1. Admission costs $8 for adults, $7 for seniors, $5 for children 6 to 17, and free for ages 5 and younger.

Many people use the words "Annapolis" and "**U.S. Naval Academy**" interchangeably. Whatever you call it, the service academy is a must-see. If you park downtown, it's a five-minute walk from City Dock via Randall Street to King George Street and Gate 1, the visitors' entrance. Since Sept. 11, 2001, tourists aren't permitted to drive onto the academy grounds (or "onboard," as the sailors say). The exception is a vehicle with a handicapped license plate or permit, which is allowed on campus through Gate 1 after an inspection. To get information before you arrive, call ☎ **410-263-6933** or visit the academy's Web site for tourists at www.navyonline.com.

Stop first at the **Armel-Leftwich Visitors Center,** just inside Gate 1 and next to the Field House, for a map and to see the short film *To Lead and to Serve.* Check out the interactive exhibits and the gift shop and stroll the waterfront promenade behind the building. You can view exhibits on life at the Naval Academy, a model of the *USS Maryland,* and the *Freedom 7* space capsule, in which Navy Commander Alan Shepard became the first American to take a suborbital flight into space. The center is open daily from 9 a.m. to 5 p.m. March through December and from 9 a.m. to 4 p.m. in January and February. It's closed Thanksgiving, Dec. 25, and Jan. 1.

Then hop onto a guided tour, which is free for preschoolers and costs $4.50 for elementary and secondary students, $5.50 for seniors older than 62, and $6.50 everyone else. June through Labor Day, the tours run from 9:30 a.m. to 3 p.m. Monday through Saturday and 12:30 to 3 p.m. Sunday. From December through March, they run Monday through Friday from 10 a.m. to 2:30 p.m., Saturday from 9:30 a.m. to 2:30 p.m., and Sunday from 12:30 to 2:30 p.m. The rest of year, the tours run Monday through Friday from 10 a.m. to 3 p.m., Saturday from 9:30 a.m. to 3 p.m., and Sunday from 12:15 to 3 p.m.

During the academic year (September through May), try to hook up with a morning tour, which allows you to see noon meal formation (about 12:10 p.m. weekdays, 12:20 p.m. weekends, weather permitting) in front of Bancroft Hall. If you're on your own, arrive a little before noon at **Tecumseh Court,** in front of Bancroft. Drills and music precede the procession into the 65,000-square-foot dining hall, which can accommodate all 4,000 midshipmen at one time.

In **Lejeune Hall,** across from the visitor center, you find athletic trophies and photographs. You may also be able to catch swim practice
in the Olympic-size pool. Close by is **Dahlgren Hall,** where a biplane
"flies" from the ceiling, the Navy's ice hockey team plays, and the site
of figure skating competitions and ice shows. Cross the yard to the
awesome **Navy Chapel** and John Paul Jones's crypt. Nearby is the
Naval Academy Museum, Preble Hall (☎ 410-293-2108), filled with 200
years of naval art and artifacts; see the ground floor Gallery of Ships,
many of which are original builder's models. The **Robert Crown Center**
is headquarters for the academy's sailing program. Bancroft Hall
(known as "Mother B") is the dormitory for all the midshipmen. For
information and tickets to athletic events, call the Naval Academy
Athletic Association (☎ 800-US-4-NAVY).

Where to dine

Café Normandie (185 Main St.; ☎ 410-263-3382), is a cozy, plant-filled
French bistro. Come for a hearty breakfast (eggs, omelets, French toast),
lunch (tomato-crab or onion soup, grilled chicken Caesar salad, crêpes),
or dinner (veal, fish, beef many ways, seafood-filled crêpes, pasta).
Except for the ice-cream or fruit-filled crêpes, the desserts are ho-hum.

From May to October, visit **Cantler's Riverside Inn** on Mill Creek
(458 Forest Beach Rd.; ☎ 410-757-1311) and dig into a pile of steamed
Maryland blue crabs. This place is packed in summer, especially on
weekends (when the restaurant won't take a reservation). The best
strategy is to arrive at off times. Have an early or late lunch or a *very*
early dinner. Otherwise, you may find the crabs AWOL. Also try the
steamed shrimp, crab-vegetable soup, soft-shell crab sandwich, and
fried or broiled fish. The inn is about a 15-minute ride from City Dock.

A bit of advice I picked up from an old crab picker: At Cantler's, order
large or jumbo males (*jimmys*). The mediums are too much work for too
little meat. The roe in the female crabs (*sooks*) puts most people off.

With its long wooden bar, chatty bartender, high-decibel noise level,
and garage-sale accessories, **Riordan's** (26 Market Space; ☎ 410-263-
5449) is a quintessential neighborhood saloon. The servers are pleasant and efficient, the food is consistent and reasonably priced, and the
beer is cold. Start with potato skins with the works or a seafood appetizer and then move on to a burger or roast beef sandwich. The soups
are, um, super, especially the New England clam chowder and crab veg-
etable. The à la carte Sunday brunch (mimosa or glass of champagne
included) is an Annapolis tradition and also a bargain, with most
entrees less than $10. At lunch and dinner, a kids' menu for the 10-and-
under set lists burgers, chicken, and pasta.

Chick and Ruth's Delly (165 Main St.; ☎ 410-269-6737) has anchored the corner of Main and Conduit streets since the '60s, before Annapolis became a yuppie outpost. Come for the breakfast platters (served all day), the tasty sandwiches (named for Maryland politicians and local characters), milkshakes, malts, or banana splits. Try the *delly fries* (home fries with plenty of pepper and onions). The kitschy decor — orange Formica countertops and bagel light-pulls are decor? — is pure 1950s. So are the cheeky waitresses and prices (most items are $2 to $9) at this friendly eatery.

Part VI
Living It Up After the Sun Goes Down: D.C. Nightlife

The 5th Wave   By Rich Tennant

"Yes, we are going to hear Pachelbel's Canon next, but maybe I should explain..."

In this part . . .

Read my lips: D.C. ain't no Vegas! For many, Washington is a place to work. Period. Some federal workers get up at 4:30 a.m. and are at their computers by 6:30 a.m. After working eight to ten hours, they may face a one- to two-hour commute into the affordable-housing suburbs. A Washington worker's idea of nightlife can be eating a peanut butter and jelly sandwich and crawling into bed.

But that doesn't mean all Washingtonians are all work and no play (remember, there are a few colleges in the District) . . . nor that you should act that way! Nightlife in Washington can mean cocktails in a quiet lounge or a warm pint in a noisy pub. You can indulge in a leisurely dinner, perhaps a movie, show, concert, or an after-dark tour. Neighborhood watering holes and music/dance clubs abound, drawing the young and awake. And D.C.'s high culture — symphony, opera, and dance — is top-notch and getting better. Whatever your pleasure (within the law), this part helps you plan your D.C. nights.

Chapter 22

Washington's Cultural Scene

. . . .

In This Chapter

▶ Getting information and tickets

▶ Dining before the curtain goes up

▶ Knowing what's hot on the cultural scene

▶ Taking in a play, concert, or dance performance

. . . .

*U*nlike the famous cherry trees, Washington's cultural scene knows no particular season and blooms year-round. Over the years, a dazzling array of theatrical venues has sprouted for residents and visitors alike.

Doing Your Research Before Taking in a Show

If you want to take in a play, concert, or dance performance during your D.C. visit, it pays to do a little homework before you arrive. Check out www.washington.org or call ☎ 202-789-7000 to gather info from the Washington, D.C. Convention and Tourism Corp. You also can peruse *The Washington Post's* daily Style section, Sunday Arts section, and Friday *Weekend* magazine or visit *The Post's* online entertainment guide at http://eg.washingtonpost.com.

Tickets, please!

Competition for tickets to a particular performance can be keen. To get the best seats (or any seats!) for a popular performance, you need to buy tickets as far in advance as possible.

If you order tickets over the phone, ask about the seat location; at the box office, ask to see a diagram of the theater.

To order tickets to most events, call **TicketMaster** (☎ 800-551-SEAT or 202-432-SEAT) or visit TicketMaster's Web site, www.ticketmaster.com. Expect to pay an outlandish surcharge.

Tickets.com (☎ 703-218-6500; Internet: www.tickets.com) pretty much covers what TicketMaster doesn't. Like TicketMaster, expect to pay an outlandish surcharge.

Located across the street from the Federal Triangle Metrorail Station, **TicketPlace** (in the Old Post Office Pavilion, 11th Street and Pennsylvania Avenue NW; ☎ 202-842-5387) sells tickets for 60 percent of their face value for same-day performances. Call first and listen to the recording of what's available and then decide whether you want to make the trip to the pavilion. TicketPlace is open Tuesday through Saturday from 11 a.m. to 6 p.m. Tickets for Sunday and Monday shows are sold on Saturday when they're available.

If your hotel has a concierge, he or she should be able to get tickets to many events. You may have to pay a surcharge, and you should tip the concierge for the service.

Some theaters set aside tickets for seniors and full-time students and sell them the day of the performance. If you don't ask, you don't get! Gamblers are advised to arrive at the box office a half-hour before curtain time; sometimes unclaimed reserved tickets are available. If you're determined to attend a performance that's sold out, ask about SRO (Standing Room Only) tickets. If someone leaves at intermission, you may get lucky and snag a seat.

Pretheater dining

If you're catching a theater performance, be seated for dinner no later than 6 p.m., as most curtains go up at 7:30 or 8 p.m. Choose someplace near the theater, in case the service is slow. (Wouldn't you rather sprint a couple of blocks than hail a cab and maybe miss Act I?) When you sit down, tell the host or waiter (or both) that you're going to an event and need to be out by a certain time. Order soon after you're seated and save the soufflé and other dishes requiring lots of preparation for a nontheater evening.

Many restaurants offer pretheater, fixed-price menus. This dinner usually includes an appetizer or salad, entree, dessert, and a nonalcoholic beverage. Pretheater specials usually are available from 4:30 or 5 p.m. to 6 or 6:30 p.m. You can spend considerably less than you would if you ordered à la carte.

If you have tickets for a show, consider the following pretheater deals:

- ✔ **The Roof Terrace Restaurant** at the Kennedy Center (☎ 202-416-8555). Available 5 to 6:30 p.m. for $38.

- ✔ **Jeffrey's,** across from the Kennedy Center in the Watergate, 2650 Virginia Ave. NW at New Hampshire Avenue (☎ 202-298-4455). Available 5 to 7:30 p.m. for $38.

✔ **Le Rivage,** near Arena Stage, at 1000 Water St. SW, between Maine Avenue and 9th Street (☎ 202-488-8111). Available 5:30 to 6:30 p.m. for $20.

✔ **701,** near the Shakespeare Theatre and Ford's Theatre, at 701 Pennsylvania Ave. (☎ 202-393-0701). Available 5:30 to 6:45 p.m. for $25. (Sometimes available all night. Ask.)

✔ **Marcel's,** 2401 Pennsylvania Ave. NW at 24th Street (☎ 202-296-1166). Serves you dinner between 5:30 and 7 p.m., sends you by limo to the Kennedy Center for your show, and then brings you back to the restaurant for dessert after the show, all for $42.

See Chapter 14 for reviews of other restaurants. Ask restaurants near your theater whether they offer a pretheater special.

Curtain calls

Some people blame it on the preponderance of bureaucrats in D.C. For whatever reason, Washingtonians are a punctual lot, so you can count on the curtain rising on time. A good general rule is to arrive at least 15 minutes early so that you can visit the restroom and buy a $2 bag of candy — ouch! (I've seen the line to the ladies room snake all the way to Kentucky five minutes before a performance.) Latecomers may not be seated until intermission.

Dressing the part

A night at the theater no longer means a suit and tie or dress and high heels. Most Washington theatergoers are a shade or two less formal and flamboyant. Knock yourself out and preen your feathers if that's your style, but the usher will show you to your seat no matter what your attire. When in doubt, follow your mother's advice and "wash behind your ears, comb your hair, and look presentable." Try slacks or a skirt, a shirt or blouse, a jacket or sweater, a tie if you want. Now, go make your entrance.

Getting the Inside Scoop on the D.C. Arts Scene

The **Kennedy Center,** with six theaters, is one of the most visited and best-attended arts centers in the nation. Home of the National Symphony and the Washington Opera, it plays host to the Washington Ballet as well as internationally acclaimed artists and such star-studded companies as the American Ballet Theatre and the Alvin Ailey American Dance Theater. D.C. also sports no less than six other professional theaters, which showcase a variety of performances, from Broadway standards to

The Performing Arts Scene in Washington, D.C.

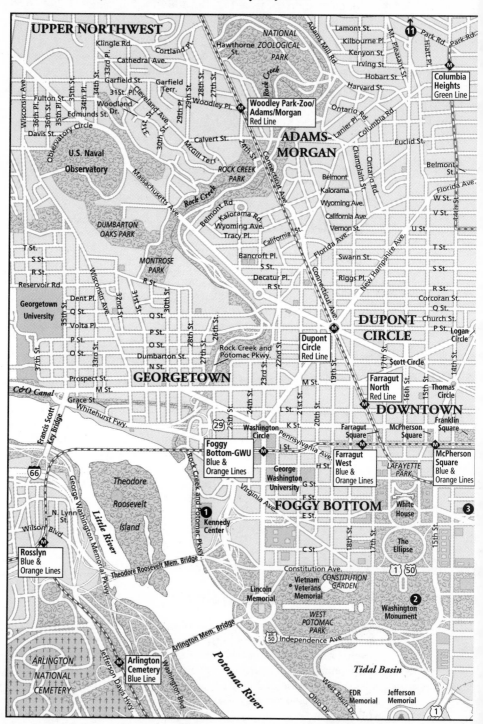

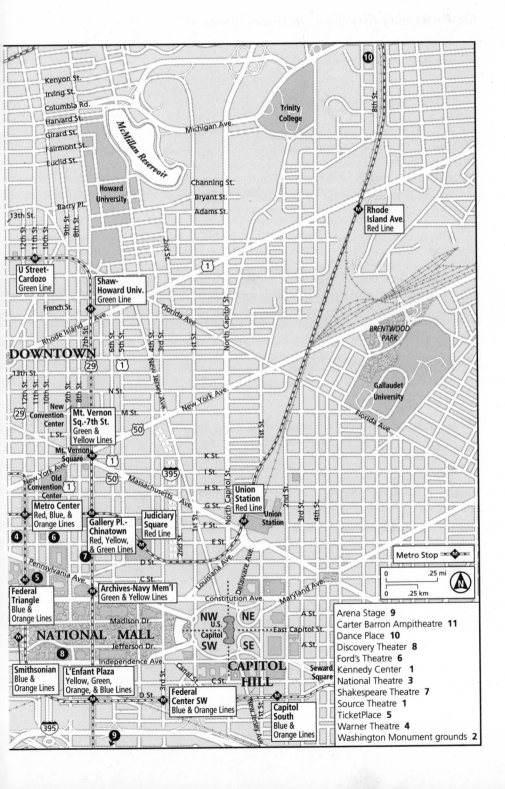

Kenyon St.
Irving St.
Columbia Rd.
Harvard St.
Girard St.
Fairmont St.
Euclid St.

McMillan Reservoir

Michigan Ave.

Trinity College

13th St.
12th St.
11th St.
10th St.
9th St.
8th St.

Barry Pl.

Howard University

Channing St.
Bryant St.
Adams St.

Rhode Island Ave
Red Line

U Street-Cardozo
Green Line

Shaw-Howard Univ.
Green Line

French St.

Rhode Island Ave.

Florida Ave.

BRENTWOOD PARK

DOWNTOWN

13th St.
12th St.
11th St.
10th St.
9th St.
8th St.

N St.

New York Ave.

Gallaudet University

Florida Ave.

New Convention Center

Mt. Vernon Sq.-7th St.
Green & Yellow Lines

M St.

L St.

Mt. Vernon Square

Old Convention Center

New York Ave.

Massachusetts Ave.

K St.

I St.

H St.

G St.

F St.

E St.

Union Station
Red Line

Union Station

2nd St.
3rd St.
4th St.

Metro Center
Red, Blue, & Orange Lines

Gallery Pl.-Chinatown
Red, Yellow, & Green Lines

Judiciary Square
Red Line

D St.

Metro Stop

Federal Triangle
Blue & Orange Lines

Pennsylvania Ave.

Archives-Navy Mem'l
Green & Yellow Lines

C St.

0   .25 mi
0   .25 km

Constitution Ave.

Louisiana Ave.
Delaware Ave.
Maryland Ave.

Madison Dr.

NATIONAL MALL

Jefferson Dr.

Independence Ave.

NW   NE
U.S. Capitol
SW   SE

East Capitol St.

A St.

A St.

CAPITOL HILL

Seward Square

Smithsonian
Blue & Orange Lines

L'Enfant Plaza
Yellow, Green, Orange, & Blue Lines

Federal Center SW
Blue & Orange Lines

Capitol South
Blue & Orange Lines

Canal St.

C St.

D St.

New Jersey Ave.

Arena Stage **9**
Carter Barron Ampitheatre **11**
Dance Place **10**
Discovery Theater **8**
Ford's Theatre **6**
Kennedy Center **1**
National Theatre **3**
Shakespeare Theatre **7**
Source Theatre **1**
TicketPlace **5**
Warner Theatre **4**
Washington Monument grounds **2**

Shakespeare to the avant-garde and experimental. Year-round, on any given day, you can count on finding performing artists on stages in Washington. (See the map in this chapter for more on the locations of the performing arts venues.)

The play's the thing

In a city that generates more than its share of political theater, dramatic and musical theater also thrives. Broadway-bound shows and resurrected classics account for much theatrical activity at the **Kennedy Center,** 2700 F St. NW, between New Hampshire Avenue and Rock Creek Parkway. (☎ **800-444-1324** or 202-467-4600; Internet: www.kennedy-center.org).

The Arena Stage, 1101 Sixth St. SW at Maine Ave. (☎ **202-488-3300;** Internet: www.arenastage.org), on the other hand, presents new works, reinterprets older works, and practices diversity. Arena celebrated its 50th anniversary in the 2000–2001 season, and it can brag about a distinguished life so far: It was the first not-for-profit theater in the United States, the first regional theater to transfer a production to Broadway, the first regional theater invited by the U.S. State Department to tour behind the Iron Curtain, and the first regional to win a Tony.

D.C.'s diminutive Theater District — I don't think I'll compare it to New York's — is downtown, east of the White House. The most active stages are

✔ **National Theatre,** 1321 Pennsylvania Ave. NW, between 13th and 14th streets; ☎ **202-628-6161;** Internet: www.nationaltheatre.org.

✔ **Warner Theatre,** 13th Street NW, between E and F streets.; ☎ **202-783-4000;** Internet: www.warnertheatre.com.

✔ **Ford's Theatre,** 511 10th St. NW, between E and F streets; ☎ **202-347-4833;** Internet: www.fordstheatre.org.

✔ **Shakespeare Theatre,** 450 7th St. NW, between D and E streets; ☎ **202-547-1122;** Internet: www.shakespearedc.org.

Don't overlook the smaller, innovative **Source Theatre,** 1835 14th St NW, between S and T streets (☎ **202-462-1073;** Internet: www.sourcetheatre.org) and the **Woolly Mammoth Theatre** (☎ **202-393-3939;** Internet: www.woollymammoth.net). As I write this book, Woolly Mammoth is performing in the Kennedy Center and other venues while a new Mammoth lair is being constructed at 7th and D streets NW.

Fabulous freebies

The best news for those traveling on a tight budget is that **free performances** are as much a part of Washington as spin doctors and negative campaign advertising. The Kennedy Center offers free performances on the Millennium Stage in the Grand Foyer daily at 6 p.m. Half-price tickets for most Kennedy Center performances are available in limited numbers to the following: full-time students first grade through graduate school, seniors 65 and older, people with permanent disabilities, enlisted military personnel in grades E1 to E4, and people on fixed low incomes. A limited number of discounted tickets are sold in advance at the box office or by mail with a form found in the Kennedy Center magazine. When available, day-of-performance discounted tickets are sold at the box office beginning at noon for matinees and 6 p.m. for evening performances. You must present evidence of eligibility when buying tickets at the box office or at the Friends Desk if you ordered by mail.

Audiences enjoy midsummer nights' freebies when the **Shakespeare Theatre** plays outdoors in Rock Creek Park's Carter Barron Amphitheatre, off 16th Street and Colorado Avenue NW. The **National Symphony** and military bands present free outdoor concerts at several sites from Memorial Day through Labor Day.

In recent summers, the Washington Monument lawn has become the theater for **"Screen on the Green."** On Monday evenings, vintage films (*Singin' in the Rain, North by Northwest, Strangers on a Train*) have been shown on a huge drive-in-type screen.

Hearing the sounds of music

The **National Symphony Orchestra** plays in the Kennedy Center Concert Hall, 2700 F St. NW between New Hampshire Avenue and Rock Creek Parkway (☎ **800-444-1324** or 202-467-4600; Internet: www.kennedy-center.org/nso). Leonard Slatkin is the conductor, with other world-renowned conductors and musicians making guest appearances. The symphony's performances frequently sell out, so make your reservations early.

Hot time: Summer in the city

If you visit Washington in summer and enjoy classical music, check out the National Symphony's **free concerts** on the West Lawn of the Capitol, on the Sunday of the Memorial Day and Labor Day weekends, and on July 4. These events are some of the top perks of summer in this city. You also can catch a free concert by the NSO several times in summer at the Carter Barron Amphitheatre in Rock Creek Park (☎ **202-426-6837**). The Capitol Lawn concerts are enormously popular, so you need to arrive early and be prepared to go through security screening.

The rousing **4th of July concert** features the National Symphony, guest artists, celebrity hosts, and an enthusiastic audience. The evening ends with a bang when the 1812 Overture accompanies the fireworks display on the Mall (or vice versa, depending on your viewpoint). Arrive early, be braced for crowds, and bring something to sit on. You can also catch a live broadcast of the concert on TV.

A night at the opera

Snagging tickets for the **Washington Opera** (☎ **800-876-7372** or 202-295-2400; Internet: www.dc-opera.org) was hard enough *before* Placido Domingo became artistic director. Now it's tougher than getting elected. Almost all seats are sold to series subscribers. Still, you can have a go at it by calling the box office in August or by getting in the standing-room-only line at the Kennedy Center Box office before 10 a.m. on Saturday during the season. SRO tickets for Saturday and the following week are sold then, one per customer, for $15 *cash* for most performances.

Due to renovation of the Kennedy Center Opera House, the Washington Opera will perform at **DAR Constitution Hall** through most of 2003, returning to the Kennedy Center in early 2004. Constitution Hall is located at 1776 D St. NW, between 17th and 18th streets, with entrances on D, C, and 18th. Free shuttle service is available from the Farragut West Metrorail station, outside the 18th Street exit, before and after performances. Before performances, the shuttle runs for one hour, beginning 75 minutes before curtain time.

Enjoying an evening of dance

The best in the dance world grace Washington's stages. Alvin Ailey, the American Ballet Theatre, the Bolshoi, Merce Cunningham, Paul Taylor, and many other stellar companies take their turns performing here. The city also is quite proud of its own **Washington Ballet** (☎ **202-362-3606**; Internet: www.washingtonballet.org). The Washington Ballet performs at several venues, including the Kennedy Center.

Located near Catholic University, **Dance Place,** 3225 8th St. NE, between Kearney and Monroe streets (☎ **202-269-1600**; Internet: www.danceplace.org), is the site of reasonably priced performances by local and visiting troupes: contemporary, postmodern, tap, ethnic, performance art, and styles as yet unnamed. Tickets to most performances are $16 general admission, $12 for seniors, college students, and professional artists, $6 for children 17 and younger, and free for children younger than 2 who sit in an adult's lap.

Finding Cool Things for the Kids

Washington offers wonderful cultural opportunities for families, especially during the school year. Look to the following for entertaining productions that are geared to youngsters:

- ✔ The **Discovery Theater,** in the Smithsonian's Arts and Industries Building, 900 Jefferson Dr. SW (☎ **202-357-1500;** Internet: discoverytheater.si.edu)

- ✔ The **Kennedy Center's** youth and family programs, 2700 F St. NW between New Hampshire Avenue and Rock Creek Parkway (☎ **800-444-1324** or 202-467-4600; Internet: www.kennedy-center.org/programs/family)

- ✔ The **National Theatre's** free children's program, "Saturday Morning at the National," 1321 E St. NW (☎ **202-783-3372;** Internet: www.nationaltheatre.org)

- ✔ The **Washington Ballet's** *Nutcracker,* performed during the Christmas season at the Warner Theatre, 13th St. NW between E and F streets (☎ **202-783-4000;** Internet: www.warnertheatre.com)

Chapter 23

Hitting the Clubs and Bars

. . . .

In This Chapter

▶ Spying the best spots to hear your favorite music

▶ Checking out clubs where you can dance the night away

▶ Taking some time out for a laugh (or two)

. . . .

Taking in Mozart at the Kennedy Center or *Hamlet* at the Shakespeare Theatre may quench your cultural appetite. But it may leave you thirsty for a chilled cocktail and some hot jazz. When your high-culture sensibilities have been fed, but you feel the urge to get down or wet your whistle, you won't lack for a place to go. Rest assured, after the lights go off in the White House, you can take the party elsewhere, such as Adams-Morgan or Georgetown. Washington's large international population has spawned clubs, bars, and other night spots that appeal to its multicultural citizenry.

Before you head off to strut your stuff, keep in mind that Metro stops running at midnight Sunday through Thursday and at 2 a.m. Friday and Saturday. Allow plenty of time to get to the station, or you may need to catch a taxi back to your hotel.

For a comprehensive listing of the entertainment scene, see the "Weekend" section of the Friday *Washington Post*. The free *City Paper* — available in bookstores, restaurants, bars, and cafes all around town — is another good source for information on what's going on.

Finding Hot Spots for Cool Jazz

D.C.'s premier jazz club is **Blues Alley** (1073 Wisconsin Ave. NW; ☎ 202-337-4141; Internet: www.bluesalley.com). All the top touring artists come here. Dizzy Gillespie, Charlie Byrd, Stanley Turrentine, Ahmad Jamal, and Ramsey Lewis cut live albums at the club. Blues Alley bills itself as a jazz supper club and serves Creole cuisine, steak, and seafood from 6 p.m. and lighter fare after 10 p.m. Reservations are recommended.

Washington, D.C. Bars & Clubs

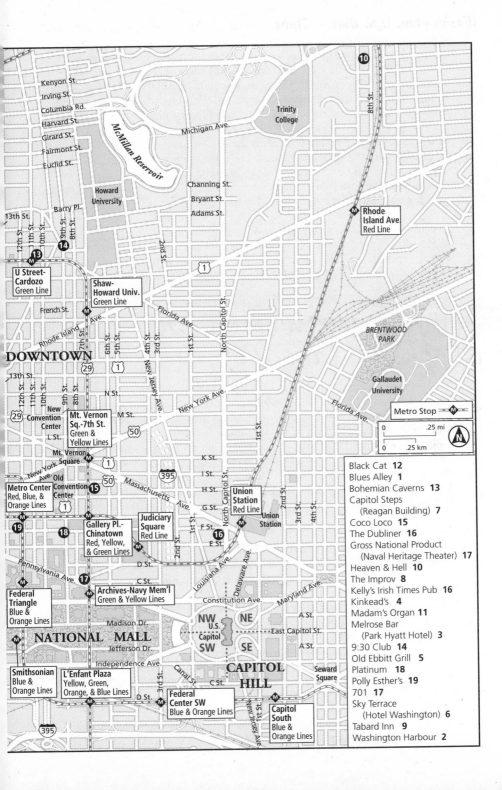

Black Cat **12**
Blues Alley **1**
Bohemian Caverns **13**
Capitol Steps
    (Reagan Building) **7**
Coco Loco **15**
The Dubliner **16**
Gross National Product
    (Naval Heritage Theater) **17**
Heaven & Hell **10**
The Improv **8**
Kelly's Irish Times Pub **16**
Kinkead's **4**
Madam's Organ **11**
Melrose Bar
    (Park Hyatt Hotel) **3**
9:30 Club **14**
Old Ebbitt Grill **5**
Platinum **18**
Polly Esther's **19**
701 **17**
Sky Terrace
    (Hotel Washington) **6**
Tabard Inn **9**
Washington Harbour **2**

The **Bohemian Caverns** (2001 11th St. NW at U Street; ☎ 202-299-0801; Internet: www.bohemiancaverns.com) is a renovation and expansion of the Crystal Caverns, which showcased such jazz greats at Duke Ellington, Pearl Bailey, Miles Davis, John Coltrane, Ella Fitzgerald, and Billie Holiday from the '20s into the '60s. A full-service restaurant resides within this multistoried jazz club. Call ahead for information on performances, which aren't scheduled every night.

In the lounge at **701,** the restaurant at 701 Pennsylvania Ave. NW at 7th Street (☎ 202-393-0701), you can listen to live jazz seven nights a week while nursing one of the bartender's signature cocktails — chocolate martini, sour apple martini, or Cosmopolitans flavored with Cointreau, peach or apricot. Or maybe you'd rather have a whisky or beer.

The informal bar and cafe on the lower level of **Kinkead's** downtown seafood restaurant features live jazz from 6:30 to 10 p.m. Tuesday through Saturday. (2000 Pennsylvania Ave. NW [actually on I Street between 20th and 21st streets]; ☎ 202-296-7700).

Feeling Groovy: Where to Go for Rock and Other Pop

The coolest felines purr at the **Black Cat** (1831 14th St. NW between S and T streets; ☎ 202-667-7960). You don't pay a cover charge in the Red Room bar, which has pool tables, pinball machines, a jukebox with an eclectic selection of music, and a laid-back atmosphere. Things can get hopping in the concert room, which showcases underground/ alternative performers and has a dance floor that holds 400. Cherry Poppin' Daddies, Foo Fighters, Korn, and Squirrel Nut Zippers — and Pete Seeger — are among the acts who have appeared here. Cover in the concert room depends on the act. A mostly vegetarian menu of light fare is available.

Sheryl Crow, Smashing Pumpkins, and Shawn Colvin have played **The 9:30 Club** (815 V St. NW between 8th and 9th streets; ☎ 202-393-0930). With a top-notch sound system and lots of dance-floor space, this premier venue is ideal for listening and dancing . . . but not sitting. This club has no seats! The cover charge depends on the act. Call to find out when performances are scheduled. Advance tickets are available through **tickets.com** (☎ 800-955-5566 or ☎ 703-218-6500; Internet: www.tickets.com) and the 9:30 Club box office, which is open Monday through Friday from noon to 7 p.m. and until 11 p.m. on show nights; Saturday from 6 to 11 p.m. on show nights; and Sunday from 6 to 10:30 p.m. on show nights.

Madam's Organ in Adams-Morgan (the owner likes puns) was named one of the 25 best bars in America by *Playboy* magazine in 2000. Madam's has a varied musical menu, with shows starting between 9 and 10 p.m. On Monday, it's funky jazz; Tuesday, delta blues; Wednesday, bluegrass (with local TV news anchor Doug McKelway sometimes sitting in on banjo); Thursday, Latin blues; and Friday and Saturday, "flaming hot blues." If you want noise, body heat, and dancing, this weekend spot is the one for you. (The club's slogan is "where the beautiful people go to get ugly.") You can get sandwiches, snacks, and "soul food" here. Redheads get half price on Rolling Rock.

Relaxing with Cocktails for Two

After a rough day of sightseeing, kicking back with your favorite aperitif can be therapeutic.

The well-worn comfort of the **Tabard Inn** (1739 N St. NW, between 17th and 18th streets; ☎ 202-833-2668) makes it a perfect spot for a drink all year round. It's even better in the winter, when you can cozy up to the fireplace. Every Sunday, live jazz plays from 7:30 to 10:30 p.m.

The **Old Ebbitt Grill** (675 15th St. NW, between F and G streets; ☎ 202-347-4800) has the feel of an old-fashioned men's club, and as the evening wears on, that feeling grows. This place is big enough and has multiple bars, so you can probably find a spot that satisfies you. You have lots of choices in the nibbles department as well.

You get a panoramic view of Washington with your cocktail at the **Sky Terrace** atop the Hotel Washington (151 15th St. NW at Pennsylvania Avenue; ☎ 202-638-5900). Between May and October, weather willing, this outdoor restaurant is a wonderful vantage point for watching the sun set over the city or the lights come on at D.C.'s landmarks.

It's always relaxing to sip a drink along the water, and a good place to do that in D.C. is at Georgetown's **Washington Harbour** complex (3000 K St. NW at Thomas Jefferson Street.). You can find a seat at **Tony and Joe's** (☎ 202-944-4545), which has terrace tables and an outdoor bar, or check out some of the other establishments along the Potomac River here.

Searching for International Sound Bites

After a thought-provoking play at the Shakespeare Theatre, walk up the street and shake your coconuts at **Coco Loco** (801 7th St. NW, between H and I streets; ☎ 202-289-2626), where you can munch tapas. And, depending on when you get here, you can listen to a live band, watch a Brazilian floor show, join a conga line or a limbo contest, take a salsa lesson, or dance to a DJ spinning Latin music.

Hanker for a taste of the Emerald Isle? Well, head on up to Capitol Hill, where **The Dubliner** (520 N. Capitol St. NW, between E and F streets; ☎ 202-737-3773) and **Kelly's Irish Times Pub** (14 F St. NW, between North Capitol Street and New Jersey Avenue; ☎ 202-543-5433) add spice to the neighborhood. You can find Irish beer, Irish food, and Irish music — some provided by professional musicians — in both hangouts.

Getting Down Tonight: Where to Shake Your Booty

Do you wanna dance? If so, see the earlier sections of this chapter for details about the Black Cat (underground/alternative rock), the 9:30 Club (usually contemporary rock), Madam's Organ (different sounds different nights), and Coco Loco (Latin).

If what you're really looking for is romantic cheek-to-cheek — maybe with dinner first — try the **Melrose Bar** in the Park Hyatt Hotel (24th Street NW at M Street; ☎ 202-789-1234), where a dance band plays from 7 to 11 p.m. Saturdays.

As you may expect, **Heaven & Hell** (2327 18th St. NW at Columbia Road; ☎ 202-667-HELL), welcomes both angels and devils. Check your wings and pitchforks at the door. Here, it's Heaven that sizzles. It's a loud dancehall on the upper level (of course) that features different styles of music on different nights, sometimes live, sometimes DJ-generated. Lines form early for the Thursday night '80s dance party. On weekends, the pearly gates don't close until 3 a.m. Hell, downstairs, is a dark bar with a pool table.

Platinum (915 F St. NW, between 9th and 10th streets; ☎ 202-393-3555; Internet: www.platinumclubdc.com) is an upscale club with three dance floors and a VIP lounge. VIP memberships are for sale, table reservations are available, and "proper attire" is required. It's open Thursday through Sunday, with a theme each night. Sunday, the music is hip-hop, R&B, and reggae. The rest of the week, it's techno, house, trance, Latin, and hip-hop. Thursday, college students get discounted admission. Friday, women get in free until midnight.

Polly Esther's (605 12th St. NW, between F and G streets; ☎ 202-737-1970) has multiple levels, too, but puts them to much different use than Platinum. It contains a '70s floor, an '80s floor, and a '90s floor. Expect many bars and much noise. As I write this book, the club is advertising a foam party, where you can dance to "hip-hop, house, high energy" music in five feet of foam.

Laughing It Up: Where to Go for Comedy

The best comedy in Washington is homegrown. **The Capitol Steps,** in fact, blossomed on the Capitol steps. They were congressional staffers who saw the humor around them and had the talent to turn it into an enduring musical act. I'm talking about songs like "It's a Whole Newt World," "Send in the Clones," "Don't Cry for Me, Judge Scalia," and the 2002 composition, "Enron-Ron-Ron." They've been doing this act since the early '80s ("The Wreck of the Walter Fritz Mondale," "Dutch, the Magic Reagan"). Now, they have a regular gig every Friday and Saturday at 7:30 p.m. in the amphitheater of the (don't you love irony?) Ronald Reagan Building, 1300 Pennsylvania Ave. NW, between 13th and 14th streets. You can purchase the $31.50 tickets (they're funny, not inexpensive) from TicketMaster (☎ **800-551-SEAT** or 202-432-SEAT; Internet: www.ticketmaster.com) or at the D.C. Visitor Information Center in the Reagan Building.

Another local comedy troupe, the **Gross National Product** (Internet: www.gnpcomedy.com), performs at the Naval Heritage Theater, 701 Pennsylvania Ave. NW at 7th Street. Call ☎ **202-783-7212** for dates, times, and reservations. Tickets are $25. This sketch troupe's past reviews have carried such titles as "Man Without A Contra," "A Newt World Order" (with a name like Newt, you've got to be funny), and "All the President's Women." (Guess which Chief Executive was featured?) The group also conducts "Scandal Tours" of Washington, which leave from the 12th Street side of the Old Post Office Pavilion, 1100 Pennsylvania Ave. NW, at 1 p.m. Saturdays from April through Labor Day. Reservations are available at the same phone number.

Headliners on the national comedy club circuit perform at **The Improv** (1140 Connecticut Ave. NW between L and M streets; ☎ **202-296-7008;** Internet: www.dcimprov.com). Ellen DeGeneres, Jerry Seinfeld, and Robin Williams have performed here. Light meals are available. Show times are Sunday through Thursday at 8:30 p.m. and Friday and Saturday at 8 and 10:30 p.m. The cover varies with the lineup. You can make reservations in person at the box office, by phone, or from the Web site.

Part VII
The Part of Tens

The 5th Wave   By Rich Tennant

"That? That's Schedule LVES-1. We've never had to use it. But, if anyone actually discovers how to grow money on trees, Uncle Sam's got a form to get his fair share of the leaves."

In this part . . .

Ah, tradition. The Part of Tens is to *For Dummies* books what monument hopping is to Washington — essential. In this part of the book, you discover the top ten views in D.C. and (gulp) the top ten reasons to drive around here.

Chapter 24

Top Ten D.C. Views

In This Chapter

▶ Finding great places to watch D.C. sunsets

▶ Checking out cool spots overlooking the capital city

S ooner or later, even the most jaded visitor succumbs to Washington's beauty. During your visit, I hope you find time to admire Washington's pretty face from one or more of the following sites. And don't forget to put the film in your camera.

Washington Monument

A rejuvenated **Washington Monument** (between Constitution Avenue NW, Independence Avenue SW, and 15th and 17th streets; ☎ 202-426-6841; Internet: www.nps.gov/wamo) reopened to the public in 2000 after three years of restoration. The view from the top didn't change. It's still the best in Washington. See the monument's listing in Chapter 16 for details on getting to its top. It's open daily from 9 a.m. to 4:45 p.m. You can call or visit the Web site for ticket information and reservations.

Old Post Office Pavilion

Ride the elevator in the tower of the **Old Post Office Pavilion** (Pennsylvania Ave. and 11th Street NW; ☎ 202-606-8691; Internet: www.nps.gov/opot). From the observation deck, 270 feet above the street, you can see a view of downtown and beyond that many people think is second only to the vista from the Washington Monument.

While you're here, take a look at the interior workings of the tower clock and bells and visit the ninth-floor exhibit room. The bells are rung on federal holidays and on special occasions declared by Congress.

Top Washington, D.C. Views

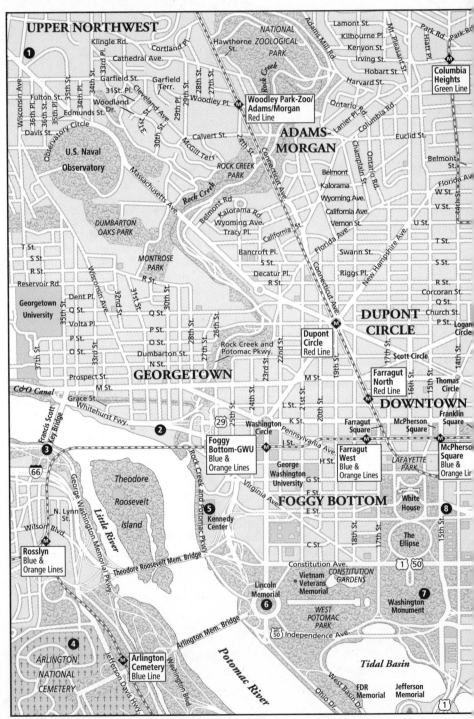

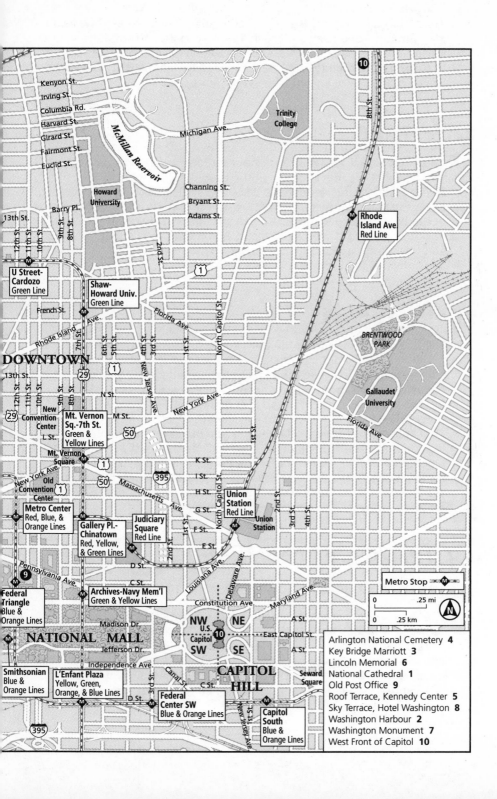

Arlington National Cemetery **4**
Key Bridge Marriott **3**
Lincoln Memorial **6**
National Cathedral **1**
Old Post Office **9**
Roof Terrace, Kennedy Center **5**
Sky Terrace, Hotel Washington **8**
Washington Harbour **2**
Washington Monument **7**
West Front of Capitol **10**

The tower is open daily 9 a.m. to 8:45 p.m. (6:30 p.m. Thursdays) early May through Labor Day and 9 a.m. to 4:45 p.m. the rest of the year. It's closed Thanksgiving, Dec. 25, and Jan. 1. The tower also closes for up to three hours when the bells are rung and in bad weather. Call ahead to make sure that it's open when you want to visit.

Sky Terrace

Come to this open-air rooftop restaurant for the view, not the food. If you do eat at the **Sky Terrace** (in the Hotel Washington, 151 15th St. NW at Pennsylvania Avenue; ☎ **202-638-5900**), pick something simple, like a sandwich. Or just have a drink. You're here for the bird's-eye view of the White House in the next block and the rest of Washington further into the distance. Arrive by 5:30 p.m. if you want to beat out the locals and other tourists for a seat. The Sky Terrace is open daily 11:30 to 1 a.m. May through October

Lincoln Memorial

Take a break from reading the Gettysburg Address on the wall and gaze at the Reflecting Pool, the Mall, the Washington Monument, and the Capitol from the steps of the **Lincoln Memorial,** 23rd Street NW between Constitution and Independence avenues (☎ **202-426-6841;** Internet: www.nps.gov/linc). From there, you can observe construction of the World War II Memorial at the other end of the Reflecting Pool and decide for yourself whether you like the location of Washington's latest monument. Then walk around to the back of Lincoln's place for a view across the Potomac River of Arlington National Cemetery and the eternal flame marking John F. Kennedy's grave. The Lincoln Memorial is open everyday except Dec. 25 from 8 a.m. to midnight. See Chapter 16 for more details.

Roof Terrace of the Kennedy Center

You don't need orchestra seats to visit the **Kennedy Center** (2700 F St. NW between New Hampshire Avenue and Rock Creek Parkway). In fact, one of the best shows in town plays night and day, and it's free. Although you may want to dine in the Roof Terrace Restaurant, the Hors D'Oeuvrerie, or the KC Café (☎ **202-416-8555** for all three), you can feast on the view from the promenade *outside* the restaurants without spending a cent. Circle the promenade once for a 360-degree vista. The center is open daily 10 a.m. until 30 minutes after the last performance. See Chapter 16 for more details.

Washington National Cathedral

Washington's highest points above sea level are the towers of the Washington National Cathedral (Massachusetts and Wisconsin avenues NW; ☎ 202-537-6200; Internet: www.cathedral.org/cathedral), so the views from those spots are among the best in the city. One way to partake of the view is to have tea in the **Pilgrim Observation Gallery**. (See Chapter 15 for details.) Or you can visit on your own. (Regular tours don't go up the towers.) The observation gallery is open Monday through Friday from 10 a.m. to 5 p.m.; Saturday from 10 a.m. to 4:30 p.m.; and Sunday 8 a.m. to 5 p.m. (See Chapter 16 for more details.)

Washington Harbour

Walk along the **riverfront promenade** at Washington Harbour, below K Street at Thomas Jefferson Street in Georgetown, and gaze across the Potomac toward Virginia. Dead ahead is Theodore Roosevelt Island. To the left, you can make out the Watergate and, beyond it, the Kennedy Center. To the right, Key Bridge connects Georgetown with Arlington, Virginia. If you're so moved, grab an outdoor seat at one of the harbour's restaurants and have a sip or a snack. This well-traveled area is fairly safe during the day and when the restaurants are open. (See a review of the Harbour Club restaurant in Chapter 14.)

West Front of Capitol

If your timing is right — maybe after an afternoon tour of the Capitol in winter or on your way to dinner in summer — you can watch the sunset over the Washington Monument, Lincoln Memorial, and Potomac River from the West Front of the Capitol. Seeing Washington's marble landmarks bathed in golden light, with purple and pink streaking the sky over the Potomac, is an awesome sight.

Arlington National Cemetery

If you don't own one, I suggest picking up a disposable panoramic camera before touring **Arlington National Cemetery** (☎ 703-607-8052; Internet: www.arlingtoncemetery.org). You can get some great shots of Washington from the Arlington House lawn (a Tourmobile stop) or from Pierre L'Enfant's grave below the house. For more on Arlington, see Chapter 16.

Key Bridge Marriott Hotel

Visitors and locals have been flocking to the top floor of the **Key Bridge Marriott** (1401 Lee Highway, Arlington, Virginia, just across the Key Bridge from Georgetown; ☎ **703-524-6400**) since it opened more than 40 years ago. Although the hotel's restaurant has gone through more lives than a cat, the outstanding vista has endured. Diners at **J.W.'s View Steakhouse** look out across the Potomac River to Georgetown and the rest of Washington's skyline. The steakhouse is open Monday through Thursday from 5 to 10 p.m.; Friday from 5 to 11 p.m.; Saturday from 6 to 11 p.m.; and Sunday from 10 a.m. to 2:30 p.m. (brunch).

Chapter 25

Driving Around D.C.

In This Chapter

▶ Finding the places worth the drive

▶ Discovering parks and parkways away from the Mall

▶ Figuring out how to get there from here

I *know*: If you've read any other chapter in this book, then you've seen my repeated warnings that you should not drive in Washington. This chapter, though, goes contrary to that advice because I'm actually giving you ten reasons *to* drive. I'll just call this chapter — as members of Congress do in the *Congressional Record* — a revision and extension of my remarks. If you happen to have a car, you can find some sights that are worth driving to. I'm not really advocating that you drive *in* central D.C. but encouraging you to use your car to reach sights and attractions that are mostly outside the District.

National Arboretum

The best time to visit the **National Arboretum** (☎ 202-245-2726; Internet: www.usna.usda.gov) is from late April into late May, when the azaleas are in full riot and crabapples, dogwoods, peonies, roses, and irises also bloom. If you can't make it during that timeframe, though, don't worry: The National Arboretum always has something to see, such as magnolias in early spring and holly berries in winter. Some manmade items will grab your attention as well, such as 22 sandstone columns that were removed from the East Portico of the Capitol during a renovation and now stand like an ancient ruin in the arboretum.

This 446-acre site is a research and educational facility of the Agricultural Department's Research Service. Stop at the Administration Building to pick up a map and guide and to find out what's blooming.

If the azaleas are in flower, you *have* to drive Azalea Road. You won't believe the cascade of colors! Pack a picnic.

From downtown D.C., go northeast on New York Avenue all the way to the arboretum's entrance (to the right). Watch carefully for the sign after you cross the big Bladensberg Road intersection. Returning to downtown is trickier because of traffic patterns. I suggest using the R Street exit from the arboretum, which is near the Administration Building. Turn left on Bladensburg and then right on Maryland Avenue, which will carry you right to the Capitol. Watch out for the jog around Stanton Park Square at 6th and C streets. Arboretum grounds are open daily (except for Dec. 25) from 8 a.m. to 5 p.m.

Clara Barton National Historic Site

Hard as it is to believe, when **Clara Barton's** last home became part of the National Park Service in 1975, it was the first National Historic Site dedicated to the accomplishments of a woman (☎ **301-492-6245;** Internet: www.nps.gov/clba). The founder of the American Red Cross lived here from Feb. 28, 1897, until she died in her bedroom on April 12, 1912, at the age of 90. Until she resigned as Red Cross president in 1904, her residence was also the Red Cross headquarters and a warehouse for disaster supplies.

Go west on M Street out of Georgetown and then turn left on Canal Road, which becomes Clara Barton Parkway. Then follow the signs to the Clara Barton National Historic Site. The interior of the house is shown by guided tour daily on the hour between 10 a.m. and 4 p.m., except Thanksgiving, Dec. 25, and Jan. 1. Admission is free.

Do not leave Washington before 9:30 a.m., when a portion of Canal Road is inbound only. Conversely, don't drive into town between 3:30 and 6:30 p.m., when the road is one-way out.

Glen Echo Park

Glen Echo Park is a very strange place, located essentially next door to the Clara Barton House. Glen Echo (☎ **301-492-6229;** Internet: www.nps.gov/glec) is an abandoned amusement park with a marvelous working carousel and a bunch of sod-roofed Mongolian *yurts* (large, wooden-framed tents lined with felt) that house arts programs.

Glen Echo was a functioning amusement park, served by trolleys, from around 1900 until 1968. That history lives in the carousel — with 40 horses, 4 rabbits, 4 ostriches, a giraffe, a deer, a lion, a tiger, 2 circus chariots, more than 1,000 lights, and lots of mirrors — and the dances still held in the ballroom. Other facilities here house quite a few arts programs, many for children. Phone or check the Web site for puppet shows and other performances for kids.

Top Destinations around Washington, D.C.

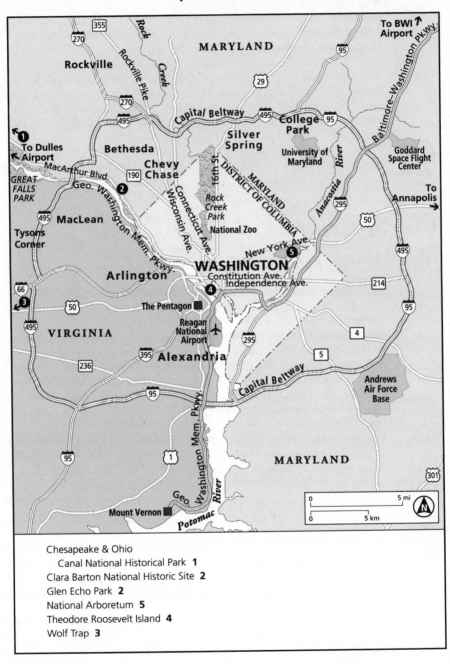

Chesapeake & Ohio
   Canal National Historical Park **1**
Clara Barton National Historic Site **2**
Glen Echo Park **2**
National Arboretum **5**
Theodore Roosevelt Island **4**
Wolf Trap **3**

Restoration of the amusement park remnants is an ongoing project. When I walk around this place — especially in winter when no one's here — I feel like an archeologist exploring some reasonably well-preserved ruin: You see the remains of the swimming pool, the abandoned bumper car pavilion, and so on.

To get to Glen Echo Park, follow the directions to the Clara Barton House. You can't miss it; it's the abandoned amusement park with the stone tower and the yurts! The park is open daily 6 a.m. to 1 a.m. The carousel operates May through September, from 11:30 a.m. to 6 p.m. weekends and 10 a.m. to 2 p.m. Wednesdays and Thursdays.

Particularly if you have kids, call to find out what activities are going on when you plan to visit. You can also picnic at the park.

Chesapeake and Ohio Canal National Historical Park

The **C&O Canal Park** (☎ **301-299-3613** or 301-767-3714; Internet: www. nps.gov/choh) actually stretches along the old canal from Georgetown to Cumberland, Maryland. In this chapter, I'm talking about the section of the park at Great Falls, Maryland. My family comes here regularly to picnic, stroll the boardwalk out to the falls, and hike along the canal and into the bordering hills. The setting is beautiful. You can brush up on your history at the visitor center in the old Great Falls Tavern, which served canal boat passengers, and you can take a 70-minute ride on a replica of a canal boat.

To get to Great Falls, follow the directions to the Clara Barton House (see the section "Clara Barton National Historic Site," earlier in this chapter), but stay on the Clara Barton Parkway until it ends at McArthur Boulevard. Follow McArthur into the park.

The schedule for the boat rides is as follows:

- ✔ **Late March:** Saturday and Sunday, 11 a.m., 1:30, p.m., and 3 p.m.

- ✔ **April through mid-June, September through mid-November:** Saturday, Sunday, and federal holidays, 11 a.m., 1:30, p.m., and 3 p.m. Wednesday through Friday 3 p.m.

- ✔ **Mid-June through August:** Saturday, Sunday, and federal holidays 11 a.m., 1:30, p.m., 3 p.m., and 4:30 p.m. Wednesday through Friday 11 a.m., 1:30 p.m., and 3 p.m.

Fares are $8 for ages 15 to 61; $6 for ages 62 and up; $5 for children ages 4 to14; and ages 3 and younger are free.

The visitor center is open Monday through Friday from 9 a.m. to 4:30 p.m. and Saturday and Sunday from 9 a.m. to 5 p.m. and is closed Dec. 25 and Jan. 1. Admission is $5 per vehicle for a three-day pass.

Great Falls Park

Great Falls Park is in Virginia, directly across the Potomac River from the C&O Canal Park's Great Falls area. You see the same falls from the opposite side, can picnic and hike, and can check out some additional history at Virginia's park (☎ **703-285-2965;** Internet: www.nps.gov/grfa). A substantial visitor center offers history and nature exhibits. Before he presided over the successful launch of a new nation, George Washington presided over a failed attempt to build a canal on this side of the Potomac. Remnants are visible.

Go west on M Street out of Georgetown, left on Canal Road, left over Chain Bridge, right on Virginia Route 123 (Chain Bridge Road), and then right on Virginia Route 193 (Georgetown Pike). Turn right at Old Dominion Drive at the sign to the park.

The park is open daily, except Dec. 25, from 7 a.m. until dark. From April 15 through October 15, the visitor center is open from 10 a.m. to 5 p.m. weekdays and 10 a.m. to 6 p.m. weekends. The rest of the year, it's open daily from 10 a.m. to 4 p.m. Admission is $5 per vehicle for a three-day pass.

Wolf Trap

The name says it all here: **Wolf Trap Farm Park for the Performing Arts** (☎ **703-255-1800;** Internet: www.nps.gov/wotr). At the Filene Center — a roofed, open-air theater with outdoor lawn seating as well — big-name artists perform before audiences of up to 7,000 from May through September. The **Meadow Pavilion** and the **Theatre in the Woods** host workshops in theater and other arts and crafts. Performances are held throughout the year in the **Barns of Wolf Trap,** a 352-seat indoor theater built in two restored 18th-century barns.

The word eclectic was created to describe Wolf Trap's performance schedule: the National Symphony Orchestra, the Wolf Trap Opera, pop, rock, country, folk, Broadway musicals, and lots of stuff for kids and for aging Boomers. My wife and I recently took my sister and her husband to see the Kingston Trio and the Smothers Brothers; the Beach Boys had performed a little earlier. Peter, Paul, and Mary are also regulars. Wolf Trap has a restaurant (reservations are strongly advised) and lots of space for picnicking — and holding festivals — on the 117 acres of farm and forest land. Call or visit the Web site to find out which performances might appeal to you.

Drive west on Constitution Avenue to westbound I-66. Watch for signs to Virginia Route 267 local exits (the Dulles Toll Road). After you're on 267, watch for signs to Wolf Trap. (*Don't* get on the toll-free Dulles Access Highway, which is restricted to airport traffic.) Fees vary with the performances.

Theodore Roosevelt Island

This little island in the middle of the Potomac River is a memorial to the 26th president's history as an outdoorsman and advocate of conservation. **Theodore Roosevelt Island Park** (☎ **703-289-2500;** Internet: www.nps.gov/this) contains 91 acres of woods, 2½ miles of trails, and a memorial plaza with an outsized statue of Roosevelt. It's a pleasant respite that's actually inside the city limits.

Drive west on Constitution Avenue and continue straight across the Theodore Roosevelt Memorial Bridge to the George Washington Memorial Parkway (northbound). The Roosevelt Island parking lot is to your right immediately after you enter the parkway. *Don't miss it!* The only entrance is from the northbound lanes. The park is open daily from sunrise to sunset, and admission is free.

George Washington Memorial Parkway

You can explore numerous interesting places along the **George Washington Memorial Parkway** (☎ **703-289-2500;** Internet: www.nps.gov/gwmp; e-mail: gwnp_superintendent@nps.gov; mailing address: George Washington Memorial Parkway Headquarters, Turkey Run Park, McLean, VA 22101), which runs along the west bank of the Potomac River from I-495 northwest of D.C. to Mount Vernon. Julie and I spent one pleasant weekend driving along the road and stopping at places we'd never visited. Write, phone, or e-mail parkway headquarters before your visit to ask for a map/brochure to be mailed to you. Otherwise, get it at parkway headquarters in Turkey Run Park, near the north end of the beltway, between 7:45 a.m. and 4:15 p.m. Monday through Friday or from outdoor boxes along the parkway at Turkey Run, Mount Vernon, Marine Corps Memorial, Netherlands Carillon, and Fort Marcy. (You also can ask whether they have parkway brochures at other National Park Service sites in the Washington area.)

Turkey Run is 700 acres of forest and hiking trails. Other parkway highlights include the following:

- ✔ **Dyke Marsh:** This 380 acres of tidal marsh, floodplain, and swamp forest comprises the largest remaining freshwater tidal wetlands in the Washington Metropolitan area and attracts birdwatchers.

- ✔ **Fort Hunt:** Batteries here guarded the river approach to Washington from 1898 to 1918.

- ✔ **Fort Marcy:** This earthenwork remnant is just one example of the many forts that surrounded Washington during the Civil War.

- ✔ **Netherlands Carillon:** Fifty-bell, 127-foot tall carillon given by the Dutch expressed gratitude to the United States after World War II. The bells strike the hour during daylight. Concerts are played on Saturdays and national holidays from 2 to 4 p.m. in May and September and 6 to 8 p.m. in June, July, and August. During concerts, visitors are welcome to go up in the tower to watch the carillonneur perform.

- ✔ **Marine Corps Memorial:** This oversized sculpture of the famous World War II photograph, by Joe Rosenthal, shows Marines raising the U.S. flag during the battle for Iwo Jima.

- ✔ **Gravelly Point:** This area is a popular spot for watching airplanes take off and land at National Airport. If you have a boat, put it in the Potomac here and view Washington's landmarks from the water.

The parkway also provides access to Arlington National Cemetery (see Chapter 16 for details), Mount Vernon (see Chapter 21), and Theodore Roosevelt Island (see earlier in this chapter). At Alexandria, the parkway runs through the city as Washington Street.

From D.C., drive west on Constitution Avenue and continue straight across the Theodore Roosevelt Memorial Bridge to the George Washington Memorial Parkway (northbound). Or drive west on Independence Avenue; as you pass the Lincoln Memorial, watch closely for signs to the Arlington Memorial Bridge. After you cross the bridge, turn right out of the traffic circle and then exit left to continue southbound or go straight to go northbound. The southbound route also will be marked to National Airport.

Do not sight-see along the parkway during rush hour. This road is a major commuter artery on weekdays. Drive here on the weekend or from mid-morning until mid-afternoon during the week. Also note: Some spots are accessible only from the northbound or southbound lanes.

Rock Creek Park

This marvelous urban park (☎ **202-895-6070;** Internet: www.nps.gov/rocr; e-mail: ROCR_superintendent@nps.gov; mailing address: 3545 Williamsburg Lane NW, Washington, DC 20008) winds its way from the Potomac River near the Kennedy Center all the way up to D.C.'s most northern tip. Write, phone, or e-mail the park headquarters before your visit to request a mailed map/brochure. In the park, you can find information desks and activities at the following locations:

✔ The Nature Center, 5200 Glover Rd. NW (open Wednesday through Sunday from 9 a.m. to 5 p.m., closed Thanksgiving, Dec. 25, Jan. 1, and July 4). The Nature Center features exhibits on plants, animals, and habitats in the park. It also offers a Discovery Room for preschool children, as well as restrooms and drink machines.

✔ Peirce Mill, Beach Drive, and Tilden Street (open Wedneday through Sunday from noon to 4 p.m.). The Mill is an actual water-powered grist mill, and visitors can see displays on 19th-century life.

✔ The Old Stone House, 305 M St. NW (open Wednesday through Sunday from noon to 5 p.m., closed Thanksgiving, Dec. 25, Jan. 1, and July 4). This restored colonial house has displays on 18th-century living, as well as tours and historical exhibits.

✔ The Park Police Station, Beach Drive south of the Military Road overpass (open daily 7 a.m. to 4 p.m.).

You can also ask at other National Park Service sites in the Washington area.

You can engage in a wide range of outdoor activities at Rock Creek Park — hiking, horseback riding, bicycling, picnicking, golf, tennis, and boating. The Nature Center, Planetarium, Pierce Mill, and Peirce Barn conduct numerous programs for children. The 4,000-seat Carter Barron Amphitheater hosts numerous outdoor performances, both paid and free, including free summer concerts by the National Symphony Orchestra and free plays by the Shakespeare Theatre.

Drive northwest on Virginia Avenue to Rock Creek Parkway. For boating on the Potomac, cross the parkway into Thompson's Boat House. For the rest of the park, turn right.

Rock Creek Parkway and Beach Drive are major commuter routes during workday rush hours. South of Connecticut Avenue, the parkway is one-way south 6:30 a.m. to 9 a.m. Monday through Friday and one-way north 3:30 p.m. to 6 p.m. those days. On weekends and holidays, portions of Beach Drive are clogged with a different kind of traffic — bicyclists, roller bladers, walkers, and runners; the drive is closed to motor vehicles from Broad Branch Road to Military Road, from Picnic

Rock Creek Park Area

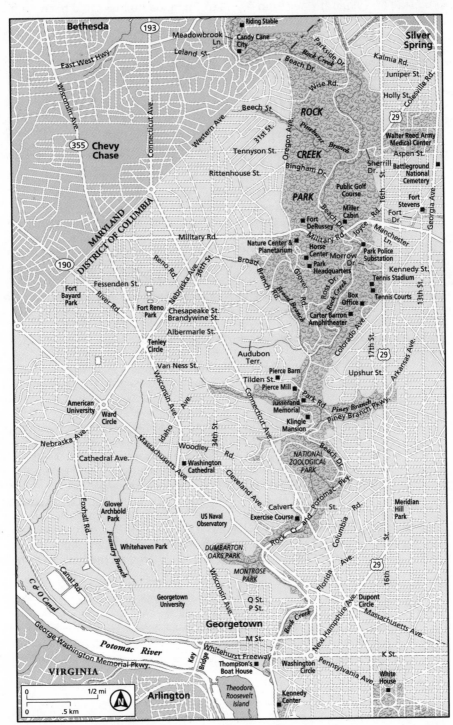

Bethesda · Silver Spring · Chevy Chase · ROCK CREEK PARK · MARYLAND · DISTRICT OF COLUMBIA · Georgetown · VIRGINIA · Arlington

Riding Stable · Meadowbrook Ln. · Candy Cane City · Parkside Dr. · Rock Creek · Kalmia Rd. · Juniper St. · Colesville Rd. · Leland St. · East West Hwy · Beach Dr. · Wise Rd. · Holly St. · Beech St. · Pinehurst Branch · Walter Reed Army Medical Center · 31st St. · Oregon Ave. · Tennyson St. · Bingham Dr. · Aspen St. · Rittenhouse St. · Public Golf Course · Sherrill Dr. · Battleground National Cemetery · Fort Stevens · Fort Dr. · Beach Dr. · Miller Cabin · Fort DeRussey · 16th St. · Military Rd. · Joyce Rd. · Manchester Ln. · Nature Center & Planetarium · Horse Center · Morrow Dr. · Park Police Substation · Park Headquarters · Glover Rd. · Ross Dr. · Kennedy St. · Tennis Stadium · Reno Rd. · Nebraska Ave. · 36th St. · Broad · Branch Rd. · Box Office · Tennis Courts · 13th St. · Fort Bayard Park · River Rd. · Fessenden St. · Fort Reno Park · Chesapeake St. · Brandywine St. · Carter Barron Amphitheater · Colorado Ave. · Albermarle St. · Tenley Circle · Audubon Terr. · 17th St. · American University · Van Ness St. · Pierce Barn · Upshur St. · Arkansas Ave. · Tilden St. · Pierce Mill · Park Rd. · Ward Circle · Nebraska Ave. · Jusserand Memorial · Piney Branch · Piney Branch Pkwy. · Cathedral Ave. · Idaho Ave. · 34th St. · Woodley Rd. · Klingle Mansion · Beach Dr. · Washington Cathedral · Cleveland Ave. · NATIONAL ZOOLOGICAL PARK · Glover Archbold Park · US Naval Observatory · Calvert · Rock Creek and Potomac Pkwy · St. · Meridian Hill Park · Foxhall Rd. · Whitehaven Park · Exercise Course · Columbia Rd. · DUMBARTON OAKS PARK · 16th St. · Foundry Branch · Georgetown University · MONTROSE PARK · Q St. · P St. · Rock Creek · New Hampshire Ave. · Dupont Circle · Massachusetts Ave. · Canal Rd. · C & O Canal · Georgetown · M St. · Wisconsin Ave. · George Washington Memorial Pkwy. · Potomac River · Key Bridge · Whitehurst Freeway · Thompson's Boat House · Washington Circle · Pennsylvania Ave. · K St. · White House · Theodore Roosevelt Island · Kennedy Center

0 · 1/2 mi · N · 0 · .5 km

Grove 10 to Wise Road, and from West Beach Drive to the D.C.-Maryland border from 7 a.m. to 7 p.m. on holidays and from 7 a.m. Saturday until 7 p.m. Sunday on weekends.

Mount Vernon, Alexandria, and Annapolis

The tenth part in this Part of Tens actually is comprised of three places that I discuss in detail earlier in the book. I'm mentioning them here because they're prime destinations for drivers.

To drive to **Alexandria** (details in Chapter 21), go west on Independence Avenue. As you pass the Lincoln Memorial, watch closely for signs to Arlington Memorial Bridge. After you cross the bridge, turn right out of the traffic circle and then exit left almost immediately, following signs to National Airport. After the parkway becomes Washington Street in Alexandria, turn left on King Street, which goes all the way to the waterfront. To preserve normal blood pressure, I suggest parking in a lot or garage rather than hunting for at-a-premium street parking.

Don't drive the parkway during rush hour.

To drive to **Mount Vernon** (details in Chapter 21), follow the preceding directions for Alexandria, but keep going straight. The parkway ends in George's front yard.

To drive to **Annapolis** (details in Chapter 21), go east on New York Avenue, which is U.S. 50, and follow 50 all the way. As you approach Annapolis, take Exit 24, Rowe Boulevard. Continue about 1 mile, hang a right at the governor's mansion, and go halfway around Church Circle. Take a right at the Maryland Inn (Duke of Gloucester Street) and follow signs to Main Street, City Dock, and the Historic District. On-street parking is 50 cents an hour, with a two-hour max. Smart drivers park in garages or at the Navy-Marine Corps Stadium (Rowe Boulevard and Taylor Avenue), where downtown shuttles run daily from 6:30 a.m. to 7 p.m. mid October through May and until 8 p.m. the rest of the year.

Quick Concierge

• •

This handy section is where you find practical information from airline phone numbers to where to get weather forecasts.

Fast Facts: Washington, D.C.

AAA

The most centrally located AAA office is at 701 15th St. NW (☎ 202-331-3000). For emergency road service, call ☎ 800-763-5500.

American Express

An American Express Travel Service office is located downtown at 1150 Connecticut Ave. NW between L and M streets (☎ 202-457-1300).

Area Codes

If you're calling a D.C. number from outside D.C., dial **202**. If you're in D.C. and calling D.C., no area code is needed. Dial **703** for suburban Virginia. For most close-in Maryland suburbs, dial **301**. Annapolis is **410**.

ATMs

It's hard to walk a block in D.C. without encountering an ATM. They're located in or near hotels, restaurants, attractions, and Metro stations. Most, if not all, banks have them. For specific locations, call Cirrus (☎ 800-424-7787) or Plus (☎ 800-843-7587).

Baby Sitters

Many hotels will secure a bonded sitter for your brood. Ask the concierge or at the front desk. White House Nannies (☎ 301-652-8088;

Internet: www.whitehousenannies.com), which has been in operation since 1985, sends sitters to hotels on short notice.

Camera Repair

If your shutter won't shut, head to Pro Photo, 1902 I St. NW (☎ 202-223-1292), or Penn Camera Exchange, 915 E St. NW (☎ 202-347-5777) and 1015 18th St. NW (☎ 202-785-7366).

Congress

Call the Capitol switchboard to locate a senator (☎ 202-224-3121) or member of the House (☎ 202-225-3121).

Convention Center

The new Washington Convention Center, scheduled to open in 2003, occupies the area between N, K, 7th, and 9th streets NW. The old convention center is located at 900 9th St. NW at H Street (☎ 202-789-1600).

Credit Cards

If your card is lost or stolen, call American Express (☎ 800-297-1000), MasterCard (☎ 800-622-7747), or Visa (☎ 800-847-2911). To obtain the phone number for other cards, call the toll-free information operator at ☎ 800-555-1212.

Customs

For information regarding U.S. Customs, call your embassy or consulate or contact the U. S. Customs office at ☎ 202-354-1000.

Dentists

In a dental emergency, call the District of Columbia Dental Society Referral Service at ☎ 202-547-7615.

Doctors

Ask your hotel's concierge or the front desk for the name of a physician who treats hotel guests. Or try the physicians referral services at George Washington University Hospital (☎ 888-449-3627), Washington Hospital Center (☎ 202-877-3627), or Georgetown University Hospital (☎ 202-342-2400).

Emergencies

For police, fire, and ambulance, call ☎ **911**. The 24-hour poison control hotline is ☎ 202-625-3333. To contact the police when it's not an emergency, dial 202-727-1010.

Eyeglasses

For same-day service on single-vision pre-scriptions, call Sterling Optical, 1900 M St. NW (☎ 202-728-1041) or 1747 Pennsylvania Ave. NW (☎ 202-466-2050).

Hospitals

For life-threatening emergencies, call ☎ **911**. For emergency-room treatment, contact one of the following hospitals: Children's National Medical Center, 111 Michigan Ave. NW (☎ 202-884-5000); George Washington University Hospital, 901 23rd St. NW (☎ 202-715-4911); Georgetown University Hospital, 3800 Reservoir Rd. NW (☎ 202-784-2119); or Sibley Hospital, 5255 Loughboro Rd. NW (☎ 202-537-4080). If you have a car, an emergency is not the time to drive in D.C. I suggest you take a taxi.

Hotlines

For help with a wide range of problems, call D.C.'s Crisis Line (☎ 202-561-7000) or the Answers Please information and referral service (☎ 202-463-6211). Other hotlines include the House of Ruth Domestic Violence Hotline (☎ 202-347-2777), the Alcohol and Drug Referral Network (☎ 888-304-9797), the D.C. Rape Crisis Center (202-333-7273), and the Poison Control Center (☎ 202-625-3333).

Information

For tourist information, contact the Washington, D.C. Convention and Tourism Corp., 1212 New York Ave. NW (☎ 800-422-8644; www.washington.org). For D.C. telephone directory information, dial ☎ 411; for telephone numbers outside the Washington area, dial the area code plus 555-1212.

Internet Access

Check your e-mail at Kramerbooks & Afterwords Café, 1517 Connecticut Ave. NW, between Dupont Circle and Q Street (☎ 202-387-1400) or at the Martin Luther King, Jr. Library, 901 G. St. NW at 9th Street (☎ 202-727-1111).

Laundry and Dry Cleaning

Many hotels provide laundry and dry-cleaning services or have coin-operated laundry facilities. For a self-service, coin-operated laundry, try Washtub Laundromat, 1511 17th St. NW between P and Q streets (☎ 202-332-9455). For same-day dry-cleaning service, go to MacDee Quality Cleaners at 1639 L St. NW, between 16th and 17th streets (☎ 202-296-6100).

Liquor Laws

You must be 21 years old to drink in D.C. Establishments can serve alcohol Monday through Thursday from 8 a.m. to 2 a.m.; Friday and Saturday from 8 a.m. to 2:30 a.m.; and Sunday from 10 a.m. to 2 a.m. Liquor stores are closed on Sunday, but grocery stores and convenience stores often sell beer and wine seven days a week.

Lost Property

You can report a loss on Metro by calling ☎ 202-962-1195, waiting until the very end of a long recording, and then leaving a message describing the lost item. You also can make a report by clicking "Lost & Found" on Metro's Internet home page, www.wmata.com. If you leave something in a taxi, call the individual company. If you forget something in a hotel room, check with the front desk or concierge.

Mail

For the nearest Post Office, ask at your hotel's front desk or call ☎ 202-635-5300. For Zip code information, call the same number.

Maps

Free city maps are available at many hotels and tourist sites and at the Washington Visitor Information Center, on the ground floor of the Ronald Reagan International Trade Center Building, 1300 Pennsylvania Ave. NW between 13th and 14th streets (☎ 202-328-4748; Internet: www.dcvisit.com).

Newspapers/Magazines

Washington's major daily newspaper is *The Washington Post. Washington City Paper* is a free weekly distributed in many places around town. *Washingtonian* magazine is published monthly.

Pharmacies

CVS pharmacies abound in Washington. It seems like you can find one on every corner. To locate the nearest one to you, call ☎ 888-607-4287. The 24-hour pharmacies are located at 1199 Vermont Ave. NW at 14th Street on Thomas Circle (☎ 202-737-3962) and on the western side of Dupont Circle (☎ 202-833-5704).

Police

In case of emergency, dial ☎ **911.** To locate the nearest police station or for non-emergency business, call ☎ 202-727-1010.

Radio Stations

Some of Washington's top AM radio stations are WTOP, 1500, news; WMAL, 630, news/talk; WTEM, 980, sports; and WOL, 1450, urban talk. Among the top FM stations are WPGC, 99.5,

urban hits; WKYS, 93.9, urban hits; WMMJ, 102.3, urban oldies; WHUR, 96.3, urban adult; WGMS, 103.5, classical; WBIG, 100.3, oldies; WJZW, 105.9, smooth jazz; WASH, 97.1, soft rock; WMZQ, 98.7, country; WWDC, 101.1, alternative rock; WRQX, 107.3, hits of the '80s, '90s, and now; WIHT, 99.5, top 40; WWZZ, 104.1, hits; WARW, 94.7, classic rock; WHFS, 99.1, rock; WAVA, 105.1, Christian; WAMU, 88.5, NPR; WPFW, 89.3, Pacifica; WCPS, 90.1, C-SPAN; and WETA, 90.9, NPR.

Restrooms

One of the great things about being a tourist in Washington is you're never far from clean, safe, and free restrooms — a particular benefit when you're traveling with young children. You can find them in all the government buildings, all the Smithsonian museums, the major monuments, and the larger food courts. One place you won't find them is inside the Metrorail system. In a truly extreme emergency, you may be able to convince a Metrorail station attendant to let you use the employee facility, but the attendants strongly resist doing so.

Safety

Especially with heightened security around federal facilities these days, the major tourist areas and Metrorail are quite safe for walking and sightseeing. At night, use the buddy system and stick to the main commercial blocks of Adams-Morgan and Capitol Hill. If Metro's service has stopped for the day and you're still out, take a taxi. Know your destination before you set out. Hold your kids' hands on city streets and sidewalks, on all Metro escalators, and on Metro platforms. Lock your hotel room door, car doors, and trunk. Don't leave luggage or other items visible in your car when you leave it. Lock valuables in a safe deposit box (if not in your room, at the front desk). Keep a tight hold on your pocketbook and camera. Hold onto your purse in a restaurant. Carry your cash and credit cards in a front pocket or a concealed money pouch. Leave the family jewels at home; what you do bring, don't flash.

Smoking

Most restaurants have smoking and non-smoking sections. State your preference when you reserve or when you meet the host or hostess.

Taxes

Sales tax on merchandise is 5.75% in D.C., 5% in Maryland, and 4.5% in Virginia. The restaurant taxes are 10% in D.C., 5% in Maryland, and 4.5% in Virginia. The hotel sales taxes are 14.5% in D.C., 5% (plus another 5 to 7% local or city tax) in Maryland, and about 10% in Virginia.

Taxis

D.C. taxis don't have meters. You're charged according to the zones you travel through — $5 within one zone, $6.90 for two, and so on. See Chapter 3 for a more detailed explanation of this complicated fare system.

Time Zone

Washington, D.C. is in the eastern time zone. For the correct time, dial ☎ 202-844-2525.

Transit Info

For Metrorail (subway) and Metrobus information, call ☎ 202-637-7000 or visit the Metro Web site, www.wmata.com.

Weather

For the D.C. weather forecast, call ☎ 202-936-1212, watch the Weather Channel, or surf over to www.weather.com.

Toll-Free Numbers and Web Sites

Airlines serving Washington area airports

Aeroflot
☎ 888-340-6400
www.aeroflot.com

Air Canada
☎ 888-247-2262
www.aircanada.ca

Air France
☎ 800-321-4538
www.airfrance.com

Air Jamaica
☎ 800-523-5585
www.airjamaica.com

AirTran
☎ 800-247-8726
www.airtran.com

Alaska Airlines
☎ 800-252-7522
www.Alaskaair.com

America West Airlines
☎ 800-235-9292
www.americawest.com

American Airlines
☎ 800-433-7300
www.aa.com

America Trans Air (ATA)
☎ 800-435-9282
www.ata.com

ANA
☎ 800-235-9262
http://svc.ana.co.jp/eng

Atlantic Coast Airlines
☎ 800-241-6522
www.atlanticcoast.com

Austrian Airlines
☎ 800-843-0002;
www.aua.com

Boston-Maine Airways
☎ 800-359-7262
www.bmairways.com

British Midland
☎ 800-788-0555
www.flybmi.com

British Airways
☎ 800-247-9297
www.british-airways.com

BWIA International Airways
☎ 800-538-2942
www.bwiacaribbean.com

Continental
☎ 800-525-0280
www.continental.com

Delta
☎ 800-221-1212
www.delta.com

Ethiopian Airlines
☎ 800-445-2733
www.flyethiopian.com

Frontier Airlines
☎ 800-432-1359
www.flyfrontier.com

Ghana Airways
☎ 800-404-4262
www.ghana-airways.com

Grupo TACA
☎ 800-535-8780
www.grupotaca.com

Icelandair
☎ 800-223-5500
www.icelandair.com

Jet Blue
☎ 800-538-2583
www.jetblue.com

KLM Royal Dutch Airlines
☎ 800-225-2525
www.klm.com/nl_en

Korean Air
☎ 800-438-5000
www.koreanair.com

Lufthansa
☎ 800-645-3880
www.lufthansa.com

Midway Airlines
☎ 800-446-4392
www.midwayair.com

Midwest Express Airlines
☎ 800-452-2022
www.midwestexpress.com

Northwest Airlines
☎ 800-225-2525
www.nwa.com

Pan Am
☎ 800-359-7262
www.panam.com

SAS
☎ 800-221-2350
www.scandinavian.net

Saudi Arabian Airlines
☎ 800-472-8342
www.saudiairlines.com

Southwest Airlines
☎ 800-435-9792
www.southwest.com

Swiss International
☎ 877/359-7947
www.swiss.com

United Airlines
☎ 800-241-6522
www.ual.com

US Airways
☎ 800-428-4322
www.usair.com

Virgin-Atlantic
☎ 800-862-8621
www.virgin-atlantic.com

Car rental agencies that serve Washington

Alamo
☎ 800-327-9633
www.goalamo.com

Avis
☎ 800-831-2847
www.avis.com

Budget
☎ 800-527-0700
www.budgetrentacar.com

Dollar
☎ 800-800-3665
www.dollarcar.com

Enterprise
☎ 800-736-8222
www.pickenterprise.com

Hertz
☎ 800-654-3131
www.hertz.com

National
☎ 800-227-7368
www.nationalcar.com

Rent-A-Wreck
☎ 800-535-1391
www.rent-a-wreck.com

Thrifty
☎ 800-847-4389
www.thrifty.com

Major hotel and motel chains that serve the Washington area

Best Western
☎ 800-780-7234
www.bestwestern.com

Comfort Inn
☎ 800-424-6423
www.hotelchoice.com

Courtyard by Marriott
☎ 800-321-2211
www.courtyard.com

Days Inn
☎ 800-329-7466
www.daysinn.com

Doubletree
☎ 800-222-8733
www.doubletree.com

Econo Lodge
☎ 877-424-6423
www.hotelchoice.com

Fairfield Inn by Marriott
☎ 800-228-2800
www.fairfieldinn.com

Hampton Inn
☎ 800-426-7866
www.hampton-inn.com

Hilton
☎ 800-445-8667
www.hilton.com

Holiday Inn
☎ 800-465-4329
www.holiday-inn.com

Howard Johnson
☎ 800-446-4656
www.hojo.com

Hyatt
☎ 800-233-1234
www.hyatt.com

Marriott
☎ 800-228-9290
www.marriott.com

Motel 6
☎ 800-466-8356
www.motel6.com

Quality Inn
☎ 877-424-6423
www.hotelchoice.com

Radisson
☎ 800-333-3333
www.radisson.com

Ramada Inn
☎ 800-272-6232
www.ramada.com

Red Roof Inn
☎ 800-733-7663
www.redroof.com

Renaissance
☎ 800-468-3571
www.renaissancehotels.com

Residence Inn by Marriott
☎ 800-331-3131
www.residenceinn.com

Sheraton
☎ 800-325-3535
www.sheraton.com

Super 8 Motel
☎ 800-800-8000
www.super8.com

Travelodge
☎ 800-578-7878
www.travelodge.com

Wyndham
☎ 877-999-3223
www.wyndham.com

Where to Get More Information

If I haven't packed enough information into this book for you, you can consult the following resources for additional info.

Call or write the Washington, D.C., Convention and Tourism Corp. (1212 New York Ave. NW; ☎ 800-422-8644) and ask for a free copy of the *Washington, D.C., Official Visitors Guide,* which contains information about visitor services, hotels, restaurants, sights, transportation, and tours. The organization's Web site (www.washington.org) also updates you on events.

For online information, check out the following Web sites:

✔ Go to the Web site www.nps.gov/parks.html to access the National Park Service Guide. You can find detailed information about all National Park Service sites, as well as individual listings for sites in the Washington area by name (Washington Monument, Lincoln Memorial). You can also find Washington's sites grouped in listings for National Capital Parks Central, National Capital Parks East, and National Mall.

✔ If you're looking for information about National and Dulles airports, go to the Web site www.metwashairports.com. It contains everything you want to know about flight schedules, flight status, ground transportation, terminal maps, and airport facilities.

✔ Visit the Smithsonian Institution Web site at www.si.edu to plan your visits to the Smithsonian museums — or to take a tour without setting foot in D.C. This Web site contains links to all the museums' Web sites, basic information about directions, hours, and facilities, and lots of online exhibits.

✔ Visit the Washington, D.C.Web site at www.dcvisit.com. Another site stuffed with current information for visitors to Washington, this one's produced by the D.C. Chamber of Commerce. Useful links take you to information on transportation providers, attractions, reservation services, and the like.

✔ At the Washington Metropolitan Area Transit Authority Web site (www.wmata.com), you can find timetables, maps, fare schedules, and more information useful to riders of Washington's buses and subway. I particularly like the online maps of the area around each station. From the home page, click Metrorail☞Stations and then the name of the station you're interested in. Then scroll down to the bottom of the page and click Neighborhood Street Map.

✔ You can find the *Washington Post* online at www.washingtonpost. com. The Web site provides up-to-the-minute news, weather, visitor information, restaurant reviews, and online discussions of various subjects. The Visitors Guide, accessible from the home page, contains information about attractions, lodging, and night spots, as well as restaurant reviews. The Entertainment section, also from the home page, tells you about concerts, theaters, night clubs, movies, and museums and also reviews restaurants.

✔ *Washingtonian Online,* D.C.'s leading local magazine, gives its take on all those things visitors would like to know, clearly indexed on the home page at www.washingtonian.com. Check out *Washingtonian's* lists of D.C.'s 100 best restaurants and the 100 best places to get an inexpensive meal. You can also access a museum guide and "What's Happening," which is a monthly tip sheet to what's going on at museums and theaters.

Making Dollars and Sense of It

Expense	Daily cost	x	Number of days	=	Total
Airfare					
Local transportation					
Car rental					
Lodging (with tax)					
Parking					
Breakfast					
Lunch					
Dinner					
Snacks					
Entertainment					
Babysitting					
Attractions					
Gifts & souvenirs					
Tips					
Other					
Grand Total					

Fare Game: Choosing an Airline

When looking for the best airfare, you should cover all your bases — 1) consult a trusted travel agent; 2) contact the airline directly, via the airline's toll-free number and/or Web site; 3) check out one of the travel-planning Web sites, such as www.frommers.com.

Travel Agency_____ Phone_____

    Agent's Name_____ Quoted fare_____

Airline 1_____ Quoted fare_____

    Toll-free number/Internet_____

Airline 2_____ Quoted fare_____

    Toll-free number/Internet_____

Web site 1_____ Quoted fare_____

Web site 2_____ Quoted fare_____

Departure Schedule & Flight Information

Airline_____ Flight #_____ Confirmation #_____

Departs_____ Date_____ Time_____ a.m./p.m.

Arrives_____ Date_____ Time_____ a.m./p.m.

Connecting Flight (if any)

Amount of time between flights_____ hours/mins

Airline_____ Flight #_____ Confirmation #_____

Departs_____ Date_____ Time_____ a.m./p.m.

Arrives_____ Date_____ Time_____ a.m./p.m.

Return Trip Schedule & Flight Information

Airline_____ Flight #_____ Confirmation #_____

Departs_____ Date_____ Time_____ a.m./p.m.

Arrives_____ Date_____ Time_____ a.m./p.m.

Connecting Flight (if any)

Amount of time between flights_____ hours/mins

Airline_____ Flight #_____ Confirmation #_____

Departs_____ Date_____ Time_____ a.m./p.m.

Arrives_____ Date_____ Time_____ a.m./p.m.

All Aboard: Booking Your Train Travel

Travel Agency_____ Phone_____

Agent's Name_____

Web Site_____

Departure Schedule & Train Information

Train #_____ Confirmation #_____ Seat reservation #_____

Departs_____ Date_____ Time_____ a.m./p.m.

Arrives_____ Date_____ Time_____ a.m./p.m.

Quoted fare_____ First class _____ Second class

Departure Schedule & Train Information

Train #_____ Confirmation #_____ Seat reservation #_____

Departs_____ Date_____ Time_____ a.m./p.m.

Arrives_____ Date_____ Time_____ a.m./p.m.

Quoted fare_____ First class _____ Second class

Departure Schedule & Train Information

Train #_____ Confirmation #_____ Seat reservation #_____

Departs_____ Date_____ Time_____ a.m./p.m.

Arrives_____ Date_____ Time_____ a.m./p.m.

Quoted fare_____ First class _____ Second class

Departure Schedule & Train Information

Train #_____ Confirmation #_____ Seat reservation #_____

Departs_____ Date_____ Time_____ a.m./p.m.

Arrives_____ Date_____ Time_____ a.m./p.m.

Quoted fare_____ First class _____ Second class

Sweet Dreams: Choosing Your Hotel

Make a list of all the hotels where you'd like to stay and then check online and call the local and toll-free numbers to get the best price. You should also check with a travel agent, who may be able to get you a better rate.

Hotel & page	Location	Internet	Tel. (local)	Tel. (Toll-free)	Quoted rate

Hotel Checklist

Here's a checklist of things to inquire about when booking your room, depending on your needs and preferences.

- ❏ Smoking/smoke-free room
- ❏ Noise (if you prefer a quiet room, ask about proximity to elevator, bar/restaurant, pool, meeting facilities, renovations, and street)
- ❏ View
- ❏ Facilities for children (crib, roll-away cot, babysitting services)
- ❏ Facilities for travelers with disabilities
- ❏ Number and size of bed(s) (king, queen, double/full-size)
- ❏ Is breakfast included? (buffet, continental, or sit-down?)
- ❏ In-room amenities (hair dryer, iron/board, minibar, etc.)
- ❏ Other_____

Places to Go, People to See, Things to Do

Enter the attractions you would most like to see and decide how they'll fit into your schedule. Next, use the "Going My Way" worksheets that follow to sketch out your itinerary.

Attraction/activity	Page	Amount of time you expect to spend there	Best day and time to go

Going "My" Way

Day 1

Hotel_____ Tel._____

Morning_____

_____

Lunch_____ Tel._____

Afternoon_____

_____

Dinner_____ Tel._____

Evening_____

_____

Day 2

Hotel_____ Tel._____

Morning_____

_____

Lunch_____ Tel._____

Afternoon_____

_____

Dinner_____ Tel._____

Evening_____

_____

Day 3

Hotel_____ Tel._____

Morning_____

_____

Lunch_____ Tel._____

Afternoon_____

_____

Dinner_____ Tel._____

Evening_____

_____

Index

See also separate Accommodations and Restaurant indexes at the end of this index.

General Index

• A •

AAA, 60, 309
AARP, 37
Access-Able Travel Source, 38
accessibility issues, 38–40
accommodations. *See also*
    Accommodations Index
  amenities, 68–69
  bed-and-breakfast, 62
  budget for, 26
  corner room, 74
  cost of, 2–3, 68–69, 77
  discounts on, 71–72, 73–74
  gay or lesbian traveler, 41
  high season, 72–73
  hotel chain, 61, 314–315
  independent hotel, 62
  inside-the-beltway, 9
  kids-stay-free option, 33
  kitchen in, 33, 36
  locations, 63–68, 94
  low season, 72
  map, 78–79
  Metrorail stations and, 59
  minibar, 29
  motel and motor inn, 62
  package deal, 48
  parking and, 127
  by price, 93
  rack rate, 68, 71
  reservation for, 62, 71, 73–74
  reservation service, 99
  room service, 29
  safe or safety deposit box, 130
  selecting, 61–62

  tax on, 29, 75, 131
  Web sites, 74
  without reservation, 75
Acela Express, 57
Adams-Morgan
  description of, 12, 86, 111
  restaurants, 137, 143, 170
  safety, 127
  shopping, 244
address, finding, 117, 118
after-dark tour, 235, 236
Aielli, Fabrizio (chef), 167
airlines. *See also* airports
  contact information, 312–314
  fares, 53–56
  flying with children, 55, 56
  travel agent and, 46
  traveling in comfort, 56
  yield management, 54
Airport Car Service, 53
airports. *See also* airlines
  Baltimore-Washington International,
    53, 110
  map, 108
  Ronald Reagan Washington National,
    50–51, 108, 109, 228
  transportation from, 107–110
  Transportation Security
    Administration, 56, 104
  Washington-Dulles International,
    51–52, 109–110
  Web sites, 315–316
A.L. Goodies General Store, 266
Alexandria Archaeology Research
  Lab, 260
Alexandria, Virginia
  attractions, 259–260
  map, 258
  Old Town, 257

• *Q* •

• *R* •

• S •